WHITNEY ON LANGUAGE

W. D. Whitney

WHITNEY ON LANGUAGE

SELECTED WRITINGS OF
WILLIAM DWIGHT WHITNEY

EDITED BY
MICHAEL SILVERSTEIN
INTRODUCTORY ESSAY BY
ROMAN JAKOBSON

The M I T Press
Cambridge, Massachusetts, and London, England

CONTENTS

v

ILLUSTRATIONS

PREFACE

A considerable portion of William Dwight Whitney's publications was directed toward establishing that in history lies the answer to the famous question with which this collection begins, 'Why do we speak as we do?' Likewise, this book is justified as part of the answer to the question, 'Why do we speak *of language* as we do?' Assembled here are representative works, which together show the range of Whitney's linguistic interests and accomplishments and give us, by implicit or overt dialectic treatment, a picture of the state of linguistic thought of his time. I do not intend to analyze each selection or to justify each separately: the choice has been made primarily to give a collection *où tout se tient.* Conspicuously absent are any purely descriptive studies of Sanskrit or of Hindu literature and astronomy, which are not suited for excerpting or condensation, though Whitney's narrowest professional interest is represented by the beautiful studies of accent in Sanskrit and the statistical treatment of imperfect and perfect tense formations. In such a volume as this, moreover, one does not shirk from reproducing what is, as we say today, 'uninsightful' by present standards.

The obligation of an editor not to include repetitions of detailed discussion appears to me obvious (though the result is not unlike Leonard Bloomfield's ideal of terseness in scientific discourse!). Therefore, in reaching the hundred-odd page condensation of *Language and the Study of Language* (originally an expanded version of twelve lectures on the subject given at the Lowell Institute in 1864–1865), I have attempted to make it a coherent statement of general principles. Thus certain important topics (for example, phonetic economy) appear to be mentioned and no more. These are taken up again in the subsequent studies, which have been arranged by area of interest. The first group continues with general topics, the 'institutional' nature of language, psychology and the origin of language, and the difficult question of linguistic mixture; and then an enigmatic piece of syntactic analysis of grammatical categories. I have placed next several phonetics studies: the unified theory of vowel and consonant, the universal transcriptional system and articulatory phonetics, and the notion of phonetic economy. Then come the Sanskrit studies already mentioned, along with a trenchant criticism of the native grammarians. Finally we have what, as Whitney himself says, 'is to make out of a joke a far too serious matter' of etymology, to illustrate his approach to criticism of Max Müller of Oxford, some of which appears in one form or another in different selections also. An Indra figure, Whitney devoted his energy time and again to 'slaying' the Vṛtra-like Müller, whose notions had become sacred cows to the English-speaking public.

The chronological distribution of the selections is from the year 1861 through 1892. During the first years of Whitney's illness (see the supplement to the autobiography) less of note was published, and therefore the late 1880s are not represented.

I have not provided each selection or group of selections with an introduction: I believe each of them to be 'relevant' today, in the most urgent sense of the word, to the debate on the nature of language and linguistics that is shaping up once again between students of rationalist grammar and students of culture. What impresses us most about this material is its fundamental sanity. It is of the nineteenth century at the time of—and an important contribution to—the spread of the empiricist ascendancy from natural to social science, from 'physical' to 'moral' science, as one would have said at the time. Much of the style of presentation may be strange for people unstudied in wider sources of the regularist historicism and belief in evolutionary progress. Here is a place for them to begin, to ask what developments prompted the particulars in the work of a man who was at the time not only one of America's most celebrated scholars (he was even elected to a list of forty 'immortals') but one of her few figures of international renown in Europe.

It is hackneyed to insist that Whitney was almost the first to stress the 'cultural' nature of language, in modern terms. Yet the reader will come to see how rich a notion this is, how wide the implications—right and wrong—that Whitney drew from his first principles, and how profoundly he appreciated what is meant by 'traditional institutions.' These include linguistics itself, which, treated as a cultural fact ('The Study of Hindu Grammar and the Study of Sanskrit' and 'On the Nature and Designation of the Accent in Sanskrit'), raises fundamental methodological questions for rationalist grammarians today.

Of specific editorial practices, there is little that need be said except that nothing has been added to the originals save silent corrections of misprints, emendation of broken, illegible type, and so on. To prepare the condensed version of the first piece, I have excised part of a sentence only if absolutely necessary for fluency of reading, including here inappropriate transitions ('thus,' 'again,' 'yet') and cross-references to topics not included. Otherwise what fluency it retains is achieved by deletion of at least whole sentences, where care has been directed of course to preserving both poles of any contrast, or a negative holding over a whole paragraph, so as not to misrepresent anything. The largest bulk of the condensation is achieved by deleting specific examples accumulated on one given point, the typological and historical details of a world language survey, and a sketch of the development of writing down to our 'historical mode of spelling.' Everything of essential and lasting nature fairly original with Whitney seems to me to be included.

I record here with thanks the kindness of the archive staffs at Yale and Harvard in providing access to letters and manuscript material. I am indebted to Karl Teeter for notice of this worthwhile opportunity. The essay summarizing Whitney's approach to language owes its existence to a request by Calvert Watkins for a guest lecture; I thank him for this kindness and encouragement. And finally, I thank here above all Roman Jakobson, who first suggested that I read Whitney when I was a junior in college, and who responded to my offer to do this work with sustained benevolent advice.

Michael Silverstein

WHITNEY ON LANGUAGE

Immediately upon his election to the Presidency of Harvard in 1869, Charles William Eliot tried to persuade William Dwight Whitney to accept a professorship there. Whitney declined the offer and remained at Yale when a chair of Sanskrit and Comparative Philology was endowed for him. Yet it is significant that Eliot should have made this one of his first offers in building the new Harvard University from Harvard College and the associated graduate schools, because comparative philology, or linguistics, as Whitney himself called its general form, was considered one of the most important of the *Geisteswissenschaften,* and Whitney was the greatest American practitioner.

The continental term *Geisteswissenschaft* was usually translated as 'moral science' (as opposed to *Naturwissenschaft,* or 'physical science'), because it dealt with the institutions of men, established and maintained by societies and reflected by the psyche of each individual in them. Crosscutting this classification, linguistics was called an 'historical science' because of the kind of causal explanation aimed at in doing research on language: by definition, facts of language are historical products only, as opposed to chemical facts, for example, which may be described with nonhistorical laws. I shall return to the notion of human institution later. I wish now to take up the historicism of Whitney and indeed all other philologists of the time. We could trace the ascendancy of historicism back quite far, since in Lyell's and Darwin's century it was predominant; this would be less satisfactory than seeing how it fits into Whitney's own conception of language.

For Whitney, clearly, a language at any given moment is unmotivated in structure—'arbitrary,' in the Saussurean idiom—because no system-internal reason can be given for the presence in a given language of particular items. Hence for Whitney explanation must be in terms of how the particular items get there, that is, in terms of how they arise, spread and become productive, and run their course to obsolescence and atavism. Furthermore, this historical explanation deals with change that is gradual and regular; it is free from catastrophes, such as the floods and crumbling towers invoked by defenders of Mosaic chronology.

Let me take this regularist historicism as valid in biography as well, and trace Whitney's intellectual development as the 'explanation' of his position on language.

Whitney was born at Northampton, Massachusetts in 1827 and attended school there, followed by three years in Williams College (he was class of 1845). Until 1849, he tried his hand at different professions but spent much of his time reading. During this early part of his life he was a naturalist par excellence, collecting specimens and participating in geological expeditions under his older brother, Josiah Whitney, later Professor of Economic Geology at Harvard. So the 'revolutions' in archaeological and geological science that were leading influences on nineteenth-century thought in general were directly a part of the scientific training of Whitney; I feel justified in attributing his historicism to his own personal appreciation of such issues in the natural sciences, rather than to a 'Zeitgeist,' from which people assume automatically the rhetoric of the dominant themes in the intellectual climate. Indeed, the geological analogy—observe that geology was considered a historical *Naturwissenschaft*—is a recurrent one in all his writings; for example, in *Language and the Study of Language* [abbreviated hereafter *LSL*], first published in 1867:

There is no way of investigating the first hidden steps of any continuous historical process, except by carefully studying the later recorded steps, and cautiously applying the analogies thence deduced. So the geologist studies the forces which are now altering by slow degrees the form and aspect of the earth's crust, wearing down the rocks here, depositing beds of sand and pebbles there, pouring out floods of lava over certain regions, raising or lowering the line of coast along certain seas; and he applies the results of his observations with confidence to the explanation of phenomena dating from a time to which men's imaginations, even, can hardly reach. The legitimacy of the analogical reasoning is not less undeniable in the one case than in the other. You may as well try to persuade the student of the earth's structure that the coal-bearing rocks lie in parallel layers, of alternating materials, simply because it pleased God to make them so when he created the earth . . . , are to be regarded as the sports of nature, mere arbitrary characteristics of the formation, uninterpretable as signs of its history—as to persuade the student of language that the indications of composition and growth which he discovers in the very oldest recorded speech, not less than in the latest, are only illusory, and that his comprehension of linguistic development must therefore be limited to the strictly historical period of the life of language. (p. 253)

Let me repeat from this one noun phrase: 'mere arbitrary characteristics of the formation, uninterpretable as signs of its history.' Notice here the polar opposition of synchronic arbitrariness and diachronic motivation, which I mentioned above: the structure which we find at time t_1 is a reflection of the historical processes from t_0 to t_1 that brought it to its present state. The sense of the regularist hypothesis is here too in the rejection of a division of prehistoric versus historic for purposes of investigation. For, the 'catastrophists' and others religiously inclined could, with a separation of the two stages, maintain that evolutionary forces operated differently in prehistory and in more recent recorded history. During the course of the nineteenth century, inductive inference back along the time axis was eliminating this means of explanation in several fields of science. Charles Lyell's *Principles of Geology* was published in 1830 (first two volumes) and 1833 (third volume). Its title in full is *Principles of geology, being an attempt to explain the former changes of the earth's surface by reference to causes now in operation.* John Lubbock's book *Prehistoric times, as illustrated by ancient remains and the manners and customs of modern savages* (1865) crystallized this approach for anthropology. Whitney's works added linguistics to these. His popular work of 1875 was entitled *The Life and Growth of Language,* capitalizing on a Darwinian analogy, which he is careful to define as analogy only. Such naïve Darwinism as that of August Schleicher, the author of pamphlets 'proving' Darwinian evolution by facts of language, came under very strong attack from Whitney in several instances.

Josiah Whitney inadvertently determined his brother's specialty by making available to him among the books he brought back from Europe the second edition of Bopp's Sanskrit grammar (1832). After studying Sanskrit at Yale during 1849 under Edward Elbridge Salisbury, whose name and endowment form the chair of Sanskrit and Comparative Philology at Yale to this day, Whitney left for Berlin to study Sanskrit with Albrecht Weber, and especially Tübingen to study with Rudolf von Roth, the Vedic scholar. Out of this last collaboration came the *editio princeps* of the Atharva Veda, one of the four principal Vedic collections, as well as Whitney's contribution of all the Atharvan material to the fundamental Petersburg Lexicon of Sanskrit (1852–1875) edited by Roth and Otto von Böthlingk. Back at Yale, starting in 1854, Whitney taught Sanskrit in the College and to the postgraduates as 'Professor of the Sanskrit language and its relations to the other languages, and of Sanskrit literature.' To support himself and family, for the next sixteen years, he taught French and German as 'instructor in modern languages' in the College and in the Sheffield Scientific School of Yale, until the funding of his chair by Salisbury to prevent the move to Harvard, whereupon this teaching became voluntary. Out of these years came several practical grammars and dictionaries of French and German. He offered for many years, until his heart attack of 1886, a senior elective course in general linguistic science in Yale College, based on his experience as lecturer on the subject and on his general books. Concurrently he held various offices in the American Oriental Society (he was elected in 1850) and was instrumental in the formative years of, among others, the American Philological Association (founded 1869), Spelling Reform Association (1876), Modern Language Association of America (1883), and the American Dialect Society (1889). Whitney's eminence in scholarship brought him to positions of what can only be described as great power—had he chosen to exercise it—in all American humanistic scholarship, which was, after all, at the time firmly based on philology. The correspondence to Whitney now preserved in the Yale archives shows clearly that appointments in various departments around the country were subject to his recommendation, if not advice and consent. His name became associated in the mind of the public at large with his advocacy of spelling reform for English through his work in the Spelling Reform Association, a form of applied linguistics whose theoretical basis lay in his belief in the enlightened, planned change of human institutions. He was also well known for his editorship of the *Century Dictionary* (1889–1891), an encyclopedic reference work published just before the Columbian Exposition and in effect summing up the nineteenth century. There he 'cast the influence of the dictionary in favor of the movement' for a 'more consistent and phonetic spelling' (p. ix) in doubtful cases. He died on June 7, 1894, at just about the time of the rise of Franz Boas's career in Washington and New York. Boas would be the next great influence in American linguistics, on the foundation of empirical anthropology and the study of 'exotic,' unwritten languages.

With all these functionary obligations, Whitney produced a steady volume of books, some already mentioned, and papers for learned journals and popular magazines such as Henry Adams's *North American Review*. This last kind of activity was, like his work in spelling reform, based on a commitment not just to inform the public on what the experts were doing, but to apply the knowledge of the experts to shaping language and language study for the future—an occupation, or rather preoccupation, now once again coming into its own. Whitney had a real belief in the intimate relationship between the cultural institutions of a people and their 'progress,' that pervasive doctrine based on historicism which is preached, for example, in Spencer. To understand the dynamics of language as it functions in a community meant that one could ascertain how to proceed in implementing an engineered reform as well as how to infer past history. As the latter was the real focus of Whitney's work, we should examine this idea in detail.

In a very direct way, the ontogeny of language and its phylogeny are parallel for Whitney, since both depend on the process of *naming*. The child learns the arbitrary and conventional signs for things according to community use around him just as a given person, in proposing a name for a new cultural object, is subject to this same constraint of the institution of usage. In other words, '. . . what we may severally choose to say is not language until it be accepted and employed by our fellows.' (*LSL*, p. 404) Note that

> This does not imply an absolute identity of dialect, down to the smallest details, among all the constituent members of a community; within certain limits . . . each one may be as original as he pleases . . . Nor must the word community, as used with reference to language, be taken in a too restricted or definite sense. It has various degrees of extension, and bounds within bounds: the same person may belong to more than one community, using in each a different idiom. (*LSL*, p. 156)

Thus not only do grammars leak, as Sapir was later to write (in 1921), but speech communities do too. There are degrees of cohesion of social groups interacting by means of language, and these

groups do not simply partition all people. Whitney shows geographical and social subcommunities to be potential separate
speech communities by just such innovations and retentions of
exclusive items as characterize small linguistic groups within a
larger one. It is very clear that his notion of historical processes,
and hence of methods of investigating them, depends on individual
items in a language, at all structural levels, rather than on some
a priori notion of structure:

> ... the history of language reposes on that of words. Language is made up
> of signs for thought, which, though in one sense parts of a whole, are in
> another and more essential sense isolated and independent entities. Each is
> produced for its own purpose; each is separately exposed to the changes and
> vicissitudes of linguistic life, is modified, recombined, or dropped, according
> to its own uses and capacities. Hence etymology, the historical study of
> individual words, is the foundation and substructure of all investigation of
> language.... (*LSL,* pp. 54–55)

The process of dialect and language formation is thus as gradual
and continuous as speciation, involving degrees of variability of
items in language over different functioning speech groups.

It becomes clear, then, that language change is a feedback
mechanism where the results of innovation in the system are
subject to selection by the community, and the external influence,
the social forces exerted by the speakers, are observable variables.
Hence in history lies the experimental paradigm for determining
the internal structural coherence of language. It is for this reason
that 'explanation' must be historical, because we cannot experiment with people in the necessary fashion. Further, since like
causes give like effects, once we recognize this as an evolutionary
feedback mechanism, then differences are explainable in a new
way: like causes give unlike effects from operating upon unlike
results of previous changes. This is the syllogism of historical
regularity, as illustrated in the accompanying diagram.

In the diagram, for the language L at time t_1, there are certain
variant formations: v_1^1 with a characteristically limited range of
uses, and v_1^2 with a wide range of uses. As the language passes into
stage L_2 (at time t_2), the same societal factors S select the variants
differentially, and in the daughter language, the corresponding
variant v_2^1 has a much wider range than v_1^1, while v_2^2 is moribund.

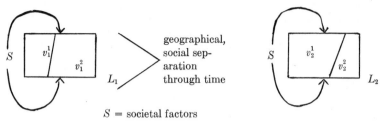

S = societal factors

L_i = language system at time t_i

v_i^j = constructions, uses variant (superscript j) at time t_i

enclosed labeled area = productivity of constructions, range of uses

But to return to the process of internal linguistic change itself, Whitney divides it into change of form and change of meaning; and further, of formal change he states:

> ... on the one hand, the production of new words and forms by the combination of old materials; on the other hand, the wearing down, wearing out, and abandonment of the words and forms thus produced, their fusion and mutilation, their destruction and oblivion—are the means by which are kept up the life and growth of language, so far as concerns its external shape and substance, its sensible body. . . . (*LSL*, p. 100)

'Combination' and 'adaptation' are the key terms in Whitney's discussion of formal processes. When two forms are combined, one always tends to become structurally subordinated to the other. We may use Schleicher's notation, capitals for syntactically independent entities ('roots') and lower case for subordinate ones ('affixes'), of which Whitney approved, and say $[A + b]$ is the historical result of $[A] + [B]$. As this combination takes place, the shapes of the two units are adapted to each other by the universal tendency to 'phonetic economy' of expression, and the result is eventually the phonetically modified $[A + b']$ and then $[A' + b'']$. The subordinated element is first subject to adaptation, and then conditions the change in the root element, itself possibly again undergoing change. The specification of what 'economy' is besides an empty, evasive term is achievable by studying a posteriori specific phonetic changes. By this process an original English *bréak fást* (transitive verb + noun) becomes *bréakfast* (verb, intransitive). The arbitrary nature of *which* units undergo such change, from the internal structural view, is indicated by the fact that an original *táke dínner* is not now ***tákedinner;* the appearance of the one but not the other is explainable only by history.

Compounding leads to the attenuation of full grammatical status of some item, which gives us a stage of productive *derivation,* and derivation gives us, by an attenuation of the lexical meaning of the affix, a productive stage of *inflection.* Once the directly syntactic value of an item is attenuated by composition or some other factor, the formation is generalized:

> ... extensibility of application is a part of the essential and indispensable character of a formative element. We have not to go over and over again with the primitive act of composition and the subsequent reduction, in each separate case. (*LSL,* p. 83)

In present-day terms, a new formative has been created; hence an element that becomes subordinated to another may become the focus for a productive morphological process in a language, adding to it a new construction type, $[\text{------} + b'] \sim [\text{------} + b'']$, with the phonological alternation probably preserved. To Whitney this demonstrates the validity of the opposition of *material* and *form* in language as two poles of a continuously variable process. Material are the grammatically independent lexical items, formal are the subordinate, grammatical affixes, of inflection especially. Certain parts of language are highly structured into formal classes, other parts not, and this can be explained by how long they have been undergoing this constant process of combination and adaptation, which seems to be a unilinear evolutionary tendency.

The implications of this are clear: first, in such a unilinear evolutionary schema it is fitting and proper to speak of Indo-European languages as the 'highest' or most developed, since no other languages investigated by his day were inflective in the same manner, and also because the farther back we trace the history of forms in, say, Indo-European, the closer we get to a completely syntactic—'formless'—tongue, the root or radical stage of language. Whitney attributes a good part of the development of the inflectional apparatus of Indo-European languages to the proto-stage itself, as shown by correspondences of elements that had already become affixes in the oldest daughter dialects. Hence families of languages can be methodologically defined by the results of comparative analysis of complex forms:

> Linguistic families, now, as at present constituted, are made up of those languages which have traceably had at least a part of their historical development in common; which have grown together out of the original radical or monosyllabic stage; which exhibit in their grammatical structure signs, still discoverable by linguistic analysis, of having descended, by the ordinary course of linguistic tradition, from a common ancestor. (*LSL*, p. 290)

The extent to which these assumptions still underlie Indo-European studies is both a measure of their correctness and an example of cultural conservatism of exactly the type Whitney spoke of as institutional. To a degree they have been unaffected by the Boasian revolution of relativism, which, dominating linguistics and anthropology under the guidance of Franz Boas and his students in America in the first half of this century, claimed that unilinear growth and progress to the single inflectional type do not have a theoretical basis.

Notice also that Whitney's is not a typological argument but an historical one. For the example of English within Indo-European can be historically distinguished from monosyllabism, the radical stage, once the dead inflective material be subjected to comparison with other languages, where it is still functioning. His explanation of the 'prevailing analogies' of composition in Indo-European, which lead to highly elaborate inflections in our classical texts and then in the further course of time again to analytic $[A] + [B]$ structures is a brilliant demonstration—startling at the time—of the use of the regularist hypothesis: the processes of combination and adaptation remain the same, but as the form of language changes, so do the 'prevailing analogies' determining the speakers' selection of efficient items. Given this necessity of history for the theory of comparative grammar, then conversely, for method, it is categorically incorrect to 'do' Indo-European from English and Hindi. Rather Old English and then Germanic dialects must be compared to Sanskrit and then Indo-Iranian dialects. We can appreciate the dilemma of the post-Boasians, then, in trying to figure out the history of the unwritten American languages. Either we must adopt some unilinear schema that insures the methodological validity of reconstructions, or, if anything is possible in the realm of structure change, we need records to indicate its directionality aforehand.

The second and third implications of Whitney's view of language change are methodological. Since there are structural features of varying degrees of generality in language, all valid comparison rests on eliminating chance resemblances by showing that particulars from language to language correspond regularly. Whitney compared paradigms as the means of proof, saying:

> Their convincing force lies in the fact that they are selected instances, examples chosen from among a host of others, which abound in every part of the grammar and vocabulary of all the languages in question, now so plain as to strike the eye of even the hasty student, now so hidden under later peculiar growth as to be only with difficulty traceable by the acute and practised linguistic analyst. (*LSL,* p. 200)

From knowing the results characteristic of dialect cleavage going on around us, we can recognize that the Indo-European evidence is of the same nature, and only of wider scope and hence more recondite.

Though he operated with regular correspondences, Whitney never formulated a principle of *Ausnahmslosigkeit* ('exceptionlessness') of sound change in so many words, as did the *Junggrammatiker* (Neogrammarians) in Germany, because in his system it is a tautology. Every change is exceptionless because every change has a context of productivity and application. Phonetic regularity is not produced at one stroke in Whitney's view, and this he even documents from his own personal history of pronunciation. Phonetic changes have an original locus of innovation as do any other kind, and spread from that locus—restricted by internal and social factors—to become general changes by the analogy of phonetic ease. (It must have been amusing to him to publish a paper on 'Examples of partial and sporadic phonetic change in English' in volume 4 (1894) of the *Indogermanische Forschungen* edited by the leading Neogrammarians Brugmann and Streitberg!) And yet he recognizes phonetic change as physiological, involving ease of articulation, relative to the existing system of sounds of a language, and subject to a notion of sequential constraints on combinations, what we called 'adaptation' of phonetic forms one to another in constructions. That such economy is definable only with reference to the repertoire of a language supports the observation that '. . . every language has its own peculiar history of phonetic development, its own special laws of mutation. . . .' (*LSL*, p. 95) So while Whitney had an explanation for the historical regularity of phonetic change, in overview, that was in keeping with the processes of the life of language in society as he outlined them, still he said of the linguist that

> He cannot tell why sounds are found in the alphabet of one tongue which are unutterable by speakers of another; why combinations which come without difficulty from the organs of one people are utterly eschewed by its neighbour and next of kin. . . . (*LSL*, p. 95)

This lacuna in explanatory power directly prepared the way for that great attempt of such pioneers as Jan Baudouin de Courtenay and Ferdinand de Saussure at the notion of a synchronic law—a mechanism of *system-internal causality*. But observe that for this we must reverse our priorities from Whitney, and look first to the system, then to the items in it. I mean here to indicate that saying '*la langue est un système*' brings the roof down on such people as the *Junggrammatiker* disciples of Whitney, because it assigns an additional referent to the word 'cause.' We are only now coming to empirical grips with Whitney's truth *and* Saussure's truth.

The final methodological implication of the Whitney model is summed up in Floyd Lounsbury's brilliant *Oneida Verb Morphology*[1] by the expression 'agglutinative analogue.' If a scientific description—hence analysis—of language deals in terms of combination and adaptation, then, in cases of non-simplex items where we do not see overtly combined the discrete units which the meaning requires, we attribute the change in form to adaptation. The synchronic picture of, say, phonological structure thus must of necessity mirror the historical process of combination and adaption which the analysis captures, in terms of one discrete axis of joining discrete units. Another cultural conservatism is represented by the reaction, documented in journals, to the

---

[1] *Yale University Publications in Anthropology*, vol. 48, 1953.

Praguean abandonment of this view in favor of a system of distinctive features. Here we have two axes of 'combination,' each sequential in construction (concatenations of distinctive features) and from the other axis appearing to be simultaneous, thus defining a matrix of features. But this latter view is possible directly to the extent that a Saussurean view of regularity of internal structure is adopted. Whitney was codifying a view of historical regularism and its implications for linguistic structure already amply illustrated by his predecessors, most immediately Franz Bopp and others in Europe. By giving it a general theoretical explanation he gave a basis for Neogrammarianism. Its adherents were expressly grateful to him, and our grammars have used this agglutination notion, of course, as the basis for phonological description.

It becomes clear, however, that in Whitney's case, as in the cases of later writers, like Franz Boas and Sapir in certain phases, this phonological 'euphony,' the dynamic alternations of shape in elements of a language in different constructions, is primarily a reflection of historical processes, the geological evidence, so to speak, of what must have gone on through time. We miss a clear idea of the independent systemic status of such alternations.

A good portion of Whitney's work (perhaps even the greater part) was in the form of reviews of work of other scholars. He read widely in Oriental studies and linguistics, and made known to his countrymen the trends and opinions in Europe. For his last twenty-five years he combated the doctrines of Max Müller of Oxford, which he found illogical and without empirical foundation. And he found Müller's textual scholarship in Sanskrit equally bad. This feud became one of the most celebrated in the cultural world. So also from his first principles he attacked and picked apart the naïve linguistic Darwinism of August Schleicher, the idealistic psycholinguistic notions of Humboldt and especially his advocate Chaim Steinthal, and the doctrine of grammatical and racial mixture in African prehistory of Richard Lepsius.

It is interesting to see that Whitney was so very consistent in applying his principles. In Schleicher, for instance, there is hypothesized a collapsing of the Indo-European and Semitic types into *internally inflected* languages, that is, languages in which the roots themselves undergo changes for inflection. On the basis of his model of combination and adaptation, Whitney concludes for Indo-European root-vowel alternations that '. . . they are called out ultimately by phonetic causes, not originated for the purpose of marking variation in meaning, though sometimes seized and applied for that purpose.' (*LSL*, p. 293) Whitney clearly gives a criterion of constant change of meaning for a given vowel change, a 'morphemic' criterion:

> . . . the change of vowel in the oldest derivatives is only an accompaniment of derivation by means of suffixes; it has no constant significance; it acquires significance only at second hand, in the manner of a result, not a cause. . . . (*LSL*, p. 294)

As he states in a review of John Peile's *An Introduction to Greek and Latin Etymology* (2nd edition, 1872),[2] it is a question of chronology within Indo-European itself, whether for Indo-European words of structure $[A' + b]$ the internal vowel change (represented by A') was historically prior and the suffixation a meaningless concomitant that eventually took over the meaning, or vice versa. The evidence points to the last possibility, on historical grounds, and so as reconstructable families Indo-European and Semitic are not of the same morphological type.

We should stress one final aspect of Whitney's approach to language as a system of subcodes and alternants in flux. This is his great concern in all his descriptive and textual work for statistical data. The empirical evidence for different subcommunities within a language is clearly the use of alternative forms, just as through time the evidence for differential productivity of competing formations is changing percentages of representation in sample corpora. Whitney's *Sanskrit Grammar*, written in 1875–1878 and revised in 1888 with the help of Charles Rockwell Lanman, is a triumph of this approach, because of the subtlety of the use of statistics on forms. Whitney is able to show from the textual evidence just when, during the long recorded course of Sanskrit, such things arose as -siṣ- aorists (built from a simple sigmatic in -s-) and -tāhe middle periphrastic futures (from -tr̥- nouns of agency + middle desinences). For Whitney, no grammar was complete unless it squarely faced the issue of produc-

---

[2] In *Transactions of the Philological Society of London*, vol. 3, 1873–1874, pp. 299–327.

tivity and stylistic appropriateness. And this is not so much a problem of history, as one of dynamics of the alternatives that every native speaker of a language controls. So on these grounds he approached the criticism of the Pāṇinian grammatical tradition of the native Hindu scholars of Sanskrit:

> If you have mastered Pāṇini sufficiently to bring to bear upon the given point every rule that relates to it, and in due succession [note the consciousness of descriptive order!], you have settled the case; but that is no easy task. For example, it takes nine mutually limitative rules, from all parts of the text-book, to determine whether a certain aorist shall be ajāgariṣam or ajāgāriṣam . . .: there is lacking only a tenth rule, to tell us that the whole word is a false and never-used formation. Since there is nothing to show how far the application of a rule reaches, there are provided treatises of laws of interpretation to be applied to them; but there is a residual rule underlying and determining the whole: that both the grammar and the laws of interpretation must be so construed as to yield good and acceptable forms, and not otherwise. . . . (*American Journal of Philology,* vol. 5, 1884, p. 280)

This fact of textual representation does not seem to be a mere accident of sampling size, since Whitney had read the whole available Vedic and post-Vedic corpus by the time he wrote those words.

Such treatment of the Hindu grammatical treatises brings us to our ultimate appreciation of Whitney's approach to the *institutions* of men. He recognized a significant level of organization of phenomena which we call now 'culture,' that this is *thesei* (by convention) in its specifics but *phusei* (by nature) in its reason for being a *faculté*—a potential of man when in society but not alone. If language, if the study of language, if literature are all part of this culture, then they must be treated as distinct in their organization from such biological givens as race and thought. Language, like any other such institution, does not exist by itself, independent of man, though the intricate feedback mechanism we saw before gives it an aspect of independence. Whitney saw that it was possible to understand the regularity of the history of language in order to continue the perfectability of mental life which culture initiates. It is significant, let us conclude, that both the Neogrammarians and Saussure, stressing each a different side of his work, took him as in their intellectual tradition.

THE WORLD RESPONSE TO WHITNEY'S PRINCIPLES OF LINGUISTIC SCIENCE

To the account of Whitney's Indological studies his Autobiographical Sketch adds that "he has also produced a couple of volumes on the general science of language." When the first of these two fundamental contributions appeared in 1867 both in London and New York, under the title *Language and the Study of Language (Twelve Lectures on the Principles of Linguistic Science)*, two learned German reviewers—Heyman Steinthal in the *Zeitschrift für Völkerpsychologie und Sprachwissenschaft*, vol. 5 (1868), and Wilhelm Clemm in *Kuhn's Zeitschrift für vergleichende Sprachforschung*, vol. 18 (1869)—warmly welcomed this comprehensive volume, and both of them emphasized its American background. As Steinthal (1823–1899), the noted promoter of ethnic and linguistic psychology, believed, one had to remember that "the author is a North American and writes for North Americans; what he says and also how he says it is conditioned by the readership for which he writes and even in the author's views certain features of his people could probably be detected." Steinthal alluded to the "different education, different inclination, and different demands" of German readership. According to the classical philologist Clemm (1843–1883), the primary orientation of Whitney's work toward American readers might seriously impede its translation.

Nevertheless Whitney's compendium was soon translated into German and Dutch, and his second book of general linguistics, *The Life and Growth of Language* (London and New York, 1875), immediately gave rise to three translations: French (Paris, 1875), Italian (Milan, 1876), and German (Leipzig, 1876). A Swedish version followed in 1880. These writings entered at once into international circulation. Thus the London publication of 1867 jointly with its German version, and likewise the English original of 1875 with its three translations of 1875 and 1876 figure among the chief references in the first pages of the *Comprehensive Program* which Jan Baudouin de Courtenay (1845–1929) published as an appendix to his trailblazing lectures of 1876–1877 at Kazan University. The relevance of these sources persisted, and in the *General Course* of comparative linguistics, read at Moscow University in 1901–1902 by the head of the Moscow linguistic school, F. F. Fortunatov (1848–1914), the first place among the few recommended manuals belongs to *The Life and Growth of Language* in the original, or in translation, preferably German. In agreement with the American scholar, Fortunatov pointed out the close relationship between language and society. His critical attitude toward August Schleicher's (1821–1868) oversimplified and mechanistic view of the Indo-European ancestor language also links him with Whitney's severe revision of the Schleicherian tenet.

A session of the First American Congress of Philologists held at Philadelphia, December 27–28, 1894, shortly after the death of W. D. Whitney (1827—June 7, 1894), was dedicated to his memory. The *Report* of that Whitney Memorial Meeting (published in Boston, 1897) bears a vivid testimony to the unforeseen difference between the American and European reactions to Whitney's attainments in general linguistics. This aspect of his activities was set aside by the domestic scholars who took part in the commemoration, whereas the responses from Europe received by the organizers of the memorial meeting rendered homage to Whitney's historic role in the astounding growth of linguistic science.

In particular, the cofounders and leaders of the influential Neogrammarian school and of its capital base in Leipzig University, the creative spirit of the new current, August Leskien (1840–1916), and his persistent disciple, the famous Indo-Europeanist Karl Brugmann (1849–1919), acknowledge the decisive impetus which the American's ideas gave to this trend from its beginning. According to Leskien's letter,

Whitney's views, particularly most recently, have effected far more in linguistics than one at first realizes. The work of the linguist proceeds for the most part in particulars, in which there is little opportunity to refer directly to Whitney. But during the last decades, even in specialized studies, and much more naturally in questions of general principles, a methodological path has been cleared that seeks to approach the true nature of things, in this case the real makeup of language; and certainly a large part of the inspiration for this comes, indirectly or directly, from Whitney.[1]

---

[1] "Whitney's Anschauungen haben, namentlich in neuster Zeit, in der Sprachwissenschaft weit mehr gewirkt, als man auf den ersten Blick bemerkt.

Brugmann insisted on the thorough indebtedness of Indo-European comparative study to Whitney's activities in Indic philology, and especially to his "indeed epoch-making" *Sanskrit Grammar*, but even more to the immense stimulations "that his consideration of the principles of language history gave to Indoger-manists" (die seine Behandlung der Principienfragen der Sprach-geschichte den Indogermanisten gegeben hat). In Brugmann's evaluation, "Whitney was, among the Indogermanists, the first to promulgate really sound essentials of language history free of any fanciful and disturbing pretense." It is significant that the champion of the Neogrammarian school assails its narrow-minded followers for their blind empiricism and aversion to theoretical questions: "Even the most gifted, if he wants to speculate on the individual events of a linguistic development, needs a knowledge of the essence of the forces by which the historical facts are produced. Only the self-control and self-criticism made possible by this more general training save him from the arbitrariness and error to which a crude empiricism is everywhere exposed." [2]

Brugmann opens his Leipzig message of November 25, 1894 "Zum Gedächtniss W. D. Whitneys" by recalling the years of initial quest for the new linguistic doctrine: "In the years when, in the homeland of Indo-European studies, we were pressing for a fundamental revision of research method and the establishment of a proper reciprocity between linguistic philosophy and special-

---

Die Arbeit der Sprachforscher bewegt sich ja zum grossen Theil in Detail-fragen, bei denen weniger Gelegenheit ist sich unmittelbar auf Whitney zu beziehen, aber selbst bei Specialuntersuchungen, noch mehr natürlich bei allgemeineren und prinzipiellen Fragen, hat sich in den letzten Jahrzehnten immer mehr eine Behandlungsweise Bahn gebrochen, die der wirklichen Natur der Dinge, d.h. hier den realen Verhältnissen der Sprache, gerecht zu werden sucht, und sicher geht ein grosser Theil der Anregung dazu mittelbar oder unmittelbar von Whitney aus."

[2] "Auch der Begabteste bedarf, wenn er über die einzelnen Ereignisse einer Sprachentwicklung speculieren will, einer Kenntniss des Wesens der Kräfte, durch die die geschichtlichen Thatsachen geschaffen sind. Nur die durch diese allgemeinere Bildung ermöglichte Selbstcontrole und Selbstkritik bewahrt ihn vor den Willkürlichkeiten und Irrtümern, denen eine rohe Empirie allenthalben ausgesetzt ist."

ized studies, Whitney was for me, as for other younger scholars, a guide in the contest of ideas, whose reliability was beyond cavil and whose hints could always be followed with much profit. And in the course of time the high opinion that I got of Whitney in my student days has only become more firmly established." [3]

When discussing the history of linguistics in a lecture of 1909, Ferdinand de Saussure (1857–1913) mentioned the date 1875 as a turning point. First, he said, Whitney's *Life and Growth of Language,* which appeared at that time in English and French, "gave the impetus." Then we witnessed the birth of "a new school," or in terms preferred by Saussure, "there arose the Neogrammarian trend" (*Cours de linguistique générale,* in R. Engler's critical edition, p. 16). Saussure spent the years 1876 and 1877 in Leipzig, which in those years was, in his judgment, "the principal center" of this "scientific movement" (see *Cahiers F. de Saussure,* vol. 17, 1960, p. 15). He audited Leskien's lectures and, at least through the mediation of Leskien, whose German translation of Whitney's *Leben und Wachstum der Sprache* was printed in Leipzig in 1876, he must have become familiar with this *Wegweiser* of the Neogrammarian pioneers.

When asked by the organizers of the Philadelphia Memorial Meeting for his appraisal of Whitney's life work, Saussure, with his usual "epistolophobia" and his growing disgust at the difficulty of writing "ten lines concerned with the facts of language and having any common sense" (letter to A. Meillet of January 4, 1894), endeavored to acknowledge and answer the invitation, and covered a notebook of some forty sheets with the draft for a reply which, however, was never finished and never sent. The notebook quoted here is kept in the Public and University Library of Geneva (Ms fr. 3951:10); only fragments were published by

[3] "War doch in jenen Jahren, da man im Mutterlande der Indogermanistik auf eine gründliche Revision der Forschungsmethode und auf die Herstellung einer angemessenen Wechselwirkung zwischen Sprachphilosophie und Spezialforschung drang, mir wie anderen jüngeren Gelehrten Whitney in Streit der Meinungen ein Wegweiser, dessen Zuverlässigkeit ausser Frage stand und dessen Winken man stets mit reichem Nutzen folgte, und hat sich mir doch die hohe Meinung, die ich von Whitney in meinen Lehrjahren gewann, im Lauf der Zeit nur befestigt."

Engler, *op.cit.*, and by R. Godel in *Cahiers F. de Saussure*, vol. 12 (1954), pp. 59ff, and in his valuable monograph *Les sources manuscrites du Cours de linguistique générale de F. de Saussure* (1957), pp. 43–46.

The rough version of Saussure's answer reads: "The thought which inspired the American Philological Association, in asking a number of [scholars], American and [European], to summarize their own opinions of the role that Whitney played in the different areas of science of their concern, seems to me a most fortunate one. Only by the comparison of opinions reached in complete freedom in absolutely different quarters will there emerge a notion of—and at the same time a full tribute to the memory of—him whose recent loss we lament along with you." [4] Saussure feels, however, overwhelmed by the task of summarizing "the work accomplished by Whitney" and ventures to open a free discussion, since "it is easier under the circumstances to give free rein to the pen" (Il est plus facile dans ces conditions de laisser courir la plume). He begins with stressing the peculiar facets in Whitney's "role and destiny":

1st. Though never having himself written a single page that one might say was intended by him to do comparative grammar, he exerted an influence on all study of comparative grammar; and this is not the case with anyone else. He is chronologically the first preceptor in the principles which will serve when applying the method in the future.

2nd. Of the different attempts between the years 1860 and 1870, which *for the first time* began to extract from the mass of results accumulated by comparative grammar some generalizations about language, all were frustrated or without general value, except that of Whitney, which from the very first was on the right track, and which today need only be patiently carried on.

Let us consider first of all this second role, for it is evident that in this way—that is to say because he showed linguists a sounder view of what

---

[4] "La pensée dont s'est inspirée l'American Philological Association, en demandant à un grand nombre de [savants], américains et [européens], de résumer selon leur propre opinion le rôle qu'a rempli Whitney dans les différents départements de la science qui les regarde, me semble une pensée des plus heureuses. De la seule comparaison de jugements portés en toute liberté de côtés absolument différents se dégagera un enseignement, en même temps qu'un hommage plus complet à la mémoire de celui dont nous avons déploré avec vous la perte récente."

was generally the object treated under the rubric of language—he induced
them to use slightly different methods in the laboratory of their day-to-day
comparative work. The two things, a good generalization about language,
which can interest just about anyone, or a sound method to propose to comparative grammar toward the precise operations of [   ], are actually the
same thing.[5]

Saussure sets off Whitney's performance against the desolate
state of the extant linguistic tradition similarly despised by both
scholars:

> For all time it will be a subject for philosophical reflection that during
> a period of fifty years linguistic science, born in Germany, developed in
> Germany, cherished in Germany by innumerable people, has never had the
> slightest inclination to reach the degree of abstraction which is necessary in
> order to dominate on the one hand *what one is doing,* on the other hand
> why what one is doing has a legitimacy and a *raison d'être* in the totality
> of sciences; but a second subject of astonishment is to see that when at
> last this science seems to triumph over her torpor, she winds up with the
> ludicrous attempt of Schleicher, which totters under its own preposter-
> ousness. Such was the prestige of Schleicher for simply having *tried* to say
> something general about language, that he even today seems an unrivaled
> figure in the history of linguistics, and one sees linguists putting on comically
> grave airs when dealing with this great figure. . . . From everything that

---

[5] "1° Que n'ayant jamais écrit une seule page qu'on puisse dire dans son
intention destinée à faire de la grammaire comparée, il a exercé une influence
sur toutes les études de grammaire comparée; et que ce n'est pas le cas
d'aucun autre. Il est en date le premier moniteur dans les principes qui
serviront en pratique de méthode à l'avenir.

"2° Que des différentes tentatives qui *pour la première fois* tendaient, entre
les années 1860 et 1870, à dégager de la somme des résultats accumulés par la
grammaire comparée, quelque chose de général sur le langage, toutes étaient
avortées ou sans valeur d'ensemble, sauf celle de Whitney, qui du premier
coup était dans la direction juste, et n'a besoin aujourd'hui que d'être
patiemment poursuivie.

"Considérons avant tout ce second rôle, car il est évident que c'est par là,
c'est-à-dire parce qu'il avait inculqué aux linguistes une plus saine vue de ce
qu'était en général l'objet traité sous le nom de langage, qu'il les
déterminait à se servir de procédés un peu différents dans le laboratoire de
leur comparaisons journalières. Les deux choses, une bonne généralisation
sur le langage, qui peut intéresser qui que ce soit, ou une saine méthode à
proposer à la grammaire comparée pour les opérations précises de [   ],
sont en réalité la même chose."

we can check, it is apparent that he was a complete mediocrity, not without pretensions.[6]

After some critical reflections upon the late American linguist, the letter of praise sketched by Saussure yields to a second, antithetic draft.

Upon receiving your esteemed letter, dated at Bryn Mawr on the 29th of October and which reached me on the 10th of Nov., I would have immediately to answer you this:

1st. You give me great honor in asking me to appraise Whitney *as a comparative philologist*. But Whitney never was a *comparative philologist*. He has left us not a single page allowing us to appraise him as a comparative philologist. He has left us only works which deduce from the results of comparative grammar a higher and general view of language: that being exactly his great originality since 1867. [   ]

2nd. As soon as it is no longer a question of mere universal statements that one can make about language, I am in agreement with no one school in general, no more with the reasonable doctrine of Whitney than with the unreasonable doctrines that he victoriously [fought]. And this disagreement is such that it admits of no compromise or shading, under penalty of finding myself obliged to write things that make no sense to me.

I would consequently have to beg you to release me immediately from the task of speaking about the oeuvre of Whitney in linguistics, even though this oeuvre is by far [the best].[7]

[6] "Ce sera pour tous les temps un sujet de réflexion philosophique, que pendant une période de cinquante ans, la science linguistique née en Allemagne, développée en Allemagne, chérie en Allemagne par une innombrable catégorie d'individus, n'ait jamais eu même la velléité de s'élever à ce degré d'abstraction qui est nécessaire pour dominer d'une part *ce qu'on fait*, d'autre part en quoi *ce qu'on fait* a une légitimité et une raison d'être dans l'ensemble des sciences; mais un second sujet d'étonnement sera de voir que lorsqu'enfin cette science semble triompher de sa torpeur, elle aboutisse à l'essai risible de Schleicher, qui croule sous son propre ridicule. Tel a été le prestige de Schleicher pour avoir simplement *essayé* de dire quelque chose de général sur la langue, qu'il semble que ce soit une figure hors pair encore aujourd'hui dans l'histoire des études linguistiques, et qu'on voit des linguistes prendre des airs comiquement graves, lorsqu'il est question de cette grande figure. . . . Par tout ce que nous pouvons contrôler, il est apparent que c'était la plus complète médiocrité, ce qui n'exclut pas les prétentions."

[7] "A la réception de votre très honorée lettre, datée de Bryn Mawr 29 Octobre et qui m'est parvenue le 10 nov., j'aurais dû immédiatement vous répondre ceci:

"1° Vous me faites le haut honneur de me demander d'apprécier Whitney *as a comparative philologist*. Mais jamais Whitney n'a voulu être un *com-*

Finally, on the last page of his notes, the Swiss scholar outlines
the third version of his planned but never accomplished reply to
the American invitation to give his view on the deceased linguist,
and this new variant is concentrated upon the historic significance
of the latter's work: "I believe that it would be the best and the
simplest homage to bestow on the oeuvre of Whitney to state how
little this oeuvre has suffered from the injuries of time." [8] Such a
eulogy, as Saussure underlines,

would be extraordinary in linguistics itself. Of all the specialized or general
books, which today are 30 years old, is there one in linguistics that has not
become irreparably obsolete for us? I look and find no other.—By which we
do not dream of saying in any way that Whitney's book is definitive, or that it
contains everything that one might want; that is something the author
himself would have rejected; but what it does contain, and what Whitney
first said in 1867, as it is universally recognized, has not been rendered void in
1894. That is a fact more instructive than much commentary, one to serve
as a touchstone in the appraisal of a thinker.[9]

---

parative philologist. Il ne nous a pas laissé une seule page permettant de
l'apprécier comme comparative philologist. Il ne nous a laissé que des travaux
qui déduisent des résultats de la grammaire comparée une vue supérieure et
générale sur le langage: cela étant justement sa haute originalité dès 1867.
[   ]

"2° Du moment qu'il ne s'agit plus que des choses universelles qu'on peut
dire sur le langage, je ne me sens d'accord avec aucune école en général, pas
plus avec la doctrine raisonnable de Whitney qu'avec les doctrines dé-
raisonnables qu'il a victorieusement [combattues]. Et ce désaccord est tel
qu'il ne comporte aucune transaction ni nuance, sous peine de me voir obligé
d'écrire des choses n'ayant aucun sens à mes yeux.

"J'aurais dû dès lors vous prier de me décharger immédiatement du devoir
de parler de l'oeuvre de Whitney en linguistique, alors même que cette
oeuvre est de beaucoup [la meilleure]."

[8] "Je crois que ce sera le meilleur et le plus simple hommage à décerner à
l'oeuvre de Whitney que de constater à quel point cette oeuvre a peu souffert
de l'injure du temps."

[9] "Un eloge de ce genre devient extraordinaire dans la linguistique proprement dite. De tous les livres, spéciaux ou généraux, qui ont aujourd'hui 30
ans de date, quel est celui qui en linguistique n'ait pas irrémédiablement
vieilli à nos yeux? Je le cherche et n'en trouve pas d'autre.—En quoi, nous ne
songeons à dire aucunement que le livre de Whitney soit définitif, ou qu'il
contienne tout ce qu'on pourrait désirer; c'est là ce que l'auteur lui-même
eût repoussé; mais ce qu'il contient, et ce que Whitney disait le premier en
1867, n'est pas encore frappé de nullité en 1894, de l'aveu universel. C'est là
un fait plus instructif que beaucoup de commentaires pour servir de pierre
de touche dans l'appréciation d'un esprit."

Saussure was pondering an extensive essayistic reply in which he could "give free rein to his pen" and which would contain such sections as "Comparative Grammar; Comparative Grammar and Linguistics; Language, a human institution (or Whitney and institutions); Linguistics, a twofold science; Whitney and the Neogrammarian school; Whitney as a phonologist." [10] The final chapter—"Definitive value"—was to have been a recognition of Whitney's merit "in having made himself sufficiently independent of comparative grammar to have taken the first philosophical view of it." [11]

Saussure's notebook of 1894 is packed with exciting, challenging preliminaries to this literary plan, abandoned as usual in his Geneva practice, and thus the Whitney Memorial Meeting impelled the eternal seeker to think over his own linguistic program and to lay it down, for the first time, in a written and perhaps most radical form.

These tentative items begin with a brief reference to Whitney's inquiry into speech sounds: "Insofar, I say, as phonology concerns linguistics, it is to be noted in this letter that several positive contributions were made to it on different occasions by Whitney, who, moreover, from the very first through his studies on the Prātiçākhyas of the different Vedas, was attentive to the details which can elucidate pronunciation." [12] From this "auxiliary science" Saussure proceeds to Whitney's endeavor to solve "a question of greater interest for linguistics. And without solving the problem (simply because he forgot one element, indeed the most decisive one, of which I cannot speak here), he made what is still by far the most reasonable statement about this question."

The essence of this striking innovation rests upon Whitney's

[10] "La Grammaire Comparée; La Grammaire Comparée et la Linguistique; Le langage, institution humaine (or Whitney et l'institution); La linguistique, science double; Whitney et l'école des néo-grammairiens; Whitney phonologiste."

[11] ". . . de s'être rendu assez indépendant de la grammaire comparée, tout pour en avoir tiré le premier une vue philosophique."

[12] "Pour autant, dis-je, que la phonologie touche à la linguistique, il est à remarquer dans cette lettre que plusieurs contributions positives y ont été apportées à différentes reprises par Whitney, d'ailleurs attentif depuis le premier moment en raison de ses études sur les Prātiçākhyas de différents Véda, à tous les détails qui peuvent éclairer la prononciation."

thesis that language is a human institution: "that changed the axis of linguistics." [13] The substantial particularity of this institution consists in the fact that "language and writing are *not founded on a natural connection of things*. There is no connection at any time between a certain sibilant sound and the form of the letter *S*, and likewise it is no more difficult for the word *cow* than for the word *vacca* to designate a *vache* ['cow']. It is this which Whitney never tired of repeating, in order better to make understood the fact that language is a pure institution." [14]

Saussure notes the American's belief that in language "there is never a trace of internal correlation between vocal signs and the idea" and underscores that "in his whole oeuvre, Whitney did not cease to take his position on these grounds." Saussure feels particularly impressed by the passage in *The Life and Growth of Language* in which Whitney stated that

men used their voices to give signs to their ideas as they would have used gesture or anything else, and because it seemed to them *more convenient* to use their voices. We consider that here, in these few lines, which seem to be a great paradox, is the most precise philosophical idea ever given about language; moreover our more day-to-day practice with the things submitted to our analysis would have everything to gain by starting from this given. For it establishes the fact that language is nothing more than a particular case of the sign, unable to be judged by itself.[15]

In his courses on general linguistics Saussure still agrees with Whitney's emphasis on the conventional character of language

[13] "Mais il y a une tentative de Whitney de résoudre une question autrement intéressante pour la linguistique. Et sans résoudre le problème (simplement parce qu'il a oublié *un* élément, il est vrai le plus décisif, dont je n'aurais pas le loisir de parler ici), il a dit, de beaucoup, ce qu'il y a encore de plus raisonnable sur cette question.

"Whitney a dit: le langage est une *Institution* humaine. Cela a changé l'axe de la linguistique."

[14] "Mais le langage et l'écriture ne sont *pas fondés sur un rapport naturel des choses*. Il n'y a aucun rapport à aucun moment entre un certain son sifflant et la forme de la lettre *S*, et de même il n'est pas plus difficile au mot *cow* qu'au mot *vacca* de désigner une vache. C'est ce que Whitney ne s'est jamais lassé de répéter, pour mieux faire sentir que le langage est une institution pure."

[15] "Whitney dit que les hommes se sont servis de la voix pour donner des signes à leurs idées comme ils se seraient servis du geste ou d'autre chose, et parce que cela leur a semblé *plus commode* de se servir de la voix. Nous

but admits a certain predisposition toward the use of vocal organs for human language.

In the shrewd reasonings of Whitney on language as an institution, Saussure detects a shortcoming to be straightened out. "The continuation would say, we believe: it is a human institution without analogue." The main reservation made by the critic is directed against the general impression one gains from Whitney's writings that "common sense were enough" to eliminate all the phantoms and to grasp the essence of linguistic phenomena: "Now this conviction is not ours. On the contrary, we are profoundly convinced that whosoever sets foot on the field of *language* can say to himself that he is abandoned by all the analogies in heaven and [earth]. That is precisely why there could be built upon language such fantastic constructions as that which Whitney demolishes, but also why there remains much to be said in another sense." [16]

Saussure answers by tracing the features which distinguish sign systems, that is, semiotic institutions, from all other human institutions, and particularly those features which specify language and writing in comparison with other semiotic patterns and thus exhibit

the very complex nature of the particular semiology called language. Language is nothing more than a *special case* of the Theory of Signs. But precisely by this fact alone it is absolutely impossible that it be a simple thing (or a thing directly perceivable by our minds in its mode of being).

The chief effect of the study of language on the theory of signs, the forever-new horizon it will have opened up, will be to have taught and revealed *a whole new aspect of the sign;* namely, that the latter begins to be really understood only when it is seen to be a thing which is not only

estimons que c'est là, en ces deux lignes, qui ressemblent à un gros paradoxe, la plus juste idée philosophique qui ait jamais été donnée du langage ; mais en outre que notre plus journalière pratique des objets soumis à notre analyse aurait tout à gagner à partir de cette donnée. Car elle établit ce fait que le langage n'est rien de plus qu'un cas particulier du signe, hors d'état d'être jugé en lui-même."

[16] "Or cette conviction n'est pas la nôtre. Nous sommes au contraire profondément convaincus que quiconque pose le pied sur le terrain de la *langue* peut se dire qu'il est abandonné par toutes les analogies du ciel et de la [terre]. C'est précisément pourquoi on a pu faire sur la langue d'aussi fantaisistes constructions que celle que démolit Whitney, mais aussi pourquoi il reste beaucoup à dire dans un autre sens."

transmittable but by its nature *destined to be transmitted* [and] modifiable. But for anyone who wants to work on the theory of language this is a hundred-fold complication.

Philosophers, logicians, psychologists have perhaps been able to teach us what is the fundamental bond between the idea and its symbol, in particular an *independent symbol* which represents it. By *independent* symbol we understand those categories of symbols whose chief character is to have visibly *no manner of connection* with the thing designated and to be no longer able to depend on it even indirectly in the course of their fortunes.[17]

Other semiotic institutions, such as rituals or fashions, imply a certain inner connection between the two aspects, *signifiant* and *signifié* (to use the terms which later, in 1911, Saussure took over from the Stoic tradition), and therefore "remain *simple* in their complications; on the contrary, it is fundamentally impossible that a single entity of language *be simple* since it presupposes the combination of two things *without connection,* an idea and a symbolic object devoid of any internal bond with this idea.

"It is exactly to the extent that the external object is a sign" and thus, implicitly, "is perceived as a sign [= *signifiant*] that it is by any right a part of language." [18]

[17] ". . . la si complexe nature de la sémiologie particulière dite langage.

Le langage n'est rien de plus qu'un *cas particulier* de la Théorie de Signes. Mais précisément par ce seul fait, il se trouve déjà dans l'impossibilité absolue d'être une chose simple (ni une chose directement saisissable à notre esprit dans sa façon d'être).

"Ce sera la réaction capitale de l'étude du langage sur la théorie des signes, ce sera l'horizon a jamais nouveau qu'elle aura ouvert, que de lui avoir appris et révélé *tout un côté nouveau du signe,* à savoir que celui-ci ne commence à être réellement connu, que quand on a vu qu'il est une chose non-seulement transmissible, mais de sa nature *destiné à être transmis* [et] modifiable.— Seulement, pour celui qui veut faire la théorie du langage, c'est la complication centuplée.

"Des philosophes, des logiciens, des psychologues, ont peut-être pu nous apprendre quel était le contrat fondamental entre l'idée et le symbole, en particulier un *symbole indépendant* qui la représente. Par symbole *indépendant,* nous entendons les catégories de symboles qui ont ce caractère capital de n'avoir *aucune espèce de lien* visible avec l'objet à désigner, et de ne plus pouvoir en dépendre même indirectement dans la suite de leurs destinées."

[18] "Les autres institutions demeurent *simples* dans leurs complications; au contraire il est fondamentalement impossible qu'une seule entité de langage soit *simple,* puisqu'il suppose la combinaison de deux choses *privées de*

Saussure's Whitney notebook opens with a fundamental semiotic statement: "The object which serves as a sign is never *'the same'* twice: from the first we need an investigation or an initial convention in order to know for what reason [and] within what limits we have the right to call it the same; there is its fundamental difference with any other object." [19]

This assertion displays a close correspondence with the continual inquiry of Charles Sanders Peirce into the relationship between *Legisigns* and *Replicas* (or *Instances*). In general Saussure's remarks on *sémiologie*, inspired by his meditations on Whitney, are essentially akin to the *semiotic* ideas of Peirce who, however, nowhere refers to his New England countryman.

Prompted by A. Sèchehaye's *Programme et méthodes de la linguistique théorique* (1908), Saussure returned to the cardinal questions of language. He asserted in his notes, as we know from R. Godel's quotations, that two Poles, Baudouin de Courtenay and M. Kruszewski (1851–1887), both still disregarded by the bulk of western scholars, "were nearer than anyone else to a theoretical view of language." He felt it necessary to adduce a third name: "The American Whitney, whom I revere, never said a single word on the same subjects which was not right; but like all the others, he does not dream that language needs systematics." [20] Saussure's notes of 1894 tried to explain this alleged lack of systematization with the help of a comparison, pursued later, between language and

---

rapport, une idée et un objet symbolique dépourvu de tout lien avec cette idée.

"Ce n'est que dans la mesure exacte où l'objet extérieur est signe (est aperçu comme signe [= *signifiant*])qu'il fait partie du langage à un titre quelconque."

[19] "L'objet qui sert de signe n'est jamais *'le même'* deux fois: il faut dès le premier moment un examen ou une convention initiale, pour savoir au nom de quoi [et] dans quelles limites nous avons le droit de l'appeler le même; là est la fondamentale différence avec un objet quelconque."

[20] "Baudouin de Courtenay et Kruszewski ont été plus près que personne d'une vue théorique de la langue, cela sans sortir des considérations linguistiques pures; ils sont d'ailleurs ignorés de la généralité des savants occidentaux.—L'Américain Whitney, que je révère, n'a jamais dit un seul mot sur les mêmes sujets, qui ne fût juste; mais comme tous les autres, il ne songe pas que la langue ait besoin d'une systématique."

a game of chess: the necessity of a clear-cut distinction between two aspects of the game, namely, the simultaneous positions of the figures and the temporal sequence of their moves. This distinction is then said to be particularly important for the science of language: among human institutions language is the only one which is not submitted "to continuous mental correction, because from the outset it does not proceed with any visible agreement between the idea and the means of expression." [21] The interconnection of these two facets is viewed by the scholar as merely conventional (Whitney's term *arbitrary,* later adopted by Saussure, was used only once and crossed out in his notebook). Consequently,

it would be truly presumptuous, from that, to believe that the history of language should resemble even distantly that of any other institution.

That language is, at every moment of its existence, *an historical product*— that much is evident. But that, at no point of language does this historical product represent anything other than the compromise (the ultimate compromise) with certain symbols that the mind accepts—this is a truth even more absolute, for without this last circumstance there would be no language. Now the manner in which the mind may employ a symbol (*if we first admit that the symbol remains unchanged*) is a whole science which has nothing to do with historical considerations. Moreover, [if the] symbol changes, then immediately there arises a new state, necessitating a new application of universal laws.[22]

As to the changes themselves, Saussure insists on their merely fortuitous character: "Everything goes on outside the mind." And

[21] "La différence de l'institution du langage d'avec les autres institutions humaines; a savoir celle-ci n'est pas soumise à la correction continuelle de l'esprit, parce qu'elle ne découle pas, depuis l'origine, d'une harmonie visible entre l'idée et le moyen d'expression."

[22] "Il serait vraiment présomptueux de croire que l'histoire du langage doive ressembler même de loin, après cela, à celle d'une autre institution.

"Que le langage soit, à chaque moment de son existence, *un produit historique,* c'est ce qui est évident. Mais qu'à aucun moment du langage, ce produit historique représente autre chose que le compromis (le dernier compromis) qu'accepte l'esprit avec certains symboles, c'est là une vérité plus absolue encore, car sans ce dernier fait il n'y aurait pas de langage. Or la façon dont l'esprit peut se servir d'un symbole (*étant donné d'abord que le symbole ne change pas*) est toute une science, laquelle n'a rien à voir avec les considérations historiques. De plus, [si le] symbole change, immédiatement après, il y a un nouvel état, nécessitant une nouvelle application des lois universelles."

above all, "in its *genesis* a process arises from some accident." If one were to cling to the comparison with a chess game, then—in Saussure's dogma—

> nothing prevents us from assuming that the player is completely absurd, as is the randomness of phonetic and other events.
>
> For many years we have maintained the conviction that linguistics is a *split* science, and so profoundly, irreparably split that one might indeed ask if there is sufficient reason to maintain under the name linguistics an artificial unity, giving rise precisely to all the errors, all the inextricable snares we are struggling against.[23]

Saussure entitled his final remarks to this question "On the Antihistoricalness of Language." He ventured to corroborate this headline:

> There is no "language" and no science of language except on the prior condition of abstracting from what has gone before, from what interconnects the periods.[. . .] It is the absolute condition for understanding what takes place—or simply what *is*—in a given state that one abstracts from what is not of that state—for example, from what preceded—especially from what preceded. But what is the result of this for generalization? Generalization is impossible. [. . .] To conceive of a generalization which would manage equally both of these things is to ask for the absurd. It is this kind of absurdity that linguistics, from its birth, has wanted to impose on the mind. Consequently, it would be impossible to discuss a single term used in linguistics in its daily work without taking up *ab ovo* the entire question of language,[24] still less to formulate an appraisal of a doctrine which, as rational as it was, did not take account [   ].[25]

---

[23] "Tout se passe hors de l'esprit."

"Par sa génèse un procédé provient de n'importe quel hasard."

". . . rien n'empêche de supposer le joueur tout-à-fait absurde comme c'est le hasard des événements phonétiques et autres."

"Nous nourissons depuis bien des années cette conviction que la linguistique est une science *double,* et si profondément, irrémédiablement double qu'on peut à vrai dire se demander s'il y a une raison suffisante pour maintenir sous ce nom de linguistique une unité factice, génératrice précisément de toutes les erreurs, de tous les inextricables pièges contre lesquels nous nous débattons."

[24] "Il n'y a pas un seul terme employé en linguistique auquel j'accorde un sens quelconque," said Saussure in his letter to Meillet quoted earlier.

[25] "Il n'y a de 'langue' et de science de la langue, qu'à la condition initiale de faire abstraction de ce qui a précédé, de ce qui relie entre elles les époques. [. . .] C'est la condition absolue pour comprendre ce qui se passe, ou seulement

It is an evident allusion to Whitney's doctrine. But, on the other hand, Saussure's belief in the preponderance or even hegemony of "nonhistorical" linguistics expressed in his notebook with such an intransigence was, nonetheless, subject throughout the nineties to recurrent and pungent hesitations. Thus even in his Whitney notebook we run into expressions of uncertainty:

It is extremely uncertain and difficult to say if it is an historical entity or rather something else, but in the current stage of trends, there is no danger in especially stressing its nonhistorical side.[26]

In the same notebook "the real question" (la vraie question) was propounded but struck out by Saussure himself:

Can one "force" language to become historical subject matter, appropriately historical?—But inversely, will it for an instant be possible to forget the historical side?[27]

One may, moreover, recall that Baudouin de Courtenay, in his Polish monograph of 1894 on phonetic alternations, blamed Saussure for a unilateral historicism and for a disregard of coexistent elements in language. The latter's introductory lectures of 1891 at the University of Geneva claimed that "everything in language is *history*, that is to say that it is an object for historical analysis,

---

ce qui *est,* dans un état que de faire abstraction de ce qui n'est pas de cet état, par exemple de ce qui a précédé; surtout de ce qui a précédé. Mais que résulte-t-il de là pour la généralisation? La généralisation est impossible. [. . .] Concevior une généralisation qui mènerait de front ces deux choses est demander l'absurde. C'est ce genre d'absurde que la linguistique, depuis sa naissance, veut imposer à l'esprit. Il serait, par suite, impossible soit de discourir sur un seul des termes usités en linguistique dans la pratique de chaque jour sans reprendre *ab ovo* la question totale du langage, soit encore moins de formuler une appréciation sur une doctrine qui n'a pas tenu compte, si rationnelle qu'elle fût, [   ]."

[26] "Il est extrêmement douteux et délicat de dire si c'est plutôt un objet historique ou plutôt autre chose, mais dans l'état actuel des tendances, il n'y a aucun danger à insister surtout sur le côté non-historique."

[27] "Peut on 'forcer' le langage jusqu'à devenir une matière historique, proprement historique?—Mais inversement, sera-t-il un seul instant possible d'oublier le côté historique?"

and not for abstract analysis," [28] and even when reviewing J. Schmidt's monograph of 1895—*Kritik der Sonantentheorie*—for the *Indogermanische Forschungen* of 1897, Saussure affirmed that

when true linguistic theory is first done, one of the very first principles which will be set down is that never, in any case, can a rule whose characteristic it is to operate in a *state of language* (= between 2 contemporaneous terms) and not in a *phonetic event* (= 2 successive terms) have more than a fortuitous validity. [. . .] And in any case, in order to put forth the rule in a true sense, one must recapture the anterior item in place of the contemporaneous one. . . .[29]

Saussure's focusing upon "states of language" alienates him from Whitney's principles of linguistic science and draws his designs and propositions nearer to Peirce's semiotic quest:

The altogether ultimate law of language is, by what we venture to say, that there is never anything which can consist in one item (as a direct consequence of the fact that linguistic symbols are without connection to what they must designate), thus that two such have their value only by their reciprocal *difference*, or that none has any value, even through a part of itself (I assume 'the root,' etc.) other than by this same network of eternally negative differences.[30]

Side by side with *différences*, the notebook uses also the term *oppositions*, most probably modeled upon Baudouin's example (*protivopolozhnosti*) and later promoted as a basic concept of Saussurian doctrine. The kernel of this doctrine emerges in the notebook: "The a priori absolute evidence that there will never be a

[28] "Tout dans la langue est *histoire*, c'est à dire qu'elle est un objet d'analyse historique, et non d'analyse abstraite."

[29] "Quand on fera pour la première fois une théorie vraie de la langue, un des tout premiers principes qu'on y inscrira est que jamais, en aucun cas, une règle qui a pour caractère de se mouvoir dans un *état de langue* (= entre 2 termes contemporains) et non dans un *événement phonétique* (= 2 termes successifs) ne peut avoir plus qu'une validité de hasard. [. . .] Et dans tous les cas, pour poser la règle sous un vrai sens, il faudra reprendre le terme antérieur au lieu d'un terme contemporain. . ."

[30] "La loi tout à fait finale du langage est à ce que nous osons dire qu'il n'y a jamais rien qui puisse résider dans un terme (par suite directe de ce que les symboles linguistiques sont sans relation avec ce qu'ils doivent désigner), donc que tous deux ne valent que par leur réciproque *différence*, ou qu'aucun ne vaut, même par une partie quelconque de soi (je suppose 'la racine' etc.), autrement que par ce même plexus de différences éternellement négatives."

single fragment of language which can be founded on anything, as an ultimate principle, other than its noncoincidence with the remainder; positive form being irrelevant, to a degree to which we have no idea [. . .] ; for this degree is tantamount to zero." [31]

Saussure's approach to the systems of correlative linguistic values permitted him to re-evaluate the achievements of such distinguished scholars as Whitney in the light of the anticipated future: "Besides, we should have no illusions. There will arrive a day where it will be recognized that the quanta of language and their relations are in their essence consistently expressible through mathematical formulas." [32] Otherwise one would have to renounce any comprehension of linguistic facts: "This is what, despite ourselves, deeply changes our point of view on the worth of everything which has been said, even by very eminent men." [33]

Both Saussure's requirement of autonomy for linguistics and his criticism of Whitney's view of this question had been anticipated one decade earlier by the paramount Czech philosopher T. G. Masaryk (1850–1937), whose treatise *Základové konkretné logiky* ('Fundamentals of Concrete Logic', 1885) tended to draft a rational systematics of sciences. Masaryk's discussion of the relation between linguistics and neighboring disciplines borders upon Whitney's "couple of volumes" which inaugurate the selection of sources recommended in the Czech treatise. Its author adheres to Whitney's view of language as a social institution but essentially modifies the latter's thesis:

The question arises whether linguistics is an independent science, and especially one might argue whether in some way it does not pertain to sociology. I think, however, that linguistics is an independent science, in

[31] ". . . l'évidence absolue, même à priori, qu'il n'y aura jamais un seul fragment de langue qui puisse être fondé sur autre chose, comme principe ultime, que sa non-coïncidence, ou sur le degré de sa non-coïncidence, avec le reste; la forme positive étant indifférente, jusqu'à un degré dont nous n'avons encore aucune idée [. . .]; car ce degré est entièrement égal à zéro."

[32] "Au reste, ne nous faisons pas d'illusions. Il arrivera un jour où on reconnaîtra que les quantités du langage et leurs rapports sont régulièrement exprimables de leur nature fondamentale par des formules mathématiques."

[33] "C'est ce qui change beaucoup, malgré nous, notre point de vue sur la valeur de tout ce qui a été dit, même par des hommes très éminents."

view of its own particular subject matter, namely language, which both in its being and buildup is distinct from the phenomena treated by sociology. However close may be the connection which ties the development of speech and writing to the genesis and development of the inner life, nonetheless it is an entirely separate theme and has to be investigated by its own science.

In his book of 1885 Masaryk condemned any superficial imitation of extraneous methods by linguists. He assailed logical incongruity and fear of theory as handicaps to the development of linguistics. In the author's vision, principles of linguistic science were to be systematically elaborated as a necessary theoretical basis of concrete linguistics—*special,* oriented toward single languages and language families, and *general,* destined to elicit and sum up the experience from the whole universe of languages. It was Whitney's latent intuition which must have furthered the thought of the twofold subdivision of the study of language—both abstract and concrete—into its synchronic (fundamental) and historical (secondary) aspects, that thought which haunted Masaryk in the eighties and Saussure in the nineties and was fraught with serious consequences for the further development of linguistic science.

The most comprehensive essay devoted to Whitney's initiatory attainments in the theory of language and to their place in the world history of ideas was written by the prominent Italian linguist Benvenuto Terracini (1886–1968). It was published, on the occasion of the fiftieth anniversary of Whitney's death, in *Revista de Filologia Hispanica,* vol. 5 (1943) under the title "W. D. Whitney y la lingüistica general." In its Italian version, "Le origini della lingüistica generale," which was included in Terracini's *Guida allo studio della linguistica storica* (Rome, 1949), Whitney is portrayed as the "initiator of general linguistics built upon historical empiricism" who still endows his readers with a feeling of "a particular charm." Especially, pervasive European discussions on the "institutionalism" and "conventionalism" of language never fail to bring forward again and again Whitney's name and creed.

In his native country, the immediate impact of Whitney's contributions to the general science of language was far weaker. For long years it looked as if students "absorbed in particulars" disregarded his prefatory warning of 1867 not to lose "sight of the grand truths and principles which underlie and give significance to their work, and the recognition of which ought to govern its course throughout." American academic publications confined their occasional tributes of respect to cursory remarks that Whitney's theoretical studies "cannot have remained wholly without effect" and that they "helped chase many a goblin from the sky" (Benjamin Ide Wheeler). New linguistic ideas which began to sprout here, mainly towards the threshold of our century, were tied to the advance of anthropology and to the methodological questions stirred by the developing research in American Indian languages, their structure, and interrelation.

If, according to Brugmann's letter, cited earlier, "a German colleague" felt the great indebtedness of European science to the New Englander Whitney, "the great departed scholar," now it was the Westphalia-born Franz Boas (1858–1942) who in 1886 transferred his versatile scientific activities from Germany to America and initiated vast descriptive, anthropologically oriented linguistic fieldwork which involved a wide team of explorers and revealed a vital need of new methods and theoretical inferences. As Leonard Bloomfield (1887–1949) wrote in his obituary of Boas, "The progress which has since been made in the recording and description of human speech has merely grown forth from the roots, stem, and mighty branches of Boas' life work."

In the succeeding generation of American scholars, the scope of linguistic interests has embraced the local native languages and the Indo-European world as well. Significantly enough, Whitney's legacy was deliberately restored by Leonard Bloomfield, whose first outline, *An Introduction to the Study of Language* (New York, 1914), is, even in its title, associated precisely with Whitney's tradition. The initial lines of Bloomfield's Preface announce that the purpose of the new publication is the same "as that of Whitney's *Language and the Study of Language* and *The Life and Growth of Language,* books which fifty years ago represented the attainments of linguistic science and, owing to their author's clearness of view and conscientious discrimination between ascertained fact and mere surmise, contain little to which we cannot today subscribe. The great progress of our science in the last half-century is, I believe, nevertheless sufficient excuse for my attempt to give a summary of what is now known about language."

Bloomfield retained his admiration for Whitney's linguistic essentials and once, in the early 1940s, he said that his first guide to a synchronic study of languages was Whitney's *Sanskrit Grammar* of 1879. It is worthy of note that A. Hillebrandt's review of 1880 recognized the novelty of this grammar in its inquiry into a state of language (*Erforschung des Sprachzustandes*), and the best translator and commentator of Saussure's *Corso di linguistica generale* (Bari, 1967), Tullio De Mauro, compared this feature of Whitney's textbook with Saussure's synchronic approach to language.

Linguistic structures are "context-sensitive": they shift their meaning correspondingly to their variable surroundings. In a similar way linguistic theories undergo modifications according to the historical environment and personal ideology of their interpreters. Thus Whitney's doctrine is differently viewed and treated by Brugmann, by Saussure, by Terracini, by Bloomfield, and presumably also by the present-day critical readers. Hitherto in all interpretations of Whitney's contributions to general linguistics, the invariant idea is that on the subjects he discussed, he made no fallacious statements, and thus in questions of general linguistics, he remarkably surpassed his predecessors and contemporaries. The variables in the appraisal of Whitney's legacy concern not so much what he said as what and how much remains to be said "dans un autre sens" and what is the relative pertinence for the science of language of that which was revealed in comparison with that which remained unvoiced.

Roman Jakobson

WHITNEY ON LANGUAGE

WILLIAM DWIGHT WHITNEY

Whitney was born on the 9th of February, 1827, at North-ampton, Mass., the second (surviving) son and fourth child of Josiah Dwight and Sarah (Williston) Whitney. The father was born in Westfield, oldest son of Abel Whitney (Harvard, 1773) and Clarissa Dwight; the family is a branch of the Whitneys of Massachusetts (to whom that of Eli Whitney, the inventor, also belongs), and unconnected with those of Connecticut and New York. The mother was daughter of Rev. Payson Williston (Yale, 1783) of Easthampton, and sister of the founder of Williston Seminary, in that town. The father was a business man, later manager, first as cashier and then as president, of the Northampton Bank, and widely and honorably known for his ability and integrity; his children mostly turned to literary pursuits: the oldest, Josiah Dwight, being a well-known scientist, long head of the California Survey and now professor of economical geology in Harvard University; the third son, James Lyman, being one of the heads of the Boston Public Library; and the fourth, Henry Mitchell, a professor in Beloit College, Wisconsin; while a daughter, Maria, is a teacher, formerly in charge of the department of modern languages at Smith College (for women) in Northampton; all the sons except our classmate are graduates of Yale.

Whitney made his preparation for college entirely in the free public schools of his native town. The teachers whom he remembers with most gratitude are Rodolphus B. Hubbard, long the head of the High School there, and John B. Dwight of New Haven (Yale, 1840). He entered the class at the beginning of Sophomore year, being examined along with Cowles. No small part of his time while in college was spent roaming over the hills and through the valleys, collecting birds for the Natural History Society and setting them up; and work of this kind has never since been entirely abandoned.

On leaving college, being undecided what occupation to turn to, he at first went provisionally into the bank, under his father, and it ended in his staying there more than three full years. During the first year, indeed, he stopped and made a feint of beginning the study of medicine—commencing service in a doctor's office one day, only to be taken down with a long fit of illness the next, and returning to his first work when this was over. He did in the three years a good deal of bird- and plant-collecting; and a case of his birds, chiefly the acquisitions of this period, now forms a part of the collection in the Peabody Museum at New Haven. He did also a good deal of studying, especially in some of the modern European languages; and finally, early in 1848, was led, partly under the influence and encouragement of his father's pastor, now Professor Geo. E. Day, of Yale, to turn his attention to Sanskrit, text-books for which were within his reach in his brother's library. In the spring of 1849, he left the bank; and the summer of that year was spent by him among the swamps and mosquitoes of Lake Superior, as "Assistant Sub-Agent" (at $2 a day) in the United States Geological Survey of that region, carried on under the care of his brother and the late J. W. Foster; he had under his charge the botany, the ornithology, and the accounts. On returning home, he went for a year to New Haven, to continue his Sanskrit studies under Professor E. E. Salisbury and in company with Professor James Hadley, and to prepare for a visit to Germany, already planned. He sailed for Bremen direct in the autumn of 1850, and returned home in July, 1853. Three winters were passed by him in Berlin, and two summers in Tübingen (in southern Germany), chiefly under the instruction of Professor Albrecht Weber and Rudolf Roth, respectively, but also of Professor Lepsius and others. Having copied in Berlin all the manuscripts of one of the oldest and most important Hindu scriptures, the Atharva-Veda, then unpublished, he planned an edition of it in conjunction with Professor Roth; and on the way home, in '53, he stopped in Paris, Oxford, and London, to collate the remaining European manuscripts. The first volume of the work, containing the text alone, was published at Berlin in 1855 and 1856; a complete Index Verborum to it was added at New Haven in 1881; a volume of notes, translations, etc., is still due. Before leaving Germany, he had accepted an invitation to return to Yale College as professor of Sanskrit; but he did not go there to remain until August, 1854, spending the interval in part in scientific work. Since '54 he has lived continuously in New Haven. The salary of the Sanskrit professorship having been for the first sixteen years a very small one, he was obliged to help support himself by teaching German and French: at the outset, partly in private classes; later, in college classes only; on the establishment of the Sheffield Scientific School, he had for some time the charge in it of the department of modern languages; nor has he entirely withdrawn from that work even down to the present time. This has led to his preparing a series of text-books, especially for the study of German, which is not yet quite complete; it consists of two German grammars, a larger (1869) and a smaller (1885), a German reader with an elaborate Vocabulary (1870), a brief German dictionary (1877), and a number of annotated German texts (from 1876 on); a French grammar is now nearly finished. He was elected a member of the American Oriental Society in 1850; in 1855 he undertook the charge of its library, remaining librarian until 1873; in 1857 he was made its corresponding secretary, and performed the duties of that office till 1884, when he was chosen its president; no small part of his work has been done in the service of the Society; from 1857 to the present time, just a half of the contents of its Journal (vols. vi.–xii.) is from his pen. In this are included four works of considerable extent: the annotated translation of a Hindu treatise of astronomy (the Sūrya-Siddhānta, 1860); the texts, translations, etc., of two Sanskrit grammatical treatises (Atharva-Veda Prātiçākhya, 1862, and Tāittirīya-Prātiçākhya, 1871: to the latter work was awarded by the Berlin Academy the Bopp prize, as the most important Sanskrit publication of the triennium); and the Atharva-Veda Index Verborum, mentioned above. Some of his minor contributions to the same Journal, along with others to various periodicals, were collected and published in two volumes of "Oriental and Linguistic Studies" (1873 and 1874). He has also produced a couple of volumes on the general science of language, entitled, respectively, "Language and the Study of Language" (1867; it was first prepared as Smithsonian and as Lowell lectures; it has been translated into German and Netherlandish), and "the Life and Growth of Language" (International Scientific Series, 1875; translated into French, Italian, German, Swedish, and Russian); and the articles on "Language" in Johnson's Cyclopædia (vol. ii., 1876), and on "Philology" in the Encyclopædia Britannica (vol. xviii., 1885), are by him. On the formation of the American Philological Association (1869), he was its first president, and has contributed extensively to its Proceedings and Transactions. He has also written an English grammar ("Essentials of English Grammar," 1877), and a Sanskrit grammar (see below: two editions, English and German)— to which last he has this year added a Supplement half as big as the work itself ("Roots, Verb-forms, and Primary Derivatives of the Sanskrit Language," Leipzig, 1885; two editions, English and German). He received the honorary degree of Doctor of Philosophy from Breslau University in 1861; that of Doctor of Laws from his Alma Mater in 1868, from William and Mary College in Virginia in 1869, and from Harvard in 1876, also from St. Andrews University in Scotland in 1874. He is further connected with many learned societies in various parts of the world: is an honorary member of the Oriental or Asiatic societies of Great Britain and Ireland, of Germany, of Bengal, of Japan, and of Peking; of the Philological Society of London; of the literary societies of Leyden, Upsala, and Helsingfors; member or correspondent of the Academies of Dublin, Turin, Rome (*Lyncci*), St. Petersburg, and Berlin; also correspondent of the Institute of France; and Foreign Knight of the Prussian order *"pour le mérite"* for Science and Arts (being elected to fill the vacancy made by the death of Thomas Carlyle)—and so on.

On the 27th of August, 1856, Whitney married Elizabeth Wooster, daughter of Roger Sherman and Emily (Perkins) Baldwin of New Haven; her father, a lawyer of the highest rank, had been Governor of Connecticut and Senator in Congress, and inherited his name from Roger Sherman, the well-known signer of the Declaration of Independence, and one of the committee charged with drawing it up, whose grandson he was. They have had six children, three sons and three daughters; of these are living one son, Edward Baldwin, a lawyer in New York city (firm Burnett and Whitney, 67 Wall street), and the three daughters, Marian Parker and Emily Henrietta and Margaret Dwight, who are still with their parents.

Very soon after their marriage, Whitney and his wife went, partly for health and partly for study, to spend somewhat less than a year in France and Italy (Nov., '56 to July, '57), passing several months at Rome. In the summer of 1875 he visited, alone,

England and Germany, mainly for the collection of further material for the Atharva-Veda. In 1878, again, having been engaged by German publishers to prepare a Sanskrit grammar, as one of a series of grammars of the principal languages related with our own, he went abroad with his wife and daughters, to write out the work and carry it through the press; and they spent fifteen months in Europe, chiefly at Berlin and Gotha, just accomplishing the prescribed task: the last proof-sheets of the Index to the volume were read in the cars on the way to the homeward steamer at Havre. Their way off the continent took them through Switzerland and across France, and at Berne they had the pleasure of falling in with Davison and his family.

The life of a college teacher is composed of uneventful years, little marked save by the succession of classes instructed and of literary labors brought to a conclusion. Only now and then comes in a noteworthy variety—as when, in 1873, Whitney was invited to take part in the summer campaign of the Hayden exploring expedition in Colorado, and passed two full months on horseback and under canvas, coursing over regions which in good part had been till then untrodden by the feet of white men, and seeing Nature in her naked grandeur—mounting some nine times up to or beyond the altitude of 14,000 feet. It is said of him, in the Report of the Survey for that year (p. 8), that he "rendered most valuable assistance to Mr. Gardner in his geographical work, for the months of July and August, without compensation from the government"—the disinterested man! His letters describing the fortunes of the summer were printed in the New York "Tribune," and afterwards gathered in one of its Supplements (Extra No. 14, Scientific Series).

[Whitney's autobiographical account in the Williams Class Record he edited mentions 1885 as the most recent date. In 1886, during the preparation of his *Practical French Grammar* (New York, 1886) he started to experience increasing pain in the arms and chest, which, when diagnosed at their severest, proved to be indicators of extensive heart disease. The last eight years of his life were lived in pain at New Haven, Whitney conserving his strength by sticking to an austere regimen prescribed for him. For

classes, he received students at his home, and was active until two
weeks before his death, which occurred in his sleep in the early
morning of June 7, 1894.

During this period, he nevertheless completed a large number of
articles for the *Journal of the American Oriental Society*, the
Proceedings and *Transactions of the American Philological Society*, the *American Journal of Philology*, and general periodi-
cals. The great *Sanskrit Grammar* appeared in a second, revised
and expanded form (Leipzig, 1889), and at the time of his death
he left a 2,459-page manuscript of Atharva Veda translation and
commentary, later edited and published by his former pupil
Charles Rockwell Lanman of Harvard (*Harvard Oriental Series*,
vols. 7–8, Cambridge, Mass., 1905). He also served as editor-in-
chief of the celebrated *Century Dictionary* (New York, 1889–91)
and personally read all of its 21,138 columns of proof.

His poor health finally forced his resignation from the presidency of the American Oriental Society in 1890, after a tenure of
six years; with his eighteen years as librarian and twenty-seven
years as corresponding secretary, this is considerable service indeed. Honors and recognition continued: add to his list in the
autobiography LHD, Columbia, 1887, LLD, Edinburgh, 1889;
Member of the Royal Danish Academy of Sciences, Fellow of the
Royal Society of Edinburgh, Foreign Member of the Royal
Society of Science and Literature of Göteborg, Member of the
National Academy of Sciences.

After his death, there took place in Philadelphia, on December
27–29, 1894, the first American Congress of Philologists, at which
the session of Friday evening, December 28, was devoted to com-
memorating the life of Whitney. From this session came the
volume on the *Whitney Memorial Meeting* (Boston, 1897; also
Journal of the American Oriental Society, vol. 19, no. 1, 1897),
with the addresses delivered, letters from foreign scholars, and a
complete bibliography up to and including the projected Atharva
Veda work.]

LANGUAGE AND THE
STUDY OF LANGUAGE

The whole subject of linguistic investigation may be conveniently summed up in the single inquiry, "Why do we speak as we do?" The essential character of the study of language, as distinguished from the study of languages, lies in this, that it seeks everywhere, not the facts, but the reasons of them; it asks, not how we speak, or should speak, but for what reason; pursuing its search for reasons back to the very ultimate facts of human history, and down into the very depths of human nature. To cover the whole ground of investigation by this inquiry, it needs to be proposed in more than one sense; as the most fitting introduction to our whole discussion, let us put it first in its plainest and most restricted meaning: namely, why do we ourselves speak the English as our mother-tongue, or native language, instead of any other of the thousand varying forms of speech current among men?

The general answer is so obvious as hardly to require to be pointed out: we speak English because we were taught it by those who surrounded us in our infancy and growing age. It is our mother-tongue, because we got it from the lips of our mothers; it is our native language, inasmuch as we were born, not indeed into the possession of it, but into the company of those who already spoke it, having learned it in the same way before us. We were not left to our own devices, to work out for ourselves the great problem of how to talk. In our case, there was no development of language out of our own internal resources, by the reflection of phenomena in consciousness, or however else we may choose to describe it; by the action of a natural impulse, shaping ideas, and creating suitable expression for them. No sooner were our minds so far matured as to be capable of intelligently associating an idea and its sign, than we learned, first to recognize the persons and things about us, the most familiar acts and phenomena of our little world, by the names which others applied to them, and then to apply to them the same names ourselves. Thus, most of us learned first of all to stammer the childish words for 'father' and 'mother,' put, for our convenience, in the accents easiest for unpractised lips to frame. Then, as we grew on, we acquired daily more and more, partly by direct instruction, partly by imitation: those who had

the care of us contracted their ideas and simplified their speech to
suit our weak capacities; they watched with interest every new
vocable which we mastered, corrected our numberless errors, explained what we but half understood, checked us when we used
longer words and more ambitious phrases than we could employ
correctly or wield adroitly, and drilled us in the utterance of
sounds which come hard to the beginner. The kind and degree of
the training thus given, indeed, varied greatly in different cases,
as did the provision made for the necessary wants of childhood in
respect to other matters; as, for instance, the food, the dress, the
moral nurture. Just as some have to rough their way by the hardest through the scenes of early life, beaten, half-starved, clad in
scanty rags, while yet some care and provision were wholly indispensable, and no child could have lived through infancy without
them—so, as concerns language, some get but the coarsest and
most meagre instruction, and yet instruction enough to help them
through the first stages of learning how to speak. In the least
favourable circumstances, there must have been constantly about
every one of us in our earliest years an amount and style of speech
surpassing our acquirements and beyond our reach, and our acquisition of language consisted in our appropriating more and more
of this, as we were able. In proportion as our minds grew in
activity and power of comprehension, and our knowledge increased, our notions and conceptions were brought into shapes
mainly agreeing with those which they wore in the minds of those
around us, and received in our usage the appellations to which the
latter were accustomed. On making acquaintance with certain
liquids, colourless or white, we had not to go through a process of
observation and study of their properties, in order to devise suitable titles for them; we were taught that these were *water* and
milk. The one of them, when standing stagnant in patches, or
rippling between green banks, we learned to call, according to
circumstances and the preference of our instructors, *pool* or
puddle, and *brook* or *river.* An elevation rising blue in the distance, or towering nearer above us, attracted our attention, and
drew from us the staple inquiry "What is that?"—the answer, "A
mountain," or "A hill," brought to our vocabulary one of the
innumerable additions which it gained in a like way. Along with

the names of external sensible objects, we thus learned also that practical classification of them which our language recognizes: we learned to distinguish *brook* and *river; hill* and *mountain; tree, bush, vine, shrub,* and *plant;* and so on, in cases without number. In like manner, among the various acts which we were capable of performing, we were taught to designate certain ones by specific titles: much reproof, for instance, doubtless made us early understand what was meant by *cry, strike, push, kick, bite,* and other names for misdeeds incident to even the best-regulated childhood. How long our own mental states might have remained a confused and indistinct chaos to our unassisted reflection, we do not know; but we were soon helped to single out and recognize by appropriate appellations certain ones among them: for example, a warm feeling of gratification and attachment we were made to signify by the expression *love;* an inferior degree of the same feeling by *like;* and their opposite by *hate.* Long before any process of analysis and combination carried on within ourselves would have given us the distinct conceptions of *true* and *false,* of *good* and *naughty,* they were carefully set before us, and their due apprehension was enforced by faithful admonition, or by something yet more serious. And not only were we thus assisted to an intelligent recognition of ourselves and the world immediately about us, but knowledge began at once to be communicated to us respecting things beyond our reach. The appellations of hosts of objects, of places, of beings, which we had not seen, and perhaps have not even yet seen, we learned by hearing or by reading, and direct instruction enabled us to attach to them some characteristic idea, more or less complete and adequate. Thus, we had not to cross the ocean, and to coast about and traverse a certain island beyond it, in order to know that there is a country *England,* and to hold it apart, by specific attributes, from other countries of which we obtained like knowledge by like means.

But enough of this illustration. It is already sufficiently clear that the acquisition of language was one of the steps of our earliest education. We did not make our own tongue, or any part of it; we neither selected the objects, acts, mental states, relations, which should be separately designated, nor devised their distinctive designations. We simply received and appropriated, as well as we could, whatever our instructors were pleased to set before us. Independence of the general usages of speech was neither encouraged nor tolerated in us; nor did we feel tempted toward independence. Our object was to communicate with those among whom our lot was cast, to understand them and be understood by them, to learn what their greater wisdom and experience could impart to us. In order to do this, we had to think and talk as they did, and we were content to do so. Why such and such a combination of sounds was applied to designate such and such an idea was to us a matter of utter indifference; all we knew or cared to know was that others so applied it. Questions of etymology, of fitness of appellation, concerned us not. What was it to us, for instance, when the answer came back to one of our childish inquiries after names, that the word *mountain* was imported into our tongue out of the Latin, through the Norman French, and was originally an adjective, meaning 'hilly, mountainous,' while *hill* had once a *g* in it, indicating its relationship with the adjective *high?* We recognized no tie between any word and the idea represented by it excepting a mental association which we had ourselves formed, under the guidance, and in obedience to the example, of those about us. We do, indeed, when a little older, perhaps, begin to amuse ourselves with inquiring into the reasons why this word means that thing, and not otherwise: but it is only for the satisfaction of our curiosity; if we fail to find a reason, or if the reason be found trivial and insufficient, we do not on that account reject the word. Thus every vocable was to us an arbitary and conventional sign: arbitrary, because any one of a thousand other vocables could have been just as easily learned by us and associated with the same idea; conventional, because the one we acquired had its sole ground and sanction in the consenting usage of the community of which we formed a part.

Our acquisition of English, however, has yet been but partially and imperfectly described.

In the first place, the English which we thus learn is of that peculiar form or local variety which is talked by our instructors and models. It is, indeed, possible that one may have been surrounded from birth by those, and those only, whose speech is wholly conformed to perfect standards; then it will have been, at least, his own fault if he has learned aught but the purest and most universally accepted English. But such cases cannot be otherwise than rare. For, setting aside the fact that all are not agreed as to whose usage forms the unexceptionable standard, nothing can be more certain than that few, on either side of the ocean, know and follow it accurately. Not many of us can escape acquiring in our youth some tinge of local dialect, of slang characteristic of grade or occupation, of personal peculiarities, even, belonging to our initiators into the mysteries of speech. These may be mere inelegancies of pronunciation, appearing in individual words or in the general tone of utterance, like the nasal twang, and the flattening of *ou* into *ău,* which common fame injuriously ascribes to the Yankee; or they may be ungrammatical modes of expression, or uncouth turns and forms of construction; or favourite recurrent phrases, such as *I guess, I calculate, I reckon, I expect, you know,* each of which has its own region of prevalence; or colloquialisms and vulgarisms, which ought to hide their heads in good English society; or words of only dialectic currency, which the general language does not recognize. Any or all of these or of their like we innocently learn along with the rest of our speech, not knowing how to distinguish the evil from the good. And often, as some of us know to our cost, errors and infelicities are thus so thoroughly wrought into our minds, as parts of our habitual modes of expression, that not all the care and instruction of after life can rid us of them. How many men of culture and eminent ability do we meet with, who exhibit through life the marks of a defective or vicious early training in their native tongue! The dominion of habit is not less powerful in language than in anything else that we acquire and practise. It is not alone true that he who has once thoroughly learned English is thereby almost disqualified from ever attaining a native facility, correctness, and elegance in any foreign tongue; one may also so thoroughly learn a bad style of English as never to be able to ennoble it into the best and most approved form of his native speech. Yet, with us, the influences which tend to repress and eradicate local peculiarities and individual errors are numerous and powerful. One of the most effective among them is school instruction. It is made an important part of our education to learn to speak and write correctly. The pupil of a faithful and competent instructor is taught to read and pronounce, to frame sentences with the mouth and with the pen, in a manner accordant with that which is accepted among the well-educated everywhere. Social intercourse is a cultivating agency hardly less important, and more enduring in its action; as long as we live, by associating with those who speak correctly, we are shown our own faults, and at the same time prompted and taught to correct them. Reading—which is but another form of such intercourse—consultation of authorities, self-impelled study in various forms, help the work. Our speech is improved and perfected, as it was first acquired, by putting ourselves in the position of learners, by following the example of those who speak better than we do. He who is really in earnest to complete his mastery of his mother-tongue may hope for final success, whatever have been his early disadvantages; just as one may acquire a foreign tongue, like German or French, with a degree of perfection depending only on his opportunities, his capacity, his industry, and the length of time he devotes to the study.

Again even when the process of training which we have described gives general correctness and facility, it is far from conferring universal command of the resources of the English tongue. This is no grand indivisible unity, whereof the learner acquires all or none; it is an aggregation of particulars, and each one appropriates more or less of them, according to his means and ability. The vocabulary which the young child has acquired the power to use is a very scanty one; it includes only the most indispensable part of speech, names for the commonest objects, the most ordinary and familiar conceptions, the simplest relations. You can talk with a child only on a certain limited range of subjects; a book not written especially for his benefit is in great part unintelligible to him: he has not yet learned its signs for thought, and they must be translated into others with which he is acquainted; or the thought itself is beyond the reach of his apprehension, the statement is outside the sphere of his knowledge. But in this regard we are all of us more or less children. Who ever yet got through learning his mother-tongue, and could say, "The work is done?" The encyclopedic English language, as we may term it, the English of the great dictionaries, contains more than a hundred thousand words. And these are only a selection out of a greater mass. If all the signs for thought employed for purposes of communication by those who have spoken and who speak no other tongue than ours were brought together, if all obsolete, technical, and dialectic words were gathered in, which, if they are not English, are of no assignable spoken tongue, the number mentioned would be vastly augmented. Out of this immense mass, it has been reckoned by careful observers that from three to five thousand answer all the ordinary ends of familiar intercourse, even among the cultivated; and a considerable portion of the English-speaking community, including the lowest and most ignorant class, never learn to use even so many as three thousand: what they do acquire, of course, being, like the child's vocabulary, the most necessary part of the language, signs for the commonest and simplest ideas. To a nucleus of this character, every artisan, though otherwise uninstructed, must add the technical language of his own craft—names for tools, and processes, and products which his every-day experience makes familiar to him, but of which the vast majority, perhaps, of those outside his own line of life know nothing. Ignorant as he may be, he will talk to you of a host of matters which you shall not understand. No insignificant part of the hundred-thousand-word list is made up of selections from such technical vocabularies. Each department of labour, of art, of science, has its special dialect, fully known only to those who have made themselves masters in that department. The world requires of every well-informed and educated person a certain amount of knowledge in many special departments, along with a corresponding portion of the language belonging to each: but he would be indeed a marvel of many-sided learning who had mastered them all. Who is there among us that will not find, on every page of the comprehensive dictionaries now in vogue, words which are strange to him, which need defining to his apprehension, which he could not be sure of employing in the right place and connection? And this, not in the technical portions only of our vocabulary. There are words, or meanings of words, no longer in familiar use, antiquated or obsolescent, which yet may not be denied a place in the present English tongue. There are objects which almost never fall under the notice of great numbers of people, or of whole classes of the community, and to whose names, accordingly, when met with, these are unable to attach any definite idea. There are cognitions, conceptions, feelings, which have not come up in the minds of all, which all have not had occasion and acquired power to express. There are distinctions, in every department of thought, which all have not learned to draw and designate. Moreover, there are various styles of expression for the same thing, which are not at every one's command. One writer or speaker has great ease and copiousness of diction; for all his thoughts he has a variety of phrases to choose among; he lays them out before us in beautiful elaboration, in clear and elegant style, so that to follow and understand him is like floating with the current. Another, with not less wealth of knowledge and clearness of judgment, is cramped and awkward in his use of language; he puts his ideas before us in a rough and fragmentary way; he carries our understandings with him, but only at the cost of labour and pains on our part. And though he may be able to comprehend all that is said by the other, he has not in the same sense made the language his own, any more than the student of a foreign tongue who can translate from it with facility, but can express himself in it only lamely. Thus the infinite variety of the native and acquired capacity of different individuals comes to light in their idiom. It would be as hard to find two persons with precisely the same limits to their speech, as with precisely the same lineaments of countenance.

Once more, not all who speak the same tongue attach the same meaning to the words they utter. We learn what words signify either by direct definition or by inference from the circumstances in which they are used. But no definition is or can be exact and complete; and we are always liable to draw wrong inferences. Children, as every one knows, are constantly misapprehending the extent of meaning and application of the signs they acquire. Until it learns better, a child calls every man *papa;* having been taught the word *sky,* it calls the ceiling of a room the *sky;* it calls a donkey or a mule a *horse*—and naturally enough, since it has had to apply the name *dog* to creatures differing far more than these from one another. And so long as the learning of language lasts, does the liability to such error continue. It is a necessity of the case, arising out of the essential nature of language. Words are not exact models of ideas; they are merely signs for ideas, at whose significance we arrive as well as we can; and no mind can put itself into such immediate and intimate communion with another mind as to think and feel precisely with it. Sentences are not images of thoughts, reflected in a faultless mirror; or even photographs, needing only to have the colour added: they are but imperfect and fragmentary sketches, giving just outlines enought to enable the sense before which they are set up to seize the view intended, and to fill it out to a complete picture; while yet, as regards the completeness of the filling out, the details of the work, and the finer shades of colouring, no two minds will produce pictures perfectly accordant with one another, nor will any precisely reproduce the original.

The limits of variation of meaning are, or course, very different in different classes of words. So far as these are designations of definite objects, cognizable by the senses, there is little danger of our seriously misapprehending one another when we utter them. Yet, even here, there is room for no trifling discordance, as the superior knowledge or more vivid imagination of one person gives to the idea called up by a name a far richer content than another can put into it. Two men speak of the *sun,* with mutual intelligence: but to the one he is a mere ball of light and heat, which rises in the sky every morning, and goes down again at night; to the other, all that science has taught us respecting the nature of the great luminary, and its influence upon our little planet, is more or less distinctly present every time he utters its name. The word *Pekin* is spoken before a number of persons, and is understood by them all: but some among them know only that it is the name of an immense city in Asia, the capital of the Chinese empire; others have studied Chinese manners and customs, have seen pictures of Chinese scenery, architecture, dress, occupation, and are able to tinge the conception which the word evokes with some fair share of a local colouring; another, perhaps, has visited the place, and its name touches a store of memories, and brings up before his mind's eye a picture vivid with the hues of truth. I feel a tolerable degree of confidence that the impressions of colour made on my sense are the same with those made upon my friend's sense, so that, when we use the words *red* or *blue*, we do not mean different things: and yet, even here, it is possible that one of us may be afflicted with some degree of colour-blindness, so that we do not apprehend the same shades precisely alike. But just so is every part of language liable to be affected by the personality of the speaker; and most of all, where matters of more subjective apprehension are concerned. The voluptuary, the passionate and brutal, the philosophic, and the sentimental, for instance, when they speak of *love* or of *hate*, mean by no means the same feelings. How pregnant with sacred meaning are *home, patriotism, faith* to some, while others utter or hear them with cool indifference! It is needless, however, to multiply examples. Not half the words in our familiar speech would be identically defined by any considerable number of those who employ them every day. Nay, who knows not that verbal disputes, discussions turning on the meaning of words, are the most frequent, bitter, and interminable of controversies?

Clearly, therefore, we are guilty of no paradox in maintaining that, while we all speak the English language, the English of no two individuals among us is precisely the same: it is not the same in form; it is not the same in extent; it is not the same in meaning.

But what, then, is the English language? We answer: It is the immense aggregate of the articulated signs for thought accepted by, and current among, a certain vast community which we call the English-speaking people, embracing the principal portion of the inhabitants of our own country and of Great Britain, with all those who elsewhere in the world talk like them. It is the sum of the separate languages of all the members of this community. Or —since each one says some things, or says them in a way, not to be accepted as in the highest sense English—it is their average rather than their sum; it is that part of the aggregate which is supported by the usage of the majority; but of a majority made in great part by culture and education, not by numbers alone. It is a mighty region of speech, of somewhat fluctuating and uncertain boundaries, whereof each speaker occupies a portion, and a certain central tract is included in the portion of all: there they meet on common ground; off it, they are strangers to one another. Although one language, it includes numerous varieties, of greatly differing kind and degree: individual varieties, class varieties, local varieties. Almost any two persons who speak it may talk so as to be unintelligible to each other. The one fact which gives it unity is, that all who speak it may, to a considerable extent, and on subjects of the most general and pressing interest, talk so as to understand one another.

A language in the condition in which ours is at present, when thousands of eyes are jealously watching its integrity, and a thousand pens are ready to be drawn, and dyed deep in ink, to challenge and oppose the introduction into it of any corrupt form, of any new and uncalled-for element, can, of course, undergo only the slowest and the least essential alteration. It is when the common speech is in the sole keeping of the uncultivated and careless speakers, who care little for classical and time-honoured usages, to whom the preferences of the moment are of more account than anything in the past or in the future, that mutation has its full course. New dialects are wont to grow up among the common people, while the speech of the educated and lettered class continues to be what it has been. But the nature of the forces in action is the same in the one case as in the other: all change in language is the work of the will of its speakers, which acts under the government of motives, through the organs of speech, and varies their products to suit its necessities and its convenience. Every single item of alteration, of whatever kind, and of whatever degree of importance, goes back to some individual or individuals, who set it in circulation, from whose example it gained a wider and wider currency, until it finally won that general assent which is alone required in order to make anything in language proper and authoritative. Linguistic change must be gradual, and almost insensible while in progress, for the reason that the general assent can be but slowly gained, and can be gained for nothing which is too far removed from former usage, and which therefore seems far-fetched, arbitrary, or unintelligible. The collective influence of all the established analogies of a language is exerted against any daring innovation, as, on the other hand, it aids one which is obvious and naturally suggested. It was, for instance, no difficult matter for popular usage to introduce the new possessive *its* into

English speech, nor to add *worked* to *wrought,* as preterit of *work,* nor to replace the ancient plural *kye* or *kine* (Anglo-Saxon *cy,* from *cu,* 'cow') by a modern one, *cows,* formed after the ordinary model: while to reverse either process, to crowd *its, worked,* and *cows* out of use by substitution of *his, wrought,* and *kine,* would have been found utterly impracticable. The power of resistance to change possessed by a great popular institution, which is bound up with the interests of the whole community, and is a part of every man's thoughts and habitual acts, is not easily to be over-estimated. How long has it taken to persuade and force the French people, for instance, into the adoption of the new decimal system of weights and measures! How have they been baffled and shamed who have thought, in these latter days, to amend in a few points, of obvious desirability, our English orthography! But speech is a thing of far nearer and higher importance; it is the most precious of our possessions, the instrument of our thoughts, the organ of our social nature, the means of our culture; its use is not daily or hourly alone, but momently; it is the first thing we learn, the last we forget; it is the most intimate and clinging of our habits, and almost a second nature: and hence its exemption from all sweeping or arbitrary change. The community, to whom it belongs, will suffer no finger to be laid upon it without a reason; only such modifications as commend themselves to the general sense, as are virtually the carrying out of tendencies universally felt, have a chance of winning approval and acceptance, and so of being adopted into use, and made language.

Thus it is indeed true that the individual has no power to change language. But it is not true in any sense which excludes his agency, but only so far as that agency is confessed to be inopera-tive except as it is ratified by those about him. Speech and the changes of speech are the work of the community; but the com-munity cannot act except through the initiative of its individual members, which it follows or rejects. The work of each individual is done unpremeditatedly, or as it were unconsciously; each is intent only on using the common possession for his own benefit, serving therewith his private ends; but each is thus at the same time an actor in the great work of perpetuating and of shaping the general speech. So each separate polyp on a coral-bank devotes himself simply to the securing of his own food, and excretes cal-careous matter only in obedience to the exigencies of his individ-ual life; but, as the joint result of the isolated labours of all, there slowly rises in the water the enormous coral cliff, a barrier for the waves to dash themselves against in vain. To pick out a single man, were he even an emperor, and hold him up to view in his impotence as proof that men cannot make or alter language, is precisely equivalent to selecting one polyp, though the biggest and brightest-coloured of his species, off the growing reef, and exclaiming over him, "See this weak and puny creature! how is it possible that he and his like should build up a reef or an island?" No one ever set himself deliberately at work to invent or improve language—or did so, at least, with any valuable and abiding re-sult; the work is all accomplished by a continual satisfaction of the need of the moment, by ever yielding to an impulse and grasp-ing a possibility which the already acquired treasure of words and forms, and the habit of their use, suggest and put within reach. In this sense is language a growth; it is not consciously fabricated; it increases by a constant and implicit adaptation to the expanding necessities and capacities of men.

This, again, is what is meant by the phrases "organic growth, organic development," as applied to language. A language, like an organic body, is no mere aggregate of similar particles; it is a complex of related and mutually helpful parts. As such a body increases by the accretion of matter having a structure homogene-ous with its own, as its already existing organs form the new addi-tion, and form it for a determinate purpose—to aid the general life, to help the performance of the natural functions, of the organized being—so is it also with language: its new stores are formed from, or assimilated to, its previous substance; it enriches itself with the evolutions of its own internal processes, and in order more fully to secure the end of its being, the expression of the thought of those to whom it belongs. Its rise, development, decline, and extinction are like the birth, increase, decay, and death of a living creature.

There is a yet closer parallelism between the life of language and that of the animal kingdom in general. The speech of each person is, as it were, an individual of a species, with its general inherited conformity to the specific type, but also with its individual peculiarities, its tendency to variation and the formation of a new species. The dialects, languages, groups, families, stocks, set up by the linguistic student, correspond with the varieties, species, genera, and so on, of the zoölogist. And the questions which the students of nature are so excitedly discussing at the present day—the nature of specific distinctions, the derivation of species by individual variation and natural selection, the unity of origin of animal life—all are closely akin with those which the linguistic student has constant occasion to treat. We need not here dwell further upon the comparison: it is so naturally suggested, and so fruitful of interesting and instructive analogies, that it has been repeatedly drawn out and employed, by students both of nature and of language.*

Once more, a noteworthy and often-remarked similarity exists between the facts and methods of geology and those of linguistic study. The science of language is, as it were, the geology of the most modern period, the Age of Man, having for its task to construct the history of development of the earth and its inhabitants from the time when the proper geological record remains silent; when man, no longer a mere animal, begins by the aid of language to bear witness respecting his own progress and that of the world about him. The remains of ancient speech are like strata deposited in bygone ages, telling of the forms of life then existing, and of the circumstances which determined or affected them; while words are as rolled pebbles, relics of yet more ancient formations, or as fossils, whose grade indicates the progress of organic life, and whose resemblances and relations show the correspondence or sequence of the different strata; while, everywhere, extensive denudation has marred the completeness of the record, and ren-

---

* For instance, by Lyell (Antiquity of Man, chapter xxiii.), who has founded upon it a lucid and able analogical argument bearing on the Darwinian theory of the mutation of species. Professor August Schleicher (Die Darwinische Theorie und die Sprachwissenschaft, Weimar, 1863) attempts absolutely to prove by its aid the truth of the Darwinian theory, overlooking the fact that the relation between the two classes of phenomena is one of analogy only, not of essential agreement.

dered impossible a detailed exhibition of the whole course of development.

Other analogies, hardly less striking than these, might doubtless be found by a mind curious of such things. Yet they would be, like these, analogies merely, instructive as illustrations, but becoming fruitful of error when, letting our fancy run away with our reason, we allow them to determine our fundamental views respecting the nature of language and the method of its study; when we call language a living and growing organism, or pronounce linguistics a physical science, because zoölogy and geology are such. The point is one of essential consequence in linguistic philosophy. We shall never gain a clear apprehension of the phenomena of linguistic history, either in their individuality or in their totality, if we mistake the nature of the forces which are active in producing them. Language is, in fact, an institution—the word may seem an awkward one, but we can find none better or more truly descriptive—the work of those whose wants it subserves; it is in their sole keeping and control; it has been by them adapted to their circumstances and wants, and is still everywhere undergoing at their hands such adaptation; every separate item of which it is composed is, in its present form—for we are not yet ready for a discussion of the ultimate origin of human speech—the product of a series of changes, effected by the will and consent of men, working themselves out under historical conditions, and conditions of man's nature, and by the impulse of motives, which are, in the main, distinctly traceable, and form a legitimate subject of scientific investigation.

These considerations determine the character of the study of language as a historical or moral science. It is a branch of the history of the human race and of human institutions. It calls for aid upon various other sciences, both moral and physical: upon mental and metaphysical philosophy, for an account of the associations which underlie the developments of signification, and of the laws of thought, the universal principles of relation, which fix the outlines of grammar; upon physiology, for explanation of the structure and mode of operation of the organs of speech, and the physical relations of articulate sounds, which determine the laws of euphony, and prescribe the methods of phonetic change; upon physical geography and meteorology, even, for information respecting material conditions and climatic aspects, which have exerted their influence upon linguistic growth. But the human mind, seeking and choosing expression for human thought, stands as middle term between all determining causes and their results in the development of language. It is only as they affect man himself, in his desires and tendencies or in his capacities, that they can affect speech: the immediate agent is the will of men, working under the joint direction of impelling wants, governing circumstances, and established habits. What makes a physical science is that it deals with material substances, acted on by material forces. In the formation of geological strata, the ultimate cognizable agencies are the laws of matter; the substance affected is tangible matter; the product is inert, insensible matter. In zoölogy, again, as in anatomy and physiology, the investigator has to do with material structures, whose formation is dependent on laws implanted in matter itself, and beyond the reach of voluntary action. In language, on the other hand, the ultimate agencies are intelligent beings, the material is—not articulated sound alone, which might, in a certain sense, be regarded as a physical product, but—sound made significant of thought; and the product is of the same kind, a system of sounds with intelligible content, expressive of the slowly accumulated wealth of the human race in wisdom, experience, comprehension of itself and of the rest of creation. What but an analogical resemblance can there possibly be between the studies of things so essentially dissimilar?

While, however, we are thus forced to the acknowledgment that everything in human speech is a product of the conscious action of human beings, we should be leaving out of sight a matter of essential consequence in linguistic investigation if we failed to notice that what the linguistic student seeks in language is not what men have voluntarily or intentionally placed there. As we have already seen, each separate item in the production or modification of language is a satisfaction of the need of the moment; it is prompted by the exigencies of the particular case; it is brought forth for the practical end of convenient communication, and with no ulterior air or object whatsoever; it is accepted by the community only because it supplies a perceived want, and answers an acknowledged purpose in the uses of social intercourse. The language-makers are quite heedless of its position and value as part of a system, or as a record with historical content, nor do they analyze and set before their consciousness the mental tendencies which it gratifies. A language is, in very truth, a grand system, of a highly complicated and symmetrical structure; it is fitly comparable with an organized body; but this is not because any human mind has planned such a structure and skilfully worked it out. Each single part is conscious and intentional; the whole is instinctive and natural. The unity and symmetry of the system is the unconscious product of the efforts of the human mind, grappling with the facts of the world without and the world within itself, and recording each separate result in speech. Herein is a real language fundamentally different from the elaborate and philosophical structures with which ingenious men have sometimes thought to replace them.* These are indeed artful devices, in which the character and bearing of each part is painfully weighed and determined in advance: compared with them, language is a real growth; and human thought will as readily exchange its natural covering for one of them as the growing crustacean will give up its shell for a casing of silver, wrought by the most skilful hands. Their symmetry is that of a mathematical figure, carefully laid out, and drawn to rule and line; in language, the human mind, tethered by its limited capacities in the midst of creation, reaches out as far as it can in every direction and makes its mark, and is surprised at the end to find the result a circle.

In whatever aspect the general facts of language are viewed, they exhibit the same absence of reflection and intention. Phonetic change is the spontaneous working out of tendencies which the individual does not acknowledge to himself, in their effects upon organs of whose structure and workings he is almost or wholly ignorant. Outward circumstances, historical conditions, progress of knowledge and culture, are recorded in speech because its

---

* For an account of some of these attempts at an artificial language, of theoretically perfect structure, and designed for universal use, see Professor Max Müller's Lectures on Language, second series, second lecture.

practical uses require that they should be so, not because any one has attempted to depict them. Language shows ethnic descent, not as men have chosen to preserve such evidence of their kindred with other communities and races, but as it cannot be effaced without special effort directed to that end. The operations of the mind, the development of association, the laws of subjective relation, are exhibited there, but only as they are the agencies which govern the phenomena of speech, unrecognized in their working, but inferrible from their effects.

Now it is this absence of reflection and conscious intent which takes away from the facts of language the subjective character that would otherwise belong to them as products of voluntary action. The linguistic student feels that he is not dealing with the artful creations of individuals. So far as concerns the purposes for which he examines them, and the results he would derive from them, they are almost as little the work of man as is the form of his skull, the outlines of his face, the construction of his arm and hand. They are fairly to be regarded as reflections of the facts of human nature and human history, in a mirror imperfect, indeed, but faithful and wholly trustworthy; not as pictures drawn by men's hands for our information. Hence the close analogies which may be drawn between the study of language and some of the physical sciences. Hence, above all, the fundamental and pervading correspondence between its whole method and theirs. Not less than they, it founds itself upon the widest observation and examination of particular facts, and proceeds toward its results by strict induction, comparing, arranging, and classifying, tracing out relations, exhibiting an inherent system, deducing laws of general or universal application, discovering beneath all the variety and diversity of particulars an ever-present unity, in origin and development, in plan and purpose. Beyond all question, it is this coincidence of method which has confused some of the votaries of linguistic science, and blinded their eyes to the true nature of the ultimate facts upon which their study is founded, leading them to deny the agency of man in the production and change of language, and to pronounce it an organic growth, governed by organic forces.

We return now, from this necessary digression, to follow onward our leading inquiry, "Why we speak as we do?" And we have to push the question a step further, asking this time, not simply how we ourselves came into possession of the signs of which our mother-tongue is made up, but also how those from whom we learned them came into possession of them before us; how the tradition from whose hands we implicitly accepted them got them in the form in which it passed them on to us; why our words, in short, are what they are, and not otherwise. We have seen that every part and particle of every existing language is a historical product, the final result of a series of changes, working themselves out in time, under the pressure of circumstances, and by the guidance of motives, which are not beyond the reach of our discovery. This fact prescribes the mode in which language is to be fruitfully studied. If we would understand anything which has *become* what it is, a knowledge of its present constitution is not enough: we must follow it backward from stage to stage, tracing out the phases it has assumed, and the causes which have determined the transition of one into the other. Merely to classify, arrange, and set forth in order the phenomena of a spoken tongue, its significant material, usages and modes of expression, is grammar and lexicography, not linguistic science. The former state and prescribe only; the latter seeks to explain. And when the explanation is historical, the search for it must be of the same character. To construct, then, by historical processes, with the aid of all the historical evidences within his reach, the history of development of language, back to its very beginning, is the main task of the linguistic student; it is the means by which he arrives at a true comprehension of language, in its own nature and in its relations to the human mind and to human history.

Furthermore, it is hardly necessary to point out that the history of language reposes on that of words. Language is made up of signs for thought, which, though in one sense parts of a whole, are in another and more essential sense isolated and independent entities. Each is produced for its own purpose; each is separately exposed to the changes and vicissitudes of linguistic life, is modified, recombined, or dropped, according to its own uses and capacities. Hence etymology, the historical study of individual words, is the foundation and substructure of all investigation of language; the broad principles, the wide-reaching views, the truths of universal application and importance, which constitute the upper fabric of linguistic science, all rest upon word-genealogies. Words are the single witnesses from whom etymology draws out the testimony which they have to give respecting themselves, the tongue to which they belong, and all human speech.

There is no word or class of words whose history does not exemplify, more or less fully, all the different kinds of linguistic change. And, as the possibility of etymological analysis depends in no small part on the nature of words as not simple entities, but made up of separate elements, this composite character of the constituents of speech may properly engage our first attention.

That we are in the constant habit of putting together two independent vocables to form a compound word, is an obvious and familiar fact. Instances of such words are *fear-inspiring, god-like, break-neck, house-top*. They are substitutes for the equivalent phrases *inspiring fear, like a god, apt to break one's neck, top of a house*. For the sake of more compact and convenient expression, we have given a closer unity to the compound word than belongs to the aggregate which it represents, by omission of connectives, by inversion of the more usual order of arrangement, but most of all by unity of accent: this last is the chief outward means of composition; it converts two entities into one, for the nonce, by subordinating the one of them to the other. Our common talk is strewn with such words, and so gradual is the transition to them from the mere collocations of the phrase, that there are couples, like *mother-tongue, well-known*, which we hardly know whether to write separately as collocations only, or with a hyphen, as loose compounds; others, like *dial-plate, well-being*, usage so far recognizes for compounds that they are always written together, sometimes with the hyphen and sometimes without; others yet, like *godlike, herself*, are so grown together by long contact, by habitual connection, that we hardly think of them as having a dual nature. And even more than this: we have formed some so close combinations that it costs us a little reflection to separate them into their original parts. Of such a character is *forehead*, still written to accord with its derivation, as a name for the *fore* part of the *head*, but so altered in pronunciation that, but for its spelling, its origin would certainly escape the notice of nineteen-twentieths of those who use it. Such, again, is *fortnight,* altered both in pronunciation and in spelling from the *fourteen nights* out of which it grew. Such, once more, is our familiar verb *breakfast.* We gave this name to our morning meal, because it *broke,* or interrupted, the longest *fast* of the day, that which includes the night's sleep. We said at first *breāk fâst*—"I broke fast at such an hour this morning": he, or they, who first ventured to say *I breakfasted* were guilty of as heinous a violation of grammatical rule as he would be who should now delare *I takedinnered,* instead of *I took dinner;* but good usage came over to their side and ratified their blunder, because the community were minded to give a specific name to their earliest meal and to the act of partaking of it, and therefore converted the collocation *breākfâst* into the real compound *brĕakfast.*

Yet once more, not only are those words in our language of composite structure, of which at first sight, or on second thought, we thus recognize the constituent elements; not a few, also, which we should not readily conjecture to be other than simple and indivisible entities, and which could not be proved otherwise by any evidence which our present speech contains, do nevertheless, when we trace their history by the aid of other and older languages than ours, admit of analysis into component parts. We will note, as instances, only a familiar word or two, namely *such* and *which.* The forms of these words in Anglo-Saxon are *swylc* and *hwylc:* with the latter of them the Scottish *whilk* for *which* quite closely agrees, and they also find their near correspondents in the German *solch* and *welch.* On following up their genealogy, from language to language of our family, we find at last that they are made up of the ancient words for *so* and *who,* with the adjective *like* added to each: *such* is *so-like,* 'of that likeness or sort'; *which* is *who-like,* 'of what likeness or sort.'

But we turn from compounds like these, in which two originally independent words are fully fused into one, in meaning and form, to another class, of much higher importance in the history of language.

Let us look, first, at our word *fearful.* This, upon reflection, is a not less evident compound than *fear-inspiring:* our common adjective *full* is perfectly recognizable as its final member. Yet, though such be its palpable origin, it is, after all, a compound of a somewhat different character from the other. The subordinate element *full,* owing to its use in a similar way in a great number of other compounds, such as *careful, truthful, plentiful, dutiful,* and the frequent and familiar occurrence of the words it forms, has, to our apprehension, in some measure lost the consciousness of its independent character, and sunk to the condition of a mere suffix, forming adjectives from nouns, like the suffix *ous* in such words as *perilous, riotous, plenteous, duteous.* It approaches, too, the character of a suffix, in that its compounds are not, like *fear-inspiring* and *house-top,* directly translatable back into the elements which form them: *plentiful* and *dutiful* do not mean 'full of plenty' and 'full of duty,' but are the precise equivalents of *plenteous* and *duteous.* We could with entire propriety form an adjective from a new noun by adding *ful* to it, without concerning ourselves as to whether the corresponding phrase, "full of so and so," would or would not make good sense. And when we hear a Scotchman say *fearfu', carefu',* we both understand him without difficulty, and do not think of inquiring whether he also clips the adjective *full* to *fu'.*

The word of opposite meaning, *fearless,* is not less readily recognizable as a compound, and our first impulse is to see in its final element our common word *less,* to interpret *fearless* as meaning *'minus fear,'* 'deprived of fear,' and so 'exempt from fear.' A little study of the history of such words, however, as it is to be read in other dialects, shows us that this is a mistake, and that our *less* has nothing whatever to do with the compound. The Anglo-Saxon form of the ending, *leas,* is palpably the adjective *leas,* which is the same with our word *loose;* and *fearless* is primarily 'loose from fear,' 'free from fear.' The original subordinate member of the compound has here gone completely through the process of conversion into a suffix, being so divorced from the words which are really akin with it that its derivation is greatly obscured, and a false etymology is suggested to the mind which reflects upon it.

Take, again, such words as *godly, homely, brotherly, lovely.* Here, as in the other cases, each is composed of two parts; but, while we recognize the one as a noun, having an independent existence in the language, we do not even feel tempted to regard the other as anything but an adjective suffix, destitute of separate significance; it appears in our usage only as an appendage to other words, impressing upon them a certain modification of meaning. What, however, is its history? Upon tracing it up into the older form of our speech, the Anglo-Saxon, we find that our modern usage has mutilated it after the same fashion as the Scottish dialect now mutilates the *ful* of *fearful*—by dropping off, namely, an original final consonant: its earlier form was *lîc*. The final guttural letter we find preserved even to the present day in the corresponding suffixes of the other Germanic languages, as in the German *lich*, Swedish *lig*, Dutch *lijk*. These facts lead us naturally to the conjecture that the so-called suffix may be nothing more than a metamorphosis of our common adjective *like;* and a reference to the oldest Germanic dialect, the Mœso-Gothic, puts the case beyond all question; for there we find the suffix and the independent adjective to be in all respects the same, and the derivatives formed with the suffix to be as evident compounds with the adjective as are our own *godlike, childlike,* and so on. Words thus composed are common in all the Germanic tongues; but we who speak English have given the same suffix a further modification of meaning, and an extension of application, which belong to it nowhere else. In our usage it is an adverbial suffix, by which any adjective whatever may be converted into an adverb, as in *truly, badly, fearfully, fearlessly.* In the old Anglo-Saxon, such adverbs were oblique cases of adjectives in *lîc,* and so, of course, were derived only from adjectives formed by this ending; the full adverbial suffix was *lîce,* the *e* being a case-termination: instances are *ânlîce,* 'only, singularly,' from *ânlîc,* 'sole, singular,' literally 'one-like'; *leôflîce,* 'lovelily,' from *leôflîc,* 'lovely.' We moderns, now, have suffered the ending to go out of use as one forming adjectives, only retaining the adjectives so formed which we have inherited from the ancient time; but we have taken it up in its adverbial application, and, ignoring both its original character and its former limitation to a single class of adjectives, apply it with unrestricted freedom in making an adverb from any adjective we choose; while, at the same time, we have mutilated its form, casting off as unnecessary the vowel ending, along with the consonant to which it was appended. The history of this adverbial suffix is worthy of special notice, inasmuch as the suffix itself is the latest addition which our grammatical system has gained in the synthetic way, and as its elaboration has taken place during the period when the growth of our language is illustrated by contemporary documents. The successive steps were clearly as follows: the adjective *like* was first added to a number of nouns, forming a considerable class of adjective compounds, like those now formed by us with *full*; then, like the latter word, it lost in a measure the consciousness of its origin, and was regarded rather as a suffix, forming derivative adjectives; one of the oblique cases of these adjectives was next often employed in an adverbial sense; and the use of the suffix in its extended form and with its modified application grew in importance and frequency, until finally it threw quite into the shade and supplanted the adjective use—and the independent adjective had become a mere adverbial ending. The mutilation of its form went hand in hand with this obliviousness of its origin and with its transferral to a new office; each helped on the other.

The examples already given may sufficiently answer our purpose as illustrations of the way in which suffixes are produced, and grammatical classes or categories of words created. The adjectives in *ful*, or the adjectives in *less*, form together a related group, having a common character, as derivatives from nouns, and derivatives possessing a kindred significance, standing in a certain like relation to their primitives, filling a certain common office in speech, an office of which the sign is the syllable *ful*, or *less*, their final member or suffix. With *ly*, this is still more notably the case: the suffix *ly* is the usual sign of adverbial meaning; it makes much the largest share of all the adverbs we have. A final *m*, added to a verbal root, in an early stage of the history of our mother-tongue, and yet more anciently an added syllable *mi*, made in like manner the first persons singular present of verbs; as an added *s*, standing for an original syllable *ti*, does even to the present day make our third persons singular. All these grammatical signs were once independent elements, words of distinct meaning, appended to other words and compounded with them— appended, not in one or two isolated cases only, but so often, and in a sense so generally applicable, that they formed whole classes of compounds. There was nothing about them save this extensibility of their application and frequency of their use to distinguish their compounds from such as *house-top, break-neck, forehead, fortnight,* and the others of the same class to which we have already referred. Yet this was quite enough to bring about a change of their recognized character, from that of distinct words to that of non-significant appendages to other words. Each passed over into the condition of a *formative element;* that is to say, an element showing the logical form, the grammatical character, of a derivative, as distinguished from its primitive, the word to which the sign was appended. There was a time when *fear-full, fear-loose, fear-free, free-making, fear-struck, love-like, love-rich, love-sick, love-lorn,* were all words of the same kind, mere lax combinations; it was only their different degree of availability for answering the ends of speech, for supplying the perceived needs of expression, that caused two or three of them to assume a different character, while the rest remained as they had been.

With but few exceptions—which, moreover, are only apparent ones—all the words of our language admit of such analysis as this, which discovers in them at least two elements, whereof the one conveys the central or fundamental idea, and the other indicates a restriction, application, or relation of that idea. Even those brief vocables which appear to us of simplest character can be proved either to exhibit still, like *am* for *as-mi,* the relic of a mutilated formative element, or, like *is* for *as-ti,* to have lost one which they formerly possessed. This, then, in our language (as in the whole family of languages to which ours is related), is the normal constitution of a word: it invariably contains a radical and a formal portion; it is made up of a root combined with a suffix, or with a suffix and prefix, or with more than one of each. In more technical phrase, no word is *unformed;* no one has been a mere significant entity, without designation of its relation, without a sign putting it in some class or category.

It is plain, therefore, that a chief portion of linguistic analysis must consist, not in the mere dismembering of such words as we usually style compounded, but in the distinction from one another of radical and formal elements; in the isolation of the central nucleus, or root, from the affixes which have become attached to it, and the separate recognition of each affix, in its individual form and office. But our illustrations have, as I think, made it not less plain that there is no essential and ultimate difference in the two cases: in the one, as in the other, our process of analysis is the re-tracing of a previous synthesis, whereby two independent elements were combined and integrated. That this is so to a certain extent is a truth so palpable as to admit of neither denial nor doubt. Had there been in the Germanic languages no such adjective as *full*, no such derivative adjectives as *fearful* and *truthful* would have grown up in them; if they had possessed no adjective *like*, they would never have gained such adjectives as *godly* and *lovely*, nor such adverbs as *fearfully* and *truly*. So also with *friendship*, with *loved*, with *am* and *is*, and the rest. No inconsiderable number of the formative elements of our tongue, in every department of grammar and of word-formation, can be thus traced back to independent words, with which they were at first identical, out of which they have grown. It is true, at the same time, that a still larger number do not allow their origin to be discovered. But we have not, on that account, the right to conclude that their history is not of the same character. In grammar, as everywhere else, like effects pre-suppose like causes. We have seen how the formative elements are liable to become corrupted and altered, so that the signs of their origin are obscured, and may even be obliterated. The *full* in *truthful* is easy enough to recognize, but a little historical re-search is necessary in order to show us the *like* which is contained in *truly*. *Hateful* is, for aught we know, as old a compound as *lovely*, but linguistic usage has chanced to be more merciful to the evidence of descent in the former cases than in the latter. A yet more penetrating investigation is required ere we discover our pronoun *me* in the word *am*, or our imperfect *did* in *I loved;* and, but for the happy chance that preserved to us the one or two fragmentary manuscripts in which are contained our only records of Mœso-Gothic speech, the genesis of the latter form would al-ways have remained an unsolved problem, a subject for ingenious conjecture, but beyond the reach of demonstration. The loss of each intermediate stage, coming between any given dialect and its remotest ancestor, wipes out a portion of the evidence which would explain the origin of its forms. If English stood all alone among the other languages of the earth, but an insignificant part of its word-history could be read; its kindred dialects, contemporary and older, help us to the discovery of a much larger portion; and the preservation of authentic records of every period of its life would, as we cannot hesitate to believe, make clear the rest. There is no break in the chain of analogical reasoning which compels the linguistic student to the conviction that his analyses are everywhere real, and distinguish those elements by the actual combination of which words were originally made up. On this conviction rests, for him, the value of his analytical processes: if they are to be regarded as in part historical and real, in part only theoretical and illusory, his researches into the history of language are baffled; he is in pursuit of a phantom, and not of truth.

Wherever, then, our study of words brings us to the recognition of an element having a distinct meaning and office, employed in combination with other elements for the uses of expression, there we must recognize an originally independent entity. The parts of our words were once themselves words.

But the same examples on which we relied to show how, and how extensively, words are compounded together and forms produced, have shown us not less clearly that mutilation and loss of the elements employed by language, and of the compounds and forms into which they enter, are also constant accompaniments of linguistic growth.

All articulate sounds are produced by effort, by expenditure of muscular energy, in the lungs, throat, and mouth. This effort, like every other which man makes, he has an instinctive disposition to seek relief from, to avoid: we may call it laziness, or we may call it economy; it is, in fact, either the one or the other, according to the circumstances of each separate case: it is laziness when it gives up more than it gains; economy, when it gains more than it abandons. Every item of language is subject to its influence, and it works itself out in greatly various ways; we will give our first consideration to the manner in which its action accompanies, aids, and modifies that of the process of composition of old material into new forms, as last set forth. For it is composition, the building up of words out of elements formerly independent, that opens a wide field to the operation of phonetic change, and at the same time gives it its highest importance as an agency in the production and modification of language. If all words were of simple structure and brief form, their alterations would be confined within comparatively narrow limits, and would be of inferior consequence as constituting one of the processes of linguistic growth. Our adjective *like,* for example, is but slightly altered in our usage from the form which it had in the Anglo-Saxon *(lîc)* and the Mœso-Gothic *(leik);* while, in the compounds into which it has entered, it is mutilated even past recognition: in the adjectives and adverbs like *godly* and *truly,* it has been deprived of its final consonant, in *such* and *which* (A.-S. *swylc, hwylc;* M.-G. *swaleik, hwaleik*), it has saved only the final consonant, and that in a greatly modified shape.

The reason which makes phonetic change rifest in linguistic combinations is the same with that which creates the possibility of any phonetic change at all in language. It is inherent in the nature of a word, and its relation to the idea which it represents. A word, as we have already seen, is not the natural reflection of an idea, nor its description, nor its definition; it is only its designation, an arbitrary and conventional sign with which we learn to associate it. Hence it has no internal force conservative of its identity, but is exposed to all the changes which external circumstances, the needs of practical use, the convenience and caprice of those who employ it, may suggest. When we have once formed a compound, and applied it to a given purpose, we are not at all solicitous to keep up the memory of its origin; we are, rather, ready to forget it. The word once coined, we accept it as an integral representative of the conception to which we attach it, and give our whole attention to that, not concerning ourselves about its derivation, or its etymological aptness. Practical convenience becomes the paramount consideration, to which every other is made to give way.

Thus—to recur to some of our former illustrations—as soon as we are ready to forego our separate memory of the constituents of such compounds as *breāk-fâst, fōre-hĕad, fourteen-night,* that we may give a more concentrated attention to the unity of signification which we confer upon them, we begin to convert them into *brĕakfast, fóre'd, fórtnĭt.* And the case is the same with all those combinations out of which grow formative elements and forms. While we have clearly in mind the genesis of *god-like, father-like,* and so forth, we are little likely to mutilate either part of them: our apprehension of the latter element as no longer coördinate with the former, but as an appendage to it, impressing upon it a modification of meaning, and our reduction of the subordinate element to *ly,* thus turning the words into *godly* and *fatherly,* are processes that go hand in hand together, each helping the other.

This brings us to a recognition of the important and valuable part played by the tendency to ease of utterance, and by the phonetic changes which it prompts, in the construction of the fabric of language. If a word is to be taken fully out of the condition of constituent member of a compound, and made a formative element, if a compound is thus to be converted into a form, or otherwise fused together into an integral word, it must be by the help of some external modification. Our words *thankful, fearful, truthful,* and their like, are, by our too present apprehension of the independent significance of their final syllable, kept out of the category of pure derivatives. Phonetic corruption makes the difference between a genuine form-word, like *godly,* and a combination like *godlike,* which is far less plastic and adaptable to the varying needs of practical use: it makes the difference between a synthetic combination, like *I loved,* and a mere analytic collocation, like *I did love.* It alone renders possible true grammatical forms, which make the wealth and power of every inflective language. We sometimes laugh at the unwieldiness of the compounds which our neighbour language, the German, so abundantly admits; words like *Rittergutsbesitzer,* 'knight's-property-possessor,' or *Schuhmacherhandwerk,* 'cobbler's-trade,' seem to us too cumbrous for use; but half the vocables in our own tongue would be as bulky and awkward, but for the abbreviation which phonetic change has wrought upon them. Without it, such complicated derivatives as *untruthfully, inapplicabilities,* would have no advantage over the tedious paraphrases with which we should now render their precise etymological meaning.

Change, retrenchment, mutilation, disguise of derivation is, then, both the inevitable and the desirable accompaniment of such composition as has formed the vocabulary of our spoken tongue.

It stands connected with tendencies of essential consequence, and is part of the wise economy of speech. It contributes to conciseness and force of expression. It is the sign and means of the integration of words. It disencumbers terms of traditional remembrances, which would otherwise disturb the unity of attention that ought to be concentrated upon the sign in its relation to the thing signified. It makes of a word, instead of a congeries of independent entities, held together by a loose bond and equally crowding themselves upon the apprehension, a unity, composed of duly subordinated parts.

But the tendency which works out these valuable results is, at the same time, a blind, or, to speak more exactly, an unreflecting one, and its action is also in no small measure destructive; it pulls down the very edifice which it helps to build. Its direct aim is simply ease and convenience; it seeks, as we have seen, to save time and labour to the users of language. There may be, it is evident, waste as well as economy in the gratification of such a tendency; abbreviation may be carried beyond the limits of that which can be well dispensed with; ease and convenience may be consulted by the sacrifice of what is of worth, as well as by the rejection of what is unnecessary. No language, indeed, in the mouths of a people not undergoing mental and moral impoverishment, gives up, upon the whole, any of its resources of expression, lets go aught of essential value for which it does not retain or provide an equivalent. But an item may be dropped here and there, which, upon reflection, seems a regrettable loss. And a language may, at least, become greatly altered by the excessive prevalence of the wearing-out processes, abandoning much which in other and kindred languages is retained and valued.

The disposition to rid our words of whatever in them is superfluous, or can be spared without detriment to distinctness of expression, has led in our language, as in many others, to curious replacements of an earlier mode of indicating meaning by one of later date, and of inorganic origin—that is to say, not produced for the purpose to which it is applied. Thus we have a few plurals, of which *men* from *man*, *feet* from *foot*, and *mice* from *mouse* are familiar examples, which constitute noteworthy exceptions to our general rule for the formation of the plural number. Comparison of the older dialects soon shows us that the change of vowel in such words as these was originally an accident only; it was not significant, but euphonic; it was called out by the vowels of certain case-endings, which assimilated the vowels of the nouns to which they were attached. So little was the altered vowel in Anglo-Saxon a sign of plurality, that it was found also in one of the singular cases, while two of the plural cases exhibited the unchanged vowel of the theme. *Man*, for instance, was thus declined:

	Singular.		Plural.	
Nom.	*man,*	'man';	*men,*	'men.'
Gen.	*mannes,*	'man's';	*manna,*	'men's.'
Dat.	*men,*	'to man';	*mannum,*	'to men.'
Accus.	*man,*	'man';	*men,*	'men.'

But the nominative and accusative singular exhibited one vowel, and the nominative and accusative plural another; and so this incidental difference of pronunciation between the forms of most frequent occurrence in the two numbers respectively came to appear before the popular apprehension as indicative of the distinction of number; its genesis was already long forgotten, as the case-endings which called it out had disappeared; and now it was fully invested with a new office—though only in a few rather arbitrarily selected cases: the word *book*, for example, has the same hereditary right to a plural *beek*, instead of *books*, as has *foot* to a plural *feet*, instead of *foots*.* The case is quite the same as if, at present, because we pronounce *nătional* (with "short *a*") the adjective derived from *nātion*, we should come finally to neglect as unnecessary the suffix *al*, and should allow *nātion* and *nătion* to answer to one another as corresponding substantive and adjective.

But every language has its own peculiar history of phonetic development, its special laws of mutation, its caprices and idiosyncrasies, which no amount of learning and acuteness could enable the phonologist to foretell, and of which the full explanation often baffles his art. His work is historical, not prescriptive. He has to trace out the changes which have actually taken place in the spoken structure of language, and to discover, so far as he is able, their ground, in the physical character and relations of the sounds

---

The plural of *bôc* in Anglo-Saxon is *bêc*, as that of *fôt* is *fêt*.

concerned, in the positions and motions of the articulating organs by which those sounds are produced. He is thus enabled to point out, in the great majority of cases, how it is that a certain sound, in this or that situation, should be easily and naturally dropped, or converted into such and such another sound. But with this, for the most part, he is obliged to content himself; his power to explain the motive of the change, why it is made in this word and not in that, why by this community and not by that other, is very limited. He cannot tell why sounds are found in the alphabet of one tongue which are unutterable by the speakers of another; why combinations which come without difficulty from the organs of one people are utterly eschewed by its neighbour and next of kin; why, for example, the Sanskrit will tolerate no two consonants at the end of a word, the Greek no consonant but *n, s,* or *r,* the Chinese none but a nasal, the Italian none at all; why the Polynesian will form no syllable which does not end with a vowel, or which begins with more than one consonant, while the English will bear as many as six or seven consonants about a single vowel (as in *splints, strands, twelfths*); why the accent in a Latin word has its place always determined by the quantity of the syllable before the last, and rests either upon that syllable or the one that precedes it, while in Greek it may be given to either of the last three syllables, and is only partially regulated by quantity; why, again, the Irish and Bohemian lay the stress of voice invariably upon the first syllable of a word, and their near relations, the Welsh and Polish, as invariably upon the penult; others still, like the Russian and Sanskrit, submitting it to no restriction of place whatever. These, and the thousand other not less striking differences of phonetic structure and custom which might readily be pointed out, are national traits, results of differences of physical organization so subtile (if they exist at all), of influences of circumstances so recondite, of choice and habit so arbitrary and capricious, that they will never cease to elude the search of the investigator. But he will not, in his perplexity, think of ascribing even the most obscure and startling changes of sound to any other agency than that which brings about those contractions and conversions which are most obviously a relief to the organs of articulation: it is still the speakers of language, and they alone, who work over and elaborate the words they utter, suiting them to their convenience and their caprice. The final reason to which we are brought in every case, when historical and physical study have done their utmost, is but this: it hath pleased the community which used this word to make such an alteration in its form; and such and such considerations and analogies show the change to be one neither isolated nor mysterious. Except in single and exceptional cases, there is no such difference of structure in human mouths and throats that any human being, of whatever race, may not perfectly master the pronunciation of any human language, belonging to whatever other race—provided only his teaching begin early enough, before his organs have acquired by habit special capacities and incapacities. The collective disposition and ability of a community, working itself out under the guidance of circumstances, determines the phonetic form which the common tongue of the community shall wear. And as, in the first essays of any child at speaking, we may note not only natural errors and ready substitutions of one sound for another, common to nearly all children, but also one and another peculiar conversion, which seems the effect of mere whim, explainable by nothing but individual caprice, so in the traditional transmission of language—which is but the same process of teaching children to speak, carried out upon a larger scale—we must look for similar cases of arbitrary phonetic transitions.

To trace out the changes of signification which a word has undergone is quite as essential a part of the etymologist's work as to follow back its changes of phonetic form; and the former are yet more rich in striking and unexpected developments, more full of instruction, than the latter: upon them depend in no small measure the historical results which the student of language aims at establishing. It may even be claimed with a certain justice that change and development of meaning constitute the real interior life of language, to which the other processes only furnish an outward support. In their details, indeed, the outer and inner growth are to a great extent independent of one another: a word may suffer modification of form in any degree even to the loss or mutation of every phonetic element it once contained, with no appreciable alteration of meaning (as in our *I* for Anglo-Saxon *ic, eye* for *eage*) ; and, again, it may be used to convey a totally different meaning from that which it formerly bore, while still maintaining its old form. Yet, upon the whole, the two must correspond, and answer one another's uses. That would be but an imperfect and awkward language, all whose expansion of significant content was made without aid from the processes which generate new words and forms; and the highest value of external change lies in its facilitation of internal, in its office of providing signs for new ideas, of expanding a vocabulary and grammatical system into a more complete adaptedness to their required uses. But change of meaning is a more fundamental and essential part of linguistic growth than change of form. If, while words grew together, became fused, integrated, abbreviated, their signification were incapable of variation, no phonetic plasticity could make of language aught but a stiff dead structure, incapable of continuously supplying the wants of a learning and reasoning people. If for every distinct conception language were compelled to provide a distinct term, if every new idea or modification of an idea called imperatively for a new word or a modification of an old one, the task of language-making would be indefinitely increased in difficulty. The case, however, is far otherwise. A wonderful facility of putting old material to new uses stands us in stead in dealing with the intent as well as the form of our words. The ideal content of speech is even more yielding than is its external audible substance to the touch of the moulding and shaping mind. In any sentence that may be chosen, as we shall find that not one of the words is uttered in the same manner as when it was first generated, so we shall also find that not one has the same meaning which belonged to it at the beginning. The phonetists claim, with truth, that any given artic-ulated sound may, in the history of speech, pass over into any other; the same may with equal truth be claimed of the ideas signified by words: there can hardly be two so disconnected and unlike that they may not derive themselves historically, through a succession of intermediate steps, from one another or from the same original.

The fundamental fact which makes words to be of changeable meaning is the same to which we have already had to refer as making them of changeable form: namely, that there is no inter-nal and necessary connection between a word and the idea designated by it, that no tie save a mental association binds the two together. Conventional usage, the mutual understanding of speakers and hearers, allots to each vocable its signficance, and the same authority which makes is able to change, and to change as it will, in whatever way, and to whatever extent. The only limit to the power of change is that imposed by the necessity of mutual intelligibility; no word may ever by any one act be so altered as to lose its identity as a sign, becoming unrecognizable by those who have been accustomed to employ it.

The word *moon*, with which are akin the names for the same object in many of the languages connected with our own, comes from a root *(mâ)* signifying 'to measure,' and, by its etymology, means 'the measurer.' It is plainly the fact—and one of some interest, as indicating the ways of thinking of our remote ancestors —that the moon was looked upon as in a peculiar sense the measurer of time: and, indeed, we know that primitive nations generally have begun reckoning time by moons or months before arriving at a distinct apprehension of the year, as an equally natural and more important period. By an exception, the Latin name *luna* (abbreviated from *luc-na*) means 'the shining one.' In both these cases alike, we have an arbitrary restriction and special application to a single object of a term properly bearing a general sense; and also, an arbitrary selection of a single quality in a thing of complex nature to be made a ground of designation for the whole thing. In the world of created objects there are a great many "measurers," and a great many "shining ones"; there are also a great many other qualities belonging to the earth's satellite, which have just as good a right as these two to be noticed in her name: yet the appellation perfectly answers its purpose; no one, for thousands of years, has inquired, save as a matter of learned curiosity, what, after all, the word *moon* properly signifies: for us it designates our moon, and we may observe and study that luminary to the end of time without feeling that our increased knowledge furnishes any reason for our changing its name. The words for 'sun' have nearly the same history, generally designating it as 'the brilliant or shining one,' or as 'the enlivener, quickener, generator.' There are hardly two other objects within the ordinary range of human observation more essentially unique than the sun and the moon, and their titles were, as nearly as is possible in language, proper names. But such they could not continue to be. No constituent of language is the appellation of an individual existence or act; each designates a class; and, even when circumstances seem to limit the class to one member, we are ever on the watch to extend its bounds. The same tendency which, as already pointed out, leads the child, when it has learned the words *papa* and *sky*, to take the things designated by those words as types of classes, and so—rightly enough in principle, though wrongly as regards the customary use of language—to call other men *papa*, and to call the ceiling *sky*, is always active in us. Copernicus having taught us that the sun is the great centre of our system, that the earth is not the point about which and for which the rest of the universe was created, the thought is at once suggested to us that the fixed stars also may be centres of systems like our own, and we call them *suns*. And no sooner does Galileo discover for us the lesser orbs which circle about Jupiter and others of our sister-planets, than, without a scruple, or a suspicion that we are doing anything unusual or illegitimate, we style them *moons*. Each word, too, has its series of figurative and secondary meanings. "So many *suns*," "so many *moons*," signify the time marked by so many revolutions of the two luminaries respectively; in some languages the word *moon* itself (as in the Greek *mēn*), in others, a derivative from it (as the Latin *mensis* and our *month*), comes to be the usual name of the period determined by the wax and wane of our satellite—and is then transferred to designate those fixed and arbitrary subdivisions of the solar year to which the natural system of lunar months has so generally been compelled to give place. By a figure of another kind, we sometimes call by the name *sun* one who is conspicuous for brilliancy and influence: "made glorious summer by this *sun* of York." By yet another, but which has now long lost its character as a figure, and become plain and homely speech, we put *sun* for *sunlight*, saying, "to walk out of the *sun*," "to bask in the *sun*," and so on. In more learned and technical phrase, the Latin name of the moon, *lune*, or its diminutive, *lunette*, is made the designation of various objects having a shape roughly resembling some one of the moon's varying phases. A popular superstition connects with these last some of the phenomena of insanity, and so the same word *lune* has to signify also, a crazy fit,' while a host of derivatives—as *lunatic, lunacy;* as *moon-struck, mooning, mooner*—attest in our common speech the influence of the same delusion.

We see that, in finding a name by which to designate a new conception, we may either pitch upon some one of the latter's attributes, inherent or accidental, and denominate it from that, limiting and specializing for its use an attributive term of a more general meaning; or, on the other hand, we may connect it by a tie of correspondence or analogy with some other conception already named, and extend so as to include it the sphere of application of the other's designation; while, in either case, we may improve or modify to any extent our apprehension of the object conceived of, both stripping it of qualities with which we had once invested it and attributing to it others, and may thus pave the way to the establishment of new relations between it and other objects, which shall become fruitful of further changes in our nomenclature. These two, in fact—the restriction and specialization of general terms, and the extension and generalization of special terms—are the two grand divisions under which may be arranged all the infinite varieties of the process of names-giving.

Every one knows that it is the usual and normal character of a word to bear a variety, more or less considerable, of meanings and applications, which often diverge so widely, and are connected so loosely, that the lexicographer's art is severely taxed to trace out the tie that runs through them, and exhibit them in their natural order of development. Hardly a term that we employ is not partially ambiguous, covering, not a point, but a somewhat extended and irregular territory of significance; so that, in understanding what is said to us, we have to select, under the guidance of the context, or general requirement of the sense, the particular meaning intended. To repeat a simile already once made use of, each word is, as it were, a stroke of the pencil in an outline sketch; the *ensemble* is necessary to the correct interpretation of each. The art of clear speaking or writing consists in so making up the picture that the right meaning is surely suggested for each part, and directly suggested, without requiring any conscious process of deliberation and choice. The general ambiguity of speech is contended against and sought to be overcome in the technical vocabulary of every art and science: in chemistry, for instance, in mineralogy, in botany, by the observation of minor differences, even back to the ultimate atomic constitution of things, and by the multiplication and nice distinction of terms, the classes under which common speech groups together the objects of common life are broken up, and each substance and quality is noted by a name which designates it, and it alone. Mental philosophy attempts the same thing with regard to the processes and cognitions of the mind; but since, in matters of subjective apprehension, it is impracticable to bring the meaning of words to a definite and unmistakable test, the difficulty of distinctly denominating one's ideas, of defining terms, amounts to an impossibility: no two schools of metaphysics, no two teachers even, agree precisely in their phraseology; nor can any one's doctrine upon recondite points be fully understood save by those who have studied longest and most thoroughly the entirety of his system—nor always even by them.

As the significant changes of language thus bring the same word to the office of designating things widely different, so they also bring different words to the office of designating the same or nearly the same thing. Thus the resources of expression are enriched in another way, by the production of synonyms, names partly accordant, partly otherwise, distinguishing different shades and aspects of the same general idea. I will refer to but a single instance. The feeling of shrinking anticipation of imminent danger, in its most general manifestation, is called *fear:* but for various degrees and manifestations of *fear* we have also the names *fright, terror, dread, alarm, apprehension, panic, tremor, timidity, fearfulness,* and perhaps others. Each of these has its own relations and associations; there is hardly a case where any one of them is employed that one or other of the rest might not be put in its place; and yet, there are also situations where only one of them is the best term to use—though the selection can only be made, or appreciated when made, by those who are nicest in their treatment of language, and though no one who does not possess unusual acuteness and critical judgment can duly describe and illustrate the special significance of each term. We are not to suppose, however, that our synonymy covers all the distinctions, in this or in any other case, that might be drawn, and drawn advantageously. On learning another language, we may find in its vocabulary a richer store of expressions for the varieties of this emotion, or a notation of certain forms of it which we do not heed. Hardly any word in one tongue precisely fills the domain appropriated to the word most nearly corresponding with it in another, so that the former may be invariably translated by the latter. The same territory of significance is differently parcelled out in different tongues among the designations which occupy it; nor is it ever completely covered by them all. The varying shades of *fear* are practically infinite, depending on differences of constitutional impressibility to such a feeling, on differences of character and habit which would make it lead to different action. Hence the impossibility that one should ever apprehend with absolute truth what another, even with the nicest use of language, endeavours to communicate to him. This incapacity of speech to reveal all that the mind contains meets us at every point. The soul of each man is a mystery which no other man can fathom: the most perfect system of signs, the most richly developed language, leads only to a partial comprehension, a mutual intelligence whose degree of completeness depends upon the nature of the subject treated, and the acquaintance of the hearer with the mental and moral character of the speaker.

All word-making by combination is closely analogous with phrase-making: it is but the external and formal unification of elements which usage has already made one in idea. The separate and distinctive meaning of the two words in *take place* is as wholly ignored by us who use the expression as is that of the two in *breakfast*; that we may allow ourselves to say *he breakfasted*, but not *it takeplaced*, is only an accident; it has no deeper ground than the arbitrariness of conventional usage. To *hit off* is as much one idea as *doff* (from *do off*), to *take on* as *don* (from *do on*), although we are not likely ever to fuse the two former into single words, like the two latter. It is clear that, as formerly claimed, the significant content of words is more plastic than their external form: while our language has nearly lost the habit, and so the "power," as we call it, of making new vocables out of independent elements, it is still able to combine and integrate the meanings of such elements, to no small extent.

But again, all form-making includes as an essential part something of the same attenuation of meaning of the formative element, the same withdrawal of its distinctive substantial significance and substitution of one which is relational and formal, which we have been illustrating in the history of independent words. The *ly* of *godly, homely, lively,* and so on, no longer means 'like'; still less does that of *fully, mostly,* etc. In the *ship* of *lordship,* the independent word *shape* is no more to be recognized by its significance than by its form. Even the *ful* of *healthful* and *cheerful* has been weakened in intent from 'full of' to 'possessed of, characterized by.' But there are other phrases which exhibit a closer resemblance and more intimate connection with form-making than any hitherto cited.

So the verb *have,* by the aid of which we form other of our past tenses, and of which the primitive significance is 'possession.' It is easy to see how "I *have* my arms stretched out" might pass into "I *have* stretched out my arms," or how, in such phrases as "he *has* put on his coat," "we *have* eaten our breakfast," "they *have* finished their work," a declaration of possession of the object in the condition denoted by the participle should come to be accepted as sufficiently expressing the completed act of putting it into that condition; the present possession, in fact, implies the past action, and, if our use of *have* were limited to the cases in which such an implication was apparent, the expressions in which we used it would be phrases only. When, however, we extend the implication of past action to every variety of case—as in "I *have* discharged my servant," "he *has* lost his breakfast," "we *have* exposed their errors," where there is no idea of possession for it to grow out of; or with neuter verbs, "you *have* been in error," "he *has* come from London," "they *have* gone away," where there is even no object for the *have* to govern, where condition, and not action, is expressed, and "you *are* been," "he *is* come," "they *are* gone" would be theoretically more correct (as they are alone proper in German)—then we have converted *have* from an independent part of speech into a purely formative element. The same word, by a usage not less bold and pregnant, though of less frequent occurrence, we make to signify causation of action, as in the phrases " I will *have* him well whipped for his impertinence," "he *has* his servant wake him every morning." And, yet once more, we turn it into a sign of future action, with further implication of necessity, as in " I *have* to go to him directly." As is well known, the modern European languages which are descended from the Latin have formed their simple futures by means of this phrase, eliminating from it the implication of necessity: the French *j'aimerai*, 'I shall love,' for instance, is by origin *je aimer ai*, i.e. *j'ai à aimer*, 'I have to love.'

It must not fail to be observed that these processes of word-making, of names-giving, in all their variety, are not, in the fullest sense, consciously performed: that is to say, they are not, for the most part, premeditated and reflective.

Sometimes the scientific man has put upon him the task of devising a terminology, as well as a nomenclature—as was the case with those French chemists, at the end of the last century, who fixed the precise scientific meaning to be thenceforth signified by a whole apparatus of formative elements, of suffixes and prefixes: for example, in *sulphuret, sulphuric, sulphurous, sulphate, sulphite, sulphide, bisulphate, sesquisulphide,* and so on. This is, indeed, of the nature of an artificial universal language, built up of precise, sharply distinguished, and invariably regular signs for the relations of ideas—such a language as some have vainly imagined it possible to invent and teach for all the infinitely varied needs of speech, and for the use of the whole human race: the chemical terminology is, in its own sphere, of universal applicability, and is adopted by chemists of various race and native tongue. But human language is not made in this way. The most important and intimate part of linguistic growth, that which affects the vocabulary of general and daily use, learned by every child, used in the common intercourse of life, goes on in a covert and unacknowledged manner; it is almost insensibly slow in its progress; it is the effect of a gradual accumulation of knowledge and quickening of insight; it is wrought out, as it were, item by item, from the mass of the already subsisting resources of expression: the mind, familiar with a certain use of a term, sees and improves a possibility of its extension, or modification, or nicer definition; old ideas, long put side by side and compared, prompt a new one; deductions hitherto unperceived are drawn from premises already known; a distinction is sharpened; a conception is invested with novel associations; experience suggests a new complex of ideas as calling for conjoint expression. Speech is the work of the mind coming to a clearer consciousness of its own conceptions and of their combinations and relations, and is at the same time the means by which that clearer consciousness is attained; and hence, it works its own progress; its use teaches its improvement; practice in the manipulation of ideas as represented by words leads the way to their more adroit and effective management. A vocabulary, even while undergoing no extension in substantial content of words and forms, may grow indefinitely in expressiveness, becoming filled up with new senses, its words and phrases made pregnant with deeper and more varied significance. It may do so, and it will, if there lie in the nature and circumstances of the people who speak it a capacity for such growth. The speech of a community is the reflex of its average and collective capacity, because, as we have already seen, the community alone is able to make and change language; nothing can become a part of the common treasure of expression which is not generally apprehended, approved, and accepted. It is not true, as is sometimes taught or implied, that a genius or commanding intellect, arising among a people, can impress a marked effect upon its language—least of all, in the earlier stages of linguistic development, or amid ruder and more primitive conditions of culture. No individual can affect speech directly except by separate items of change in respect to which he sets an example for others to follow and an example which will be followed in proportion as the changes are accordant with already prevailing usage and naturally suggested by it: the general structure and character of language are out of his reach, save as he can raise the common intellect, and quicken and fertilize the minds of his fellows, thus sowing seed which may spring up and bear fruit in language also. If he attempt anything like innovation, the conservatism of the community will array itself against him with a force of resistance against which he will be powerless. The commanding intellect has much the better opportunity to act effectively in a cultivated and lettered people, inasmuch as his inciting and lifting influence can be immediately exerted upon so many more of his fellows, and even upon more than one generation.

Especially is it true that all form-making is accomplished by a gradual and unreflective process. It is impossible to suppose, for instance, that, in converting the adjective *like* into the adverbial suffix *ly*, there was anything like intention or premeditation, any looking forward, even, to the final result. One step simply prepared the way for and led to another. We can trace the successive stages of the transfer, but we cannot see the historical conditions and linguistic habits which facilitated it, or tell why, among all the Germanic races, the English alone should have given the suffix this peculiar application; why the others content themselves without any distinctive adverbial suffix, nor feel that their modes of expressing the adverbial relation are less clear and forcible than ours. And so in every other like case. An aptitude in handling the elements of speech, a capacity to perceive how the resources of expression can be applied to formative uses, a tendency toward the distinct indication of formal relations rather than their implication merely—these, in their natural and unconscious workings, constitute the force which produces grammatical forms, which builds up, piece by piece, a grammatical system, more or less full and complete. Every language is the product and expression of the capacities and tendencies of a race as bearing upon the specific work of language-making; it illustrates what they could do in this particular walk of human effort; and the variety of product shows the difference of human endowment in this regard, even more strikingly than the variety of the art-products of different peoples exhibits their diverse grade and kind of artistic power to conceive and execute.

For, as has been already pointed out, and must here again be insisted on, every single act in the whole process of making words and forming language, at every period of linguistic development, has been a human act. Whether more or less deliberately performed, it was always essentially of the same kind; it was something brought about by the free action of men. Its reasons lay in human circumstances, were felt in human minds, and prompted human organs to effort. No name was ever given save as a man or men apprehended some conception as calling for expression, and expressed it. Every idea had its distinct existence before it received its distinctive sign; the thought is anterior to the language by which it is represented. To maintain the opposite, to hold that the sign exists before the thing signified, or that a conception cannot be entertained without the support of a word, would be the sheerest folly; it would compel us to assert that *galvanism* could not be recognized as a new form of natural force, hitherto undescribed, until its discoverers had decided what to style it; that Neptune was not visible in the astronomer's glass till it had been determined after which of the Grecian divinities it should be christened; that the spinner's *mule* and *jenny* were not built till the inventor had chosen a name for them; that the aniline colours made upon the eye no impressions distinguishable from those of hues long familiar until the battle-fields had been pitched upon whose names they should bear; that the community had no appreciation of the frequent tediousness and impertinence of official forms until they had agreed to call it *red tape;* that the human race did not see that the colour of growing things like leaves and grass was different from those of the clear sky, of blood, of earth, of snow, until, from the name for *growing,* they had worked out for it a name *green,* as well as, by some similar process, like names for the others. Men do not lay up in store a list of ideas, to be provided with spoken signs when some convenient season shall come; nor do they prepare a catalogue of words, to which ideas shall be attached when found: when the thing is perceived, the idea conceived, they find in the existing resources of speech the means of its expression—a name which formerly belonged to something else in some way akin with it; a combination of words, a phrase, which perhaps remains a phrase, perhaps is fused into, or replaced by, a single word.

Thus it is that the reason why anything is called as we are accustomed to call it is a historical reason; it amounts to this: that, at some time in the past—either when the thing was first apprehended, or at some later period—it was convenient for men to apply to it this name. And the principal item in this convenience was, that certain other things were already named so and so. Until we arrive at the very beginnings of speech every name comes, by combination, derivation, or simple transfer of meaning, from some other name or names: men do not create new words out of hand; they construct them of old material. At the time and under the circumstances, then, when each term acquired its given significance, the possession of certain other resources of expression, combined with certain usages of speech and habits of thought, and influenced by external circumstances, caused men's choice to fall upon it rather than upon any other combination of sounds. Thus every word has its etymology or derivation, and to trace out its etymology is to follow up and exhibit its transfers of meaning and changes of form, as far back and as completely as the nature of the case allows.

We study, then, the history of words, not in order to assure ourselves of our right to employ them as we do, but to satisfy a natural curiosity respecting the familiar and indispensable means of our daily intercourse, and to learn something of the circumstances and character of those who established them in use. It is because every act of word-making is a historical act, the work of human minds under the guidance of human circumstances, that the investigation of language is an inquiry into the internal and external history of men.

But etymological reminiscences, while thus of the highest value to him who reflects upon language and examines its history, are, as regards the practical purposes of speech, of very subordinate consequence; nay, they would, if more prominent before our attention, be an actual embarrassment to us. Language would be half spoiled for our use by the necessity of bearing in mind why and how its constituents have the value we give them. The internal development of a vocabulary, too, would be greatly checked and hampered by a too intrusive etymological consciousness. All significant transfer, growth of new meanings, form-making, is directly dependent upon our readiness to forget the derivation of our terms, to cut loose from historical connections, and to make the tie of conventional usage the sole one between the thing signified and its spoken sign. Much the greater part of the resources of expression possessed by our language would be struck off at a blow, if a perceived bond of meaning between etymon and derivative were a requisite to the latter's existence and use. Those, then, are greatly in error who would designate by the name "linguistic sense" (*sprachsinn*) a disposition to retain in memory the original *status* and value of formative elements, and the primary significance of transferred terms; who would lay stress upon the maintenance of such a disposition, and regard its wane as an enfeeblement, a step downward toward the structural decay of language. On the contrary, the opposite tendency is the true principle of lively and fertile growth, both of the form and content of speech, and, as we shall see hereafter, it prevails most in the languages of highest character and destiny. A certain degree of vividness, of graphic and picturesque quality, it is true, is conferred upon a term which has been applied by a metaphor to a mental or philosophic use, by the continued apprehension of the metaphor; but vividness is a quality which is dearly bought at the expense of any degree of objective clearness, of dry and sober precision; and it can always be attained, when really wanted, by new figures, after old figures have become prosaic appellations. As we rise, too, in the scale of linguistic use, from that which is straightforward and unreflective to that which is elaborate, pregnant, artistic, etymological considerations in many cases rise in value, and constitute an important element in that suggestiveness which invests every word, giving it its delicacy of application, making it full of significance and dignity where another term, coarsely synonymous with it, would be tame and ineffective. A pregnant implication of etymologic meaning often adds strikingly to the force and impressiveness of an expression. Yet this is but one element among many, and its degree of consequence is, I am convinced, apt to be over-estimated.

Now the particular modes and departments of linguistic change are so diverse that no one cause, or kind of causes, can affect them all, or affect them all alike, either to quicken or to retard them. But the plainest and most apprehensible influence is that which is exerted by change of external circumstances, surroundings, mode of life, mental and physical activity, customs and habits. How powerfully such causes may act upon language: it expands and contracts in close adaptation to the circumstances and needs of those who use it; it is enriched and impoverished along with the enrichment or impoverishment of their minds. But it is needless to insist farther upon a truth so obvious: no one will think of denying that the content of any language, in words and phrases and their meanings, must correspond with and be measured by the mental wealth of the community to whom it belongs, and must change as this changes. It is but the simplest corollary from the truth which we have already established, that men make their own language, and keep it in existence by their tradition, and that they make and transmit it for their own practical uses, and for no other end whatsoever.

A vastly more subtle and difficult question is, in what shall consist the linguistic growth which change of circumstance demands, or to which varying character and choice impel: how far shall it lie in the accession or withdrawal of words and meanings of words, and how far in development or decay of linguistic structure? Change of vocabulary, while it is the most legitimate and inevitable of any that a language undergoes, is also the least penetrating, touching most lightly the essential character of speech as the instrument of thought. Such words as *photograph* and *telegraph* are brought in and naturalized, fitted with all the inflectional apparatus which the language possesses, without any further consequences. Such are mere additions to speech, which may affect the sum and aggregate value of its resources of expression, often to a considerable extent, without modifying its organism, or altering its grammatical form, its apprehension of relations and command of the means of signifying them. And yet, the same circumstances which lead to the great and rapid development of a vocabulary—especially where it takes place out of native resources, and in a less conscious and artificial way—may have an indirect effect upon grammatical development also; where so much change is going on, so much that is new coming into use, the influence will naturally be felt in some measure in every part of the language. Hints of such a possibility are discoverable even in the modern history of our own speech: *ism*, though of ultimate Greek origin, and coming to us through the French, has become a thoroughly English suffix, admitting of the most familiar and extended application in forming new words. So distinct, indeed, is our apprehension of the specific value of the ending *ism* that we are able to cut it off and make an independent word of it, talking of a person's *isms,* or of his favourite *ism.*

The variation of language in space, its change from one region to another, is a not less obvious fact than its variation in time, its change from one epoch to another. The earth is filled with almost numberless dialects, differing from one another in a greater or less degree, and some of them, at least, we know by historical evidence to be descendants of a common original. This state of things finds its ready and simple explanation in the principles which have been already laid down.

If communication is the assimilating force which averages and harmonizes the effects of discordant individual action on language, keeping it, notwithstanding its incessant changes, the same to all the members of the same community, then it is clear that everything which narrows communication, and tends to the isolation of communities, favours the separation of a language into dialects; while all that extends communication, and strengthens the ties which bind together the parts of a community, tends to preserve the homogeneity of speech. Suppose a race, occupying a certain tract of country, to possess a single tongue, which all understand and use alike: then, so long as the race is confined within narrow limits, however rapidly its language may yield to the irresistible forces which produce linguistic growth, all will learn from each, and each from all; and, from generation to generation, every man will understand his neighbour, whatever difficulty he might find in conversing with the spirit of his great-grandfather, or some yet remoter ancestor. But if the race grows in numbers, spreading itself over region after region, sending out colonies to distant lands, its uniformity of speech is exposed to serious danger, and can only be saved by specially favouring circumstances and conditions. And these conditions are yet more exclusively of an external character than those which, as we lately saw, determine the mode and rate of linguistic change in general: they consist mainly in the kind and degree of culture enjoyed and the effects which this naturally produces. In a low state of civilization, the maintenance of community over a wide extent of country is altogether impracticable; the tendency to segregation is paramount; local and clannish feeling prevails, stifling the growth of any wider and nobler sense of national unity and common interests; each little tribe or section is jealous of and dreads the rest; the struggle for existence arrays them in hostility against each other; or, at the best, the means of constant and thorough communication among individuals of the different parts of the country is wanting, along with the feelings which should impel to it. Thus all the diversifying tendencies are left to run their course unchecked; varieties of circumstance and experience, the subtler and more indirect influences of climate and mode of life, the yet more undefinable agencies which have their root in individual and national caprice, gradually accumulate their discordant effects about separate centres, and local varieties of speech arise, which grow into dialects, and these into distinct and, finally, widely dissimilar languages. The rate at which this separation will go on depends, of course, in no small degree, upon the general rate of change of the common speech; as the dialects can only become different by growing apart, a sluggishness of growth will keep them longer together—and that, not by its direct operation alone, but also by giving the weak forces of an imperfect and scanty communication opportunity to work more effectively in counteraction of the others. Thus all the influences which have already been referred to as restricting the variation of a language from generation to generation are, as such, equally effective in checking its variation from portion to portion of a people. But the most important of them also contribute to the same result in another way, by directly strengthening and extending the bonds of community. Culture ånd enlightenment give a wonderful cohesive force; they render possible a wide political unity, maintenance of the same institutions, government under the same laws; they facilitate community of memories and traditions, and foster national feeling; they create the wants and tastes which lead the people of different regions to mix with and aid one another, and they furnish the means of ready and frequent intercourse: all of which make powerfully for linguistic unity also. A traditional literature, sacred or heroic, tends effectively in the same direction. But of more account than all is a written literature, and an organized and pervading system of instruction, whereby the same expressions for thought, feeling, and experience are set as models before the eyes of all, and the most far-reaching and effective style of linguistic communication is established.

Moreover, that same necessity of mutual understanding which makes and preserves the identity of language throughout a community has power also to bring forth identity out of diversity. No necessary and indissoluble tie binds any human being to his own personal and local peculiarities of idiom, or even to his mother-tongue; habit and convenience alone make them his; he is ever ready to give them up for others, when circumstances make it worth his while to do so. The coarse and broad-mouthed rustic whom the force of inborn character and talent brings up to a position among cultivated men, wears off the rudeness of his native dialect, and learns to speak as correctly and elegantly, perhaps, as one who has been trained from his birth after the best models. Those who come up from among the dialects of every part of Britain to seek their fortune in the metropolis acquire some one of the forms of English speech which flourish there; and, even if they themselves are unable ever to rid themselves wholly of provincialisms, their children may grow up as thorough cockneys as if their families had never lived out of hearing of Bow bells. Any one of us who goes to a foreign land and settles there, identifying himself with a community of strange speech, learns to talk with them, as well as his previously formed habits will let him, and between his descendants and theirs there will be no difference of language, however unlike they may be in hue and feature. If adventurers of various race and tongue combine themselves together in a colony and take up their abode in some wild country, their speech at once begins to undergo a process of assimilation, which sooner or later makes it one and homogeneous: how rapidly this end shall be attained, and whether some one element shall absorb the rest, or whether all shall contribute equally to the resulting dialect, must be determined by the special circumstances of the case. Of the multitudes of Germans whom emigration brings to our shores, some establish themselves together in considerable numbers: they cover with their settlements a tract in the West, or fill a quarter in some of our large towns and cities. They form, then, a kind of community of their own, in the midst of the greater community which surrounds them, having numerous points of contact with the latter, but not absorbed into its structure: there are enough speakers of English among them to furnish all the means of communication with the world about them which they need; they are proud of their German nationality and cling to it; they have their own schools, papers, books, preachers—and their language, though sure to yield finally to the assimilating influences which surround it, may be kept up, possibly, for generations. So also with a crowd of Irish, clustered together in a village or suburb, breeding in and in, deriving their scanty instruction from special schools under priestly care: their characteristic brogue and other peculiarities of word and phrase may have an indefinite lease of life. But, on the other hand, families of foreign nationality scattered in less numbers among us can make no effective resistance to the force which tends to identify them thoroughly with the community of English speakers, and their language is soon given up for ours.

There is evidently no limit to the scale upon which such fusion and assimilation of speech may go on. The same causes which lead an individual, or family, or group of families, to learn and use another tongue than that which they themselves or their fathers have been accustomed to speak, may be by historical circumstances made operative throughout a whole class, or over a whole region. When two communities are combined into one, there comes to be but one language where before there were two. A multiplication and strengthening of the ties which bind together the different sections of one people tends directly toward the effacement of already existing varieties of dialect, and the production of linguistic uniformity.

Such effacement and assimilation of dialectic varieties, not less than dissimilation and the formation of new dialects, are all the time going on in human communities, according as conditions favour the one or the other class of effects; and a due consideration of both is necessary, if we would comprehend the history of any tongue, or family of tongues.

It will be noticed that we have used the terms "dialect" and "language" indifferently and interchangeably, in speaking of any given tongue; and it will also have been made plain, I trust, by the foregoing exposition how vain would be the attempt to establish a definite and essential distinction between them, or give precision to any of the other names which indicate the different degrees of diversity among related tongues. No form of speech, living or dead, of which we have any knowledge, was not or is not a dialect, in the sense of being the idiom of a limited community, among other communities of kindred but somewhat discordant idiom; none is not truly a language, in the sense that it is the means of mutual intercourse of a distinct portion of mankind, adapted to their capacity and supplying their needs. The whole history of spoken language, in all climes and all ages, is a series of varying and successive phases; external circumstances, often accidental, give to some of these phases a prominence and importance, a currency and permanence, to which others do not attain; and according to their degree of importance we style them idiom, or *patois*, or dialect, or language. To a very limited extent, natural history feels the same difficulty in establishing the distinction between a "variety" and a "species": and the difficulty would be not less pervading and insurmountable in natural than in linguistic science, if, as is the case in language, not only the species, but even the genera and higher groups of animals and plants were traceably descended from one another or from common ancestors, and passed into each other by insensible gradations. Transmutation of species in the kingdom of speech is no hypothesis, but a patent fact, one of the fundamental and determining principles of linguistic study.

One or two recent writers upon language* have committed the very serious error of inverting the mutual relations of dialectic variety and uniformity of speech, thus turning topsy-turvy the whole history of linguistic development. Unduly impressed by the career of modern cultivated dialects, their effacement of existing

---

* I refer in particular to M. Ernest Renan, of Paris, whose peculiar views upon this subject are laid down in his General History of the Semitic Languages, and more fully in his treatise on the Origin of Language (2nd edition, Paris, 1858, ch. viii.)—a work of great ingenuity and eloquence, but one of which the linguistic philosophy is in a far higher degree constructive than inductive. Professor Max Müller, also, when treating of the Teutonic class of languages (Lectures on Language, first series, fifth lecture), appears distinctly to give in his adhesion to the same view.

dialectic differences and production of homogeneous speech throughout wide regions, and failing to recognize the nature of the forces which have made such a career possible, these authors affirm that the natural tendency of language is from diversity to uniformity; that dialects are, in the regular order of things, antecedent to language; that human speech began its existence in a state of infinite dialectic division, which has been, from the first, undergoing coalescence and reduction. Such comparison and inference as we have been illustrating constitute the method of linguistic research of the comparative philologists, among whom they too desire to count themselves. Only they fail to note that the whole sum of dialectic difference is made up of instances like these, and that, if the latter point back, in detail, to an original unity, the former must, in its entirety, do the same. "As there were families, clans, confederacies, and tribes," we are told,* "before there was a nation, so there were dialects before there was a language." The fallacy involved in this comparison, as in all the reasoning by which is supported the view we are combating, is that it does not go back far enough; it begins in the middle of historic development, instead of at its commencement.

It is true, again, that a certain degree of dialectic variety is inseparable from the being of any language, at any stage of its history. We have seen that even among ourselves, where uniformity of speech prevails certainly not less than elsewhere in the world, no two individuals speak absolutely the same tongue, or would propagate absolutely the same, if circumstances should make them the founders of independent linguistic traditions. However small, then, may have been the community which laid the basis of any actually existing language or family of languages, we must admit the existence of some differences between the idioms of its individual members, or families. And if we suppose such a community to be dispersed into the smallest possible fragments, and each fragment to become the progenitor of a separate community, it might be said with a kind of truth that the languages of these later communities began their history with dialectic differences already developed. The more widely ex-

* Max Müller, *l.c.*

tended, too, the original community before its dispersion, and the more marked the local differences, not inconsistent with mutual intelligibility, existing in its speech, the more capital, so to speak, would each portion have, on which to commence its farther accumulation of dialectic variations. But these original dialectic differences would themselves be the result of previous growth, and they would be of quite insignificant amount, as having been able to consist at the outset with unity of speech; they might be undistinguishable even by the closest analysis among the peculiarities of idiom which should have arisen later; and it would be the grossest error to maintain either that these last were original and primitive, or that they grew out of and were caused by the first slight varieties: we should rather say, with entire truth, that the later dialects had grown by gradual divergence out of a single homogeneous language.

The continuity and similarity of the course of linguistic history in all its stages, and the competency of linguistic correspondences, wherever we find them, to prove unity of origin and community of tradition, are truths which we need to bear in mind as we proceed with our inquiries into language. If we meet in different tongues with words which are clearly the same word, notwithstanding differences of form and meaning which they may exhibit, we cannot help concluding that they are common representatives of a single original, once formed and adopted by a single community, and that from this they have come down by the ordinary and still subsisting processes of linguistic tradition, which always and everywhere involve liability to alteration in outer shape and inner content. It is true that there are found in language accidental resemblances between words of wholly different origin: but exceptions like these do not make void the rule; the possibility of their occurrence only imposes upon the etymologist the necessity of greater care and circumspection in his comparisons, of studying more thoroughly the history of the words with which he has to deal. It is also true that real historical correspondences may exist between isolated words in two languages without implying the original identity of those languages, or anything more than a borrowing by the one out of the stores of expression belonging to the other. Our own tongue, for instance, aside from its wholesale composition out of the tongues of two different races, draws more or less of its material from nearly every one of the languages of Europe, and from not a few of those of Asia, Africa, and America. Yet it is evident that such borrowing has its limits, both of degree and of kind, and that it may be within the power of the linguistic student readily to distinguish its results from the effects of a genuine community of linguistic tradition.

The following table will set forth, it is believed, in a plain and apprehensible manner some of the correspondences of which we have been speaking. For the sake of placing their value in a clearer light, I add under each word its equivalents in three of the languages—namely Arabic, Turkish, and Hungarian—which, though neighbours of the Indo-European tongues, or enveloped by them, are of wholly different kindred.

English	two	three	seven	thou	me	mother	brother	daughter
Germanic:								
Dutch	twee	drie	zeven		mij	moeder	broeder	dóchter
Icelandic	tvŏ	thriu	siŏ	thu	mik	modhir	brodhir	dottir
High-German	zwei	drei	sieben	du	mich	mutter	bruder	tochter
Moeso-Gothic	twa	thri	sibun	thu	mik		brothar	dauhtar
Lithuanic	du	tri	septyni	tu	manen	moter	brolis	dukter
Slavonic	dwa	tri	sedmi	tŭ	man	mater	brat	dochy
Celtic	dau	tri	secht	tu	me	mathair	brathair	dear(??)
Latin	duo	tres	septem	tu	me	mater	frater	
Greek	dŭo	treis	hepta	sŭ	me	meter	phrater	thugater
Persian	dwa	thri	hapta	tum	me	matar		duhitar
Sanskrit	dwa	tri	sapta	twam	me	matar	bhratar	duhitar
Arabic	ithn	thalath	sab	anta	ana	umm	akh	bint
Turkish	iki	ŭch	yedi	sen	ben	ana	kardash	kiz
Hungarian	ket	harom	het	te	engem	anya	fiver	leany

I have selected, of course, for inclusion in this table, those words of the several classes represented which exhibit most clearly their actual unity of descent: in others, it would require some detailed discussion of phonetic relations to make the same unity appear. Thus, the Sanskrit *panca*, the Greek *pente*, the Latin *quinque*, and the Gothic *fimf*, all meaning 'five,' are as demonstrably the later metamorphoses of a single original word as are the varying forms of the primitive *tri*, 'three,' given above: each of their phonetic changes being supported by numerous analogies in the respective languages. The whole scheme of numeral and pronominal forms and of terms of relationship is substantially one and the same in all the tongues ranked as Indo-European.

These facts, of themselves, would go far toward proving the original unity of the languages in question. To look upon correspondences like those here given as the result of accident is wholly preposterous: no sane man would think of ascribing them to such a cause. Nor is the hypothesis of a natural and inherent bond between the sound and the sense, which would prompt language-makers in different parts of the earth to assign, independently of one another, these names to these conceptions, at all more admissible. The existence of a natural bond could be claimed with even the slightest semblance of plausibility only in the case of the pronouns and the words for 'father' and 'mother'; and there, too, the claim could be readily disposed of—if, indeed, it be not already sufficiently refuted by the words from stranger tongues which are cited in the table. Mutual borrowing, too, transfer from one tongue to another, would be equally far from furnishing an acceptable explanation. Were we dealing with two or three neighbouring dialects alone, the suggestion of such a borrowing would not be so palpably futile as in the case in hand, where the facts to be explained are found in so many tongues, covering a territory which stretches from the mouths of the Ganges to the shores of the Atlantic. A modified form of the hypothesis of mutual borrowing is put forth by some who are indisposed to admit the essential oneness of Indo-European speech. Some tribe or race, they say, of higher endowments and culture, has leavened with its material and usages the tongues of all these scattered peoples, engrafting upon their original diversity an element of agreement and unity. But this theory is just as untenable as the others which we have been reviewing. Instances of mixture of languages—resulting either from the transmission of a higher and more favoured culture, or from a somewhat equal and intimate mingling of races, or from both together—have happened during the historical period in sufficient numbers to allow the linguistic student to see plainly what are its effects upon language, and that they are very different from those which make the identity of Indo-European language. The introduction of culture and knowledge, of art and science, may bring in a vocabulary of expressions for the knowledge communicated, the conceptions taught or prompted; but it cannot touch the most intimate fund of speech, the words significant of those ideas without whose designation no spoken tongue would be worthy of the name. If we could possibly suppose that the rude ancestors of the Indo-European nations, more brutish than the Africans and Polynesians of the present day, were unable to count their fingers even until taught by some missionary tribe which went from one to the other, scattering these first rudiments of mathematical knowledge, we might attribute to its influence the close correspondence of the Indo-European numeral systems; but then we should have farther to assume that the same teachers instructed them how to address one another with *I* and *thou,* and how to name the members of their own families: and who will think of maintaining such an absurdity? All the preponderating influence of the Sanskrit-speaking tribes of northern India over the ruder population of the Dekhan, to which they gave religion, philosophy, and polity, has only resulted in filling the tongues of the south with learned Sanskrit, much as our own English is filled with learned Latin and Greek. Even that coalescence of nearly equal populations, languages, and cultures out of which has grown the tongue we speak, has left the language of common life among us—the nucleus of a vocabulary which the child first learns, and every English speaker uses every day, almost every hour—still overwhelmingly Saxon: the English is Germanic in its fundamental structure, though built higher and decorated in every part with Romanic material. So is it also with the Persian, in its relation to the Arabic, of whose material its more learned and artificial styles are in great part made up; so with the Turkish, of which the same thing is true with regard to the Persian and Arabic. But most of all do these cases of the mingling of different tongues in one language, and every other known case of a like character, show that the grammatical system, the apparatus of inflection and word-making, the means by which vocables, such as they stand in their order in the dictionary, are taken out and woven together into connected discourse, resists longest and most obstinately any trace of intermixture, the intrusion of foreign elements and foreign habits. However many French nouns and verbs were admitted to full citizenship in English speech, they all had to give up in this respect their former nationality: every one of them was declined or conjugated after Germanic models. Such a thing as a language with a mixed grammatical apparatus has never come under the cognizance of linguistic students: it would be to them a monstros-

ity; it seems an impossibility. Now the Indo-European languages
are full of the plainest and most unequivocal correspondences of
grammatical structure; they show abundant traces of a common
system of word-formation, of declension, of conjugation, however
disguised by the corruptions and overlaid by the new developments of a later time: and these traces are, above all others, the
most irrefutable evidences of the substantial unity of their linguistic tradition. We will notice but a single specimen of this kind
of evidences, the most striking one, perhaps, which Indo-European
grammar has to exhibit. This is the ordinary declension of the
verb, in its three persons singular and plural. In drawing out the
comparison, we cannot start, as before, from the English, because
the English has lost its ancient apparatus of personal endings: we
must represent the whole Germanic branch by its oldest member,
the Mœso-Gothic. The table is as follows:*

English	'I have'	'thou hast'	'he has'	'we have'	'ye have'	'they have'
Moeso-Gothic	*haba*	*habai-s*	*habai-th*	*haba-m*	*habai-th*	*haba-nd*
Mod. Persian	*-m*		*-d*	*-m*	*-d*	*-nd*
Celtic	*-m*		*-d*	*-m*	*-d*	*-t*
Lithuanic	*-mi*	*-si*	*-ti*	*-me*	*-te*	*-ti*
Slavonic	*-mi*	*-si*	*-ti*	*-mu*	*-te*	*-nti*
Latin	*habeo*	*habe-s*	*habe-t*	*habe-mus*	*habe-tis*	*habe-nt*
Greek	*-mi*	*-si*	*-ti*	*-mes*	*-te*	*-nti*
Sanskrit	*-mi*	*-si*	*-ti*	*-masi*	*-tha*	*-nti*

Fundamental and far-reaching as are the correspondences, of
material and of form, which have thus been brought forward, it is
not necessary that we insist upon their competency, alone and
unaided, to prove the Indo-European languages only later dialectic forms of a single original tongue. Their convincing force
lies in the fact that they are selected instances, examples chosen
from among a host of others, which abound in every part of the
grammar and vocabulary of all the languages in question, now so
plain as to strike the eye of even the hasty student, now so hidden

* Owing to the difficulty of finding a single verb which shall present the
endings in all the different languages, the verb *to have* has been selected, and
given in full in the two languages in which it occurs, the terminations alone
being elsewhere written. These are not in all cases the most usual endings
of conjugation, but such as are found in verbs, or in dialects, which have
preserved more faithfully their primitive forms.

under later peculiar growth as to be only with difficulty traceable by the acute and practised linguistic analyst. He who would know them better may find them in such works as the Comparative Grammars of Bopp and Schleicher and the Greek Etymologies of Curtius. An impartial examination of them must persuade even the most sceptical that these tongues exhibit resemblances which can be accounted for only on the supposition of a prevailing identity of linguistic tradition, such as belongs to the common descendants of one and the same mother-tongue. On the other hand, all their differences, great and widely sundering as these confessedly are, can be fully explained by the prolonged operation of the same causes which have broken up the Latin into the modern Romanic dialects, or the original Germanic tongue into its various existing forms, and which have converted the Anglo-Saxon of a thousand years ago into our present English. Besides its natural divergent growth, the original Indo-European tongue has doubtless been in some degree diversified by intermixture here and there with languages of other descent; but there is no reason for believing that this has been an element of any considerable importance in its history of development. At some period, then, in the past, and in some limited region of Europe or Asia, lived a tribe from whose imperfect dialect have descended all those rich and cultivated tongues now spoken and written by the teeming millions of Europe and of some of the fairest parts of Asia.

Its dialects have a range, in the variety of their forms and in the length of the period of development covered by them, which is sought elsewhere in vain. They illustrate the processes of linguistic growth upon an unrivalled scale, and from a primitive era to which we can make but an imperfect approach among the other languages of mankind. Portions of the Chinese literature, it is true, are nearly or quite as old as anything Indo-European, and the Chinese language is in some respects more primitive in its structure than any other human tongue; but what it was at the beginning, that it has ever since remained, a solitary example of a language almost destitute of a history. Egypt has records to show of an age surpassing that of any other known monuments of human speech; but they are of scanty and enigmatical content, and the Egyptian tongue also stands comparatively alone, without descendants, and almost without relatives. The Semitic languages come nearest to offering a worthy parallel; but they, too, fall far short of it. The earliest Hebrew documents are not greatly exceeded in antiquity by any others, and the Hebrew with its related dialects, ancient and modern, fills up a linguistic scheme of no small wealth; yet Semitic variety is, after all, but poor and scanty as compared with Indo-European; Semitic language possesses a toughness and rigidity of structure which has made its history vastly less full of instructive change; and its beginnings are of unsurpassed obscurity. The Semitic languages are rather a group of closely kindred dialects than a family of widely varied branches: their whole yield to linguistic science is hardly more than might be won from a single subdivision of Indo-European speech, like the Germanic or Romanic. None of the other great races into which mankind is divided cover with their dialects, to any noteworthy extent, time as well as space; for the most part, we know nothing more respecting their speech than is to be read in its present living forms. Now it is so obvious as hardly to require to be pointed out, that a science whose method is prevailingly historical, which seeks to arrive at an understanding of the nature, office, and source of language by studying its gradual growth, by tracing out the changes it has undergone in passing from generation to generation, from race to race, must depend for the soundness of its methods and the sureness of its results upon the fulness of illustration of these historical changes furnished by the material of its investigations. It is true that the student's historical researches are not wholly baffled by the absence of older dialects, with whose forms he may compare those of more modern date. Something of the development of every language is indicated in its own structure with sufficient clearness to be read by analytic study. Yet more is to be traced out by means of the comparison of kindred contemporaneous dialects; for, in their descent from their common ancestor, it can hardly be that each one will not have preserved some portion of the primitive material which the others have lost. Thus—to illustrate briefly by reference to one or two of our former examples—the identity of our suffix *ly*, in such words as *godly* and *truly*, with the adjective *like* might perhaps have been conjectured from the English alone; and it is made virtually certain by comparison with the modern German (*göttlich, treulich*) or Netherlandish (*goddelijk, waarlijk*); it does not absolutely need a reference to older dialects, like the Anglo-Saxon or Gothic, for its establishment. Again, not only the Sanskrit and other ancient languages exhibit the full form *asmi,* whence comes our *I am,* but the same is also to be found almost unaltered in the present Lithuanian *esmi.* But, even if philological skill and acumen had led the student of Germanic language to the conjecture that *I loved* is originally *I love-did,* it must ever have remained a conjecture only, a mere plausible hypothesis, but for the accident which caused the preservation to our day of the fragment of manuscript containing a part of Bishop Ulfilas's Gothic Bible. And a host of points in the structure of the tongues of our Germanic branch which still remain obscure would, as we know, be cleared up, had we in our possession relics of them at a yet earlier stage of their separate growth. The extent to which the history of a body of languages may be penetrated by the comparison of contemporary dialects alone will, of course, vary greatly in different cases; depending, in the first place, upon the number, variety, and degree of relation of the dialects, and, in the second place, upon their joint and several measure of conservation of ancient forms: but it is also evident that the results thus arrived at for modern tongues will be, upon the whole, both scanty and dubious, compared with those obtained by comparing them with ancient dialects of the same stock. Occasionally, within the narrow limits of a single branch or group, the student enjoys the advantage of access to the parent tongue itself, from which the more recent idioms are almost bodily derived: thus, for example, our possession of the Latin gives to our readings of the history of the Romanic tongues, our determination of the laws which have governed their growth, a vastly higher degree of definiteness and certainty than we could reach if we only knew that such a parent tongue must have existed, and had to restore its forms by careful comparison and deduction. Next in value to this is the advantage of commanding a rich body of older and younger dialects of the same lineage, wherein the common speech is beheld at nearer and remoter distances from its source, so that we can discover the direction of its currents, and fill out with less of uncertainty those parts of their network of which the record is obliterated. This secondary advantage we enjoy in the Germanic, the Persian, the Indian branches of Indo-European speech; and, among the grander divisions of human language, we enjoy it to an extent elsewhere unapproached in the Indo-European family, that immense and varied body of allied forms of speech, whose lines of historic development are seen to cover a period of between three and four thousand years, as they converge toward a meeting in a yet remoter past.

Herein lies the sufficient explanation of that intimate connection, that almost coincidence, which we have noticed between the development of Indo-European comparative philology and that of the general science of language. In order to comprehend human language in every part, the student would wish to have its whole growth, in all its divisions and subdivisions, through all its phases, laid before him for inspection in full authentic documents. Since, however, anything like this is impossible, he has done the best that lay within his power: he has thrown himself into that department of speech which had the largest share of its history thus illustrated, and by studying that has tried to learn how to deal with the yet more scanty and fragmentary materials presented him in other departments. Here could be formed the desired nucleus of a science; here the general laws of linguistic life could be discovered; here could be worked out those methods and processes which, with such modifications as the varying circumstances rendered necessary, should be applied in the investigation of other types of language also. The foundation was broad enough to build up a shapely and many-sided edifice upon. Yet the study of Indo-European language is not the science of language. Such is the diversity in unity of human speech that exclusive attention to any one of its types could only give us partial and false views of its nature and history. Endlessly as the dialects of our family appear to differ from one another, they have a distinct common character, which is brought to our apprehension only when we compare them with those of other stock; they are far from exhausting the variety of expression which the human mind is capable of devising for its thought; the linguist who trains himself in them alone will be liable to narrowness of vision, and will stumble when he comes to walk in other fields. We claim only that their inner character and outer circumstances combine to give them the first place in the regard of the linguistic scholar; that their investigation will constitute in the future, as it has done in the past, a chief object of his study; and that their complete elucidation is both the most attainable and the most desirable and rewarding object proposed to itself by linguistic science.

The grand means, now, of modern etymological research is the extensive comparison of kindred forms. How this should be so appears clearly enough from what has been already taught respecting the growth of dialects and the genetical connections of languages. If spoken tongues stood apart from one another, each a separate and isolated entity, they would afford no scope for the comparative method. As such entities the ancient philology regarded them; or, if their relationship was in some cases recognized, it was wrongly apprehended and perversely applied—as when, for instance, the Latin was looked upon as derived from the Greek, and its words were sought to be etymologized out of the Greek lexicon, as corrupted forms of Greek vocables. In the view of the present science, while each existing dialect is the descendant of an older tongue, so other existing dialects are equally descendants of the same tongue. All have kept a part, and lost a part, of the material of their common inheritance; all have preserved portions of it in a comparatively unchanged form, while they have altered other portions perhaps past recognition. But, while thus agreed in the general fact and the general methods of change, they differ indefinitely from one another in the details of the changes effected. Each has saved something which others have lost, or kept in pristine purity what they have obscured or overlaid: or else, from their variously modified forms can be deduced with confidence the original whence these severally diverged. Every word, then, in whose examination the linguistic scholar engages, is to be first set alongside its correspondents or analogues in other related languages, that its history may be read aright. Thus the deficiencies of the evidence which each member of a connected group of dialects contains respecting its own genesis and growth are made up, in greater or less degree, by the rest, and historical results are reached having a greatly increased fulness and certainty. The establishment of a grand family of related languages, like the Indo-European, makes each member contribute, either immediately or mediately, to the elucidation of every other.

But the comparative method, as we must not fail to notice, is no security against loose and false etymologizing; it is not less liable to abuse than any other good thing. If it is to be made fruitful of results for the advancement of science, it must not be wielded arbitrarily and wildly; it must have its fixed rules of application. Some appear to imagine that, in order to earn the title of "comparative philologist," they have but to take some given language and run with it into all the ends of the earth, collating its material and forms with those of any other tongue they may please to select. But that which makes the value of comparison—namely, genetical relationship—also determines the way in which it shall be rendered valuable. We compare in order to bring to light resemblances which have their ground and explanation in a real historical identity of origin. We must proceed, then, as in any other genealogical inquiry, by tracing the different lines of descent backward from step to step toward their points of convergence. The work of comparison is begun between the tongues most nearly related, and is gradually extended to those whose connection is more and more remote. We first set up, for example, a group like the Germanic, and by the study of its internal relations learn to comprehend its latest history, distinguishing and setting apart all that is the result of independent growth and change among its dialects, recognizing what in it is original, and therefore fair subject of comparison with the results of a like process performed upon the other branches of the same family. It needs not, indeed, that the restoration of primitive Germanic speech should be made complete before any farther step is taken; there are correspondences so conspicuous and palpable running through all the varieties of Indo-European speech, that, the unity of the family having been once established, they are at a glance seen and accepted at their true value. But only a small part of the analogies of two more distantly related languages are of this character, and their recognition will be made both complete and trustworthy in proportion as the nearer congeners of each language are first subjected to comparison. If English were the only existing Germanic tongue, we could still compare it with Attic Greek, and point out a host of coincidences which would prove their common origin; but, as things are, to conduct our investigation in this way, leaving out of sight the related dialects on each side, would be most unsound and unphilological; it would render us liable to waste no small share of our effort upon those parts of English which are peculiar, of latest growth, and can have no genetic connection whatever with aught in the Greek: it would expose us, on the one hand, to make false identifications (as between our *whole* and the Greek *holos*, 'entire') ; and, on the other hand, to find diversity where the help of older dialectic forms on both sides would show striking resemblance. What analogy, for instance, do we discern between our *bear*, in *they bear*, and Greek *pherousi?* but comparison of the other Germanic dialects allows us to trace *bear* directly back to a Germanic form *berand*, and Doric Greek gives us *pheronti*, from which comes *pherousi* by one of the regular euphonic rules of the language; the law of permutation of mutes in the Germanic languages exhibits *b* as the regular correspondent in Low German dialects to the original aspirate *ph;* and the historical identity of the two words compared, in root and termination, is thus put beyond the reach of cavil.

Yet more contrary to sound method would it be, for example, to compare directly English, Portuguese, Persian, and Bengali, four of the latest and most altered representatives of the four great branches of Indo-European speech to which they severally belong. Nothing, or almost nothing, that is peculiar to the Bengali as compared with the Sanskrit, to the Persian as compared with the ancient Avestan and Achæmenidan dialects, to the Portuguese as compared with the Latin, can be historically connected with what belongs to English or any other Germanic tongue. Their ties of mutual relationship run backward through those older representatives of the branches, and are to be sought and traced there.

But worst of all is the drawing out of alleged correspondences, and the fabrication of etymologies, between such languages as the English—or, indeed, any Indo-European dialect—on the one hand, and the Hebrew, or the Finnish, or the Chinese, on the other. Each of these last is the fully recognized member of a well-established family of languages, distinct from the Indo-European. If there be genetic relation between either of them and an Indo-European language, it must lie back of the whole grammatical development of their respective families, and can only be brought to light by the reduction of each, through means of the most penetrating and exhaustive study of the dialects confessedly akin with it, to its primitive form, as cleared of all the growth and change wrought upon it by ages of separation. There may be scores, or hundreds, of apparent resemblances between them, but these are worthless as signs of relationship until an investigation not less profound than we have indicated shall show that they are not merely superficial and delusive.

Let it not be supposed that we are reasoning in a vicious circle, in thus requiring that two languages shall have been proved related before the correspondences which are to show their relationship shall be accepted as real. We are only setting forth the essentially cumulative nature of the evidences of linguistic connection. The first processes of comparison by which it is sought to establish the position and relations of a new language are tentative merely. No sound linguist is unmindful of the two opposing possibilities which interfere with the certainty of his conclusions: first, that seeming coincidences may turn out accidental and illusory only; second, that beneath apparent discordance may be hidden genetic identity. With every new analogy which his researches bring to view, his confidence in the genuineness and historic value of those already found is increased. And when, examining each separate fact in all the light that he can cast upon it, from sources near and distant, he has at length fully satisfied himself that two tongues are fundamentally related, their whole mutual aspect is thereby modified; he becomes expectant of signs of relationship everywhere, and looks for them in phenomena which would not otherwise attract his attention for a moment. When, on the contrary, an orderly and thorough examination, proceeding from the nearer to the remoter degrees of connection, has demonstrated the position of two languages in two diverse families, the weight of historic probability is shifted to the other scale, and makes directly against the interpretation of their surface resemblances as the effect of anything but accident or borrowing.

We see, it may be farther remarked, upon how narrow and

imperfect a basis those comparative philologists build who are content with a facile setting side by side of words; whose materials are simple vocabularies, longer or shorter, of terms representing common ideas. There was a period in the history of linguistic science when this was the true method of investigation, and it still continues to be useful in certain departments of the field of research. It is the first experimental process; it determines the nearest and most obvious groupings, and prepares the way for more penetrating study. Travellers, explorers, in regions exhibiting great diversity of idiom and destitute of literary records—like our western wilds, or the vast plains of inner Africa—do essential service by gathering and supplying such material, anything better being rendered inaccessible by lack of leisure, opportunity, or practice. But it must be regarded as provisional and introductory, acceptable only because the best that is to be had. Genetic correspondences in limited lists of words, however skilfully selected, are apt to be conspicuous only when the tongues they represent are of near kindred; and even then they may be in no small measure obscured or counterbalanced by discordances, so that deeper and closer study is needed, in order to bring out satisfactorily to view the fact and degree of relationship. Penetration of the secrets of linguistic structure and growth, discovery of correspondences which lie out of the reach of careless and uninstructed eyes, rejection of deceptive resemblances which have no historical foundation—these are the most important part of the linguistic student's work. Surface collation without genetic analysis, as far-reaching as the attainable evidence allows, is but a travesty of the methods of comparative philology.

Another not infrequent misapprehension of etymologic study consists in limiting its sphere of action to a tracing out of the correspondences of words. This is, indeed, as we have called it, the fundamental stage, on the solidity of which depends the security of all the rest of the structure; but it is only that. Comparative etymology, like chemistry, runs into an infinity of detail, in which the mind of the student is sometimes entangled, and his effort engrossed; it has its special rules and methods, which admit within certain limits of being mechanically applied, by one ignorant or heedless of their true ground and meaning. Many a man

is a skilful and successful hunter of verbal connections whose
views of linguistic science are of the crudest and most imperfect
character. Not only does he thus miss what ought to be his highest
reward, the recognition of those wide relations and great truths to
which his study of words should conduct him, but his whole work
lacks its proper basis, and is liable to prove weak at any point.
The history of words is inextricably bound up with that of human
thought and life and action, and cannot be read without it. We
fully understand no word till we comprehend the motives and
conditions that called it forth and determined its form. The word
money, for example, is not explained when we have marshalled
the whole array of its correspondents in all European tongues, and
traced them up to their source in the Latin *moneta:* all the historical circumstances which have caused a term once limited to an
obscure city to be current now in the mouths of such immense
communities; the wants and devices of civilization and commerce
which have created the thing designated by the word and made it
what it is; the outward circumstances and mental associations
which, by successive changes, have worked out the name from a
root signifying 'to think'; the structure of organ, and the habits of
utterance—in themselves and in their origin—which have meta-
morphosed *monéta* into *móney:*—all this, and more, is necessary to
the linguistic scholar's perfect mastery of this single term. There
is no limit to the extent to which the roots of being of almost every
word ramify thus through the whole structure of the tongue to
which it belongs, or even of many tongues, and through the history
of the people who speak them: if we are left in most cases to come
far short of the full knowledge which we crave, we at least should
not fail to crave it, and to grasp after all of it that lies within our
reach.

We have been regarding linguistic comparison as what it primarily and essentially is, the effective means of determining genetical relationship, and investigating the historical development
of languages. But we must guard against leaving the impression
that languages can be compared for no other purposes than these.
In those wide generalizations wherein we regard speech as a human
faculty, and its phenomena as illustrating the nature of mind, the
processes of thought, the progress of culture, it is often not less

important to put side by side that which in spoken language is analogous in office but discordant in origin than that which is accordant in both. The variety of human expression is well-nigh infinite, and no part of it ought to escape the notice of the linguistic student. The comparative method, if only it be begun and carried on aright—if the different objects of the genetic and the analogic comparison be kept steadily in view, and their results not confounded with one another—need not be restricted in its application, until, starting from any centre, it shall have comprehended the whole circle of human speech.

The present structure of language has its beginnings, from which we are not yet so far removed that they may not be clearly seen. Our historical analysis does not end at last in mere obscurity; it brings us to the recognition of elements which we must regard as, if not the actual first utterances of men, at least the germs out of which their later speech has been developed. It sets before our view a stage of expression essentially different from any of those we now behold among the branches of our family, and serving as their common foundation.

It must be premised that this belief rests entirely upon our faith in the actuality of our analytical processes, as being merely a retracing of the steps of a previous synthesis—in the universal truth of the doctrine that the elements into which we separate words are those by the putting together of which those words were at first made up. With the disguising and effacing effects of the processes of linguistic change fully present to our apprehensions, we shall not venture to conclude that those cases in which our historical researches fail to give us the genesis of both the elements of a compound form are fundamentally different from those in which it fully succeeds in doing so. The difference lies, not in the cases themselves, but in our attitude toward them; in our accidental possession of information as to the history of the one, and our lack of it as to that of the other. This reasoning, however, obviously applies not to Germanic speech alone; it is equally legitimate and cogent in reference to all Indo-European language. We cannot refuse to believe that the whole history of this family of languages has been, in its grand essential features, the same; that their structure is homogeneous throughout. There is no reason whatever for our assuming that the later composite forms are made up, and not the earlier; that the later suffixes are elaborated out of independent elements, and not the earlier. So far back as we can trace the history of language, the forces which have been efficient in producing its changes, and the general outlines of their modes of operation, have been the same; and we are justified in concluding, we are even compelled to infer, that they have been the same from the outset. There is no way of investigating the first hidden steps of any continuous historical process, except by carefully studying the later recorded steps, and cautiously applying the analogies thence deduced.

The conclusion is one of no small consequence. Elements like *voc*, each composing a single syllable, and containing no traceable sign of a formative element, resisting all our attempts at reduction to a simpler form, are what we arrive at as the final results of our analysis of the Indo-European vocabulary; every word of which this is made up— save those whose history is obscure, and cannot be read far back toward its beginning—is found to contain a monosyllabic root as its central significant portion, along with certain other accessory portions, syllables or remnants of syllables, whose office it is to define and direct the radical idea. The roots are never found in practical use in their naked form; they are (or, as has been repeatedly explained, have once been) always clothed with suffixes, or with suffixes and prefixes; yet they are no mere abstractions, dissected out by the grammarian's knife from the midst of organisms of which they were ultimate and integral portions; they are rather the nuclei of gradual accretions, parts about which other parts gathered to compose orderly and membered wholes; germs, we may call them, out of which has developed the intricate structure of later speech. And the recognition of them in this character is an acknowledgment that Indo-European language, with all its fulness and inflective suppleness, is descended from an original monosyllabic tongue; that our ancestors talked with one another in single syllables, indicative of the ideas of prime importance, but wanting all designation of their relations; and that out of these, by processes not differing in their nature from those which are still in operation in our own tongue, was elaborated the marvellous and varied structure of all the Indo-European dialects.

Such is, in fact, the belief which the students of language have reached, and now hold with full confidence. New and strange but a few years ago, it commands at present the assent of nearly all comparative philologists, and is fast becoming a matter of universal opinion.

Thus is it, also, as regards the division of the roots into two classes, pronominal and verbal: this division is so clearly read in the facts of language that its acceptance cannot be resisted. Some are loth to admit it, and strive to find a higher unity in which it shall disappear, the two classes falling together into one; or to show how the pronominal may be relics of verbal roots, worn down by linguistic usage to such brief form and unsubstantial significance; but their efforts must at least be accounted altogether unsuccessful hitherto, and it is very questionable whether they are called for, or likely ever to meet with success. As regards the purposes of our present inquiry, the double classification is certainly primitive and absolute; back to the very earliest period of which linguistic analysis gives us any knowledge, roots verbal and roots pronominal are to be recognized as of wholly independent substance, character, and office.

It is not possible to regard them as the worn-down relics of a previous career of inflective development. The English, it is true, has been long tending, through the excessive prevalence of the wearing-out processes, toward a state of flectionless monosyllabism; but such a monosyllabism, where the grammatical categories are fully distinguished, where relational words and connectives abound, where every vocable inherits the character which the former possession of inflection has given it, where groups of related terms are applied to related uses, is a very different thing from a primitive monosyllabism like that to which the linguistic analyst is conducted by his researches among the earliest representatives of Indo-European language; and he finds no more difficulty in distinguishing the one from the other, and recognizing the true character of each, than does the geologist in distinguishing a primitive crystalline formation from a conglomerate, composed of well-worn pebbles, of diverse origin and composition, and containing fragments of earlier and later fossils. If the English were strictly reduced to its words of one syllable, it would still contain an abundant repertory of developed parts of speech, expressing every variety of idea, and illustrating a rich phonetic system. The Indo-European roots are not parts of speech, but of indeterminate character, ready to be shaped into nouns and verbs by the aid of affixes; they are limited in signification to a single class of ideas, the physical or sensual, the phenomenal, out of which the intellectual and moral develop themselves by still traceable processes; and in them is represented a system of articulated sounds of great simplicity.

The first beginning of polysyllabism seems to have been made by compounding together roots of the two classes already described, pronominal and verbal. Thus were produced true forms, in which the indeterminate radical idea received a definite significance and application. The addition, for example, to the verbal root *vak*, 'speaking,' of pronominal elements *mi, si, ti* (these are the earliest historically traceable forms of the endings: they were probably yet earlier *ma, sa, ta*), in which ideas of the nearer and remoter relation, of the first, second, and third persons, were already distinguished, produced combinations *vakmi, vaksi, vakti*, to which usage assigned the meaning 'I here speak,' 'thou there speakest,' 'he yonder speaks,' laying in them the idea of predication or assertion, the essential characteristic which makes a verb instead of a noun, just as we put the same into the ambiguous element *love* when we say *I love*. Other pronominal elements, mainly of compound form, indicating plurality of subject, made in like manner the three persons of the plural: they were *masi* (*ma-si*, 'I-thou,' i.e. 'we'), *tasi* (*ta-si*, 'he-thou,' i.e. 'ye'), and *anti* (of more doubtful genesis). A dual number of the same three persons was likewise added; but the earliest form and derivation of its endings cannot be satisfactorily made out. Thus was produced the first verbal tense, the simplest and most immediate of all derivative forms from roots. The various shapes which its endings have assumed in the later languages of the family have already more than once been referred to, in the way of illustration of the processes of linguistic growth: our *th* or *s*, in *he goeth* or *goes*, still distinctly represents the *ti* of the third person singular; and in *am* we have a solitary relic of the *mi* of the first. Doubtless the tense was employed at the outset as general predicative form, being neither past, present, nor future, but all of them combined, and doing duty as either, according as circumstances required, and as sense and connection explained; destitute, in short, of any temporal or modal character; but other verbal forms by degrees grew out of it, or allied themselves with it, assuming the designation of other modifications of predicative meaning, and leaving to it the office of an indicative present.

To follow back to its very beginnings the genesis of nouns, and of the forms of nouns, is much more difficult than to explain the origin of verbal forms. Some nouns—of which the Latin *vox* (*voc-s*), 'a calling, a voice,' and *rex* (*reg-s*), 'one ruling, a king,' are as familiar examples as any within our reach—are produced directly from the roots, by the addition of a different system of inflectional endings; the idea of substantiation or impersonation of the action expressed by the root being arbitrarily laid in them by usage, as was the idea of predication in the forms of the verb. The two words we have instanced may be taken as typical examples of the two classes of derivatives coming most immediately and naturally from the root: the one indicating the action itself, the other, either adjectively or substantively, the actor; the one being of the nature of an infinitive, or abstract verbal noun, the other of a participle, or verbal adjective, easily convertible into an appellative. Even such derivatives, however, as implying a greater modification of the radical idea than is exhibited by the simplest verbal forms, appear to have been from the first mainly made by means of formative elements, suffixes of derivation, comparable with those which belong to the moods and tenses, and the secondary conjugations of the verb. Precisely what these suffixes were, in their origin and primitive substance, and what were the steps of the process by which they lost their independence, and acquired their peculiar value as modifying elements, it is not in most cases feasible to tell. But they were obviously in great part of pronominal origin, and in the acts of linguistic usage which stamped upon them their distinctive value there is much which would seem abrupt, arbitrary, or even perhaps inconceivable, to

one who has not been taught by extensive studies among various
tongues how violent and seemingly far-fetched are the mutations
and transfers to which the material of linguistic structure is often
submitted—on how remote an analogy, how obscure a suggestion,
a needed name or form is sometimes founded. Verbal roots, as
well as pronominal, were certainly also pressed early into the same
service: composition of root with root, of derived form with form,
the formation of derivative from derivative, went on actively,
producing in sufficient variety the means of limitation and indi-
vidualization of the indeterminate radical idea, of its reduction to
appellative condition, so as to be made capable of designating by
suitable names the various beings, substances, acts, states, and
qualities, observed both in the world of matter and in that of mind.

This class of derivatives from roots was provided with another,
a movable, set of suffixes, which we call case-endings, terminations
of declension. Where, as in the case of our two examples *vox* and
rex, the theme of declension was coincident with the verbal root,
the declensional endings themselves were sufficient to mark the
distinction of noun from verb, without the aid of a suffix of derivation. They formed a large and complicated system, and were
charged with the designation of various relations. In the first
place, they indicated case, or the kind of relation sustained by the
noun to which they were appended to the principal action of the
sentence in which it was used, whether as subject, as direct object,
or as indirect object with implication of meanings which we express by means of prepositions, such as *with, from, in, of.* Pronominal elements are distinctly traceable in most of them, and
may have assumed something of a prepositional force before their
combination. The genitive affix is very likely to have been at the
first, like many genitive affixes of later date in the history of the
Indo-European languages, one properly forming a derivative adjective: and it is not impossible that the dative ending was of
the same nature.

The conditions of that primitive period, and the degree in which
they might have been able to quicken the now sluggish processes of
word-combination and formation, are so much beyond our ken that
even our conjectures respecting them have—at least as yet—too
little value to be worth recording. What may have been the

numbers of the community which laid the foundation of all the Indo-European tongues, and what its relation to other then existing communities, are also points hitherto involved in the deepest obscurity. But we know that, before the separation, whether simultaneous or successive, of this community into the parts which afterward became founders of the different tongues of Europe and south-western Asia, the principal part of the linguistic development had already taken place—enough for its traces to remain ineffaceable, even to the present day, in the speech of all the modern representatives of the family: the inflective character of Indo-European language, the main distinctions of its parts of speech, its methods of word-formation and inflection, were elaborated and definitely established.

But, though we cannot pretend to fix the length of time required for this process of growth, in terms of centuries or of thousands of years, we can at least see clearly that it must have gone on in a slow and gradual manner, and occupied no brief period. Such is the nature of the forces by which all change in language has been shown to be effected, that anything like a linguistic revolution, a rapid and sweeping modification of linguistic structure, is wholly impossible—and most especially, a revolution of a constructive character, building up a fabric of words and forms. Every item of the difference by which a given dialect is distinguished from its ancestor, or from another dialect having the same ancestry, is the work of a gradual change of usage made by the members of a community in the speech which they were every day employing as their means of mutual communication, and which, if too rapidly altered, would not answer the purposes of communication. It takes time for even that easiest of changes, a phonetic corruption or abbreviation, to win the assent of a community, and become established as the law of their speech: it takes decades, and even generations, or centuries, for an independent word to run through the series of modifications in form and meaning which are necessary to its conversion into a formative element. That the case was otherwise at the very beginning, we have not the least reason for believing. The opinion of those who hold that the whole structure of a language was produced "at a single stroke" is absolutely opposed to all the known facts of linguistic history; it has no inductive basis whatever; it rests upon arbitrary assumption, and is supported by *à priori* reasoning. There must have been a period of some duration—and, for aught we know, it may have been of very long duration—when the first speakers of our language talked together in their scanty dialect of formless monosyllables. The first *forms*, developed words containing a formal as well as a radical element, cannot have come into existence otherwise than by slow degrees, worked out by the unconscious exercise of that ingenuity in the adaptation of means to ends, of that sense for symmetry, for finished, even artistic, production, which have ever been qualities especially characterizing our division of the human race. Every form thus elaborated led the way to others: it heiped to determine a tendency, to establish an analogy, which facilitated their further production. A protracted career of formal develop-ment was run during that primitive period of Indo-European history which preceded the dispersion of the branches: words and forms were multiplied until even a maximum of synthetic com-plexity, of fullness of inflective wealth, had been reached, from which there has been in later times, upon the whole, a gradual descent and impoverishment.

Here we must pause a little, to consider an objection urged by some linguistic scholars of rank and reputation against the truth of the views we have been defending, as to the primitive mono-syllabism of Indo-European language, and its gradual emergence out of that condition—an objection which has more apparent legitimacy and force than any of those hitherto noticed. It is this. In ascending the current of historical development of the lan-guages of our family, say the objectors, instead of approaching a monosyllabic condition, we seem to recede farther and farther from it. The older dialects are more polysyllabic than the later: where our ancestors used long and complicated forms, we are content with brief ones, or we have replaced them with phrases composed of independent words. Thus, to recur once more to a former example, for an earlier *lagamasi* we say *we lie;* thus, again, for the Latin *fuisset*, the French says simply *fût*, while we ex-press its meaning by four distinct words, *he might have been*. Modern languages are full of verbal forms of this latter class, which substitute syntactical for substantial combinations. The relations of case, too, formerly signified only by means of declensional endings, have lost by degrees this mode of expression, and have come to be indicated by prepositions, independent words. This is what is well known as the "analytical" tendency in linguistic growth. Our own English tongue exhibits its effects in the highest known degree, having reduced near half the vocabulary it possesses to a monosyllabic form, and got rid of almost all its inflections, so that it expresses grammatical relations chiefly by relational words, auxiliaries and connectives: but it is only an extreme example of the results of a movement generally perceptible in modern speech. If, then, during the period when we can watch their growth step by step, languages have become less synthetic, words less polysyllabic, must we not suppose that it was always so; that human speech began with highly complicated forms, which from the very first have been undergoing reduction to simpler and briefer shape?

This is, as we have confessed, a plausible argument, but it is at the same time a thoroughly unsound and superficial one. It skims the surface of linguistic phenomena, without penetrating to the causes which produce them. It might pass muster, and be allowed to determine our opinions, if the analytical tendency alone had been active since our knowledge of language began; if we had seen old forms worn out, but no new forms made; if we had seen words put side by side to furnish analytic combinations, but no elements fused together into synthetic union. But we know by actual experience how both synthetic and analytic forms are produced, and what are the influences and circumstances which favour the production of the one rather than of the other. The constructive as well as the destructive forces in language admit of illustration, and have been by us illustrated, with modern as well as with ancient examples. Both have been active together, during all the ages through which we can follow linguistic growth. There have never been forms which were not undergoing continual modification and mutilation, under the influence of the already recognized tendencies to forget the genesis of a word in its later application, and then to reduce it to a shape adapted to more convenient utterance; there was also never a time when reparation was not making for this waste in part by the fresh development of true forms out of old materials. Nor has the tendency been everywhere and in all respects downward, toward poverty of synthetic forms, throughout the historic period. If the Greek and Latin system of declension is scantier than that of the original language of the family, their system of conjugation, especially the Greek, is decidedly richer, filled up with synthetic forms of secondary growth; the modern Romanic tongues have lost something of this wealth, but they have also added something to it, and their verb, leaving out of view its compound tenses, will bear favourable comparison with that which was the common inheritance of the branches. Some of the modern dialects of India, on the other hand, having once lost, in the ordinary course of phonetic corruption, the ancient case-terminations of the Sanskrit, have replaced them by a new scheme, not less full and complete than its predecessor. The Russian of the present day possesses in some respects a capacity of synthetic development hardly, if at all, excelled by that of any ancient tongue. For example, it takes the two independent words *bez Boga,* 'without God,' and fuses them into a theme from which it draws a whole list of derivatives. Thus, first, by adding an adjective suffix, it gets the adjective *bezbozhnüï,* 'godless'; a new suffix appended to this makes a noun, *bezbozhnik,* 'a godless person, an atheist'; the noun gives birth to a denominative verb, *bezbozhnichat,* 'to be an atheist'; from this verb, again, come a number of derivatives, giving to the verbal idea the form of adjective, agent, act, and so on: the abstract is *bezbozhnichestvo,* 'the condition of being an atheist'; while, once more, a new verb is made from this abstract, namely *bezbozhnichestvovat,* literally 'to be in the condition of being a godless person.' A more intricate synthetic form than this could not easily be found in Greek, Latin, or Sanskrit; but it is no rare or exceptional case in the language from which we have extracted it; it rather represents, by a striking instance, the general character of Russian word-formation and derivation.

It is obviously futile, then, to talk of an uninterrupted and universal reduction of the resources of synthetic expression among the languages of the Indo-European family, or to allow ourselves to be forced by an alleged pervading tendency toward analytic forms into accepting synthesis, inflective richness, as the ultimate condition of the primitive tongue from which they are descended. If certain among them have replaced one or another part of their synthetic structure by analytic forms, if some—as the Germanic family in general, and, above all, the English—have taken on a prevailing analytic character, these are facts which we are to seek to explain by a careful study of the circumstances and tendencies which have governed their respective development. If, moreover, as has been conceded, the general bent has for a long time been toward a diminution of synthesis and a predominance of analytic expressions, another question, of wider scope, is presented us for solution; but the form in which it offers itself is this: why should the forces which produce synthetic combinations have reached their height of activity during the ante-historic period of growth, and have been gradually gained upon later, at varying rates in different communities, by those of another order?

When once, after we know not how long a period of expectation and tentative effort, the formation of words by synthesis had begun in the primitive Indo-European language, and had been found so fruitful of the means of varied and distinct expression, it became the habit of the language. The more numerous the new forms thus produced, the greater was the facility of producing more, because the material of speech was present to the minds of its speakers as endowed with that capacity of combination and fusion of which the results in every part of its structure were so apparent. But the edifice after a time became, as it were, complete; a sufficient working-apparatus of declensional, conjugational, and derivative endings was elaborated to answer the purposes of an inflective tongue; fewer and rarer additions were called for, as occasional supplements of the scheme, or substitutes for lost forms. Thus began a period in which the formative processes were more and more exclusively an inheritance from the past, less and less of recent acquisition; and as the origin of forms was lost sight of, obscured by the altering processes of phonetic corruption, it became more and more difficult to originate new ones, because fewer analogies of such forms were present to the apprehension of the language-makers, as incentives and guides to their action. On the other hand, the expansion of the whole vocabulary to wealth of resources, to the possession of varied and precise phraseology, furnished a notably increased facility of indicating ideas and relations by descriptive phrases, by groups of independent words. This mode of expression, then, always more or less used along with the other, began to gain ground upon it, and, of course, helped to deaden the vitality of the latter, and to render it yet more incapable of extended action. That tendency to the conscious and reflective use of speech which comes in with the growth of culture especially, and which has already been repeatedly pointed out as one of the main checks upon all the processes of linguistic change, cast its influence in the same direction; since the ability to change the meaning and application of words, even to the degree of reducing them to the expression of formal relations, is a much more fundamental and indefeasible property of speech than the ability to combine and fuse them bodily together. Then, when peculiar circumstances in the history of a language have arisen, to cause the rapid and general decay and effacement of ancient forms, as in our language and the Romanic, the process of formative composition, though never wholly extinct, has been found too inactive to repair the losses; they have been made up by syntactical collocation, and the language has taken on a prevailingly analytic character.

No living language ever ceases to be constructed, or is less rapidly built upon in ages of historic activity: only the style of the fabric is, even more than the rate, determined by external circumstances. It is because the very earliest epochs of recorded history are still far distant from the beginnings of Indo-European language, as of human language generally, that we find its peculiar structure completely developed when it is first discovered by our researches. We have fully acknowledged the powerful influence exerted by culture over the growth of language: but neither the accident of position and accessibility to other nations that at a certain time brings a race forward into the light of record, and makes it begin to be an actor or a factor in the historic drama, nor its more gradual and independent advance to conspicuousness in virtue of acquired civilization and political power, can have any direct effect whatever upon its speech. The more thorough we are in our study of the living and recent forms of human language, the more rigorous in applying the deductions thence drawn to the forms current in ante-historic periods, the more cautious about admitting forces and effects in unknown ages whereof the known afford us no example or criterion, so much the more sound and trustworthy will be the conclusions at which we shall arrive. It is but a shallow philology, as it is a shallow geology, which explains past changes by catastrophes and cataclysms.

Much of that which has been demonstrated to be true respecting Indo-European speech is to be accepted as true respecting all human speech. Not that its historical analysis has been everywhere made so complete as to yield in each case with independent certainty the same results which the study of this one family has yielded. But nothing has been found which is of force to prove the history of language otherwise than, in its most fundamental features, the same throughout the globe; while much has been elicited which favours its homogeneousness: enough, indeed, when taken in connection with the theoretical probabilities of the case, to make the conclusion a sufficiently certain one, that all the varied and complicated forms of speech which now fill the earth have been wrought into their present shape by a like process of gradual development; that all designation of relations is the result of growth; that formative elements have been universally elaborated out of independent words; that the historical germs of language everywhere are of the nature of those simple elements which we have called roots; moreover, that roots have generally, if not without exception, been pronominal and verbal; and that, in the earliest stages of growth, forms have been produced especially by the combination of roots of the two classes, the verbal root furnishing the central and substantial idea, the pronominal indicating its modifications and relations.

Linguistic families, now, as at present constituted, are made up of those languages which have traceably had at least a part of their historical development in common; which have grown together out of the original radical or monosyllabic stage; which exhibit in their grammatical structure signs, still discoverable by linguistic analysis, of having descended, by the ordinary course of linguistic tradition, from a common ancestor. We shall see hereafter indeed, that the science of language does not and cannot deny the possible correspondence of some or all of the families in their ultimate elements, a correspondence anterior to all grammatical development; but neither does she at present assert that correspondence. She has carried her classification no farther than her collected material, and her methods of sober and cautious induction from its study, have justified her in doing; she has stopped grouping where her facts have failed her, where evidences of common descent have become too slight and vague to be longer depended upon: and the limit of her power is now, and is likely ever to be, determined by coincidences of grammatical structure. The boundaries of every great family, again, are likely to be somewhat dubious; there can hardly fail to be branches which either parted so early from the general stock, or have, owing to peculiar circumstances in their history, varied so rapidly and fundamentally since they left it, that the tokens of their origin have become effaced almost or quite beyond recognition. There was a time when the Celtic languages were thus regarded as of doubtful affinity, until a more penetrating study of their material and structure brought to light abundant and unequivocal evidence of their Indo-European descent. The Albanian, the modern representative of the ancient Illyrian, spoken by the fierce and lawless race which inhabits the mountains of north-western Greece, is still in the same position; linguistic scholars are divided in opinion as to whether it is yet proved to be Indo-European, though with a growing preponderance upon the affirmative side. Examples of excessive and effacing differentiation are not wanting in existing speech. There are now spoken among barbarous peoples in different parts of the world—as on some of the islands of the Pacific, among the African tribes, and the aborigines of this continent—dialects in which the processes of linguistic change, the destruction and reconstruction of words and forms, are going on at a rate so abnormally rapid, that a dialect, it is said, becomes unintelligible in a generation or two; and in a few centuries all material trace of affinity between idioms of common descent may become blotted out. Such exceptional cases do not take away the value of the genetic method of investigation, nor derogate from the general certainty of its results in the classification of languages. But they do cause the introduction, cautiously and to a limited extent, of another indication of probable relationship:

namely, concordance in the general method of solution of the linguistic problem. It is found that the great families of related languages differ from one another, not only in the linguistic material which they employ, in the combinations of sounds out of which, back to the remotest traceable beginning, they make their radical and formative elements, and designate given meanings and relations, but also, and often to no small degree, in their way of managing their material; in their apprehension of the relations of ideas which are to be expressed by the combination of elements, and in the method in which they apply the resources they possess to the expression of relations: they differ in the style, as well as the substance, of their grammatical structure. It is evident that the style may be so peculiar and characteristic as to constitute valid evidence of family relationship, even where the substance has been altered by variation and substitution till it presents no trustworthy coincidences. Morphological resemblance is the ground on which the claim of Scythian unity is chiefly founded; their fundamental common characteristic is that they follow what is styled an *agglutinative* type of structure. That is to say, the elements out of which their words are formed are loosely put together, instead of being closely compacted, or fused into one; they are aggregated, rather than integrated; the root or theme is held apart from the affixes, and these from one another, with a distinct apprehension of their separate individuality. As Professor Müller well expresses it, while Indo-European language, in putting two roots together to compose a form, sinks the individuality of both, the Scythian sinks that of but one, the suffix. The process is not, in its first stages, diverse in the two families, since every Indo-European form began with being a mere collocation, and, in a large proportion of cases, the root maintains to the end its integrity of form and meaning: the difference is one of degree rather than of kind; of the extension and effect, rather than the essential nature, of a mode of formation: and yet, it is a palpable and an important difference, when we compare the general structure of two languages, one out of each family.

The simple possession in common of an agglutinative character, as thus defined, would certainly be a very insufficient indication of the common parentage of the Scythian tongues; mere absence

of inflection would be a characteristic far too general and indeterminate to prove anything respecting them. They do, however,
present some striking points of agreement in the style and manner
of their agglutination, such as might supplement and powerfully
aid the convincing force of a body of material correspondences
which should be found wanting in desired fullness.

There can be no question that, of all the modes of classification
with which linguistic scholars have had to do, the one of first and
most fundamental importance is the genetical, or that which
groups together, and holds apart from others, languages giving
evidence of derivation from the same original. It underlies and
furnishes the foundation of all the remaining modes. There can be
no tie between any two dialects so strong as that of a common
descent. Every great family has a structural character of its own,
whereby, whatever may be the varying development of its members, it is made a unit, and more or less strikingly distinguished
from the rest. Whatever other criterion we may apply is analogous in its character and bearings with the distinction of apetalous,
monopetalous, and polypetalous, or of monogynous, digynous, etc.,
or of exogenous and endogenous, or of phenogamous and cryptoga-
mous, in the science of botany—all of them possessing real importance in different degrees, variously crossing one another, and
marking out certain general divisions; while the arrangement of
linguistic families corresponds with the division of plants into
natural orders, founded upon a consideration of the whole complicate structure of the things classified, contemplating the sum of
their characteristic qualities; fixing, therefore, their position in the
vast kingdom of nature of which they are members, and determining the names by which they shall be called. The genetical classification is the ultimate historical fact which the historical method
of linguistic study directly aims at establishing. With its establishment are bound up those more general historical results, for
the ethnological history of mankind, which form so conspicuous a
part of the interest of our science.

How language proves anything concerning race, and what it
does and does not prove, was brought clearly to light in the course
of our earliest inquiries into its nature and history. What we then
learned respecting the mode of acquisition and transmission of

each man's, and each community's, "native tongue" was sufficient to show us the total error of two somewhat different, and yet fundamentally accordant, views of language, which have been put forth and defended by certain authorities—the one, that speech is to man what his song is to the bird, what their roar, growl, bellow are to lions, bears, oxen; and that resemblances of dialect therefore no more indicate actual genetic connection among different tribes of men than resemblances of uttered tone indicate the common descent of various species of thrushes, or of bears, inhabiting different parts of the world; the other, that language is the immediate and necessary product of physical organization, and varies as this varies; that an Englishman, a Frenchman, and a Chinaman talk unlike one another because their brains and organs of articulation are unlike; and that all Englishmen talk alike, as do all Frenchmen, or all Chinamen, because, in consequence of their living amid similar physical conditions, and their inheritance of a common race-type, their nervous and muscular systems minutely correspond.

From this it also follows that no individual's speech directly and necessarily marks his descent; it only shows in what community he grew up. Language is no infallible sign of race, but only its probable indication, and an indication of which the probability is exposed to very serious drawbacks. For it is evident that those who taught us to speak, of whose means of expression we learned to avail ourselves, need not have been of our own kith and kin. Not only may individuals, families, groups of families, of almost every race on earth, be, as at present in America, turned into and absorbed by one great community, and made to adopt its speech, but a strange tongue may be learned by whole tribes and nations of those who, like our Negroes, are brought away from their native homes, or, like the Irish, have lived long under a foreign yoke, or, like the Celts of ancient Gaul and Spain, have received laws, civilization, and religion from another and a superior race. Languages unnumbered and innumerable have disappeared from off the face of the earth since the beginning of human history; but only in part by reason of the utter annihilation of the individuals who had spoken them; more often, doubtless, by their dispersion, and incorporation with other communities, of other speech. Everywhere,

too, where the confines of different forms of speech meet, there
goes on more or less of mixture between them, or of effacement of
the one by the other. Yet, on the other hand, mixture of language
is not necessary proof of mixture of race. We can trace the genesis
of a very large part of our own vocabulary to the banks of the
Tiber, but hardly the faintest appreciable portion of our ancestry
is Roman. We obtained our Latin words in the most strangely
roundabout way: they were brought us by certain Germanic
adventurers, the Normans, who had learned them from a mixed
people, the French, chiefly of Celtic blood; and these, again, had
derived them from another heterogeneous compound of Italican
races, among whom the Latin tribe was numerically but a feeble
element.

It still remains true that, upon the whole, language is a tolerably
sure indication of race. Since the dawn of time, those among whom
individuals were born, of whom they learned how to express their
mental acts, have been usually of their own blood. Nor do these
difficulties place linguistic evidence at any marked disadvantage
as compared with physical. They are, to no small extent, merely
the effect, on the side of language, of the grand fact which comes
in constantly to interfere with ethnological investigations of every
kind: namely, that human races do not maintain themselves in
purity, that men of different descent are all the time mingling,
mixing their blood, and crossing all their race-characteristics.
Fusion and replacement of languages are impossible, except when
men of different native speech are brought together as members
of the same community, so that there takes place more or less of
an accompanying fusion of races also; and then the resulting
language stands at least a chance of being a more faithful and
intelligible witness of the mixture than the resulting physical type.
The physicists claim that there may be a considerable infusion of
the blood of one race into that of another, without perceptible
modification of the latter's race-type; the intruded element, if not
continuously supplied afresh, is overwhelmed and assimilated by
the other and predominant one, and disappears: that is to say, as
we may interpret the claim, its peculiarities are so diluted by
constant remixture that they become at last inappreciable. In any
such case, then, traces discoverable in the language may point out

what there is no other means of ascertaining. It is true that, on the other hand, the spread and propagation of a language may greatly exceed that of the race to which it originally belonged, and that the weaker numerical element in a composite community may be the one whose dialect becomes the common tongue of all. Thus the Latin swept away the primitive tongues of a great part of southern and central Europe, and has become mingled with the speech of all civilized nations, in the Old World and the New. But we are not rashly to infer that such things have happened over and over again in the history of the world. We have rather to inquire what influences make possible a career like that of the Latin, what lends the predominant and assimilating force to a single element where many are combined.

If the limitations and imperfections of the two kinds of evidence are thus in certain respects somewhat evenly balanced, there are others in which linguistic evidence has a decidely superior practical value and availability. The differences of language are upon a scale almost infinitely greater than those of physical structure. They are equal in their range and variety to those found in the whole animal kingdom, from the lowest organisms to the highest, instead of being confined within the limits of the possible variation of a single species. Hence they can be much more easily and accurately apprehended, judged, and described. Two persons may readily be culled from two diverse races who shall be less unlike than two others that may be chosen from the same race. While, on the contrary, words and phrases taken down from the lips of an individual, or written or engraved by one hand, can be no private possession; they must belong to a whole community.

Language tells so much more respecting races than lies within the reach or scope of the physicist. In every part and particle, it is instinct with history. It is a picture of the internal life of the community to which it belongs; in it their capacities are exhibited, their characters expressed; it reflects their outward circumstances, records their experiences, indicates the grade of knowledge they have attained, exhibits their manners and institutions. Being itself an institution, shaped by their consenting though only half-conscious action, it is an important test of national endowment and disposition, like political constitution, like jural usage, like national art. Even where it fails to show strict ethnic descent, it shows race-history of another sort—the history of the influence which, by dint of superior character and culture, certain races have exercised over others. The spread of the Latin has swept away and obliterated some of the ancient landmarks of race, but it has done so by substituting another unity for that of descent; its present ubiquity illustrates the unparalleled importance of Rome in the history of humanity.

For these reasons, and such as these, the part which language has to perform in constructing the unwritten history of the human race must be the larger and more important. There are points which physical science alone can reach, or upon which her authority is superior: but in laying out and filling up the general scheme, and especially in converting what would else be a barren classification into something like a true history, the work must chiefly be done by linguistic science.

Linguistic science is not now, and cannot hope ever to be, in condition to give an authoritative opinion respecting the unity or variety of our species. For we cannot venture to say how long a time the formation of roots may have demanded, or during what period universal language may have remained nearly stationary in this its inceptive stage. It is entirely conceivable that the earliest human race, being one, should have parted into disjoined and henceforth disconnected tribes before the formation of any language so far developed and of so fixed forms as to be able to leave traceable fragments in the later dialects of the sundered portions. These possibilities preclude all dogmatic assertion of the variety of human species on the part of the linguist. Among all the known forms of speech, present and past, there are no discordances which are not, to his apprehension, fully reconcilable with the hypothesis of unity of race, allowing the truth of that view of the nature and history of speech which is forced upon him by his researches into its structure. It is certain that no one, upon the ground of linguistic investigations alone, will ever be able to bear witness against the descent of all mankind from a single pair. As the linguist is compelled to allow that a unique race may have parted into branches before the development of abiding germs of speech, so he must also admit the possibility that the race may have clung together so long, or the development of its speech have been so rapid, that, even prior to its separation, a common dialect had been elaborated, the traces of which no lapse of time, with all its accompanying changes, could entirely obliterate. I claim that investigation, limited as its range and penetration have hitherto confessedly been, has already put us in condition to declare the evidence incompetent, and the thesis incapable of satisfactory proof.

The fact is well established, that there are no two languages upon the face of the earth, of however discordant origin, between which may not be brought to light by diligent search a goodly number of false analogies of both form and meaning, seeming indications of relationship, which a little historical knowledge, when it is to be had, at once shows to be delusive, and which have no title to be regarded as otherwise, even if we have not the means of proving their falsity. It is only necessary to cast out of sight the general probabilities against a genetic connection of the languages we are comparing (such as their place and period, their nearer connections, and the pervading discordance of their structure and material), and then to assume between them phonetic transitions not more violent than are actually proved to be exhibited by other tongues—and we may find a goodly portion of the vocabulary of each hidden in that of the other. Dean Swift has ridiculed the folly which amuses itself with such comparisons and etymologies, in a well-known caricature, wherein he derives the names of ancient Greek worthies from honest modern English elements, explaining *Achilles* as 'a kill-ease,' *Hector* as 'hacked-tore,' *Alexander the Great* as 'all eggs under the grate!' and so on. This is very absurd; and yet, save that the absurdity of it is made more palpable to us by being put in terms of our own language and another with which we are somewhat familiar, it is hardly worse than what has been done, and is done, in all soberness, by men claiming the name of linguistic scholars. It is even now possible for such a man to take an African vocabulary, and sit deliberately down to see what words of the various other languages known to him he can explain out of it, producing a batch of correspondence like these: *abetele*, 'a begging beforehand' (which he himself defines as composed of *a*, formative prefix, *be*, 'beg,' and *tele,* 'previously'), and German *betteln,* 'beg' (from the simpler root *bit, bet,* our *bid*); *idaro,* 'that which becomes collected into a mass,' and English *dross; basile,* 'landlord' (*ba* for *oba,* 'master,' *si,* 'of,' and *ile,* 'land'), and Greek *basileus,* 'king': and the comparer, who is specially versed in the mathematical doctrine of chances, gravely informs us that the chances against the merely accidental character of the last coincidence are "at least a hundred million to one." More than one unsound linguist has misled himself and others by calculating, in the strictest accordance with mathematical rules, how many thousand or million of chances to one there are against the same word meaning the same thing in two different and unconnected languages. The calculation is futile, and its result a fallacy. The relations of language are not to be so simply reduced to precise mathematical expression. If words were wholly independent entities, instead of belonging to families of connected derivatives; if they were of such precise constitution and application as so many chemical formulas; if the things they designated were as distinct and separate individualities as are fixed stars, or mineral species, or geographical localities—then the calculations of chances would be in place respecting them. But none of these things are true. The evidences on which linguistic science relies to prove genetical connection are not identities of form combined with identities of meaning: forms may differ as much as *hijo* and *filius;* meanings may differ as much as German *bekommen,* 'get,' and English *become,* 'come to be,' and *become,* 'suit'; form and meaning may differ together to any extent, and yet the words may be one and the same, and good evidences of relationship between the languages to which they respectively belong. Not literal agreement, but such resemblances, nearer or more distant, cleared or more obscure, as are proved by supporting facts to have their ground in original identity, make satisfactory evidence of common descent in language.

Here, then, is the practical difficulty in the way of him who would prove all human speech a unit. On the one hand, those fortuitous coincidences and analogies which any given language may present with any other with which it is compared form a not inconsiderable body, an appreciable percentage of its general stock of words. On the other hand, the historical coincidences and analogies traceable between two languages of common descent are capable of sinking to as low, or even to a lower, percentage of its vocabulary. That is to say, there may be two related tongues, the genuine signs of whose relationship shall be less numerous and conspicuous than the apparent but delusive signs of relationship of two others which derive themselves from independent origins. The former have been so long separated from one another, their changes in the mean time have been so pervading, that their inherited points of resemblance are reduced in number and obscured in character, until they are no longer sufficient to create a reasonable presumption in favour of their own historical reality; they are undistinguishable from the possible results of chance. Evidences of genetic connection are cumulative in their character; no single item of correspondence is worth anything until there are found kindred facts to support it; and its force is strengthened with every new accession. And, in the comparison of languages, the point is actually reached where it becomes impossible to tell whether the few coincidences which we discover are the genuine traces of a community of linguistic tradition, or only accidental, and evidence of nothing. When we come to holding together the forms of speech belonging to the diverse families, linguistic testimony fails us: it no longer has force to prove anything to our satisfaction.

To demonstrate that this is so, we do not need to enter into a detailed examination of two tongues claimed to be unrelated, and show that their correspondences fall incontestably short of the amount required to prove relationship: we may take a briefer and directer argument. We have seen that the established linguistic families are made up of those dialects which exhibit traceable signs of a common historic development; which have evidently grown together out of the radical stage (unless, as in the case of the monosyllabic tongues, they have together remained stationary in that stage); which possess, at least in part, the same grammatical structure. There are some linguistic scholars who cherish the sanguine hope that trustworthy indications of this kind of correspondence may yet be pointed out between some two or three of the great families; but no one whose opinion is of one straw's weight thinks of such a thing with reference to them all. So discordant is the whole growth of many of the types of speech that we can find no affinities among them short of their ultimate beginnings: if all human speech is to be proved of one origin, it can only be by means of an identification of roots. To give the investigation this form, however, is virtually to abandon it as hopeless. The difficulties in the way of a fruitful comparison of roots are altogether overwhelming. To trace out the roots of any given family, in their ultimate form and primitive signification, is a task whose gravity the profoundest investigators of language are best able to appreciate. Apparent resemblances among apparent roots of the different families are, indeed, to be found: but they are wholly worthless as evidences of historical connection. To the general presumption of their accidental nature is to be farther added the virtual certainty that the elements in which they appear are not ultimate roots at all, but the products of recent growth. There is nothing, it may be remarked, in the character of ultimate roots which should exempt them from the common liability to exhibit fortuitous coincidences, but rather the contrary. The system of sounds employed in the rudimentary stage of linguistic growth was comparatively scanty, the circle of ideas represented by the roots was narrow and limited, the application of each root more vague and indeterminate; hence accidental analogies of form and meaning might even more reasonably be looked for between the radical elements of unconnected families than between their later developed words.

But if linguistic science must thus observe a modest silence with regard to the origin of the human race, what has it to say respecting the origin of language itself? We have been engaged in analyzing and examining the recorded facts of language, in order to find what answer we could to our leading question, "why do we speak as we do?" and we have been brought at last to the recognition of certain elements called roots, which we clearly see to have been the germs whence the whole development of speech has proceeded, but which we do not dare affirm to have been absolutely the first utterances of speaking men. These, then, are the historical beginnings of speech; and historical research will take us no farther. The question as to what were the actual first utterances, and how they were produced, must be decided, if at all, in another way—by general considerations and analogies, by inferences from the facts of human nature and the facts of language, taken together, and from their relations to one another. And our attention must evidently first be directed to the inquiry whether those same inventive and shaping powers of man which have proved themselves capable of creating out of monosyllabic barrenness the rich abundance of inflective speech were not also equal to the task of producing the first poor hoard of vocables.

Language, articulate speech, is a universal and exclusive characteristic of man: no tribe of human kind, however low, ignorant, and brutish, fails to speak; no race of the lower animals, however highly endowed, is able to speak: clearly, it was just as much a part of the Creator's plan that we should talk as that we should breathe, should walk, should eat and drink. The only question is, whether we began to talk in the same manner as we began to breathe, as our blood began to circulate, by a process in which our own will had no part; or, as we move, eat, clothe and shelter ourselves, by the conscious exertion of our natural powers, by using our divinely-given faculties for the satisfaction of our divinely-implanted necessities. Our recognition of language as an institution, as an instrumentality, as no integral system of natural and necessary representatives of thought, inseparable from thought or spontaneously generated by the mind, but, on the contrary, a body of conventional signs, deriving their value from the mutual understanding of one man with another; and, farther, our recognition of the history of this institution as being not a mere succession of changes wrought upon something which still remains the same in essential character, but a real development, effected by human forces, whose operations we can trace and understand—these take away the whole ground on which the doctrine of the divine origin of language, as formerly held, reposed. The origin of language is divine, in the same sense in which man's nature, with all its capacities and acquirements, physical and moral, is a divine creation; it is human, in that it is brought about through that nature, by human instrumentality.

Speech, we know, is composed of external audible signs for internal acts, for conceptions—for ideas, taking that word in its most general sense. But why create such signs? The doctrine, now, is by no means uncommon, that thought seeks expression by an internal impulse; that it is even driven to expression by an inward necessity; that it cannot be thought at all without incorporation in speech; that it tends to utterance as the fully matured embryo tends to burst its envelop, and to come forth into independent life. The doctrine is, in my view, altogeter erroneous: I am unable to see upon what it is founded, if not arbitrary assumption, combined with a thorough misapprehension of the relation between thought and its expression. It is manifestly opposed to all the conclusions to which we have been thus far led by our inquiries into the nature and office of speech. Speech is not a personal possession, but a social; it belongs, not to the individual, but to the member of society. No item of existing language is the work of an individual; for what we may severally choose to say is not language until it be accepted and employed by our fellows. The whole development of speech, though initiated by the acts of individuals, is wrought out by the community. That is a word, no matter what may be its origin, its length, its phonetic form, which is understood in any community, however limited, as the sign of an idea; and their mutual understanding is the only tie which connects it with that idea. It is a sign which each one has acquired from without, from the usage of others; and each has learned the art of intimating by such signs the internal acts of his mind. Mutual intelligibility, we have seen, is the only quality which makes the unity of a spoken tongue; the necessity of mutual intelligibility is the only force which keeps it one; and the desire of mutual intelligibility is the impulse which called out speech. Man speaks, then, primarily, not in order to think, but in order to impart his thought. His social needs, his social instincts, force him to expression. A solitary man would never frame a language.

Language, then, is the spoken means whereby thought is communicated, and it is only that. Language is not thought, nor is thought language; nor is there a mysterious and indissoluble connection between the two, as there is between soul and body, so that the one cannot exist and manifest itself without the other. There can hardly be a greater and more pernicious error, in linguistics or in metaphysics, than the doctrine that language and thought are identical.

52066

In every department of thought, the mind derives from the possession of speech something of the same advantage, and in the same way, as in mathematical reasoning. The idea which has found its incarnation in a word becomes thereby a subject of clearer apprehension and more manageable use: it can be turned over, compared, limited, placed in distinct connection with other ideas; more than one mind, more than one generation of minds, can work at it, giving it shape, and relation, and significance. In every word is recorded the result of a mental process, of abstraction or of combination; which process, being thus recorded, can be taught along with its sign, or its result can be used as a step to something higher or deeper. There are grades of thought, spheres of ratiocination, where our minds could hardly work at all without the direct aid of language; as there are also those where they could not surely hold and follow the chain of reason and deduction without the still further assistance afforded by writing down the argument. It may be freely conceded that such mental processes as we are in the constant habit of performing would be too difficult for us to compass without words—as they certainly also lie far beyond what would have been our mental reach had we not been trained through the use of language to orderly thought, and enriched with the wealth of mental acquisitions accumulated by our predecessors and stored up in words. But this is a very different thing from acknowledging that thought is impossible without language.

True it is that the individual mind, without language, would be a dwarfed and comparatively powerless organ: but this means simply that man could develop his powers, and become what he was meant to be, only in society, by converse with his fellows. He is by his essential nature a social being, and his most precious individual possession, his speech, he gets only as a social being. The historical beginnings of speech, therefore, were no spontaneous outbursts, realizing to the mind of the utterer the conceptions with which he was swelling; they were successful results of the endeavour to arrive at signs by which those conceptions should be called up also in the minds of others.

Recognizing the external and non-essential nature of the bond which unites every constituent of language to the idea represented by it, and also the external nature of the force which brings about the genesis of the sign, we are enabled to reduce the inquiry to this form: how should the first language-makers, human beings gifted like ourselves, with no exceptional endowments, but with no disabilities other than that of the non-development of their inherent capacities, have naturally succeeded in arriving at the possession of signs by which they could understand one another? The one thing necessary is, that thought, tending irresistibly toward expression under the impulse to communication, should find the means of intelligibly expressing itself. With the mental powers and social tendencies which men have, they would, even if unendowed with voice, have nevertheless put themselves in possession of language—language less perfect and manageable, to be sure, than is our present speech; but still, real language. Resort, doubtless, would first have been had to gesture: it is hardly less natural to men to use their hands than their tongues to help the communication of their ideas; the postures of the body, the movements of the face, can be made full of significance; the resources of pantomime are various and abundant, and constitute a means of expression often successfully employed, between those who are unacquainted with the conventional signs of one another's spoken language. It is past all reasonable question that, in the earliest communication between human beings, gesture long played a considerable, if not the principal, part, and that our race learned only by degrees the superior capacities of spoken signs, and by degrees worked them out to a sufficiency for all the ordinary needs of expression; when gesture was relegated to the department of rhetoric, to the office of giving individual colouring and intensity to intellectual expression—as, in all well-developed languages, has been the case with tone also.

Language begins with analysis, and the apprehension of characteristic qualities. Not what the mind first consciously contemplated, but what was most readily capable of being intelligibly signified, determined the earliest words. Now a concrete object, a complex existence, is just as much out of the immediate reach of the sign-making faculty as is a moral act or an intellectual relation. As, during the whole history of language, designations of the latter classes of ideas have been arrived at through the medium of names for physical acts and relations, so have appellations for the former been won by means of their perceived characteristics. In the case of a word like *splash*, used to imitate and call up before the mind the fall of a stone into water—the collision of the stone and the water would be the immediate suggestion; but a natural act of association might make the sign mean the stone, or the water, or the act of throwing, or the fall. One sign would turn more readily to the designation of a property or action, another to that of a concrete thing, an actor, according to the nature of each, and the exigencies of practical use as regarded it; but both would be inherently a kind of indifferent middle, capable of conversion to either purpose: and, in the poverty of expression and indistinctness of analysis belonging to the primitive stage of linguistic growth, would doubtless bear various offices at once. In short, they would be such rudiments of speech, rather than parts of speech, as we have already found the radical elements of language to be.

Especially great and undeniable are the capabilities of the onomatopoetic principle. Since qualities or acts are the immediate objects of the first designations, and since the voice is the appointed means of designating, audible acts, utterances or accompanying noises, would be most naturally chosen to be designated. That words have been and may be formed through the medium of imitation of natural sounds is palpably true; every language has such to show in its vocabulary. That, for example, an animal can be named from its cry, and the name thus given generalized and made fertile of derivatives, is shown by such a word as *cock*, which is regarded by etymologists as an abbreviated imitation of chanticleer's *cock-a-doodle-doo!* and from which come, by allusion to the bird's pride and strut, the words *coquette, cockade,* the *cock* of a gun, to *cock* one's eye, to *cock* the head on one side, a *cocked* hat, and so on. Through all the stages of growth of language, absolutely new words are produced by this method more than by any other, or even almost exclusively; there is also to be seen an evident disposition to give an imitative complexion to words which denote matters cognizable by the ear; the mind pleases itself with bringing about a sort of agreement between the sign and the thing signified. Both theory and observed fact, therefore, unite to prove the imitative principle more actively productive than any other in the earliest processes of language-making.

But neither is a noteworthy degree of importance to be denied to the exclamatory or interjectional principle. It is, beyond all question, as natural for the untaught and undeveloped man to utter exclamations, as to make gestures, expressive of his feelings; and as, in the absence of a voice, the tendency to gesture might have been fruitful in suggesting a language of significant motions, so we may most plausibly suppose that the tendency to exclaim was not without value in aiding men to realize that they had in their voices that which was capable of being applied to express the movements of their spirits. Perhaps the principal contribution of exclamations to the origin of language was made in this way, rather than by the furnishing of actual radical elements: for the latter work, their restricted scope, their subjective character, their infertility of relations, would render them less fitted.

There is no real discordance between the onomatopoetic and interjectional theories, nor do the advocates of either, it is believed, deny or disparage the value of the other, or refuse its aid in the solution of their common problem. The definition of the onomatopoetic principle might be without difficulty or violence so widened that it should include the interjectional. We must, indeed, beware of restricting its action too narrowly. It is by no means limited to a reproduction of the sounds of animate and inanimate nature: it admits also a kind of symbolical representation—as an intimation of abrupt, or rapid, or laborious, or smooth action by utterances making an analogous impression upon the ear.

It is quite unnecessary that we should attempt to determine the precise part played by these principles, or these different forms of the onomatopoetic principle, in generating the germs of speech. We cannot go far astray, either in overestimating or in underestimating the value of each one of them, if we bear always distinctly in mind the higher principle under which they all alike exercised their influence: namely, that the language-makers were not attempting to make a faithful depiction of their thought, but only to find for it a mutually intelligible sign; and that everything which conduced to such intelligibility would have been, and was, resorted to, and to an extent dependent on its degree of adaptedness to the purpose—the extent being a fair matter for difference of opinion, and for ascertainment by further detailed investigation, both theoretical and historical. There are many ideas which would be much more clearly intimated by a gesture, a grimace, or a tone, than by a word; and, as has been already remarked, we cannot doubt that tones, grimaces, and gestures constituted no small portion of the first sign-language, both as independently conveying meaning, and as helping to establish the desired association between articulate signs and the ideas which they were intended to signify.

Onomatopœia, in all its varieties of application, thus came in at the outset, aided and supplemented by tone and gesture, to help the language-makers to find intelligible signs, but ceased to control the history of each sign when once this had become understood and conventionally accepted; while the productive efficiency of the principle gradually diminished and died out as a stock of signs was accumulated sufficient to serve as the germs of speech, and to increase by combination and differentiation. Thus, as mutual intelligibility had been before proved to be the only test of the unity of language, and its necessity the force that conserved linguistic unity, it was further demonstrated that the desire to understand and be understood by one another was the impulse which acted directly to call forth language. In all its stages of growth alike, then, speech is strictly a social institution; as the speaking man, when reduced to solitude, unlearns its use, so the solitary man would never have formed it. We may extol as much as we please, without risk of exaggeration, the advantage which each one of us derives from it within his inmost self, in the training and equipment of his own powers of thought: but the advantage is one we should never have enjoyed, save as we were born members of a community: the ideas of speech and of community are inseparable. If each human being had to begin for himself the career of education and improvement, all the energies of the race would be absorbed in taking, over and over again, the first simple steps. Language enables each generation to lay up securely, and to hand over to its successors, its own collected wisdom, its stores of experience, deduction, and invention, so that each starts from the point which its predecessor had reached, and every individual commences his career, heir to the gathered wealth of an immeasurable past.

So far, now, as this advantage comes to us from the handing down, through means of speech, of knowledge hoarded up by those who have lived before us, or from its communication by our contemporaries, we appreciate with a tolerable degree of justness its nature and value. We know full well that we were born ignorant, and have by hearing and reading possessed ourselves in a few short years of more enlightenment than we could have worked out for our own use in many long centuries; we can trace, too, the history of various branches of knowledge, and see how they have grown up from scanty beginnings, by the consenting labour of innumerable minds, through a succession of generations. We are aware that our culture, in the possession of which we are more fortunate than all who have gone before us, is the product of historical conditions working through hundreds, even thousands, of years; that its germs began to be developed in the far distant East, in ages so remote that history and tradition alike fail to give us so much as glimpses of their birth; that they were engendered among exceptionally endowed races, in especially favouring situations, and were passed on from one people to another, elaborated and increased by each, until, but a thousand years ago, our own immediate ancestors, a horde of uncouth barbarians, were ready to receive them in their turn—and that this whole process of accumulation and transfer has been made possible only by means of speech and its kindred and dependent art of record. What we are far less mindful of is the extent to which we derive a similar gain in the inheritance of language itself, and that this very instrumentality is in like manner the gradually gathered and perfected work of many generations—in part, of many races. We do not realize how much of the observation and study of past ages is stored up in the mere words which we learn so easily and use so lightly, and what degree of training our minds receive, almost without knowing it, by entering in this way also into the fruits of the prolonged labour of others. To this point, then, we owe a more special consideration.

Learning to speak is the first step in each child's education, the necessary preparation for receiving higher instruction of every kind. So was it also with the human race; the acquisition of speech constituted the first stage in the progressive development of its capacities. We, as individuals, have forgotten both the labour that the task cost us and the enlightenment its successful accomplishment brought us: the whole lies too far back in our lives to be reached by our memories; we feel as if we had always spoken, as directly and naturally as we have thought. As a race, too, we have done the same thing: neither history nor tradition can penetrate to a period at all approaching that of the formation of language; it was in the very childhood of our species, and men learned thinking and talking together, even as they learn them now-a-days: not till they had acquired through language the art of wielding the forces of thought, were they qualified to go on to the storing up of various knowledge. Into a few years of instruction are now crowded, for the young student, the net results of as many tens of centuries of toiling after wisdom on the part of no small portion of mankind; and, in like manner, into the language-learning of the first few months and years is crowded the fruit of as many ages of language-making. Men invent language, their mental instrument, as truly as they invent the mechanical appliances whereby they extend and multiply the power of their hands; but it would be as impossible for a man, or a generation, to invent a language like one of those which we know and use, as, for example, to invent a locomotive engine. The invention of the engine may be said to have begun when the first men learned how to make a fire and keep it alive with fuel; another early step (and one to which many a living race has not even yet ascended) was the contriving of a wheel; command was won, by degrees, of the other mechanical powers, at first in their simplest, then in their more complicated, forms and applications; the metals were discovered, and the means of reducing and working them one after another devised, and improved and perfected by long accumulated experience; various motive powers were noted and reduced to the service of men; to the list of such, it was at length seen that steam might be added, and, after many vain trials, this too was brought to subjection—and thus the work was at length carried so far forward that the single step, or the few steps, which remained to be taken, were within the power of an individual mind. When one of us now undertakes to invent a language (as in fact happens from time to time), it is as if one who had been all his life an engineer should sit down to invent a steam-engine: he does nothing but copy with trifling modifications a thing which he is already familiar with; he rearranges the parts a little, varies their relative dimensions, uses new material for one and another of them, and so on—perhaps making some improvements in matters of minor detail, but quite as probably turning out a machine that will not work. To call upon a man who has never spoken to produce a complete language is like setting a wild Fijian or Fuegian at constructing a power-loom or a power-press: he neither knows what it is nor what it will be good for. The conditions of the problem which is set before the language-makers are manifest: man is placed in the midst of creation, with powers which are capable of unlocking half its secrets, but with no positive knowledge either of them or of himself; with apprehensions as confused, with cognitions as synthetic, as are those of the lower animals; and he has to make his way as well as he can to a distinct understanding of the world without and the world within him. He accomplishes his task by means of a continuous process of analysis and combination, whereof every result, as soon as it is found, is fixed by a term, and thus made a permanent possession, capable of being farther elaborated, and communicated by direct instruction. It is necessary to study out what needs to be expressed, as well as the means of its expression. Even the naming of concrete objects, as we saw, demands an analysis and recognition of their distinctive qualities; and to find fitting designations for the acts and relations of the external sensible world, and then, by an acute perception of analogies and a cunning transfer, to adapt those designations to the acts, states, and relations of the intellectual and moral world within the soul, was not an easy or rapid process; yet, till this was measurably advanced, the mind had no instrument with which it could perform any of the higher work of which it was capable. But as each generation transmitted to its successor what it had itself inherited from its predecessor, perfected and increased by the results of its own mental labour, the accumulation of language, accompanying the development of analytic

thought and the acquisition of knowledge, went steadily and successfully forward; until at last, when one has but acquired his own
mother-tongue, a vocabulary of terms and an understanding of
what they mean, he already comprehends himself and his surroundings; he possesses the fitting instrument of mental action,
and can go on intelligently to observe and deduce for himself. Few
of us have any adequate conception of the debt of gratitude we
owe to our ancestors for shaping in our behalf the ideas which we
now acquire along with the means of their expression, or of how
great a part of our intellectual training consists in our simply
learning how to speak.

One thing more we have to note in connection herewith. The
style in which we shall do our thinking, the framework of our
reasonings, the matters of our subjective apprehension, the distinctions and relations to which we shall direct our chief attention,
are thus determined in the main for us, not by us. In learning to
speak with those about us, we learn also to think with them: their
traditional habits of mind become ours. In this guidance there is
therefore something of constraint, although we are little apt to
realize it. Study of a foreign language brings it in some measure
to our sense. He who begins to learn a tongue not his own is at
first hardly aware of any incommensurability between its signs for
ideas and those to which he has been accustomed. But the more
intimately he comes to know it, and the more natural and familiar
its use becomes to him, so much the more clearly does he see that
the dress it puts upon his thoughts modifies their aspect, the more
impossible does it grow to him to translate its phrases with satisfactory accuracy into his native speech. The individual is thus
unable to enter into a community of language-users without some
abridgment of his personal freedom — even though the penalty be
wholly insignificant as compared with the accruing benefit. Thus,
too, each generation feels always the leading hand, not only of the
generation that immediately instructed it, but of all who have
gone before, and taken a part in moulding the common speech;
and, not least, of those distant communities, hidden from our
view in the darkness of the earliest ages, whose action determined
the grand structural features of each tongue now spoken. Every
race is, indeed, as a whole, the artificer of its own speech, and

herein is manifested the sum and general effect of its capacities in this special direction of action; but many a one has felt through all the later periods of its history the constraining and laming force of a language unhappily developed in the first stages of formation; which it might have made better, had the work been to do over again, but which now weighs upon its powers with all the force of disabling inbred habit. Both the intellectual and the historical career of a race is thus in no small degree affected by its speech.

Letter from Whitney to C. R. Lanman, December 19, 1875. Whitney's criticism of Max Müller became a *cause célèbre* through articles in popular journals in 1875, culminating in Müller's "In Self-Defense," pp. 473–549 in volume 4 of his *Chips from a German Workshop* (London, 1875). Virtually all of Whitney's publications in 1876 were devoted to answering (see pp. 336–349), beginning with the letter referred to in *The Academy* issue of January 1, 1876. (By permission of Harvard University Archives and Mrs Robert A. Cushman.)

down by him; my prevailing sentiment is that of
disgust, and of utter astonishment that a man
having a reputation to be careful of should dare to
put forth such a production. It is disingenuous and
dishonest beyond anything I ever saw in controversy, to say nothing of its scurrility & insolence. He
has not made a single point fairly against me.
I have sent a brief & very moderate letter to the
Academy, casting a little light on its spirit: what
I shall do further is not yet decided; nor, indeed,
whether I shall do anything: much will depend
on how the thing is received in Europe. If we had
a philological journal here, I should take up the
varying Sanskrit points and turn the tables on
him, as it would be very easy to do. You will, I
am sure, put in a word on my behalf here and there,
as opportunity offers.

VIII. — Φύσει or Θέσει — Natural or Conventional?

BY WILLIAM D. WHITNEY,

PROFESSOR OF SANSKRIT AND COMPARATIVE PHILOLOGY IN YALE COLLEGE.

THE Greeks, it is well known, disputed of old with one
another whether the names of things existed φύσει, 'by nature,'
or θέσει, 'by attribution' — that is, as we should say, 'by
convention.' Into the history of this dispute, into the question as to what philosophers took ground on the one side and
on the other, with what arguments they supported their
views, and how near they came to a final agreement, there

is no need that we enter. Their basis of argument was so much more restricted than ours that their discussions would have for us only a historical interest; and the inquiry itself is still a living one. Notwithstanding all the progress that linguistic science has made in this century, general opinion — nay, even the opinion of linguistic scholars, of writers upon language — is still so far at variance that both answers are given. This may be, at least in part, not so much from a real essential difference of view, as from a different understanding of the meaning of the terms used. But, whichever it be, the discordance is not to the credit of the new science of language : if that science has not been able yet to settle so fundamental a question, between views as different as white and black, it cannot claim to have accomplished much ; it is still in its infancy.

It may be sufficient to quote, as the starting-point of our own inquiry, the expressed opinion of one well-known and highly meritorious author, Archbishop Trench, of Dublin. In his " Study of Words " (p. 173, note), he remarks, after noting the fact of the dispute, whether words were θέσει or φύσει, " it is needless to say that the last is the truth " ; and one seems to see on his face the smile of conscious superiority to those poor Greeks, who labored so long over a matter which could be settled in half a sentence, by a mere unargumentative " it is needless to say," without statement of reasons or explanation of meaning. And the Archbishop is supported, solidly and heartily, by that immense majority of the human race who know each his own language alone, and who are persuaded that only those that speak it really speak at all. Every linguistic scholar is aware how wide-spread and deep-rooted this feeling has been and still is ; how it has been the foundation of many a race-name, assumed by the race to itself as self-asserted ' speakers,' all outsiders being " barbarians " or ' babblers.' And it would be very easy to find even in our enlightened communities men who, though they may know that other people have other names for things than their own, yet believe, outspokenly or in their secret hearts, that those are mere nicknames, only their own being the real thing.

Doubtless we should do wrong to assume that Trench and his fellows hold names in this sense to exist *φύσει*: that is to say, that for every conception there exists a single "natural" name, all the others being "unnatural," or "artificial," or whatever else they may choose to set up as opposed to "natural."

For, as every well-informed person is aware nowadays, there are for our current conceptions as many different names, names somewhat unlike or totally diverse, as there are languages in the world — let us say, a thousand; and, apparently, each one of the thousand has as good a right to claim that it exists *φύσει* as any of the other nine hundred ninety and nine. Can any good reason be discovered why the term applies to one more than to another? or why it belongs alike to all?

Each of the thousand plainly has its own supporting community, its constituency. Perhaps, then, each corresponds to the peculiar nature of its community, comes *φύσει* to every individual member thereof. There are, in plenty, differences of race-endowment, differences of common circumstance and education, of community atmosphere; with some of these the differences of expression may be correlated. May be so, certainly; but are they so? As regards race, it is indeed true to a very considerable extent that men of the same race employ more or less kindred expressions for a good part of their common conceptions. But then, there are ways enough of accounting for this without involving the answer *φύσει*; and there are also exceptions enough to make us cast out this answer as impossible. Take, for example, the full-blooded Celt of Ireland who uses only English names for things, the one of Wales who uses only Celtic, the one of France (there must probably be such, if there were only a test by which we could discover him.) who uses only Romanic. Take the Jew of pure lineage, talking just as the community talks with whom his lot happens to be cast. Note what names the African uses, in the various lands of his former or present servitude, while bearing in his aspect the most convincing marks of undiluted descent. Or come into an

American community, and pick out, by a little careful examination or genealogic inquiry, the representatives of a dozen
diverse nationalities, and find them all calling the same
things by the same names, knowing no other. This does not
look very much as if names came by any kind of φύσις that is
characteristic of a race. As for one that should be characteristic of a grade of ability, a cast of personal disposition
and character, a tone of education and enlightenment, that is
still more out of the question; every one knows that in any
single community of accordant speakers such discordances,
in all possible kind and degree, are abundantly found.

But if, weary of this superficial and empirical inquiry, we
look more deeply to see how such a state of things comes
about, we shall find a not less total absence of φύσις. We shall
see that every normally constituted human being that comes
into the world has a linguistic faculty amounting simply to
this: that he is able to learn to speak, by acquiring those
particular signs for ideas, and those methods of their use,
which are established and current in the community into whose
midst he is born. The whole consideration of the process
by which the individual gets his " native language " teaches
us this; and there is no other way of accounting for the fact
that each person grows up to speak the tongue of his own
community, and of his own special class of the community,
without any regard to the race from which he comes, or to
the capacity and disposition with which he is endowed, or to
the grade of culture which he attains. If there be — we will
leave that possibility open for the present, to take it up again
later — a mode of expression that is natural to the individual
as such, that forms a part of his φύσις, it is at any rate
overborne and stifled by that other unnatural mode which his
teachers impose upon him. It is difficult to see how, without
laying himself open to the charge of an absurd disregard of
patent facts, any one can put forth a different doctrine; can
maintain, for example, that the child creates his speech by
independent action, but creates it in necessary accordance
with the speech of those about him. As well maintain that
he creates certain melodies, devises certain trades, develops

certain branches of knowledge, dances certain combinations of steps, without learning them, but by a spontaneous mental action, which some mysterious, undefined and indefinable, force brings into wonderful accordance with the like action of his fellows.

It may be asserted, I believe, without any chance of successful contradiction, that not a single item of the traditional English speech received by us from our forefathers has a vestige of right to claim to exist *φύσει* in any one of the innumerable individuals that employ it, to have been produced by him under government of an internal, instinctive impulse, that made it what it is and no other. The tie existing between the conception and the sign is one of mental association only, a mental association as artificial as connects, for example, the sign 5 with the number it stands for, or π with $3.14159+$.

That a system of signs won after the openest and most conscious fashion in this way is capable of answering to us the purposes of a language may be clearly shown in the acquisition of a foreign tongue. One may take a grammar and a dictionary, and commence, by the tedious method of translating into his own set of familiar signs that set which the French or the German child learns by a directer process, and may keep so long at it that a French or German page is as readily and surely intelligible to him as an English one; moreover, by going among the people who use that other set, and practicing himself in the use of them, he may " get them loose," as the Germans say, may mobilize them, associate them in such fashion with his conceptions that they will come into his mind, at first not less readily than his old English signs, and then even more so; and when this last takes place, he has deposed his first acquisition in favor of a second. If the process of substitution be not begun too late, after the habits of thought and habits of utterance have become too far fixed to be altered, it may go on even to the oblivion of one's " native speech," and to the winning of a command of the " foreign tongue " not inferior to that of any person to whom the latter is " native." In fact, *native tongue* means simply ' tongue first acquired ": acquired under peculiar circumstances, and therefore in its own peculiar way; and having upon the mental powers, in respect to training and development, an effect which no second acquisition can have in anything like the same degree.

There are, it is true, differences between the conceptions attached in different languages to words that seem synonymous. But these have nothing to do with determining the peculiar form of the varying signs. So there are marked differences between the conceptions of individual speakers of the same language. Every child begins with using a host of signs of which he is far enough from apprehending the meaning in fullness and with accuracy; and this imperfection of apprehension cleaves to him, in greater or less degree in different parts of his vocabulary, to the end. However much an idea may expand and grow clearer in his mind, or in that of the whole community, there is no corresponding change of the sign.

But there are not a few pictorial, imitative, onomatopoetic signs in our speech: is not the case otherwise with them? do not they, at least, have in them something of a φύσει character Yes, in a certain sense; but not at all as the term φύσει is meant in the controversy which we are judging. So, among the mathematical signs we use, a round mark, reminding one of a hole, may be said to be more suggestive of vacancy or nothingness, and a single straight mark of unity, than the other figures are suggestive, each of its own meaning; they have in them an element of what we may call onomatopoetic force. But there is no necessity about this; nothing that makes the signs in question, to the exclusion of others, the "natural" representatives of their meaning. If there were no other sign for 'naught' would be acceptable; and we should have to signify 'two' by two strokes, and 'three' by three strokes — as, in fact, the Romans and Chinese have done — and so on. Just so, when it is pointed out, we see that there is a kind of adaptedness in two parallel lines ($=$) to signify equality, especially when compared with $>$ and $<$ as used to signify superiority and inferiority; yet, in the great majority of cases, the signs used (like $+$ and $-$) are purely conventional, and answer their purpose precisely as well; and these particular purposes would be answered just as well by other signs, if once established in use for them. There is no such thing as a " natural" symbol for nonentity, or unity, or plurality; it is only that, in casting about for signs for this whole class of conceptions, we find certain ones for certain uses more readily suggested than others, which would have served equally well: the effective use is not dependent on any such considerations. That a certain bird is called a *cuckoo*, by a rude imitation of its note (for the bird really utters neither proper *k* sound nor *oo* sound, and its distinct interval of musical tone is lost in our reproduction), is an obvious and generally intelligible onomatopœia; but if the word *cuckoo* were *φύσει* the name of the animal, then the other animals that make imitable sounds would have also to get their names from them. And there is certainly no *φύσις* in calling, for example, the related American species by the same name, since they do not utter the same note. So the *crack* and *crash*, the *hiss* and *whiz* and *buzz*, and all their kin, have a like pictorial character, of a like value: it is by no means essential to their usefulness as signs, but is rather ornamental, giving them an added attraction. Such words testify to a disposition which is an interesting and a highly important one in language-making, and has to be taken carefully into account especially by those who are discussing the problem of the origin of language — the disposition, namely, to form and use signs that have about them an immediate suggestiveness, inside those rather narrow limits, imposed by the nature of the thing signified and the instrumentality employed for signifying it, within which it is practicable so to do. These imitative signs are by no means all primitive; the disposition toward their use also leads to their production from time to time, or, in the history of manifold change in the form of words, acts as a shaping force. It is essentially the same with the disposition which expresses itself in such lines as those celebrated ones of Pope: —

> When Ajax strives some rock's vast weight to throw,
> The line too labors, and the words move slow.
> Not so when swift Camilla scours the plain,
> Flies o'er the unbending corn and skims along the main. etc.

Its office is not unlike that belonging to tone and gesture in our ordinary speech — impressive, decorative, artistic, but not indispensable in order to mutual intelligence, which is the great object of speech, and is fully attained by the use of signs respecting which we only know that others have formed with them the same associations as ourselves, and will, when we use them, think what we are thinking and desiring them to think. There is not one of these onomatopoetically signified conceptions which is not in other languages, or even also in our own, intimated by signs possessing no trace of an imitative character.

In full view, therefore, of the not wholly insignificant list of onomatopœic words existing in English, we may still maintain that the English names of things do not exist φύσει, that they are the results of a θέσις, of a θέσις which each one of us is led to make under government of the example or the direct instruction of others.

There is, however, another department of expression in which we might plausibly look for the clearest signs of a φύσις: namely, among the interjections, which should be, not the medium of signification of conceptions and judgments, but direct intimations of will and outbursts of emotion; and which thus lie upon the border between human speech and animal expression. Yet even here the effects of educated habit show themselves in the most perplexing manner. Speech is so essentionally conventional that its character infects even our exclamations: which, after all, are not so much means of relieving feeling as of signifying to others that we have such and such feeling. The Englishman, accordingly, does not say *ach* and *weh* and *so*, like the German, nor *fi* and *bah*, like the Frenchman. So far as consonants and vowels are concerned, we have no available evidence that the untrained, the purely natural, human animal would give vent to any definite system of utterances in order to express any definable variety of emotions. As regards, indeed, the tone of utterance, the case is very different. The capacity of tone to serve as the immediate expression of feeling, intelligible to all human beings without explanation and without training, is beyond dispute. This is even added as a powerful auxiliary, along with the other natural means of expression, to our conventional speech. Language without it loses half its power to move and sway, to incite and persuade. Here we seem to touch the true sphere of instinctive expressiveness. And this kind of utterance shades off into those universal acts of expression which belong to man purely as an animal, the laugh and the cry, the groan and the sob, involuntary movements of the muscles, which are analogous with the shiver, the rise of the hair and falling of the jaw, the smile, the watering or beaming of the eye, and all the other physical movements which make the countenance, the arms, the whole body, indicative of a felt emotion.

So far, then, as our present audible speech is concerned, we are able to find in it nothing but the added tone, the modulation of the voice, which can be said to have its existence and its value *φύσει*, by its own intrinsic nature. But the question still remains whether this must be regarded as the only possible sphere of natural expression: May there not be, after all, a connection between some part of the muscular apparatus and the intellectual action of the soul or inner self, whereby an idea, a conception, a judgment, has also its corresponding external and sensible action? If these meddling teachers, with their elaborated systems of conventional signs, would only keep out of the way, might not each human being, as fast as it formed ideas, produce a natural language for their expression?

In investigating this question, we are cut off from the aid of direct experiment. Every child does actually grow up in the company of trained and practiced speakers; it hears them speaking together; and, long before it can govern its own organs of utterance so as to reproduce the signs they make, it understands what many of these mean; it crows and prattles in imitation of them. To get at even a little community of two or three persons untaught to speak seems an impossibility; for humanity forbids us to bring up human beings in utter ignorance, like mere animals, merely to satisfy our curiosity; to deny them the fundamental human privilege

of instruction in speech, in order that we may see how they
would act. And accident neither has created nor is likely to
create, the necessary conditions of the experiment. The
nearest approach to it is made in the case of individuals who
by exceptional causes are cut off from the ordinary education
of their kind. This may be by isolation, or it may be by
deafness. Cases of the former kind, of wild and solitary men,
are exceedingly rare, and the accounts given of them are
of doubtful authenticity or competency. But the deaf are
abundantly found and easily observed; and the ordinary name
of *deaf-mute*, by which we know them, shows what is their
condition in reference to speech. One of this class ordinarily
differs from a normal human being only by the disabling
of a single nerve, that which is sensitive to the vibrations of
the tympanum, and reports them to the brain as sound, or
else in the more external organs that produce the vibration.
The apparatus of mental action is perfect, the apparatus of
articulate utterance is also perfect; nothing is amiss with the
mechanism which connects the two and coördinates their
movements. Here, then, is quite what the φύσει theorist
wants; a human being cut off from the disturbing influences
of linguistic education, but accessible to light of every other
kind, so far as it is not dependent on that education. He is
placed in the midst of human society, which the great apostle
of the φύσει theory, Steinthal, declares* to be the only condition
indispensable to the development of speech. If, now, the deaf
person produces. articulate utterances as distinct permanent
signs of his conceptions, if deaf persons of the same race or
community produce utterances accordant with one another,
such as are those of the ordinarily educated individuals in a
community, if deaf persons of different race or community
produce utterances that vary by differences resembling those
found to prevail among existing dialects and languages, then
the φύσει theory has a basis of observed fact to rest on; if
otherwise, it has none. And that the case is otherwise does
not need to be pointed out. Even the man isolated by solitude
gets by degrees, in the conflict between his higher than

Abriss der Sprachwissenschaft, i. 83, 84.

merely animal powers and the circumstances of his life, a certain amount of education by experience: he learns to know and classify the objects of his daily observation, to appreciate rudely the operations of the more obvious natural causes, to connect and separate and anticipate, in a manner which, if far short of what is easily within our reach, is at least beyond what any other animal can compass: he ought, then, if language is an instinctive human product, to have something of a language for his entertainment and his aid. It is certainly more important to him than to others, since he is debarred most of the means of improvement which are open to them. Yet, as we have seen, even Steinthal does not venture to claim that he will talk, but rather postulates society as the only medium in which the heaven-implanted germs of speech can develop themselves. I do not question that he is right as to the fact; but his admission appears to me a virtual abandonment of the *φύσει* theory.

As the anomalies of linguistic life thus seem to furnish no evidence of a power of immediate natural expression, we have next to examine the regular progress of the history of language, and see if this exhibits any traces of such a power. If there were a natural adaptedness of certain signs to certain ideas, we ought to be able to discover its influence among the variety of those which govern the development of speech. But, in the first place, it seems to make decidedly against the existence of the influence that there is such utter discordance among the names given by different communities to the same conception. Within the sphere of emotional expression, as pointed out above, the elements are of kindred character in all beings, and universally intelligible. The laugh, the scream of pain, the tone of anger or of grief, need no interpreter. But it is far otherwise with the signs of ideas. Languages, words, are absolutely unintelligible to him who has not learned to speak them. It is all in vain to appeal to the inner sense of meaning to help the explanation, for instance, of a Lycian or an Etruscan inscription; he who should attempt it would be simply laughed at. In the changes of form and changes of sense which constitute the main growth of speech, we equally fail to find any regulating princple of the kind here referred to. Let us take as an example our word φύσις itself. It contains as its central element the root φυ (*phü*, a *p* with an audible *h*, a puff or flatus, following it), altered, it is believed, from a yet earlier *bhû*, and having the sense of 'grow.' That there is in any human organization a state of things conditioning *bhû* or φυ as the natural expression of the conception of 'growing,' no one probably, will be bold enough to maintain. Far from this, we do not even know whether that sense was absolutely the earliest one belonging to the word, whether it was not obtained by a transfer, even a distant one, from some other sense. Were it not for Greek usage, the root would seem rather to signify simple existence (Skt. *bhû*, Lat. *fu-i*, our *be*); and all the acuteness of the φύσει theorists would have been incompetent to demonstrate the transfer. The ending σι which makes the derived word is altered from an earlier *ti*; the same element is found, still otherwise altered, in our *grow*TH. Here, again, if there had been any natural adaptedness in the syllable *ti* to express, in combination with a root, the particular modification which this actually expresses, it ought to have exerted a conservative influence, keeping the element unchanged in form, or allowing it to alter only in a certain way, in accordance with the change of the idea. But no such thing is true here; nor anywhere else in language. The word *bhûti* has become φύσι- without any reference to meaning; the transformations of its *bh* and *u* and *t* are due to phonetic influences which wrought equally through the whole language, regardless of the sense of a single element affected by them. Comparative philologists have not seldom claimed that the onomatopoetic character of a word has protected it from phonetic change; but no one has ever detected a similar protective influence as exercised by the sense of the word. Nor can we discover any conservation in the opposite direction — any, namely, that has prevented a transfer of meaning, as being inconsistent with the unchanged audible form. Of the absence of such an influence we may find evidence enough in the history of this same word φύσις and its relatives. Φύσις, we have seen, means most literally the 'action of growing'; and how far this lies from its other uses, so much more wide and indefinite as they are, needs not to be pointed out. The addition of a simple adjective ending makes the derivitive φυσικός; and while *physics* and *physical* and *physicist* show only a development of meaning akin with that which has taken place in φύσις itself, *physic* and *physician* and *metaphysics* exhibit curious movements in quite other directions. We have noted above the change, in Sanskrit and Latin and Germanic, of the signification of the root from 'grow' to 'be.' And *bhûti*, the close analogue of φύσις in Sanskrit, has taken the prevailing sense of 'prosperity,' instead of 'nature.' *Nature* itself, our equivalent for φύσις, is a word of Latin origin. It likewise has a root at its centre; and the oldest form of this is *ga* or *gan*, 'be born.' Relics of the *g* which was once the main stay and support of the meaning are to be seen in *cognate*, *agnate*, and their like. All, then, that is left in *nature* of the significant syllable which lay at the foundation of its history is the initial *n*, which many etymologists, not without a certain reason, look upon as a secondary addition, forming *gan* from a more original *ga*; the rest is a mere accumulation of formative elements, suffixes. And though there may be a degree of analogy between the conceptions 'be born' and 'grow,' it is by no means such as should by any necessity lead to the development out of both of a name for 'nature.' The Latin derivatives which have most analogy in point of formation with φύσις are *natio* from the altered root and *gens* (*genti*) from its more primitive form; and how unlike they are in meaning to φύσις, and even to one another, is plain enough; while from *gens* we get in our language, secondarily, such curious varieties as *gentle, genteel*, and *gentile*, in defiance of all laws of the connection of sound and sense.

And so, if we were to extend our search, we should find it to be, through the whole domain of language: the utmost conceivable variety of expression of the same idea in different tongues; a great diversity of derivation of the expressions for any given idea; a bewildering multifariousness of meaning in families of related words: nowhere in the known history of language-development any trace of a domination of sound by sense, or of sense by sound. Not by any means that there are not reasons, and in a host of cases discoverable reasons, why things are called as they are; but they are reasons founded, not in natural connection, but in previously formed associations, in already established conventions. When we nowadays want to signify a new conception, we have recourse to the (as above shown) purely conventionally used material lying within our reach, in our own tongue or elsewhere. We make a transfer of meaning, without other change, in a word already in use, as in *gravity;* or a derivative, as *galvanism;* or a compound, as *lightning-rod;* or we go deliberately to the anciently used stores of expression of some extinct tongue, and piece together a new vocable, as *thermometer;* or we variously combine two or more of these methods. There is always involved in the act some change of form, or of meaning, or of both; but the single underlying principle is that the new designation is obtained where, according to the existing habits of the language, it can most conveniently be found. No one ever sits down to let the idea strike in upon his soul and evoke an answering utterance: the very suggestion of such a thing is ludicrous; nor does the utterance ever slip out instinctively, without premeditation. It is all a process of the development and multiplication of usages. People having been in the habit of doing so and so, they are led, when occasion arises, to do this and that also: the new habit being connected with the old by some tie of association, it matters little what. To follow the history of this development is a task of the highest interest; in it are bound up the most valuable results of the science of language; by its aid we trace the evolution of knowledge, of thought, of institutions. But it does not bring us to—nor even, in my opinion, toward—a condition of things where we recognize the existence of any natural tie between the conception and its expression, between the idea and the word. On the contrary, we are led thereby to see the more clearly the essential congruence, in the midst of their more adventitious characteristics and their circumstances, of all the various processes of language-getting

and language-making. He, in the first place, who acquires a
"foreign language" finds, by the ear or by the eye, certain
combinations of sounds, which he is able more or less
accurately to reproduce, and which he learns to associate with
their several ideas, and to use in combination with one
another, familiarly and freely, and also " correctly " : that is,
according to the methods usual in a given community, methods
which might just as well be otherwise, if the common consent
only willed it so. Again, the child learning to speak does
only the same thing: he too hears and imitates certain
combinations of sounds, associates them with rudimentary
conceptions which he is led to form, and puts them together,
at first imperfectly and awkwardly, into the phrases which
the usage of his community accepts. And, in the third place,
through the whole traceable development of language, the
language-makers have not been giving vent to natural and
directly intelligible utterances; they have, rather, been
increasing, by methods of whose nature and results they were
themselves only dimly conscious, their store of conventional
signs, elaborating new combinations of sounds which should
henceforth be associated with certain ideas, and used as their
representatives. It makes, properly speaking, no difference to
the users whence their sign is obtained; only, as this is
intended for the general use of a community, and as it must
pass the ordeal of their acceptance before it can become a part
of language, it is gained in such a way as involves the least
practicable change of existing habits, the least possible shock
to prevailing preferences—or prejudices, if we choose to call
them so. We express this prosaic fact in imaginative form
by saying that it must not be " opposed to the genius of the
language." This does not, however, prevent the tie of
association whereby the new sign is connected with the old
from being often a very slender, a remote, even a fantastic or
senseless one. Such cases, to be sure, are the exceptions, and
to be explained by the special circumstances of each, if we
can only command knowledge of them; but they have a high
theoretic importance, as showing what the practical end of
word-making is, and how it justifies even the most questionable

means. On the whole, the body of expression grows and changes by an almost insensible process, step following step, each new sign attaching itself quite closely to an old one.

It is only by taking this view of the history of speech that we can explain its leading facts, and especially that capital fact, the oblivion of etymologies. In any given language, it is but a part of its words, often only a very small part, which even the skilled etymologist can carry back through even a few steps of their history, toward their ultimate roots. And as for the generality of speakers, they are ignorant and heedless of all etymological connections; to them, the word means the thing, and that is the end of it. For a time, and in a measure, the relation between primitive and derivative maintains itself; but it is by the mere power of inertia; if there were a positive conservative force involved, if its maintenance were essential or important, it would not be let go. As things are, it is of great consequence to the practical usefulness of language as an instrument of communication and of thought that the oblivion in question do take place, that our signs for ideas be not encumbered with etymological reminiscences. And the changes of form and of meaning, under the government solely of convenience, do go on unchecked, and independent of one another: there is no limit to the extent to which a word may change its form while retaining its old meaning, or its meaning while retaining its old form; or to which it may wander from its primitive condition, both inner and outer.

We do not find, then, in the traceable history of language, any more than in its present condition, evidence that the names of things exist φύσει. No such principle is called for in order to explain the facts; none such seems even admissible, as reconcilable with the facts. It now only remains to inquire whether there was or must have been something different at the outset, in the actually primitive period, that of the origin of language. Each existing conventional usage or habit founds itself upon a predecessor of the same character, as far back as we can go: was the absolutely lowest course of the foundation of another character? are we to recognize there a real internal correspondence of sound to sense? If there be any such thing in language, it is to be found only there.

But, as hardly needs to be pointed out, if this last be true, there is a strong presumption against its being found there, any more than elsewhere. What we can discover no traces of in all the later periods of speech, we may well despair of detecting in the earliest. To assume it out of hand, as the manner of some is, without even deigning to attempt its proof, but simply setting down as superficial or mechanical those who hold any other view, is certainly in the highest degree unreasonable. On the contrary, it may properly enough be claimed that if any sufficient and satisfactory way can be made out, of accounting for the origin of speech without bringing in as a factor any natural correspondence of sound to sense, but by appealing only to those forces which are seen in action in the later periods, and in their recognized and usual modes of action—then that account of origin will have the whole body of probabilities overwhelmingly in its favor.

And certainly, such an explanation lies close at hand, and is easy enough to find. We need only to recognize the impulse to communication as the force most immediately active in the production of speech, to acknowledge that man spoke primarily in order to make his feeling or thought known to his fellows, and all difficulty is removed. It will then follow that whatever would most readily conduce to mutual intelligence would be made the first foundation of expression: whether a reproduction of the natural tones and cries expressive of emotion, or an imitation of the sounds of nature, living or lifeless, or any other kind of imitation; whether, again, by tones addressed to the ear, or by gestures or grimaces addressed to the eye—for the theory would fully combine and turn to account all the known varieties of expression, leaving that one which experience should show the most available for its purposes to win the preference over the rest, and finally, perhaps, to well-nigh crowd them out of use. The beginnings thus made would certainly be of a rude character—even as sticks and stones for instruments, as fig-leaves and skins for garments, as caves and holes in the ground for dwellings, as scratches with sharp points and daubs of colored earth for pictorial art, as yells and groans for musical art: and so on. To adopt the theory of origin here proposed is equivalent to paralleling speech with these other human acquisitions and branches of culture, as being an instrumentality, gradually wrought out by the exercise of the peculiar powers with which man is endowed, and answering purposes which are human only ; as brought into its present state of perfection, greatly different in different races, by slow accumulation, improvement, evolution, according to the various gifts and circumstances of each race. This view of language doubtless appears to some to be lacking in dignity ; but if it is supported by all the facts and inferences of language-history, a sentimental prejudice can avail nothing against its reception.

And that it is so supported appears to me true beyond all reasonable question. If there is any other acceptable theory, I know not who has set it forth and given it a solid foundation. Those who reject it have wholly failed to realize that the burden of proof rests upon them, to show, or make probable, that there is, or ever was, a power of natural expression in men whereby certain combinations of articulate sounds are produced as the instinctive signs of certain articulate conceptions. I cannot see that they have produced any good evidence that there exists such a thing as the natural uttered sign of a conception. As has been pointed out above, the natural utterances of man do not signify conceptions ; they intimate only feelings, emotions. If a human being feels a certain kind of lively pleasure, he laughs ; if the contrary, he cries, or groans, or sighs, or something of the sort ; if he is struck with astonishment or horror at the sight of anything, he may utter an exclamation ; but it will only signify his feeling in view of it, not the thing itself. So much as this is instinctive, subjective ; but it is not of the nature of human language ; it is on the same plane with the ordinary utterances of the lower animals. There is no conversion of it into language until that motive is added which is the dominant and almost the only conscious one through the whole after-history of language: namely, the intent to communicate. This, by a change which is almost imperceptibly slight at first, while yet of deep and wide-reaching importance, lifts the whole action up to a higher plane. It inaugurates an instrumentality which, though cut loose from any internal connection with the operations of the mind, yet makes itself their ally and aid, and is, precisely on account of its extraneousness and its conventionality, capable of indefinite increase, development, refinement. It is like the production of instruments, in place of a sprouting out of new arms and legs, to answer to the higher needs of the more skilled workman. It comes to bear a wonderful part in the development of the individual mind, and in the cultural progress of the race.

There is nothing really derogatory to the creative power and self-centred action of the human soul in making it thus dependent for its development upon what seems a slight and extraneous motive: nothing, at any rate, more than in making man's development in all other respects dependent upon his position as a social being. It is confessed that the wholly solitary man would never be anything but an utterly wild savage ; in the collision, the emulation, the mutual helpfulness, that come of sociality, are born all the arts of life. The greatness of man consists in what he was capable of becoming, not in what he actually was at the outset. In his low estate he was accessible to only the lower motives. He is, at the best, a short-sighted being, capable of taking but one step forward at a time, and never quite knowing where that will lead him ; but also capable of maintaining the ground he has won, finding out what it is worth to him, and in due time taking another step. All his grand acquisitions have had their small beginnings and their slow growth, each generation adding to what it had received from its predecessor ; and language just as much and just as plainly as the rest.

The doctrine of those who deliberately answer *φύσει* to our question I cannot help regarding as mainly a prejudice, and resting on a foundation of misapprehension. Because, in the history of development of human expression, the voice has come to be the greatly-prevailing, the well-nigh exclusive, instrument of expression, therefore they hastily conclude that there is a special natural relation between the mental apparatus of conception and judgment and the physical apparatus of sound-making—a relation which, as we have seen, is wholly imaginary. They talk learnedly about the reflex-motor action of the nerves, and assume that, when an impression comes over one, it causes him to utter or imagine a responsive sound, somewhat as a sense of the ludicrous calls forth a laugh, a sensation of fear, a crawling feeling, a dash of cold water, a shiver, and the like. They overlook certain essential differences between the two cases: in the first place, that these reflex-motor actions are the intimation of subjective conditions only, which conditions confessedly give rise also to utterances—but these utterances are not language, are not even its beginnings, but only its suggestion and preparation ; and, in the second place, that the actions referred to are actually seen and demonstrated in living men, of every race, that they are substantially the same in all, that they may be controlled, but not altogether obliterated, much less interchanged and varied, under purely social influences, without regard to race ; while the variety of expression of ideas is unlimited, and its choice dependent on nothing but education. To support the φύσει doctrine by quoting sporadic efforts at independent expression on the part of children growing up in the midst of speaking men is quite futile. Children are imitative beings, and sometimes a little wayward ; they catch soon from their surroundings the trick of applying names to things, and, being aware of no particular reason for those they are taught, they try now and then a new one of their own making, enjoying the exercise of a degree of independent ingenuity. Nothing more than this is needed, I believe, to explain away all the scanty array of alleged facts which have ever been brought up in defense of the theory of natural expressiveness. To give that theory a real basis, it would be necessary to show that a child growing up alone, or among mutes, would also produce a body of articulate utterances, of definite meaning and application : or (what has been noted above as a much more accessible proof) that the deaf do the same thing.

Eminent knowledge in psychology, in physiology, in phonetics, in any of the single departments which contribute their part, or their aid, to the science of language, does not by any means lead necessarily to correct views in linguistic philosophy. One may, for example, be the greatest living phonetist, and yet be still puzzling himself with the question what is, after all, the real tie of connection between sound and sense in language. One may be a profound metaphysician, and yet wholly mistake the same connection, taking with regard to the most essential points in the history of language an untenable, even absurd, position. It would not be difficult to cite individual examples of both these classes.

Our conclusion then is, that there is no proper sense in which the names of things can be said to exist φύσει; not only now, and through the ages of recorded speech, but even back to its very beginning, every name has been the result of a θέσις, an act of human attribution.

And yet, there is at least a certain sense in which the θέσις itself may be said to be performed φύσει; and it is in great part owing to a misapprehension of this sense that the answer φύσει has been so often given to the main question. It is undoubtedly, in a manner, " natural" to man to speak. We have to say " a certain sense," " in a manner," because the naturalness does not consist in man's individual nature alone, but also in his circumstances; with all his gifts just as they are, he would not speak unless placed in the company of his fellows. It is in just the same sense " natural" to man to live in houses, to wear clothes, to make instruments, to form societies, to establish customs and laws; yet hardly any one would think on that account of maintaining that, for example, coats and telescopes existed φύσει: while it is nevertheless quite as true of them as of nouns and verbs.

He who answers φύσει, therefore, to the question we have been discussing, lays himself open to the charge of total misapprehension of the most fundamental facts of language-history; he who answers θέσει needs only to show by due explanation that he does not mean to imply that any individual can successfully fasten any name he pleases upon any idea he

may choose to select ; since every change must win the assent
of a community before it is language, and the community will
ratify no arbitrary and unmotivated changes or fabrications.
It is in this action of the community that another great part
(besides that spoken of above) of the difficulty resides for
those who hesitate to admit the doctrine of θέσις: they see so
clearly that no man can do what he will with language that
they are led to deny the action of individuals on language
altogether.   To do this is to mistake the nature of the
conservative force which resists change : in reality, this force
all resolves itself into the action of individuals, working under
the same guidance and limitation, of motives and of circumstances, by which each of us is directed, and of which each
one may, if he set himself rightly at work, become fully
conscious.

before saying you may. Though I ought to add
further, that I should look upon the sum-
mons as much less imperative that might
be one of another character. I am teaching
German and French chiefly as a bread-work,
because I have no other means of support.
But it is not my mission: that is the study
of the old tongues and institutions of the
far East, and of language itself as one of
the oldest and most important of institutions.
An invitation to teach in these lines would

Letter from Whitney to C. W. Eliot, June 14, 1869. Eliot had proposed that Whitney give a language course in his 'University Lectures' (now 'extension') series. This was not to Whitney's taste, and he eventually (spring 1870) gave a course on the history of the Germanic languages instead. The offer of a permanent appointment (see p. 260) was really what Eliot had in mind. (By permission of Harvard University Archives and Mrs. Robert A. Cushman.)

Steinhal on the Origin of Language

W. D. WHITNEY

Art. II. — *Abriss der Sprachwissenschaft.* Von Dr. H. Stein-thal, etc. Erster Teil. *Die Sprache im Allgemeinen.* Also with separate title : *Einleitung in die Psychologie und Sprachwissenschaft.* Von Dr. H. Steinthal, etc. Berlin. 1871. 8vo. pp. xxiii, 487.

Hajjim Steinthal, though little known to the general English-reading public, is one of the leading linguistic scholars of Germany. He represents, as professor extraordinary, the general science of language in the Berlin University. He is joint editor, with Professor Lazarus of Berne, of the *Zeitschrift für Völkerpsychologie und Sprachwissenschaft*, which is now in its seventh volume. His more important separate works have been his *Grammatik, Logik, und Psychologie* (1855), the *Charakteristik der hauptsächlichsten Typen des Sprachbaues* (1860), the *Geschichte der Sprachwissenschaft bei den Griechen und Römern* (1863), and *Die Mande-Neger-Sprachen psychologisch und phonetisch betrachtet* (1867), of which the *Charakteristik*, especially, has necessarily lain upon the table of every deeper student of language. He was also the *rédacteur* of Heyse's *System der Sprachwissenschaft* (1856), and has put forth a considerable number of valuable lesser works and essays, the titles of which need not be given here. Nothing of his, so far as we know, has ever been translated into English. This is not, indeed, to be wondered at, since he habitually writes for a limited circle of readers, and not at all in a style calculated to be taking with the general public, either of England and America or of any other country. His point of view and method of treatment are distinctively and highly metaphysical, and what he produces is wont, therefore, to be hard reading, even for the practised linguistic scholar. He has been, in particular, the disciple, interpreter, and continuer of Wilhelm von Humboldt, a man whom it is nowadays the fashion to praise highly, without understanding or even reading him ; Steinthal is *the* man in Germany, perhaps in the world, who penetrates the mysteries, unravels the inconsistencies, and expounds the dark sayings, of that ingenious and profound, but unclear and wholly unpractical, thinker.

The present work is intended by its author to be a new elaboration and digest of his former contributions to linguistics, the summary of his philosophy of language. Its first part, now published, is founded mainly on his *Grammatik, Logik, und Psychologie;* the parts to follow will be an expansion rather of the *Charakteristik*, treating of the ethnological peculiarities of the different families of language, our own in particular, and adding the history of languages, especially of the Greek, Latin, and Germanic ; the whole forming three or four volumes. All students of language, we are sure, will thank us for bringing to their notice this comprehensive and systematic work of a writer who is worthy of careful attention.

It is not our intention to give here a comprehensive analysis and criticism of Steinthal's first volume, nor to set forth the general features of his scientific system. We prefer to take up but a single subject or chapter, namely, the Origin of Language, and, by discussing that in detail, to get an impression of the author's way of working. No more central and telling subject, certainly, could be selected than this for attaining such a purpose ; its exposition ought to bring to light the strength or the weakness that is in him, and enable us to see how fruitful of advantage to science his labors are likely to prove.

The Origin of Language is treated in the fifth and last chapter of the Introduction (pp. 72 – 90). The subjects of the previous chapters have been : 1. Scientific knowledge in general, the task of philosophy, and that of linguistic philosophy in particular; 2. Extent and division of the science of language ; 3. Relation of this science to other sciences ; 4. Speaking and thinking, grammar and logic. In entering upon this one, the author remarks that he comes at last to the more precise determination of the task which is to occupy him in the present work. " How could one hope," he asks, " to discover the principle of grammar, without having exactly analyzed and thoroughly investigated the essential character of language and its manifold relations to the mental activities, its function in the mental economy, its efficiency for the development of the mind ? But these researches we have to begin with the investigation of the origin of language." It is characteristic of Steinthal's synthetic and *aprioristic* way of working, that he thinks it necessary to settle thus, at the very outset, the most recondite and difficult question in the whole science, one that most scholars would doubtless prefer to put off to the end of their work, as what might be settled by inference when everything else was established, and the way thus duly prepared for it. But, as we have hinted already, he is nothing if not metaphysical, and the metaphysical method requires that one get behind the facts he deals with, and evolve them by a necessity out of some predetermining principle. This is the opposite of the current scientific method, which is proud to acknowledge its dependence on facts, and prefers to proceed by cautious induction backward from the known and familiar to the obscure and unknown. Both methods ought to come to the same thing in the end, and will do so, provided the scientific be conducted with sufficient reach and insight, and the metaphysical with sufficient moderation and caution ; we are used, however, to seeing the metaphysical, when it comes to deal with concrete facts and their relations, fail by labored obscurity and feebleness or by forced and distorting treatment. The result alone can decide which is the better, as applied to language.

Men ask for a definition of language, we are now told ; but very improperly, since things of such immense content are not to be defined ; and moreover, a definition, like a picture, can represent only something at rest, or only a moment in an action ; while language is manifold, and constantly growing and developing. If, then, we inquire how it is with language, the proper answer follows, " It is what it is becoming " (*sie ist, was sie wird*). Surely, it was hardly worth while to moot the point, only to come to so barren a result as this. Locomotives, likewise, are numerous and various, and their mode of construction is all the time changing ; yet it is possible to give a plain man a reply to the question, " What is a locomotive ? " When a definition of language is called for, men expect the answer, " It is audible thinking ; it is the body of which thought is the soul ; it is the spoken instrumentality of thought ; it is a body of uttered signs for conceptions," or something of the kind, drawn out with more or less fulness, enough to show us, in a preliminary way, what the answerer's general idea of language is. The author might have left out the paragraphs he devotes to this little discussion, and nobody would have missed them ; we only refer to the matter because it illustrates a vexatious way he sometimes has of startling and rebuffing a common-sense inquirer with a reply from a wholly different and unexpected point of view : as when you ask a physician, " Well, doctor, how does your patient promise this morning ? " and he answers, with a wise look and an oracular shake of the head, " It is not given to humanity to look into futurity ! " The effect is not destitute of the element of *bathos*.

Next we are called on to note that the way in which a problem is stated is of the highest consequence, often half involving the solution ; and it is proposed to determine " what demand this present question contains, what significance it can alone have."

And, to lead the way to such a statement, our author gives

a sketch of the discussions respecting the origin of language, as they were carried on, in an especially lively manner, during the last century. Some maintained that language was invented by man, under the pressure of necessity and convenience, as a means of communicating with his fellows and securing their assistance. " He, the much-inventive man, has, among many other remarkable works, invented language also." And it was not at the outset so perfect a work that rude and uncultivated men should not have been equal to its production ; having been improved and perfected later, somewhat as the means of navigation have been, from the first hollowed-out trunk of a tree to the modern ship of a hundred cannon. The opposing party referred to the languages of the negroes and of our Indians, as being so cunningly devised products as to imply a degree of reflection (*Nachdenken*) of which such savages were not capable. Moreover, the invention of language would require reason (*Vernunft*), and before the possession of language men could have had no reason. Therefore language must have been given by God ; it is no human invention, but a divine communication.

According to Steinthal, those who defended the human invention of speech show a revolting triviality and rudeness of conception and view ; while the upholders of the divine origin saw deeper. From his sketch of the argument, indeed, we should draw quite the contrary conclusion ; but this may pass, as of small consequence. Of much more consequence is it to notice that he makes no reference of any kind, anywhere in his chapter, to a view of the nature and origin of language which is held by a whole school of linguistic students at the present day, and which is akin with the one first stated above, only modified to accord with the better knowledge and deeper insight of modern times. An adherent of that view would be likely to urge that it is an easy matter to cast reproach and ridicule upon the last-century form of it ; but that to carry from the latter an inferential condemnation over to its present form is much more easy and convenient than fair and ingenuous ; and he would be justified in adding that its present opponents are in the habit of combating it in that way, and in that alone. This also, however, only by the way ; what concerns us here is rather what our author does than what he leaves undone.

He declares, namely, that he cannot join the other party, who assume for language a divine origin, notwithstanding their deeper insight; and that, "for one general reason and two special reasons," which he proceeds to set forth. We give the general reason in his own words : —

"Of God, the philosophy of religion, founded on metaphysics, has to take account. It has to determine how far, in order to the understanding of every being and of every occurrence, in order to the full and true apprehension of all actuality, we are to add in our thoughts the idea of God. All other sciences are unauthorized to bring in God as a means of explanation. The philosophy of religion teaches πάντα θεῖα ; the special sciences teach φυσικά or ἀνθρώπινα πάντα ; and the two may not contradict one another."

We fail to appreciate the force or to see the appositeness of this objection. If to bring in the idea of God is the monopoly of religious philosophy, then, whenever that idea comes in, religious philosophy comes also; and the latter is called upon in this case to help solve a problem which science finds insoluble. Religious philosophy and the special sciences may be so distinct as not even to have in common the idea of a God; but, at least, the same person may be both special scientist and (even without knowing it) religious philosopher; and what he cannot do in the one character he may attempt to do in the other. If Steinthal chooses to say that it is not scientific to appeal to a divine author, that it only shows the weakness of the scientist, whose problem is really soluble without such appeal, then we shall understand what he means, and perhaps agree heartily with him; but to claim that God cannot have originated language because, in our classification of knowledge, we put the idea of God under another rubric than the linguistic, seems to us a mere verbal quibble.

In the "two special reasons," also, we find force and pertinence equally wanting. God, we are told, must either have created language in man, or taught it to him. But the latter is impossible; because, although much may be taught man by means of language, teaching is only possible by that means, and therefore language itself cannot be taught. This, we remark, in spite of the fact that every child learns language without being previously possessed of language whereby to acquire it! To be sure, Steinthal does not, as we shall see hereafter, believe that children do learn language, in the ordinary sense of that term ; yet, whatever the precise nature of the process, why should not God, in a confessedly supernatural or miraculous way, have been to the first human beings what they were, and what human parents have in general since been, to their children ? This assumption, however, is in a manner involved and answered in our author's further reasoning, in refutation of the alternative theory, that God created language in men, — that is to say, made it a part of their nature or constitution. Language, he says, is evidently not created in us ; it is certain and evident that the child " appropriates " (*sich aneignet*) the language of the community in which it grows up. And he goes on : —

" God, then, would have to be regarded as having created language in the first human pair alone, while the succeeding generations learned to speak, each from its own parents. But this assumption also is impossible. For what man can learn, that he can also bring forth as original out of himself, without instruction ; for all learning is merely facilitated, supported, and for that very reason limited creation. But what one man should receive from God as an exceptional endowment, that no other man would be able to learn from him. If, therefore, language had been created in the first human beings, their children never could have appropriated it. If they were in fact able to do this, then the language of the first human beings could not have been an exceptional endowment of theirs, and their children must have been able also to create it independently for themselves. If, then, in order to man's possession of language, he absolutely must have had the power to create it, the first man in like manner with all his successors, why should it in only a single case have been created in him by God ? "

We have given this in Steinthal's own words, because we feared not being able to do him justice in a paraphrase or summary. We think the inaptness of the reasoning, in spite of its obscure intricacy, will at once strike almost every one. The assumption is impossible, because — why should things have been so ? We may retort, it is possible, because — why should n't they ? What the Creator might or might not have thought it proper to do for the first human beings in order to give the race a fair start in life, we would rather not claim to decide. And as to the impossibility of transmission claimed to be involved, it amounts simply to this, that a miracle contravenes the laws of nature. But that, we imagine, is involved in the very idea of a miracle. Our author might just as well assert that water could not be miraculously converted into wine, because there are certain chemical elements in wine which water does not contain; and because, if it had once been so converted, then all water would have to be so convertible, which every one knows not to be the case. The assumption of the divine origin of language does not, as we understand it, deny that each man, as a part of his human nature, possesses the capacity to learn and use and make language; it only implies that, whereas this capacity might be indefinitely or infinitely long in developing itself so as to produce languages like those we know, the first men were miraculously put by anticipation in possession of its perfected fruits. It is a part, and a natural part, of the view which supposes the first human beings to have been produced in the maturity of growth and in a condition of high culture, by a direct and anomalous fiat of the Almighty. We are ourselves just as far as Steinthal from accepting the theory that language was a miraculous gift to the first human beings; but our objections to it would be of a wholly different character from his. Here, it seems to us, he again shows the same remarkable incapacity already once noticed, of getting upon the same plane with the holders of an opinion which he opposes, and of so constructing his argument that it shall be understood and received by those against whom it is directed.

We are now led on by our author to a more serious attempt at breaking through the low and trivial assumed conditions of the problem as looked at by the controversialists of the last century. Our views of man, he says, have undergone a complete revolution since that time. As what a little, petty creature was he then regarded! born in the mire, ever crawling on the earth, a prey to want, from which he was all the time devising ways to extricate himself; driven by the pressure of necessity from one improvement of his at first rough work to another; nothing wise and great in his development; indeed, no inward development at all! "Of the primeval powers of the human spirit, out of which the institutions of social life have grown, and from which they continually draw the juices of life, those people knew nothing; unknown was the creative force from which religious and moral ideas flow forth unsought, for the human being's own gratification."

Here, again, is seen Steinthal's complete antagonism with the inductive and scientific tendencies of the day. We should have said that the prevailing movement of modern thought was precisely the reverse of what is thus described; that only the philosophers of the eighteenth century and those who in the nineteenth inherit their spirit could regard the first human being as having walked the earth with lofty tread and gaze uplifted, letting grand ideas and noble institutions flow forth spontaneously from the deep springs of his soul, and enjoying their flow; comprehending by intuition the Creator and his works, and worshipping him with a pure adoration; meditating on problems of psychology, and giving birth to soulful expression as naturally and unconsciously as he walked or moved his arms. Modern science, on the contrary, claims to be proving, by the most careful and exhaustive study of man and his works, that our race began its existence on earth at the bottom of the scale, instead of at the top, and has been gradually working upward; that human powers have had a history of development; that all the elements of culture — as the arts of life, art, science, language, religion, philosophy — have been wrought out by slow and painful efforts, in the conflict between the soul and mind of man on the one hand, and external nature on the other, — a conflict in which man has, in favored races and under exceptional conditions of endowment and circumstance, been triumphantly the victor, and is still going on to new conquests. For ourselves, we heartily hold this latter view, deeming it to be established already on a firm basis, soon to be made impregnable; and we regard the other as the mere dream of a psychologist, who, in studying the growth of humanity, descends into the depths of his own being — a being developed in the midst of the highest culture produced by thousands of years of united efforts on the part of the whole race — instead of appealing to the facts of history. Why our author should feel his conception of the dignity of humanity insulted by the belief that the first men were a prey to necessity, and rose by diht of earnest and persistent endeavor to escape its cruel yoke, we do not precisely see, inasmuch as the great majority of men are still bent beneath that yoke, and the number of those who realize his ideal is hardly more than infinitesimal. It would appear that he must hold the doctrine of a " fall " of the race, mental and moral, in its extremest form.

It is, then, only with a feeling of discouragement, of expectation devoid of hope, that we go on from this capital misapprehension to examine Professor Steinthal's further inquiries into the origin of language. We cannot but fear that here, again, he has mistaken the nature and bearings of the question he undertakes to discuss.

The succeeding paragraph warns us against being content with that half-view of language which would come from our merely regarding it, as well as poetry and the like, with wonder and admiration, as springing forth from the unfathomable depths of human nature, and which might lead us to explain it as the product of an " instinct "; some persons, in fact, having attributed the differences of Semitic and Indo-European speech, as of Semitic monotheism and Indo-European polytheism, to a difference in the linguistic and religious " instincts " of those races respectively ; which is a mere play of words.

For, our author goes on, besides the " recognition of the creative power of man," we have in this century the advantage of a rational psychology, which strives to discover a mechanism in the movements of consciousness, laws in mental life, and so on ; since all the creations of man will be found not less subject to the dominion of rational laws than are the productions of nature. Now we also, on our part, expect decided advantage to the study of language, as of every other human production, from an improved comprehension of the operations of the human mind, as of all the other determining conditions of a difficult problem. But whether the advance of psychology is or is not to bring about a revolution in the science of language, is a question depending on the manner and degree in which language is a " mental production " (*geistiges Erzeugniss*). It is very possible here to fall into the serious error of looking upon words and phrases as an immediate emanation of the mind, and so of settling the laws of mental action, and out of them evolving the events of language-history. The soul of man and its powers and operations are, after all, the mystery of mysteries to us ; the phenomena of language are one of its external manifestations, and comparatively a simple matter ; the light which these shall cast upon the soul must probably be greater than that which they shall receive from our comprehension of the soul. If the linguistic student, in his devotion to psychology, shall invert this relation, he is very likely to add one more to the already numerous instances in which metaphysics has shown its inaptitude for dealing with facts of observation and induction. Only the result can decide, and that we will proceed to test.

In order, then, to exhibit the complete change of aspect of the question in this century, Professor Steinthal enters upon a detailed comparison between the " invention " of language and that of some product of mechanical ingenuity, as a watch, a steam-engine, gunpowder. And he first points out that men regard the original invention of a thing with much more interest than the succeeding manufacture of the thing invented ; since invention is the grand difficulty, while imitation and reproduction are comparatively easy. So people have been talking about the invention of language by the first human beings ; and that, even down to the present day ; though now they change the name, and style it production instead of invention ; the acquisition of speech by children they have regarded as a reproduction or later manufacture. They have, therefore, been curious to ascertain how and when this invention was made. They have wanted to know how Adam and Eve chatted together in Paradise, and, as they had no other way of getting at the desired knowledge, they dreamed it out.

We object *in toto* to this way of opening the inquiry. No one with any sense or learning has, within the memory of this generation, thought of regarding language as a thing invented or produced by anybody at any time. Whom is Steinthal arguing against ? Whom does he wish to convince ? Is it the shallow theorists of the last century, with here and there a last-century man, who has by some mischance failed to

get himself yet laid beneath the sod ?   Surely, there are involved in the origin of language a plenty of real living questions contended about by live men ; it is hardly better than
trifling to descend into the sepulchre for one's antagonists.   Or
can it be that he does not realize the measureless absurdity of
the view he is opposing, that he thinks it calls for rectification
rather than summary rejection ?   We shall see as we go on.

Our author confesses that first invention is more important
than later reproduction ; but he doubts whether the history of
first manufacture is more attractive than that of later or present manufacture.   What, at any rate, is more important and
more attractive than either is to comprehend the laws of nature
which underlie and determine the working of the thing invented, both at the outset and ever since.   The latter is merely
temporary and in part even accidental : the former are fundamental and eternal.   Whoever knows that a certain monk
named Schwarz, experimenting in his laboratory, perhaps in
search of the philosopher's stone, invented powder, knows
merely anecdotes : suppose another to be ignorant of this, but
to understand the chemical composition and resolution of powder and the reason of the effects it produces, does not this one
know what is better worth knowing ?   So as regards language :
" it is more important and more attractive to investigate the
laws according to which it both originally lived and subsisted,
and at this very day subsists and lives ; and to know the specific
circumstances under which its first production may have taken
place is a matter of less moment."

If, now, a comparison is to be enlightening and instructive,
there needs to be at least a degree of analogy between the
things compared ; and such analogy we must confess ourselves
unable here to discover.   If there be any man living, or dead
since the rise of linguistic science, who holds that language
was invented, or produced, or created, or evolved, by an individual, as powder by Schwarz, or the watch by some one else,
let him be brought forward that we may stare at him for a
wonder, as we do at the *megalonyx* and the *ichthyosaurus ;* but
do not let us spend paper and ink in reasoning him down.
And if we must perforce refute him, let us do it by pointing
out the fundamental error of his understanding of language, not

by letting that pass unnoticed, and taking exceptions to a point of wholly subordinate consequence. But what, after all, does Steinthal's objection amount to ? Simply to this : that it is a grander thing to be a chemist or physicist than to be a student of human culture as exhibited in the history of mechanical inventions. That may be so ; it were useless to discuss the question of relative dignity ; but, at any rate, the two are quite different, and there is room and occupation for both of them. The historical student does not fully comprehend his task without the help of the physicist to teach him the nature of the practical problems which human ingenuity has solved, one after another ; yet he is an independent worker in a separate branch of inquiry, in which the physicist may be as little versed as he in physics. In like manner, it may be a far grander thing to be a psychologist than an historical student of language ; yet the two are not engaged in the same work, and the eminent psychologist may show himself but a blunderer when he comes to deal with the facts and principles of linguistic history.

Indeed, although Professor Steinthal does not appear to understand the bearing of the comparison with which he is dealing, he yet goes on to set forth something like what we have just been stating. No single invention, he says, comes without due preparation, consisting in previous inventions and the capacity and insight arising from familiarity with them ; and it falls fruitless and is forgotten unless it serves certain definite purposes, founded in the necessities and aspirations of the age in which it makes its appearance. In order to understand the invention of powder or of printing, we need to set the bare facts in relation with the whole history of the times of their production. Undoubtedly ; nothing could be plainer than this. And what follows from it ? Why, that we study the history of that department of human culture which includes the use of instruments and inventions, comprehensively and in detail, and through the medium of the facts themselves, though at the same time heeding carefully what mechanical science has to say in part explanation of the facts ; we trace up invention after invention, inferring, as well as we may in the imperfection of the record, out of what preparation each one grew, and what new conditions it created to favor the production of its successor. And at last, as it now appears, going back from the almost miraculous appliances of modern culture to simpler and simpler instruments, from iron to bronze, from bronze to stone, we find the beginnings of human effort in this direction to have been pebbles and flakes of flint-stone, and rods and clubs of wood ; and one grand department of man's activity, of the utmost importance in its bearings on the progress, mental as well as physical, of the race, is laid before us, most interestingly and instructively, in at least the main outlines of its development. Such knowledge lies outside the sphere of the physicist, and is unattainable by his methods ; one might study the laws of mechanical force and of chemical combination till doomsday, without advancing a step nearer to its possession. Thus is it, also, with language. A close and instructive analogy really exists between the two subjects, if rightly looked at ; and in failing to discover this, and to put it in place of the other and false analogy, Steinthal has, as it seems to us, failed to draw any valuable result from the whole discussion. What in linguistics corresponds to the invention of a particular machine, or application of force, or useful combination of elements, is not the production of language in general ; far from it ; it is the production of an individual word or form. Every single item of existing speech had its own separate beginning, a time when it first came into men's use ; it had its preparation, in the already subsisting material and usages of speech, and the degree of culture and knowledge in the community where it arose, and it obtained currency and maintained itself in existence because it answered a practical purpose, subserving a felt need of expression. The history of the development of language is nothing more than the sum and result of such single histories as this. The scientific student of language, therefore, sets himself at work to trace out the histories of words and forms, determining, so far as he is able, the chronological place and reason and source of each one, and deriving by induction from the facts thus gathered a comprehension, in no other way attainable, of the gradually advancing condition of mind and state of knowledge of the language-makers and language-users. And if he can determine what, or even of what sort, were the very first elements of language used by men, and why these instead of other possible elements were used, he has solved the problem of the origin of language; and the history of this other, even grander and more important department of human productiveness, is also laid before us in its main features, though with infinite work yet remaining to be done upon it in detail. All the questions involved in it are primarily historical, to be investigated by studying and comparing the recorded facts of language. Psychology has just as much to do with it as theoretical mechanics and chemistry have to do with the study of human inventions; it is invaluable as critic and aid, but worthless as foundation and substitute. Which of all the innumerable events of linguistic history is accessible to us by the *a priori* method? What word or form in any language under the sun could we have prophesied, from the laws of action of the human mind and soul?

We are obliged, accordingly, to dissent utterly from Steinthal's conclusion, which is expressed in these words: " For us, then, the investigation of the origin of language is nothing else than this, to acquaint ourselves with the mental culture which immediately precedes the production of language, to comprehend a state of consciousness and certain relations of the same, as conditions under which language must break forth, and then to see what the mind gains by means of it, and how under the government of law it further develops itself." Our author, like others before him, here suffers the psychologist to overbear and replace in him the linguistic scholar; he ignores the essential character of the questions with which he deals, and substitutes subjective for objective methods of investigation. So far as we can see, he breaks not less decidedly with the inductive school of linguistics than he has broken before with the inductive school of anthropology. The origin and history of language is a mere matter of states of mind. Neither here nor anywhere else in the chapter do we find acknowledgment of the truth that speech is made up of a vast number of items, each one of which has its own time, occasion, and effect, nor anything to show that he does not regard it as an indivisible entity, produced or acquired once for all, so that when, under due favoring conditions, it has " broken forth," it *has* broken forth, and that is the end of the matter: than which, certainly, a grosser error in the view of the historical student of language cannot possibly be committed. If such is to be the result of the full admission of psychology into linguistic investigation, then we can only say, may Heaven defend the science of language from psychology! and let us, too, aid the defence to the best of our ability.

We see pretty clearly, by this time, how much and how little we have to expect from Professor Steinthal toward the solution of the real question of the origin of language. It is important, however, that we continue to follow his reasonings and note to what result they actually come.

He next calls upon us to observe that, as regards the so-called invention of speech, natural laws and mental conditions are one and the same thing. " The mental condition and the relations of consciousness are here the actual forces themselves which produce language." But our observation refuses to show us any such thing. Speech is a body of vocal signs, successions of vibrations produced in the atmosphere by the organs of utterance, and apprehended by the organs of hearing. Are the lungs, the larynx, the tongue, the palate, the teeth, the lips, even the air about us, parts of the mind? If so, what is the body? and what are its acts, as distinguished from those of the mind? So far as we can see, the word "jump" is just as much and just as little an act of the mind as jumping over a fence is ; each is an act of the body, executed under direction of the mind indeed, but by bodily organs, namely, the muscles. The mind's immediate products are conceptions, judgments, feelings, volitions, and the like ; pyschology, surely, ought to teach that. An utterance is like nothing else in the world so much as a gesture or motion of the arms, hands, fingers. The latter is in like manner the effect of an act of will upon bodily organs that are obedient to the will ; it differs only in being brought through another medium, the luminiferous ether, to the cognizance of another receptive organ, the eye. The hands can make an indefinite number of such motions, and combine them in every conceivable variety ; and the mind, acting on and developing the hints afforded by what may be called the natural gestures, is capable of using these motions as instrumentalities for the expression of its thoughts; and it does so use them when circumstances limit it to this kind of instrumentality. In like manner, the voice can utter an indefinite number of articulate sounds, and can put them together into combinations practically infinite; and here, again, founding on the natural cries and on imitative sounds (perhaps also on other bases, the whole to an extent and in a manner not yet fully determined, and the determination of which would be the real and final solution of the remaining questions as to the origin of language), the human mind has been able to avail itself of this instrumentality in order to the expression of its acts; and it does so avail itself in every normally constituted human being. There is no more intimate connection between the mind and the articulating apparatus than between it and the fingering apparatus; words are just as extraneous to the mind — only lying within its convenient reach, and so capable of being put to use by it at pleasure — as are twistings of the fingers and brandishings of the arms or feet. These truths seem to us so plain, so self-evident, that we are at a loss to conceive how they can be opposed by any valid argument; we never have seen anything brought against them that could stand a moment's critical examination. That there is, therefore, any such wide and essential difference as our author would postulate between the material of speech and those purely physical and independently existing substances which the mechanically inventive mind turns to its purposes, does not appear. The difference is in reality great enough, and for that very reason does not require to be exaggerated. To contract it one way, and identify words outright with sticks and stones and metals, is at the very least no worse than to stretch it the other way, and to identify them with mental acts.

Steinthal's inferential assumption, then, from which we have necessarily to set forth in order to the further prosecution of our inquiries, is this: "that a certain condition of mental culture must be given, in which there lies a certain material, and which is governed by such laws that speech must necessarily come into being." We should state what of truth there seems to us to be in this in a very different manner, somewhat thus: A certain state of mind being given, consisting in the apprehension of an idea that calls for expression, and in the desire to express it, and a certain material lying ready at hand, or being producible and habitually produced in indefinite quantity, the laws which govern human action in general in the adaptation of means to ends cause the production of an item of speech ; and speech in general is made up of such items, so produced.   I employ the words " locomotive " and " spectroscope " now simply by imitation, because some one else has employed them before me ; the man who first employed them did so because his " mental culture," by reason of the invention of the one or the other instrument, had got into such a " condition " that he wanted a name to call them by ; and he knew where to find it.   Does Professor Steinthal believe that states of mental culture and laws of consciousness actually produced the two words in question ?   We hardly credit it ; although it would seem a necessary inference from what he says.   Perhaps he would not allow that these are parts of " language " at all, in the peculiar and psychological sense of that term.   But we do not know where, in that case, he would stop, in excising and amputating the members of the body of speech.   The queer new word *apperception*, which makes such a figure in his writings and in those of his school, would, for aught that we can see, have to go too.   More probably, he has never brought his doctrine to the test of actual fact in recent times at all ; and he would perhaps claim that productions of words in these modern degenerate days are of a very different character from those of earlier ages.   That is to say, he would fly with his pet theory from the clear light of the present into the dimness of the past ; and the further back into the dark he got, the more confident he would be of its truth and sufficiency.   For our part, we think no explanation of the facts of language which does not account for the nearest present just as well as for the remote past has any good claim to acceptance.   Of course, some of the important determining circumstances and conditions have been in constant change since the beginning, and this change requires to be fully allowed for ; it is to be read in the antecedent forms of language, as we reconstruct them by taking away, one after another, the productions of the later time.   And we need not absolutely deny the possibility that other principles have been at work than those we now perceive working ; only, they have to be inductively established before we shall accept them, and not simply " assumed " as part of a doctrine which appears not less inconsistent with the former than with the present phenomena of linguistic growth.

Our author proceeds : —

" This means, then, that language is not an invention, but an origination or creation in the mind, not a work to which the understanding has furnished the means, not an intentional application of a means sought after and found for the relief of a conscious necessity, nor even the happy turning to account of an accident for the enrichment of mental working (for this also presupposes reflection or consciousness as to the possible utilization of what had thus turned up), but language has come to be without being willed into existence. The laws which, while remaining unconscious, yet govern the elements of consciousness, operate, and execute the creation."

There are statements in this paragraph to which we can yield a partial assent. That men have willed language, as language, into existence, or, in its production, have labored consciously for the enrichment of their mental working, we do not believe, any more than Professor Steinthal does. But consciousness has its various spheres and degrees. The first man who, on being attacked by a wolf, seized a club or a stone and with it crushed his adversary's head, was not conscious that he was commencing a series of acts which would lead finally to rifles and engines, would make man the master (comparatively speaking) instead of the slave of nature, would call out and train some of his noblest powers, and be an essential element in his advancement to culture. He knew nothing either of the laws of association and the creative forces in his own mind that prompted the act, or of the laws of matter which made the weapon accomplish what his fist alone could not. The psychologist and the physicist, between them, can trace out now and state with exactness those laws and forces ; can formulate the perceptions and apperceptions and reflex actions on the one hand ; can put in terms of a and b and x and y the additional power conferred, on the other hand ; and can even maintain, as we infer, that those laws and forces and formulas produced the man's act ; while all that he himself knew was that he was defending himself in a sudden emergency. We are not loath to admit that all the later advances in mechanics have been made in a similar way, each to meet some felt necessity, and to seize and realize an advantage which the possession of what had been done before him enabled the inventor to perceive as within his reach ; and all the mental progress of the race (which is founded on physical well-being, since there could be no philosophers until there was spare fruit of other men's ruder labors to feed and support them), and all science and art, have depended in great part on those advances in mechanics, and have come as their unforeseen results. Professor Steinthal, as we have seen above, does not relish or accept this view, and thinks it a part of the philosophy of the last century. What man does not win directly, by the free play of his inherent creative forces, is to him only such a degradation of human nature as psychology spurns. While he remains in this frame of mind, we have no hope that he will accept our view of the history of origination and development of language, which is closely akin with what we have just laid down respecting that of mechanical invention. Men have not, in truth, produced language reflectively, or even with consciousness of what they were doing ; they do not, in general, even so use it after it is produced. The great majority of the human race have no more idea that they are in the habit of " using language," than M. Jourdain had that he " spoke prose " ; all they know is that they can and do talk. That is to say, language exists to them for the purpose of communication simply ; of its value to the operations of their own minds, of its importance as an element in human culture, of its wonderful intricacy and regularity of structure, nay, even of the distinction of the parts of speech, they have not so much as a faint conception, and would stare in stupid astonishment if you set it forth to them. And we claim that all the other uses and values of language come as unforeseen consequences of its use as a means of communication. The desire of communication is a real living force, to the impelling action of which every human being, in every stage of culture, is accessible ; and, so far as we can see, it is the only force that was equal to initiating the process of language-making, as it is also the one that has

kept up the process to the present time. It works both consciously and unconsciously: consciously, as regards the immediate end to be attained ; unconsciously, as regards the further
consequences of the act. When two men of different speech
meet, they fall to trying simply to understand one another ; so
far as this goes, they know well enough what they are about ;
that they are thus making language they do not know : that
is to say, they do not think of it in that light. The man who
beckons to his friend across a crowded room, or coughs or
hems to attract his attention, commits, consciously and yet unconsciously, a rude and rudimentary act of language-making,—
one analogous doubtless with innumerable acts that preceded
the successful initiation of the spoken speech which we have.
No one consciously makes language, save he who uses it most
reflectively, who has his mind always filled with its character
and worth, — indeed, hardly even he ; perhaps (to take an
extreme case) the man who produced *apperception* itself only
knew that he was finding a sign for a conception which he had
formed, in order to use it as a factor, a kind of x, or π, or O_2,
in his reasonings. And so men have gone on from the beginning, always finding a sign for the next idea, stereotyping the
conception by a word, and working with it till the call for
another came ; and the result, at any stage of the process, is
the language of that stage. Precisely here, then, is where
comes in the operation of those " unconscious laws which gov
ern consciousness," to the direct action of which our author
would vainly ascribe the whole production ; they shape into a
regular and well-ordered whole the congeries of items thus miscellaneously and as it were accidentally produced ; they create
out of words a language ; they give, in a perfectly unconscious
way, that completeness, adaptedness, and proportion which
make the instrumentality represent the nature and answer the
higher uses of the minds from which it proceeds.

In the creative forces of the human soul, as by their free and
spontaneous action the producers of spoken language, we have,
then, no faith or belief whatever ; indeed, to our unpsychologi-
cal apprehension, there is something monstrous in the very
suggestion or implication that a word is an act of the mind.
Conceptions and judgments, these and their like are what the

mind forms; for them it finds, under the social impulse to communication, signs, in those acts of the body which experience shows to be best suited to its use; and the sum of these signs is language. Whether we shall call language-making invention, or production, or creation, or giving birth, is quite immaterial, provided we understand what the process really is, and how far it is faithfully represented by any or all of those terms. "Invention" is doubtless a name invested with too much false suggestiveness to be conveniently used; yet we are confident that many of those who have used it were much nearer the truth in their conception of what they thus denominated than is Professor Steinthal. "Growing organism," "unfolding germ," which he goes on in the immediate sequel to apply, — though also innocent enough, if employed with a full realization of how far they are figurative merely, — are far more dangerously misleading. That they mislead him into some strange ways and hard places, we shall have no difficulty in proving.

He next proceeds, namely, to abolish the distinction which he had before laid down so sharply between the first coming into being of language and its later acquisition by children. That, it appears, was a provisional concession to our weakness; a kind of scaffolding, by the aid of which we should rise a step in the argument he was constructing. Only, it must be confessed, the scaffolding is to our mind so much more substantial than the main structure, that we shall prefer to cleave to it, and stand or fall with it. Hear him: —

"Respecting language, it has been already observed that it no more admits of being taught and learned than seeing and hearing do. Who, I pray, has ever observed that children were taught to speak? Many a one, however, has perhaps already noticed how vain is the effort sometimes expended in teaching the child. But I assume with certainty that every one who has had occasion to watch a child from the second to the fourth year of life has often enough been astonished to see with what startling suddenness (*wie urplötzlich*) the child has used a word or a form. One seldom knows where the child got that. He has grasped it at some opportunity or other, and to grasp is to create" (*ergreifen heisst erzeugen*)!

Prodigious! Then, doubtless, the man we lately imagined, who "grasped" the stick or stone for purposes of self-defence, really created it; and the said stick or stone was his mental act! If we can go on smoothing away differences and effecting identifications at this rate, we shall soon have all the elements of the discussion reduced to a condition of chaotic nebulosity out of which we may evolve just what suits our individual taste. Seriously, we should not have supposed any man, at this age of the world, capable of penning the sentences we have quoted. To deny that children learn their language from those about them is to abandon definitely and finally the ground of sound reason and common sense. What if you cannot sit down with spectacles on nose, and book and ferule in hand, and " teach " a child to speak? Is that the only way of teaching? Then we do not " learn " a tune, for example, which we have heard from the street-organs till our souls are weary of it; we are simply brought into such a condition of mental culture that our creative forces in their unconscious workings produce the tune. Would this statement be a whit less absurd than that which our author makes about language? It has even become with us an item of popular wisdom, as attested by a proverb, that example teaches better than precept. Children do, indeed, " grasp" just what they can, what they best understand and are prepared for, of the language which is current in their hearing, and we cannot follow the movements of their minds closely enough to tell beforehand what that will be; although we can act upon the hints their imperfect efforts give us, and help and correct till the step they are striving to take is taken. Does any one before whom some unforeseen new acquisition is blurted out by a child doubt that the child has heard it somewhere, at some time, and is simply reproducing it by imitation? If otherwise, why are not the current expressions of another language sometimes generated by the creative forces of the childish soul? Put the German child, along with its German-speaking parents and brothers and sisters, in an English-speaking community, so that it hears both languages every day, and almost every hour, and it acquires (or produces) both, apparently as well and as easily as it would have acquired (or produced) either alone under other circumstances. Is there nothing like learning there? Then how would Professor Steinthal explain it ? But he proceeds : " We have no right whatever, then, to speak of the learning of language on the part of children. For where there is no teaching, there there is no learning." Most true, indeed ; there never yet was an effect where there was not a cause. But then we assert with equal confidence, that where there is learning, there there is also teaching ; because, where the effect is, there we know there is a cause, if we can only find it ; and the cause in this case is not hard to discover, if one will but open his eyes. Further : " What the gardener does with seeds out of which he wishes to rear plants, is all that we do with our children in order to bring them to speech : we bring them into the necessary conditions of mental growth, — namely, into human society. But as little as the gardener makes the seed grow, do we make or teach the child to speak : in accordance with the laws, in one case of nature, in the other of mind, does the flower spring up on the one hand, the language in the consciousness of the child on the other." We are heartily tired, we must say, of these comparisons that go limping along on one foot, or even on hardly the decent stump of a foot, deficient in the essentials of an instructive analogy, fit only to confuse and mislead. Let Professor Steinthal show us, if he can, a seed which in the forest would send up an oak, in the orchard an apple-tree, in the garden a tulip or an onion, according to the bed in which you planted it, or whose product, if planted in a bed of mingled tulips and onions, would be both a tulip and an onion at the same time ; and then we will acknowledge that he has found something analogous with the child that grows up a user of language. What right, again, has he to assume that human society is the one necessary condition of mental growth ? Mere physical growth, with the experience and observation it brings, brings also mental growth ; but even our author, apparently, does not hold that it would bring language, or certainly not any given language. No ; the one thing above all others that human society affords the young child, is the opportunity to acquire the form of human culture possessed by that society, of whatsoever kind or degree it may be ; and because language is a part of culture, it, too, with all the incalculable advantages it brings, is acquired along with the rest.

Our author here quits for a moment his similitude of a seed, to point out "how rude the view was which regarded the invention of language as that of a machine, and the learning to speak of the present day as a new fabrication of an invention previously made." No doubt; we got past that long ago; only we were less impressed by the rudeness of the view itself than by the inutility of quoting and opposing it, and the helplessness of the reasoning by which it was opposed. If we have got to put in place of it the view that language is a growing organism or a sprouting germ, we shall wish that we had our old adversary back again. Next, reverting to and adopting an idea which he had in an earlier paragraph expressly repudiated, as a mere "playing with words," he pronounces language an invention to which men were impelled by a mental "instinct," and which is continually reproduced by the same "instinctive" powers; and declares that if we know these latter, we know also the first invention. To this we demur: comprehending the forces in action is a very different thing from comprehending the history of their action, and knowing what were its first products. These same identical forces, in their present observable modes of action, produce some hundreds or thousands of wholly dissimilar linguistic "inventions." Which of all these was the first invention like, or how did it differ from them all? The question, in short, is one of fact, and our author would fain treat it as one of theory only. The infinite diversity of human speech ought alone to be a sufficient bar to the assertion that an understanding of the powers of the soul involves the explanation of speech. There are current in the world say a thousand different names for *mind*, or *love*, or *finger*, or *two*, and each of them is current, not among minds of a certain degree of culture everywhere, but within certain geographical limits among minds of every grade; which of them is the product of an instinctive action of mental forces, and which of them could have been determined *a priori* by a knowledge, however penetrating and intimate, of those forces?

Did pine forests, continues Professor Steinthal, have to wait for man to plant them? Did they not grow of old after the same laws as when we now plant them? Then the language of the first men grew out of a like germ, and by the same laws, with that of every child of the present generation. We have already seen how "rude" this analogy is, and to how little valuable knowledge it conducts us. We pass it here, then, and go on to consider the further arguments by which it is followed up, and which are as extraordinary as anything in this extraordinary chapter.

We quote our author's own words: —

"But, it will be said, the conditions into which the germ fell were not the same, for the children of later generations come into the society of speakers, while the primitive man had to do at first with non-speakers. That is so. Still, from it follows only that the primitive man learned to speak under more unfavorable circumstances than our children now produce their speech ; namely, there was wanting to the conditions in which the former lived a single circumstance, the language of the society in which he lived. But this circumstance is not essential.[!] It is human society alone that is indispensable to man. If he has this, he will either learn to speak along with it, in case it is not yet able to speak, or, if it already possesses speech, he will necessarily create his own speech entirely after the analogy of that which his society has."

Here, we acknowledge, Professor Steinthal occupies a position one step nearer the truth than that of those who maintain, or imply, that a solitary man would form a language for himself. But he occupies it only by the sacrifice of consistency. Where are those creative forces of the human soul which the present century has learned to recognize as doing such wonderful things ? Shall we push the botanical parallel a little further, and say that the flowers which our "germ" produces are diœcious, or triœcious, or polyœcious, and cannot be expected to reproduce from a single individual ? The additional strain thus put upon it would be, to our sense at least, hardly perceptible. The burden of proof obviously rests upon those who hold that, while the creative force, as regards language, of the soul A, and the soul B, and the soul C is each equal to nothing, that of $A + B + C$ is of such immense power that only the nineteenth century has been found able to estimate it. Perhaps if Steinthal would really look into the question otherwise than psychologically, he would find that the only thing which human society furnishes, and which nothing else can furnish, toward the production of language, is the impulse to communication; and that no other inducement than this has operated or can operate to draw out the powers of the human soul in the direction of language, and bring them to action and to consciousness. Where, again, resides the " necessity " which compels the creative soul of each new member of a community to produce a language precisely accordant with that of the community? Individuals of every variety of endowment are born in every community, in every class of the community; why does each one grow up to talk after the same fashion as those with whom he associates; speaking not only their speech, but their dialect, with their limitations, their least peculiarities of tone and phrase, even their mispronunciations and grammatical irregularities and blunders? Here, too, if our author would study the facts and learn what they teach him, instead of trying to get above and domineer them, he might soon convince himself that children really do, as he himself maintained in an earlier part of the chapter, "appropriate" their speech; that they *learn* it, as much as they do mathematics or philosophy, only by a different process.

We quote the remainder of the paragraph, the last which we shall find it necessary to treat thus : —

" With reference to what has been set forth, we can already say what will become yet plainer hereafter ; man learns not so much to speak as to understand. Neither the primitive man nor the child of later generations makes or creates language, but it rises and grows in man ; he gives it birth (*er gebiert sie*). When it is born, he has to take up his own child, and learn to understand it. The primitive man in the primitive society, like the child in later times, has to learn, not to speak, but to understand. The latter learns to understand the developed speech of later generations ; the former, the language that is just breaking forth, just coming out into the air ; and as the child has not created the language which he learns, so also the primitive man learns·the primitive speech which he in like manner has not created ; which is, rather, only born from the soul of the primitive society."

This may be called the climax of the chapter. We have now our solution of the question complete. Do you ask what was the origin of language? Why, there was once a primitive society, and (more fortunately endowed than " corporations " in our days) it had a primitive soul ; and this soul possessed primitive creative powers, which were not possessed by the souls of the individuals composing the community, although these too were creative ; and these powers, not by creation, or invention, or making of any kind, but simply obstetrically, gave birth to primitive speech. But that is not the sole origin ; the same obstetrical process repeats itself each day in the soul of every new member of the human race ; language " originates " anew in every individual. Are you satisfied now ?

Could there be more utter mockery than this ? We ask for bread, and a stone is thrown us. What have these statements to do with the origin of language ? Why all this long talk in order to arrive at a result so simple ? We could have conceded at the outset that it is the powers with which man is endowed that produce language, and that they are on the whole the same powers in every individual of the race, and powers which, through the whole history of the race and of language, act on the whole in the same way. Yet their products, in different communities and in different ages of the same community, are exceedingly different. There are thousands of dialects to-day, the speakers of each of which are unintelligible to those of every other ; and each is so unlike its own ancestor, from time to time back in the past, that no one would be intelligible to the speakers of any other. What is the reason of all this ? and what was the still earlier and unrecorded condition out of which each, or all together, arose ? Respecting each word of every language now existing, we know that it is used by the new individuals born into its community because it was used before, and the new-comer had only to imitate his predecessors, to do as they set him the example. Now what did the first speaking individuals do, who had no predecessors to set them an example ? What, or of what kind, were the significant utterances they used, and how did these obtain their significance ? To reply to these questions is to determine the origin of language ; and Professor Steinthal does not so much as lift his finger toward answering them. He shows the same incapacity of appreciation respecting the main point as we had to notice in regard to one or two preliminary points at the commencement of the discussion. We have an historical inquiry before us, and he wants to force it into a metaphysical form.

He ignores all that has been accomplished in our day by the historical study of language; there is not a sentence in the chapter, so far as we have observed, which implies the existence of such a branch of knowledge as comparative philology. Whatever he may have learned and done in that direction, he keeps it out of sight here, and lets us behold only the psychologist. He ignores all that has been done by anthropology, in tracing out the history of other departments of human culture, and determining the general character of the process of development by which man has become what he is. We can hardly say that his theory is antagonistic to these sciences, or inconsistent with them, so much as that it has nothing in common with them. It belongs to the period before they came into being. Born in the latter half of the nineteenth century, it is nevertheless the child of the eighteenth, or of any earlier century you may choose. There was needed to produce it only an exalted idea of the creative forces of the human soul; and that, we venture to say, might have been found in at least a few exalted heads among the philosophers of any age. This may be, after all, the deeper reason why it seeks its antagonists among the linguistic theorizers of another century than ours. Views similar to those which we have been sustaining in opposition to it have been within not many years drawn out in a systematic and consistent form, based upon the established facts of linguistic and anthropological science, and extended by inductive methods over the whole ground of linguistic study, from the present time back to the beginning; and here, it might fairly be thought, Professor Steinthal would have found foes better worth contending with, and an opportunity to test the soundness of his views by seeing how effectively they could be made to confront the living and aggressive views of others; but he does not take the slightest notice of them, direct or implied. References, it is true, to other students of language, of any class, are very rare in the volume ; the psychologic method is mainly independent of all aid, save from the soul of the investigator.

There remains, however, one more shift of ground for our author to make in the progress of his ratiocination. As he has successively set up the provisional assumptions that language is an invention and a product, and, after reasoning awhile upon them, has got above and discarded them, so he now treats in the same way his last thesis, that language is a birth. Noting that speech does not exist in grammar and dictionary, but in the actual use and utterance of men, he pronounces it " no abiding existence, but a fleeting activity." It is " a mere possibility, which under due circumstances expresses itself, is exercised, and then becomes reality, but only for the moment. . . . . Language is not a something, like powder, but an occurrence, like the explosion ; it is not an organ, like the eye and ear, but a capacity and activity, like seeing and hearing." All this, again, is in our opinion very verbiage, mere turbid talk, and mainly growing out of the fact that our author does not distinguish between language as a faculty, or the power to speak, and language as an actual concrete possession, or the set of audible signs which we first hear, then understand, then learn ourselves to make and use. The lack of this distinction underlies a considerable part of the false reasoning of the whole chapter, but it is especially fatal here and in what follows. The fault, it must be confessed, is in no small measure that of language itself. If the term *sprache* in German, and " speech " and " language " in English, did not apply indifferently to both things, if we were compelled to use one word where we meant the faculty, and another where we meant our current phraseology, the words and forms we make, half the mistaken views of language now in vogue would lose their foundation, and become even transparently absurd. The power to say " water " and to use it as the sign of a certain conception is a part of my human nature, shared by me with every normally constituted human being ; it is a " capacity and activity," though in a sense so different from those of seeing and hearing that we can only marvel at Professor Steinthal's mentioning them together, and fear that there is unsoundness in his psychology as well as in his linguistic philosophy. Seeing and hearing are capacities with which the will has nothing directly to do ; they are passive, receptive ; only refrain from shutting our eyes and ears, and visible and audible things cannot but impress the sense, and impress it practically alike in all men ; while, on the other hand, an act of the will is necessary to every sound we utter, as much as to every gesture we make. In short, we have here one more of those unfortunate comparisons of which our author is so prolific in this chapter. But the word "water" is neither a capacity nor an activity; it is a *product*, not less so than is a machine, though in quite another way; it is capable of being first originated, or produced, or invented, at a given time, and thenceforward reproduced by learning and imitation; it is capable of being described, and depicted, and represented, and set down in dictionary, and its use regulated by grammar. Think of a grammar of capacity, a dictionary of activities! And of such products as "water" is all human speech, in the concrete sense of the term, composed. When, then, the paragraph goes on to say, "Such was and is language at all times. The primitive man saw not otherwise and spoke not otherwise than we at the moment when we speak," we answer that the statement is either a truism or a falsity, according as it is understood; and that, as the writer appears to suppose it has both senses, he is partly right and partly wrong; but that the truth is a worthless one, and all the point lies in the part that is false. That the primitive man had a mind like ours and used organs like ours, and that their joint working was after much the same fashion as in us, is so palpably true as to be almost impertinent; but that he said "water," as we do, and for the reason that he had heard some one else say it before him, is not true; and we crave to know whether he said anything when he had formed the conception of water (a conception which he was fully capable of forming without speech); and, if he did, what it was, and why.

That which follows is in the same strain. There is, we are told, absolutely no essential distinction between the original creation of language, the process of children's learning to speak, and the speaking which now goes on daily and hourly everywhere where human beings are to be found. There is no origin of language, otherwise than as it originates anew in every word we utter. And now all is finished. To adopt one of our author's favorite comparisons, the question of origin is not a substantial thing, like powder; it is a mere fleeting aspect, like the explosion; a little smouch, a momentary bad smell, and it is over; we are left with only the mortification of having concerned ourselves about a matter in which there was absolutely nothing.

Here, for the first time, Professor Steinthal is seized with a slight misgiving. May not his conclusions strike some persons as paradoxical? May it not appear that he arrives at this general identification of everything in language by ignoring essential distinctions? We seem to hear from his readers one universal cry of assent. But it does not reach his ears; and he proceeds to reason down his misgiving, after his peculiar fashion. Accepting, apparently, as impregnably established the general impression that there must be something deep and wonderful about the origin of language, he endeavors to remove any possible scruples on our part as to the identity of everything else with it, by proving that these everythings are also deep and wonderful, each in its way. In the first place, he assumes that any one of us who is profound enough will have already convinced himself that children's learning to speak is just as mysterious as the primitive man's creation of speech. We confess, however, that we are not profound enough for that; that the acquisition of language by children does not seem to us any mystery at all. We stand in an attitude of constant wonder and admiration before the human mind, with its wealth of endowments, its infinite acquirements, and the unlimited possibilities of its future; but that a child, after hearing a certain word used some scores or hundreds of times, comes to understand what it means, and then, a little later, to pronounce and use it, perhaps feebly and blunderingly at first, — this does not seem to us any more astonishing than the exercise of the same child's capacities in other directions; in acquiring, for instance, the command of a musical instrument, or mastering the intricacies of mathematics. Our admiration is called out in a much higher degree by considering what this simple instrumentality finally comes to be in the matured man, what power it gives him over himself and others, and the secrets of the world about him. And we wonder most of all when we consider the history of language, and see how its growth has gone hand in hand with the cultural development of the race, at once the result and the efficient aid of the latter. In fact, we think our appreciation of the wondrous character of language a vastly higher one than Professor Steinthal's; for, while he holds that any two or three human beings, putting their heads together, in any age and under any circumstances, not only can, but of necessity must, produce it in all its essential features, we think it a possible result only of the accumulated labors of a series of generations, working on step by step, making every acquired item the means of new acquisitions. But let us see what he has to say in the way of setting forth the deep mystery of our daily speech, that we may be thereby led to regard ourselves as the true originators of language. " Only notice how, on the one hand, a person speaking in a strange tongue, *with which he is not very familiar,* gathers the words laboriously together in his memory and combines them with reflection; and how, on the other hand, when we use our mother-tongue, the words flow in upon us one after another in right order and in proper form." Well, we notice it, as directed; but we fail to see the mystery. On the contrary, we think our author has unwittingly solved the whole problem by the suggestion which we have italicized; the one language is familiar, the other is not. So the practised pianist sits down at his instrument with a sheet of dots and lines before him, which to another are devoid of all meaning, a mere intricate puzzle; and his fingers move over the white and black keys as if they went of themselves, without the direction of his will, and the puzzle is translated, at first sight, into ravishing music. But give him a new-fangled method of notation, " with which he is not familiar," and turn his key-board the other way, so that the tones go down in the scale from left to right, and behold, how changed! now he labors painfully from note to note, stumbling and tripping at every step. Or change the mathematician's whole system of signs and symbols, and see what a weight you have hung at his heels, until he shall have worn it out by sheer dint of dragging it over hard places. Let one pass, however, a series of years in complete divorcement from his mother-tongue, and in the enforced daily and hourly practice of another, and the balance of familiarity is shifted; the latter becomes the one which he wields with ease and adroitness, the former the one in whose use he stumbles, and has to labor and reflect. Is there anything in all this that is not fully explainable on the supposition that language is an acquired instrumentality? Is there, indeed, anything that is explainable on any other supposition ? Here, once more, as it appears to us, our author has failed to see the point of his illustration, and draws from it an unwarranted conclusion. All our readiness to appreciate the wonders of language will not lead us to see anything marvellous in the fact that one manages a great and intricate instrument with which he is familiar better than one with which he is unfamiliar. Next we are called upon to observe that the difficulties and imperfections of some men's expression in their own mother-tongue show us how admirable is that gift of speech by which the word flows forth of itself. Very well ; but what follows further ? Simply that men's gifts are various. Just so one person can never learn to be more than a passable pianist, if even that ; and there is an immense difference in the skill and effect with which two individuals will wield the resources of the higher mathematics. We by no means jump from this to the conclusion that music and mathematics did not have their weak beginnings and their slow development, and that the living musician or mathematician is in essentially the same position with every one of his craft from the beginning, and really produces or brings to birth all that they have recorded for him to learn.

And so our author goes on from item to item, where it would be tedious to follow him ; everywhere missing the true analogy and suggesting in its place a false one, and therefore deducing from it an argument which is overthrown as soon as stated. We will pass over all of them excepting the last, where he points out that " many a one who at other times is but a stammerer, becomes eloquent when he falls under the influence of passion (*in Leidenschaft gerät*). Just in an excited condition of mind, then, when the clearness of his consciousness is diminished, when he is carried away, the fount of speech flows fullest ; for [reverting suddenly to his favorite obstetrical parallel], the more painful the throes, the easier the birth." Disregarding the slightly paradoxical character of the last statement (as if the throes were not a part of the process of birth itself), as well as the characteristic weakness of the comparison in the essential point (for, to make it good, a violent headache, or severe wrenches of rheumatism, or a sound whipping, ought to make labor easy), we would urge in reply that excitement, up to a certain point, has never been looked upon as dulling the powers of action, either mental or physical. The man who in the exaltation of passion would show a capacity of doing and daring, of exerting powers of attack and defence, of judging and deciding, which in his cooler moments he never dreamed himself to possess, need not feel that there is anything mysterious in his heightened power of expression under such circumstances. If he can wield the club or discourse upon the musical instrument the better for his passion, he may also better wield the word, without our needing to infer thence that the word is anything more than the instrument of the mind's acts. This, of course, without implying that there are not kinds and degrees of passion which may lame one's powers, either of speech or of action.

We must pronounce, then, Professor Steinthal's attempt to explain away the paradoxical character of his universal identification a complete failure, a mere continuation of the same sophistical reasonings by which he originally arrived at it.

After all this he declines to maintain " that, notwithstanding the essential likeness between the speaking of the primitive man and that of the child and the adult, there are not also, on the other hand, accompanying conditions which modify these three processes, and give to each a peculiar character. Only the differences cannot be understood except on the basis of the similarity." And so, it was necessary to lay down as a foundation that speech is always a creation, its origin the eternal and unchangeable origin of a power and activity in the consciousness of men ; then to proceed to find the point of mental development at which speech necessarily breaks forth, and, to this end, to plunge into a psychological development of the processes of human thought. Accordingly, the title of the first succeeding part is " Psychical Mechanics," followed later by " History of Psychical Development."

That this is a direct reversal of the true process we are fully convinced. We repeat in summary the truths which we have endeavored above to establish: that language in the concrete sense, the sum of words and phrases by which any man expresses his thought, is an historical product, and must be studied, before all and above all, in an historical method. The mental development which it accompanies, and of which it is at once the result and the aiding cause or instrument, is also an historical one, and involves among its elements the whole sum of human knowledge and variety of human institutions. The soul of man has grown from what it was once only potentially to what it is now actually, only by means of its own gradual accumulations of observation and reasoning, of experience and deduction. This historical growth is not to be read in the growth at the present day of an individual soul, surrounded from its birth by all the appliances of culture, with instructors on every hand, with the results of others' labors piled about it for it to grasp, in a profusion that defies its highest powers of acquisition. It is to be read only in the recorded and inferable facts of human history itself; these are to be first striven after and determined by every possible means; and from these we are to reason back to the states of mind that produced them. Doubtless a comprehension of the workings of the human soul under its present conditions will be an aid of high importance, but it will be only an aid. As well found the study of the history of astronomy on that of the laws of planetary perturbations as the study of the history of language on psychology. Psychology may be a valuable handmaid to linguistic science, but it must be a harmful mistress; it may follow alongside of historical investigation, guarding and checking every conclusion, but it has no right to claim to go on in advance and lead the way.

Or, if the case be not so, let it be shown to be otherwise; only do not ask us to accept the reasonings of this chapter, or anything like them, as in the least degree proving it otherwise. If this is the best that can be said in behalf of what we may call the psychologico-obstetrical theory of language, then that theory is an irretrievable failure. We have gone through our author's reasonings in detail, quoting in his own words all the principal passages, that there might be no chance of our misinterpreting his meaning, or of omitting what was essential to the right understanding of the rest; and it is seen with what result. We have not found telling expositions, arguments generally sound and cogent, with here and there a slip or a flaw; we have found nothing but mistaken facts and erroneous deductions. The chapter is not entitled to be called able; even a false doctrine ought to admit of a better defence; we almost feel that we ought to apologize for occupying with its refutation so much of the time of our readers. But we know not where to find at present anything better on this side. Steinthal would, we imagine, be put forward by his party as their strongest man. It is, then, as the representative of a school and a tendency in linguistics that we have taken him up; to show how laming and disabling is the system and method in which he, with his coadjutors, works. Some will say, doubtless, that the fault lies with the metaphysical attitude of mind; that the metaphysician, in his efforts to get into the *a priori* position, to face and dominate his facts, really turns his back upon the foremost of them, as they surround him and drag him on in the opposite direction to that in which he fancies himself to be moving. We would not go so far as that; we are willing to allow, at least provisionally, that metaphysical inquiry carries one up into heights and down into depths that are not otherwise attainable, and that in its pursuit is the loftiest exertion and the keenest enjoyment of which man is capable; the metaphysicians say so, and surely they ought to know. We only demand that when they come down, or up, on to middle ground, when they take hold of matters that lie within the ken of common sense, their views and conclusions shall square with those of common sense; or, if it be not so, that they shall be able to show us why it is not, and to convince our common sense by their uncommon. The upholders of views akin with Steinthal's still constitute — as we hold, merely by force of tradition from the centuries of darkness — the largest and most influential body of writers on the theory of language, and they look down with contempt upon the opposing party as lost in the mazes of superficiality and philisterism. In our view, their profundity is merely subjective, and their whole system is destined to be swept away and succeeded by the scientific, the inductive. This alone is in unison with the best tendencies of modern thought; this alone can bring the science of language into harmonious alliance with the other branches of knowledge respecting man, his endowments and his history.

W. D. WHITNEY.

TRANSACTIONS

OF THE

AMERICAN PHILOLOGICAL ASSOCIATION,

1881.

***

I. — *On Mixture in Language.*

By W. D. WHITNEY,

PROFESSOR IN YALE COLLEGE.

A few years ago (1876), there appeared in England a
volume (8vo. pp. viii., 126) on Mixed Languages, by a Mr.
Clough, who calls it a " prize essay," though without betray-
ing who should have awarded it a prize. It takes for its text
a quotation from M. Müller, to this effect : " In the course of
these considerations, we had to lay down two axioms, to
which we shall frequently have to appeal in the progress of
our investigations. The first declares grammar to be the
most essential element, and therefore the ground of classification in all languages which have produced a definite grammatical articulation ; the second denies the possibility of a
mixed language." (Lectures, 1st series, 6th edition, p. 86.)
Mr. Clough's work is meant to be a refutation of this doctrine of Müller's ; and he enters upon his task thus :

" Certain philologists have stated that a mixed language is an impossibility, but the truth of the axiom may well be doubted ; indeed,
as it would, perhaps, be impossible to find any modern language
which contains no foreign elements, it is evident that the principles
involved in the question are fundamental.

" Language consists of three parts — sounds, words, and grammar ;
and a mixture in any one of these points produces a mixed language."

Mr. Clough, it will be seen, absolutely declines to take his stand upon the same point of view with Mr. Müller, and therefrom to criticise, and if possible prove unfounded, the latter's statements ; he will look only on his own side of the shield. For Müller, in the next paragraph to that quoted as above by his opponent, goes on to say : " There is hardly a language which in one sense may not be called a mixed language. No nation or tribe was ever so completely isolated as not to admit the importation of a certain number of foreign words. In some instances these imported words have changed the whole native aspect of the language, and have even acquired a majority over the native element." And, a page or two later : " There is, perhaps, no language so full of words evidently derived from the most distant sources as English." Only he adds, still further on (p. 89) : " Languages, however, though mixed in their dictionary, can never be mixed in their grammar." Müller's view, then, plainly admits of being laid down in this form : 1. There is a certain part of every language, namely its grammar, which appears to be inaccessible to mixture ; 2. In virtue of this fact, a mixed language is an impossibility ; 3. Hence, the unmixableness of language is an axiom of linguistic science. Mr. Clough should have set before him the doctrine in some such form as the above, and then have addressed himself in an orderly manner to its refutation. Instead of so doing, he goes laboriously onward, gathering evidences of mixture, according to his definition of the term, which do not at all touch his antagonist ; since the latter, acknowledging them all, nevertheless declares that they do not constitute mixture according to *his* definition of the term. Mr. Clough does not disengage the merely verbal question — whether any one has good and sufficient reason for denying the name of "mixed" to a language which may have imported so much foreign material as to have " its whole native aspect changed " thereby — from the real question, as to whether there are in fact any limits to mixture, and if so, what and why ; and on this account, as well as by reason of his generally loose and credulous method, his work must be admitted to contribute nothing of value to the elucidation of the subject.

That the subject, however, urgently calls for further elucidation, will hardly be denied. Thus, Lepsius, in the Introduction to his recent Nubian Grammar (p. lxxxv.), says: "It is at present an assumption usually made, that the vocabulary of one language may indeed to a great extent be transferred to another, but not its grammatical forms and their use. The linguistic history of Africa . . . shows this to be a prejudice;" and he sets up a theory of the relations of African languages which seems to imply grammatical mixture on a very large scale. It is, indeed, this so sharp antithesis between the views of two highly considered authorities — the one stigmatizing as an assumption and a prejudice what the other lays down as an axiom — that has suggested the preparation of the present paper.

As regards, now, in the first place, the axiomatic character of any view that we may come to hold concerning the mixableness or unmixableness of language, the sooner such a claim is abandoned the better. The use of the term "axiom" is probably not to be seriously pressed against Mr. Müller. If not a mere slip of the pen (which it can hardly be, as he has let it stand in edition after edition since objection was raised against it), it is at any rate only one of those pieces of genial inaccuracy which, as he often pleads, he "has permitted himself." He means no more than that the doctrine under discussion seems so well established and is so generally accepted that it does not enter into his own mind to question it. He perhaps would designate it more deliberately as a fundamental principle, comparable not with "things equal to the same thing are equal to one another," but rather with, for instance, "the sum of the angles of a triangle equals two right angles." Even this, however, would be a great deal too much. It would imply that Müller, or some one else, had so grounded the unmixableness of grammar on the bottom facts of human nature and of the nature of language, had so demonstrated its inevitableness from the acknowledged laws of linguistic growth, that no well informed and sound-minded man could

have any inclination to doubt it.   How far that is from being
so is shown by the circumstance that Lepsius unceremoni-
ously rejects it.   No writer on geometry could throw over
the principle that the angles of a triangle equal two right
angles, and expect to command any attention for his reasonings.   But Lepsius's theory of African language is received,
as it well deserves to be, with all respect, as one that calls
for the most careful examination, and may perhaps be found
to compel acceptance.   It is interesting to see how Müller
himself handles his "axiom."   After asserting, as quoted
above, that "languages can never be mixed in their grammar,"
he immediately adds : "Hervas was told by missionaries that,
in the middle of the eighteenth century, the Araucans used
hardly a single word which was not Spanish, though they
preserved both the grammar and the syntax of their own
native speech."   This, from its position and bearings, must
be meant as an example of the evidence of the doctrine : a
curious "axiom" that, certainly, which rests in part upon
what some missionaries told somebody: perhaps they did
not know ; or perhaps neither party realized the importance
and wide bearing of the point in question.   Müller goes on
in the next paragraph : "This is the reason why grammar
is made the criterion of the relationship and the base of the
classification in almost all languages ; and it follows, therefore, as a matter of course, that in the classification and in
the science of language, it is impossible to admit the existence of a mixed idiom."   These statements seem neither
exact nor clear.   The value of grammar as a criterion by no
means rests solely on its unmixableness ; nor does that value
furnish a reason for denying the possibility of mixture : to
assert this is simply to reason in a circle.   There is no need,
however, of spending any more time upon the point.   To set
up the unmixableness of grammar as an axiom is to provoke
and justify its rejection as a prejudiced assumption ; if it is
to be forced on us, without discussion and exposition, as
something intuitive, it may be discarded in like manner,
without refutation, by one to whose inner sense it does not
commend itself.

In opposition to Müller's view, it may be claimed, without any fear of successful contradiction, that what we hold and are justified in holding as to the mixture of languages is a pure scientific induction from the observed facts of mixed languages, dependent for its authority and its extensibility to further cases, on the one hand, upon the number and variety of the cases already observed, and, on the other hand, upon the degree of success with which the facts they present have been reasoned out and put in connection with the fundamental principles of language-using and language-making. That, in either of these essential respects, the subject has been fully worked up, no one would be justified in asserting; yet there is a considerable body of knowledge respecting it, enough to establish among students of language a prevalent doctrine, held with a fair degree of confidence, though also held open to modification by further evidence, or by the bringing-in of examples radically different from those thus far taken into account. What this doctrine is, what are its foundations, and what its limitations, a brief exposition may here help to show.

The general *rationale* of the process of borrowing out of one language into another is simple enough, and may be illustrated from any tongue. It rests, of course, with everything else in linguistic science, upon these fundamental principles: that spoken signs have nothing to do with conceptions except historically (that is, there is no internal, substantial, necessary tie between a given conception and a given sign for it); and that, consequently, a language has nothing to do except historically with a given race, but is, like any other element of acquired civilization, transmissible not only from generation to generation, but also, under favoring circumstances, from community to community, from race to race. The individual man is everywhere only seeking after a sign — not one existing φύσει, but one usable θέσει — by means of which he may communicate with his fellow-man respecting some object of common knowledge and conception; and he is always ready to take it where he finds it handiest. If, then, we learn of or introduce to our own use something new from

outside our borders, unnamed in our speech, we are likely
enough, instead of making a name for it out of our own resources, to adopt along with it some more or less successful
imitation of its native name : it may be some concrete thing,
like *tobacco, tea, canoe, shawl, alcohol ;* or something more ideal,
institutional, like *sabbath, jubilee, algebra, taboo, check* (and
check and *checker* and *exchequer* are a striking example of the
exuberant life which such a chance adoption may win), and so
on. There needs only a knowledge on the part of the speakers of one language of a designation used in another language
and then a sufficient inducement to its use by themselves also,
and they proceed to use it : nothing in the nature of language
stands in the way of such an appropriation ; it is in strictest
accordance with the method by which every speaker has acquired every expression he employs. Hence, wherever two
tongues come in contact, each is liable to borrow something
from the other ; and more or less, according to wholly inde-
terminable circumstances : the measure and nature of the
intercourse, the resources of the respective tongues, their
degree of facilitating kinship or structural accordance, and so
forth. And there are (as was noticed above) few tongues in
the world which are not to this extent mixed. The language
of a civilized people like our own, having intercourse with
nearly all the other peoples of the globe, and laying them all
under contribution to its comfort or entertainment or zeal for
knowledge, shows a wonderful variety of items of speech thus
borrowed. The degree is different in different divisions of
our language : thus, the English of India has quite a vocabulary of native Hindu terms which are either unknown or unfamiliar to us and to most of the English-speakers of Britain ;
the same is true of the English of South Africa ; and the
same is true, to a certain extent, of the English of America.

This might be called the sporadic or fortuitous method of
borrowing. It is, however, only the same process on a larger
scale that goes on when any community makes itself the
pupil of another in respect to any part of its civilization.
Where institutions, beliefs, ceremonies, arts, sciences, and the
like, pass from race to race, names cannot help going with

them. The leading examples of this which history offers are familiar to all, and need only be alluded to. The spread of Christianity over Europe carried with it a certain number of Hebrew words, from the dead tongue of the Old Testament; but a vastly greater number of Greek and Latin words, from the living tongue of the New Testament, and from those of the European peoples who propagated the new religion. And who propagated also a higher civilization along with it; the two are not to be separated from one another; it is their joint influence that made the Greek and Latin vocabularies mines from which all the languages of Europe should freely draw new resources of expression. The extension of Mohammedanism has made Arabic occupy a similar position in reference to the tongues of all Mohammedan peoples: greatly varied in detail, according to the variety of circumstances of each case, the combination of religious with general cultural instruction, and actual mixture of races. The relation of Chinese to Japanese and some other neighboring tongues is probably the next most striking example; then that of Sanskrit to the vernaculars of India in general; and as minor instances may be cited the influence of Swedish upon Finnish, and of German upon Hungarian. There is no definable limit to the amount of accessions that may be brought in this way into a language; but they can hardly fail to leave untouched its forms, and the central kernel of its vocabulary, its words of commonest use.

A somewhat different case is that in which there takes place a noteworthy mixture of peoples: that is, a mingling in the same larger or smaller community of persons of discordant inherited speech. But here, too, the special circumstances are infinitely varied, with corresponding variety in the linguistic result. The circumstance which most directly represents the disturbing cause is the comparative number of the one and of the other element of population in the mixed community; yet this appears practically to be of minor consequence only. The blood of a people may, for example, become prevailingly different from what it was, by a process of gradual mixture, such as is now bringing a never ending current of immigration to our American shores, with only a minimal effect on the original speech ; and, on the other hand, the great bulk of a community may give up its old tongue for that of a small intruded element, as in the case of the countries of southern Europe which were Romanized and in consequence Latinized : and between these two extremes lie numberless intermediates. We may say, in a general way, that the outcome of a mixture of population is of three kinds. First, under the government of peculiar isolating conditions, the elements of the mixed population maintain each its own linguistic independency, with perhaps no more mixture of speech than takes place between separate communities : as is the case, on a large scale, under Moslem domination in the border-lands of Turkish, Armenian, Persian, Syriac, and Arabic speech, where almost every individual is bilingual, speaking his own inherited dialect along with that of a neighbor, or with the general official language added ; while another curious example is said to have been furnished at a certain period by the discordant speech of the Carib warriors and their captured wives. Secondly, as in the case of the Latinized countries of southern Europe, referred to above, and in numerous others, the language of one division of the mixed community becomes, almost without mixture, the language of the whole. We can trace in a measure, but only in a measure, the particular influences, with their mode of action, that have brought about such a result as this ; much about them is obscure and surprising. Thirdly, there arises a notably mixed language, containing abundant elements derived from both the one and the other of the tongues whose speakers were brought together to form the community.

This last case is evidently the only one with which we have to concern ourselves here ; and of it a very conspicuous example is our own English. There is no known mixed language of developed structure and of high cultivation in which the process of mixture has gone further. The two composing elements were, so far as one could have estimated them in advance, of nearly equal force ; which of them would win the upper hand might have appeared doubtful — as, indeed, it long did appear doubtful. We may expect to find English, then, a normal illustration of the processes of language-mixture. It ought to be the instance most thoroughly studied and best understood in all its parts; for the original ingredients of the mixture are perfectly known, being both recorded in earlier literatures ; and the steps of combination are set forth all along in contemporary documents. It is, perhaps, better understood than any other similar case in language-history ; yet that is far from implying that it is fully mastered, or that opinions are not still at variance respecting matters of prime importance connected with it : thus, for example, as to how much of the decay and loss of former Germanic structure in English is due to the mixture ; as to whether the process has or has not extended to the grammar of the language ; as to the effect of foreign influence on the structure and arrangement of the English sentence ; and so on. The subject still calls for skilful and wary investigation, in order to be comprehended in its details ; but some of the main results for the general theory of language-mixture may perhaps already with sufficient certainty be gathered off the surface of the phenomena it exhibits.

The first and most important of these is, that the case is not, after all, essentially different from those already noticed. We have still one language, namely the Anglo-Saxon or native English, borrowing and incorporating crude material from the other, the intrusive Norman French. Of a meeting of the two ingredients on equal terms, and their amalgamation in any part, either of grammar or of vocabulary, the one contributing an element and the other another element of the same kind, there is no sign whatever. This appears most clearly in the system of inflection : not a trace of Romanic conjugation or declension shows itself in the new mixed speech ; the imported verbs and nouns are assimilated entirely to those of the borrowing tongue, being varied in form with whatever apparatus the latter has still left. But it appears also in the system of derivation : such suffixes and prefixes as native English retained in actual living use for the making of new words, it proceeded to apply to the borrowed material ; and the derivatives so made are no more to be accounted as of "mixed" character than are the inflectional forms with Romanic stems and Germanic endings. And the same thing is to be seen not less clearly in the stock of words: here, too, whatever is more formal or structural in character remains in that degree free from the intrusion of foreign material. Thus, of the parts of speech, the pronouns and articles, the prepositions and conjunctions, continue to be purely Germanic; and, in the more general vocabulary, the same is true of the numerals. In brief, the borrowing is of the grosser elements of speech, of raw material, to be worked into proper syntactical shape for direct use by the word-making processes of the borrower. The exemption of "grammar" from mixture is no isolated fact; the grammatical apparatus merely resists intrusion most successfully, in virtue of its being the least material and the most formal part of the language. In a scale of constantly increasing difficulty it occupies the extreme place.

Now what is thus true of English is believed to be essentially true also of every other observed case of language-mixture. Such a thing as the adoption on the part of one tongue, by a direct process, of any part or parts of the formal structure of another tongue has, so far as is known, not come under the notice of linguistic students during the recorded periods of language-history. So far as these are concerned, it appears to be everywhere the case that when the speakers of two languages, A and B, are brought together into one community, there takes place no amalgamation of their speech, into A B; but for a time the two maintain their own several identity, only as modified each by the admission of material from the other in accordance with the ordinary laws of mixture: we may call them A^b and B^a; and finally, one of these two prevails over the other, and becomes the speech of the whole community: this is still either A^b or B^a, and not A B.

This, then, is at least a general principle, derived by legitimate deduction from a considerable number and variety of cases. Into an absolute law of universal language, however, it can be converted only by a successful analysis of the psychological processes involved, and a demonstration that in no conceivable case could their action lead to a different result. And until that work is accomplished, we shall doubtless meet now and then with the claim that such and such a case presents peculiar conditions which separate it from the general class, and that some remote and difficult problem in language-history is to be solved by admitting promiscuous mixture. Any one advancing such a claim, however, does it at his peril; the burden of proof is upon him to show what the peculiar conditions might have been, and how they should have acted to produce the exceptional result; he will be challenged to bring forward some historically authenticated case of analogous results; and his solution, if not rejected altogether, will be looked upon with doubt and misgiving until he shall have complied with these reasonable requirements.

It also seems a fair and obvious inference that the more discordant the structure of the borrowing language and the language borrowed from, the less will be the chance that any items of structure should be transferred from the one to the other. As between two nearly related dialects of the same tongue, the possibility of transfer would be greatest; the slight existing differences might be with least difficulty disregarded. French and English, though ultimately related, and corresponding with one another in all the main features of structure, were yet, as we have seen, sufficiently held apart by their difference in details to prevent structural mixture — just as effectively, indeed, as Arabic and Persian, or Turkish and Arabic or Persian, where the discordance is much profounder. If we dispute, therefore, the validity of an *à priori* claim that a prefix-language and a suffix-language — as, for example, a South African and a Hamitic tongue — might mingle in a manner seen to be impracticable in the case of two Indo-European dialects, we do not at all set up unmixableness of grammar as a self-evident truth; we are only refusing to admit the more difficult of two processes until the less difficult shall be proved possible.

It appears, then, that in Müller's alleged "axiom" there is

perhaps (until the contrary be shown) so much legitimately deduced truth as this : that two languages never meet and mingle their grammar on equal terms. But in the form in which he puts it, that "languages can never be mixed in their grammar," it must be refused acceptance ; for grammatical mixture by a secondary process actually does take place, and its effects are clearly to be seen in English — as we may next proceed to notice.

Whenever crude material of foreign origin is introduced by borrowing into the full vernacular use of a language, it becomes an integral part of that language, undistinguished, except to reflective and learned study, from the native material. It enters, for example, into the mind of no ordinary English speaker to recognize some of his words as coming from a Romanic source and others from a Germanic. To him, the relation of *pure* and *purity* and of *envy* and *envious* is the same with that of *good* and *goodness* and of *child* and *childish.* But he has in everyday use so many words plainly made from others by the added endings *ness* and *ish* that those endings are distinctly before his mind as by their addition impressing certain modifications of meaning ; and he therefore goes on to make with them, by analogy, new words like those already in his use. It needs, then, only that he have taken in pairs enough like *pure, purity,* and *envy, envious,* and he will in the same manner and for the same reason make new words with *ity* and *ous* — heedless, because ignorant, whether the primitives to which he applies those endings are Romanic or Germanic by origin. Such new words are made, to be sure, more freely and abundantly from Romanic primitives, both because the analogies are in themselves closer and more suggestive, and because the making is in part by the learned, who know and are mindful of the proprieties of combination, and whose influence is cast against the admission and retention of what they deem improper combinations ; and hence we have, of words not French, but made of French elements on our own soil, *duty* beside *beauty,* and *duteous* and *beauteous* beside *envious,* and so on in abundance. But we have also not a few like *oddity* and *murderous,* made with

Romanic formatives from Germanic primitives : well known examples showing other affixes are *atonement, eatable, talkative, disbelief, retake, derail.* Such cases are in part isolated ones, too sporadic and fortuitous to prove much respecting the character of the tongue in which they occur ; but in part also they are specimens of classes, and unmistakable evidences that the resources of formation of a Romanic tongue have been adopted by a Germanic tongue and made its own resources of formation likewise. Perhaps the most notable of their class are the trio *ize, ist, ism,* which have become real living English formative elements, used with constantly increasing freedom in making new words, and for popular as well as for learned use.

No language of which this can be said has the right to claim that it has successfully maintained against mixture the purity of its grammar. For there is no good reason whatever for limiting (as Müller, in order to save his " axiom " from being proved untrue even as a fact, seems inclined to do) the name of grammar to the inflective apparatus of a language ; it belongs equally to the derivative apparatus. There is no line to be drawn between the added elements that make a person or tense or number, and those that make a degree of comparison, or an ordinal, or an adverb, or a noun or adjective. Moreover, it is not inconceivable that a foreign mode of inflection should get itself introduced into a language, after the same fashion as a foreign mode of word-making. We have received into English some classical singulars and plurals together — such as *phenomenon* and *phenomena, stratum* and *strata ;* and there is no necessary reason, none inherent in the nature of things, why these cases might not be numerous enough to prompt an extension by analogy to new formations. Doubtless this is more difficult, and less likely to occur, than the extension of use of derivative endings ; but so is the latter more difficult and less likely than the taking in of new words ; and if the one difficulty has actually been overcome by the pressure of circumstances, the other can by sufficient pressure be in like manner overcome.

While, therefore, we find no warrant in the historically

authenticated facts of language for admitting a mixture of the grammar of two languages by a first process, we see clearly that any language having a developing structure may become mixed in grammar secondarily, by processes of growth involving the use of borrowed material. In whatever department there is growth, thither the foreign elements can penetrate. This appears equally in those parts of the vocabulary which are most akin with grammatical structure. Form-words are no more taken in directly than are formative parts of words ; yet there is hardly a class of such in English that has not come to allow intrusion from the French. It is part of the living growth of English expression to make prepositions and conjunctions out of other material — nouns and adjectives and adverbs; and hence we have Latin stuff in so common an adverb-preposition as *around*, and, still more strikingly, in *because*, one of the commonest and most indispensable of our subordinating conjunctions. No force of which we have knowledge could have brought an adverb of degree — for example, *très* in its older form — straight out of French use into English ; but its present equivalent, *very*, is a pure French word ; and the equally French word *real* is in vulgar use undergoing a precisely similar reduction to the same value (in " that's *real* good," and the like). Into the very citadel of that most exclusive class of words, the numerals, has been intruded the Romanic ordinal *second;* and the use of an indefinite pronoun, *one* (in " *one* must not believe all *one* hears," and the like), appears at least to rest in considerable measure on the French phrases with *on*, by a half-blundering literary imitation. And these are but specimens of a considerable class of similar facts.

It must not fail to be noticed that the structural elements thus taken into our language from a foreign source are only such as are analogous with others already in use among us : suffixes, having the same office with Germanic suffixes, form-words corresponding in their value with those of native origin ; and so on. This follows, indeed, from the method of analogy with existing formations by which, as already explained, the new elements are brought in. There is nothing in English borrowing to give any support to the doctrine that one tongue can learn from another a grammatical distinction, or a mode of its expression, formerly unknown : for instance, the prepositional construction of nouns, period-building with help of conjunctions, formation by affix of comparatives or abstracts or adverbs, or of tenses or numbers or persons. Whether, however, the possibility of this, or of any part of it, is to be rejected altogether, under all circumstances, is another question, to which we may well be slow to return a categorical answer. To take a simple illustration or two : ought we to suppose that a tongue having no diminutives could take in from another words enough like *lamb* and *lambkin, brook* and *brooklet, goose* and *gosling*, to have this distinction of degree so impressed and taught as to lead to its independent use? or that something of a "sense for gender" could be caught from borrowed couplets like *prince* and *princess, tiger* and *tigress?* Or, again, is it conceivable that there may have been a period in the history of Chinese when the borrowing of plainly agglutinated words was able to quicken the Chinese itself into the adoption of agglutinative processes? While perhaps unwilling to say either yes or no, until after a more complete collection and better comprehension of the phenomena of universal mixture, we may at any rate assert that no unquestionable instances of such results from the cause in question have yet been brought to notice, and that their occurrence would appear to stand at the very summit of the scale of difficulty. A necessary part of this whole investigation is the determination of a general scale of comparative ease or difficulty for immediate borrowing, and for the indirect effects of borrowing; upon which might follow in any given case the ascertainment of how far its degrees had been surmounted, and under the pressure of what special circumstances. By universal consent, what is most easily transferred from one tongue to another is a noun ; the name of a thing is language-material in its most exportable form. Even an adjective, an attributive word, has a more marked tinge of formal character, and is less manageable ; and a verb, a predicative word, still more : this part of speech is, in fact, to no small extent wanting in human languages. In English borrowing, to be sure, it has been comparatively easy to add adjectives and verbs to nouns, because of the direct convertibility of our nouns into adjectives (a *gold* watch, a *leather* medal, etc.), and of our nouns and adjectives into verbs (to *tree* a raccoon, to *grass* a plot of ground, to *brown* a complexion, to *lower* a price, etc.), without any change of form; but under different circumstances the degree of difficulty may be quite other; and we see the Persian, for example, receive no Arabic verb, but always add an auxiliary of native growth to an Arabic adjective or noun, in order to make a *quasi*-Arabic verbal expression. Next to the verb, among parts of speech, would come the adverb, with the yet more formal prepositions and conjunctions, and the pronouns ; and, not far from these, the formative elements proper, the prefixes and suffixes, first of derivation and then of inflection ; and last of all, the fundamental features of grammatical distinction. Respecting all these, it is extremely questionable whether they ever pass from tongue to tongue by a direct process ; and no transfer of the last of them, even by a secondary process, has ever yet been demonstrated.

As to the effect which mixture may have on the yet less material parts of a language, as the order of its words and its modes of construction, we cannot speak with too much caution. Here is where real results are hardest to analyze and trace to their causes, and where claims lightly and thoughtlessly made are least easy to disprove. Of claims thus made, the study of language affords an abundance. There are those who seem to hold that a language is, as it were, always watching its neighbors, ready to imitate whatever in them it sees to be worthy of imitation. If, for example, the Persian uses an *i* to connect a noun with its qualifying adjective, the construction must be modelled on a Semitic one; if the Rumanian or Scandinavian has a suffixed article, its suggestion came from Turkish or Finnish speech ; and so on.[1]

---

[1] Striking illustrations of this are to be found in Edkins's "China's Place in Philology" (a model of nearly everything that is unsound in language-study). Thus, speaking of gender, it says : "this characteristic of the Sanskrit, Greek, and Latin tongues has been derived from the influence of the earlier Semitic

Such explanations betray an absolute and utter failure to comprehend the way in which languages live and grow, and are able to influence one another. The users of language in general are neither grammarians nor comparative philologists; they cannot describe the usages of their own tongue; they are wholly unaware of and supremely indifferent to the usages of another tongue, even of one with which they have some practical acquaintance. That analysis and comparison which should point out differences and suggest imitation is the work only of reflective study. A prefix-language, for example, might live in contact with a suffix-language forever without finding out the latter's character, and without adopting a single item of its methods — until, perchance, it should have borrowed suffix-words enough to create in its own usage an analogy which it might proceed in entire unconsciousness to follow. Where there is learned cultivation, deliberate investigation of language and imitation of literature, the case is of course somewhat changed; here there may take place a conscious and artificial borrowing, or imitation, which will remain on the whole confined to the learned class and to learned styles, although something of it may perhaps filter through by degrees into popular usage. In this way, for example, Latin and Greek have had a certain influence on the literary usages of various European languages, and French has affected English and possibly German; but how small is the amount! and how little of it, if anything, has reached the phraseology of common life!

If we would realize the baselessness of the assumption of syntactical imitation, we have only to consider an actual case or two of the kind, in its bearing on ourselves. The French has a trick (it may fairly be called so) of putting the object of a verb, provided it be a pronoun, before the verb, instead of after it, as is the case with a noun-object: now can any one conceive of the English or the German as catching that trick,

---

type " (p. 101). Further: "the Greek seems to be specially founded on the Chinese in regard to tones" (p. 359); "the syntax of the European languages is a mixture: it contains Chinese, Semitic, and Turanian principles " (p. 358) — with much more of the same sort.

notwithstanding the geographical contact on either hand, and all the knowledge and admiration of French style that accompanies it? Again, the German has striking peculiarities as regards the position of its verbs, putting an infinitive or participle at the end of a clause, though at the cost of remote separation from the auxiliary which it ought to accompany, and also setting the personal verb itself at the end of the clause, far from its subject, provided the clause be a dependent one; and these peculiarities, less marked at an earlier stage of the language, were establishing themselves more firmly at the very time when German was, as it were, groaning under the oppressive influence of French, to the structure of whose sentences both were alike repugnant; and here, again, any one may be defied to imagine a process by which English or French should be led to copy the German arrangement. Yet such a result would be vastly more easily attained than the production by imitation of a suffixed article.

A sample point, one of those not infrequently brought up in connection with this subject of the influence of one language on another, is the place of the genitive (so-called) with reference to the noun qualified by it, as either preceding or following that noun: thus, in Latin, *patris filius* or *filius patris;* in German, *des Mannes Sohn* or *Sohn des Mannes;* or, in uninflected juxtaposition, whether in a given language 'a ring for the finger' is *finger ring* or *ring finger;* the varying arrangement in related tongues is wont to be referred to mixture as cause. But there are a multitude of special questions involved here, which would have to be settled before we assumed to decide any particular case. Is there any such thing, in the first place, as a natural order for two nouns standing in such a relation to one another? It would seem, rather, to be a matter of indifference until the formation of a habit of speech accepting the one order in preference to the other; at the outset, the natural relation of the two objects named would be a sufficient guide to what was meant by naming them together: thus, for example, as between *house* and *top*, the latter is so obviously the thing belonging to the other that ' top of a house' is, in default of a linguistic usage to the contrary, equally signifiable by *house top* and by *top house*. Then, what is the relation of genitive-position in a given tongue to adjective-position, to the order of compounded words (if such are formed), and to the other usual modes of arrangement? Further, has a genitive its distinctive and sufficient sign, independent of position; and if so, of what origin is the sign, and what influence has that origin contributed to the determination of usual position? How obligatory is the law of position? Is there any difference in the treatment of genitives of different kinds: of those used more attributively and those used more appositively, of the possessive genitive and the partitive, of the subjective and the objective, of a short genitive and a long one, of the genitive of a common and of a proper noun, of the genitive of a noun and of a pronoun — and so on? Finally, are any changes of habit in any of these respects to be traced during the historical period of the language in question, provided there be such a period? All these matters fall so fully into the category of established usages, gradually fixed and gradually modifiable by causes arising within the language itself, that an extremely careful and far-reaching investigation would appear to be called for before we decide what value should be attributed in any given case to the place of the genitive, or whether it should be regarded as of any value at all in the history of the language, in the way of indicating either relationship or mixture.

Another syntactical point which has been brought into the discussion of mixture is the order of the essential elements of the sentence — the subject, the verb, and the modifiers of the latter, especially its object. Lepsius, in his Introduction already quoted (p. lxxxiii.), speaks of it thus: " Of essential consequence in two languages which are to come to a mutual understanding (*die sich verständigen sollen*) is the same order of words. If, therefore, this is different in the two, the one must give way and the other prevail. In the negro languages everywhere, the verb stood originally in the simple sentence between subject and object. This position is maintained in most of the mixed languages [i. e. in the languages of the great central zone of Africa, which Lepsius holds to have taken shape by mixture of South-African and Hamitic elements], with exception of the most eastern ones . . . where, evidently under Hamitic influence, it is given up and replaced by the Hamitic order [namely, with the verb at the end]."

In the expression here used, of two languages "coming to a mutual understanding," as in some of those employed by the same author in other places, is implied a theory of mixture quite different from that which, as explained above, is suggested by all the best-understood historical examples of mixture. He compares it (p. lxxxii.) with what "still happens every day, when two individuals of different tongue are thrown together and obliged to understand one another:" all grammar, namely, is laid aside, or represented only by gesture and grimace, and the names of things and of the commonest acts, in a mutilated form, are adopted in common use. Now something like this is undoubtedly the case when the two individuals have a chance meeting, or when they fall in with one another only from time to time; but not at all, if they come to live together (like Robinson and Friday): in that case, it will inevitably be found after a while that one of them has learned to understand and use the language of the other; they will speak the same tongue, indeed, but it will be no mixed jargon ; it will be substantially the original language of one of the two individuals, somewhat modified (but not mixed) in its grammar, and with more or less of material brought in from the other language. That is to say : the result will be precisely accordant with that which, as was seen above, has been found normally to follow when two communities mix: not A B, but either A^b or B^a. The one party, after a certain period of fluctuation and struggle, abandons its own tongue and puts in its place the strange tongue which it has learned. When members of two communities, each of which maintains its own speech for its own purposes, meet occasionally for special ends, there can grow up a jargon for their joint use, like the "pigeon English" of the counting-houses of China; but no such barbarous result has ever been shown to come from that more intimate association which makes a family or a community; and until such an instance is found, no one has a right to assume that two grammatical systems, or two vocabularies, can meet and mingle on equal terms. The resistance of one of the two parties to accepting frankly and fully the speech-usages of the other is practically less in every instance than their joint resistance to a mixture of usages. And when one — be he individual or community — learns a new language, he learns not its individual signs only, but also its phraseology, its inflections, its syntax, the order of its words: these are all part and parcel of the same process. That the new speakers may show a degree of tendency, while their speech is still a broken one, to cast the new material into their own familiar order, need not be denied; but it is in the highest degree improbable that their errors in this respect should have any traceable influence on the usages of the rest of the community: after subsisting for a while as errors, they will disappear. The language which proves strong enough to impose itself on those to whom it is not native will have no noticeable difficulty in making them accept its own order of arrangement.

On the whole, we are justified in refusing for the present to admit the power of mixture to change the order of words in a language, except in the same secondary and subordinate way in which the formative apparatus may come to be changed in consequence of mixture : namely, by contributing to the forces which are slowly and almost insensibly determining the growth of a language an element which may finally work itself out into visible consequences. If the French can have come to violate the primeval law of Indo-European position [1] so far as to put its adjectives prevailingly after the nouns they qualify; if the German can establish so peculiar rules of place for some of its sentence-elements by internal development, against the example and influence (assuming that it be proper to speak of such) of all the languages about it, related and unrelated — then it must be very dangerous to charge upon foreign influence a difference of arrangement

---

[1] See Delbrück's *Syntaktische Forschungen,* iii. 35.

which any tongue in any part of the world may exhibit as compared with its relations.

These, it seems to me, are the conclusions respecting mixture to which we are led by a consideration of the facts thus far brought to light.   What is needed in order further to advance our comprehension of the subject is, first of all, a new and more penetrating examination of the facts themselves, with a distinct eye to the general principles that are in question.   Nothing could be a better introduction to this than an exhaustive study of the English as a mixed language (for nothing deserving such a name has ever yet been made) ; to which would be added a like study of the other notable historical cases : and thus the way would be prepared for a thorough discussion of the philosophy of mixture.   But it is altogether probable that the result would only be to establish on a firmer basis the principles provisionally stated above, and to cut off all possibility of the assumption, for any stage or period in the history of language, of a mingling in the same tongue of diverse structural elements, forms or form-words, otherwise than by the same secondary process, of growth involving borrowed and assimilated material, which we see to have brought Romanic ingredients into the grammatical structure of English words and sentences.

II. — *The Varieties of Predication.*

By WILLIAM D. WHITNEY,

PROFESSOR IN YALE COLLEGE.

THE simplest complete sentence is composed of two members, each a single word : the subject noun and the predicate verb. For the noun as subject, there are various possible substitutes, but not for the verb as predicate ; in languages like ours, there is no predication without a verb-form, and the office of predication is the thing, and the only thing, that makes a word a verb. There is no other acceptable, or even tolerable, definition of a verb than as that part of speech which predicates. The point is one of no small consequence in grammar, in view of the long-standing currency of other and false definitions ; and it may fairly be denied that one who is not right in regard to it can call himself a grammarian. What has confused men's minds respecting it is especially the inclusion of infinitives and participles in the verbal system, as the non-finite parts of the verb ; while in fact they are merely nouns and adjectives, retaining that analogy with the verb in the treatment of their adjuncts which has been lost by the great body of ordinary nouns and adjectives ; and the line that separates them from the latter is indistinct and variable.

The primary predicative relation, then, is that sustained by the verb to its subject. Its formal establishment, by setting apart certain combinations of elements to express it and it alone, appears to have been the first step in the development by our family of languages of the sentence out of those formless entities of expression which we are accustomed to call roots. Any other variety of predication is of later date and of secondary origin.

In the developing syntax of the language, namely, the adjuncts of the predicate verb gain in logical significance at the cost of the verb itself; the latter forfeits more or less of its primary value, and becomes a "verb of incomplete predication": that is to say, in the actual usage of the language, it is not enough in itself to stand as a member of the sentence, but craves a complement; though still indispensable, it has lost its absoluteness and independence. In one direction of this development, the extreme is reached when certain verbs are attenuated in meaning to the value of a "copula," or assume the office of indicating merely the mental act of predicating, the whole logical significance of the predication lying in the added word or words, which, from being originally adjuncts of the verb, have now grown to be qualifiers of the subject of the sentence. Thus we come to have predicate nouns and adjectives; they are definable only as being by means of the copula made descriptive of the subject, or predicated of the subject through the instrumentality of a verb.

Then it comes to be possible to analyze every predicate verb into two parts: the copula, which expresses the act of predication, and a noun or adjective, which expresses the substance of what is predicated; as, *he is running,* for *he runs ; he was a sufferer,* for *he suffered.* This analysis is a real one, and for certain purposes important; but it is mere artificiality and pedantry to impose it, as some systems do, upon every verb, in the description of the sentence. To do this is to do violence to the history of language. No tongue ever arrived at the possession of a copula by incorporating in a form-word the act of predication. Languages which have no verbs have no copula, as a matter of course; a word used predicatively is their substitute for a verb: a word capable of standing in a variety of uses, and pointed out as predicative in this particular case, either merely by the requirements of the sense as gathered from the totality of expression, or by its position relative to the other items of expression; or, it might possibly be, by a "particle" — which then has only to grow on to the predicatively used word in order to make a predicate form, or a verb. A copula verb is only made, as everything in language that is formal is without exception made, by the gradual wearing down to a formal value of verbs that originally had material significance — the latest case close at hand being the reduction of Lat. *stabat* to Fr. *était;* this is but a single example of a most pervasive and characteristic mode of growth in language.

Since the grammatical structure of language is indeed a growth, and all its distinctions the product of gradual differentiation, grammar is everywhere full of imperfect classifications and transitional forms and constructions ; and so it is also in the department of predication. The copula is, as we may say, a verb of extirpated predication, and the words that follow it are descriptive purely of the subject ; others are verbs of more or less incomplete predication, with predicative complements, these latter being partly qualifiers of the subject, but partly also modifiers of the verb itself. Examples are, *he stands firm, she walks a queen, it tastes sour, they look weary.* Such constructions occasion much difficulty to mechanical analyzers of the sentence, and the difficulty is sought to be avoided in various ways. To see their true character, we must apply the definition already laid down : the noun or adjective is predicative so far as it is made through the verb descriptive of the subject ; it is an adjunct to the verb, or adverbial, so far as it describes the action of the verb itself. Thus, *she walks a queen* means partly that ' she has a queenly walk,' and partly that ' she is shown by her walk to be a queen.' If it is worth while (and it seems to be so) to distinguish these transitional cases from the normal predicate, and to mark them by a name, nothing can so suitably express their double character as the term " adverbial predicate."

Yet another variety of predication comes into use, in connection with the object of the verb. A most important kind of incompleteness of mere verbs as predicates is shown by those which demand the complement of a direct object. This object originally (as seems altogether probable) denotes that to or at which the action expressed by the verb immediately directs itself; it finds incorporation in a special case, the accusative, which then becomes the most frequent and important of the oblique cases. Then verbs expressing certain actions come to be so usually followed by an expression of the recipient of the action that they acquire the character of "transitive" verbs, and appear to lack something when no object is added. And the sentence-form subject-verb-object becomes as prevalent in our languages as the sentence-form subject-copula-predicate (noun, etc.).

Next are developed in many languages modes of expression which, without turning the sentence into a really compound or complex one, yet virtually make the object a subject of further predication. Thus, for example, *I make him fall* means 'he falls, and I bring it about,' or 'I cause that he falls'; and *I see him fall*, or *I hear him fall*, and so on, are of the same character. Such phrases are not at the outset different in character from the equivalent ones, *I cause his fall, I see him falling*, and the like ; but out of them grows in some languages an important and conspicuous construction, that of an infinitive with its subject-accusative (most used in Latin, of the languages familiar to us) : a construction which is at first strictly limited to a governing verb, but gradually acquires a degree of independence, and becomes a new clause-form, and almost a new sentence-form. A sort of analogy to this, and a very instructive one, is seen in such English sentences (not elegant, nor strictly correct, yet common enough in familiar speech) as *for him to do so would be quite insufferable*, where the *him* has come to seem to us a virtual subject to *to do*, instead of object of the preposition *for*, which connects it with the adjective *insufferable*.

A case of kindred character, though not leading to so important results in the development of the sentence, is that by which a noun or adjective (or its equivalent) is made directly predicative to an object noun. Examples are, *I make him a ruler, I make it black*. That the logical value of the words *ruler* and *black* in these little sentences is that of predicates to *him* and *it* respectively, is past all question. The fact appears from every test that can be applied, in the way of transfer into other and equivalent forms of expression : ' I cause that *he* be a *ruler*' (change to a subordinate substantive clause with its regular subject and predicate) ; 'I cause *it* to be *black*' (change to accusative-subject with an infinitive copula and following predicate); 'it is made black' (change to passive form, with object turned into subject, and the adjective etc. becoming an ordinary predicate to it as such); and so on. The predicate word is also often absorbable into the verb itself: thus, 'I blacken it'; which is analogous to 'I fell it,' i. e. 'make it fall' — one of the points of contact between denominative and causative formations. That is to say, *fell* is analyzable into *fall*, as the material part of the predication, and a copula of causation instead of the ordinary copula of existence; and *blacken*, in like manner, into the same copula with the adjective *black*, as the material part of the predication. And not only logically, but by fundamental definition, are the words of which we are treating predicates; since they are, like the other cases considered above, words which by and through the verb of the sentence are made descriptive of something: only this time of the object, instead of the subject. Here then we have one more kind of predicate, quite different from the rest; if we name it after its essential characteristic, we shall call it an "objective predicate," or "predicate of the object." It occurs oftenest and most plainly with the verb *make;* but there are many others with which it may appear: thus, verbs which virtually involve the idea of making, as "I *choose* him ruler," "they *appointed* him consul"; verbs of considering and the like, as "we *thought* him honest"; "men *call* her handsome"; and various less classifiable cases, instanced by "I *saw* her safe home," "we *heard* the water trickling," "he *keeps* his mouth shut"; and so on. The construction shades off into one in which the added adjective or noun is merely appositive, as in "they found him sleeping," and the like.

There is also in English, as in some other languages, the interesting case of a verb used factitively, or in the sense of causing or making by means of the action represented by it in its ordinary use, and necessarily accompanied by an objective predicate belonging to its object: thus, "he *wiped* his face *dry*," "you will *walk* yourself *lame*," "he *struck* his enemy *dead* at his feet," and so on. To trace the beginnings and development of this idiom in English, and to define its limits, would be an interesting subject for a special study in the history of English constructions.

This last kind of predicate, the objective, calls for the more notice, inasmuch as it is apt to be either ignored, or indistinctly and inconsistently treated, in the grammars. I have not noticed that any English grammar (excepting, of course, my own) gives an account of the construction accordant with that above. Goold Brown, for example, after noting one or two cases, and the difficulties of other grammarians in disposing of them, says, " I pronounce them cases of apposition." K. F. Becker calls the noun or adjective thus used simply a "factitive": "The object is conceived as an effect of the action; this relation is called the relation of the *factitive.*" He does not, so far as I see, use the term "factitive object"; yet the language quoted, and his putting his treatment of it under the head of "the object," fairly justify those who have so called it after him and as if by his authority. This both ignores the essentially predicative character of the construction, and leaves out of sight the employment in it of an adjective; since no adjective can properly be called the object of a verb. But Kühner likewise, in both his Latin and Greek grammars, puts the case under the head of "two accusatives"; as if an accusative object with an adjective describing it could properly be so classified. He calls, to be sure, the second accusative an "accusative of the predicate," thus recognizing its real character; but it is not noticed under the head of predicative constructions. Even Madvig's account is open to criticism. He says that a verb may have, "besides its object, the accusative of a substantive or adjective, which constitutes a predicate of the object, and serves to complete the notion of the verb (strictly speaking, this accusative forms an apposition to the object)." The essential syntactical relation is here accurately defined in the first instance; but the definition is rather spoiled by the added parenthesis, which seems to imply that in a higher sense the relation is appositive rather than predicative. If Madvig had said, instead, that the construction is by its historical origin appositive, and still shades off into that, he would have been more nearly right.

2. *On the Relation of Vowels and Consonants.*

The question of the mutual relation of vowels and consonants, of what constitutes the essential distinction of either class from the other, is one of primary interest as regards the theory of the alphabet, and does not appear to me ever to have been taken up and discussed in a wholly satisfactory manner. In my criticism of Prof. Lepsius's Standard Alphabet, to which he has replied in the above letter, I set forth, in a somewhat brief and cursory manner, my own views upon the subject. But inasmuch as they do not seem to have won his assent, and as the exposition of them there given may appear equally unconvincing to others who might possibly be won over by their fuller discussion, I propose in this place to state and defend them anew.

The mode of production of the consonants in general, involving a consideration of the positions taken up by the mouth-organs in uttering them, and the character of the material furnished for them by the lungs and throat, whether intonated or unintonated, is a comparatively easy subject, and is now pretty thoroughly worked out; only a few doubtful and difficult points remaining, concerning the character of certain more rare and exceptional sounds, or concerning what are the essential and what the accidental characteristics of others. The vowels are a more difficult subject, and only the most recent investigations of such men as Willis, Kempelen, Ellis, Helmholtz, Brücke, have been successful in giving us anything like an exact scientific definition of what makes an *a*, an *i*, an *u*, etc., as distinguished from one another; and, approximately, by what physical action they receive their peculiar and characteristic quality. I say approximately, because the differences of position in the mouth-organs by which they are produced are in part so slight, so obscure, and so complicated, that they may for a long time, if not always, continue to elude exact observation. For all present practical purposes, however, so far as concerns the needs of the historical student of language, the comparative philologist, the physical system of sounds may be regarded as, in all its parts, fairly understood.

In all its parts, I cannot but think, better than in its totality as a system. Those who study the spoken alphabet have been content, for the most part, to treat the vowels and consonants as two independent bodies, partners in the work of articulate expression, indissolubly married together for the uses of speech, yet distinct individuals, to be classed, arranged, and described separately, and afterward set side by side. Now it is, certainly, theoretically conceivable that the products of the organs of articulation should be thus of two distinct kinds; just as the human race is composed of two distinct sexes, each having its own part to play in the work of the race, any true intermediate form or combination of the two being impossible, any apparent one a monstrosity. But is this actually the case in the spoken alphabet? I think decidedly not. The simple fact of the occurrence in our phonological vocabulary of the term "semivowel" is of itself enough to shake such a theory to its foundation. Think of a woman who should be a "semi-man!" There is, on the one hand, a not inconsiderable class of sounds, known by various names—as semivowels, liquids, nasals—in which, though we generally reckon them as consonants, we recognize a special kindred with the vowels, insomuch that they even sometimes assume vocalic value: they are especially *l, m, n, r.* On the other hand, there are two vowels, *i* and *u,* which are so closely allied to consonants that, when we put them in the same syllable before another vowel, we can hardly keep them from passing into sounds which we are accustomed to represent by *y* and *w,* regarding them as consonantal, and not vocalic. These are the principal facts which seem to oppose the theory of the independence of vowel and consonant, and compel us to inquire more narrowly into what we are to understand respectively by a vocalic and a consonantal character.

Probably no better and more truly descriptive designation than "consonant" could be found for the class of sounds to which we assign that name. It means 'sounding along with' a letter of the other class, a vowel. By this is not at all intended, however, that a consonant cannot be uttered except in combination with a vowel: every consonant can be so uttered; the semivowels, sibilants, spirants are continuable sounds, not less than the vowels; one may utter an *l,* an *s,* a *v,* or their like, as long as his breath will hold out; and even the mutes may be made distinctly audible by explosion with breath alone, with a mere puff of unarticulated air. The epithet is a historical one, not a theoretical. In the actual usage of language, consonants never do occur independently: no word is composed of consonants alone; a vowel is a necessary constituent of every one of those items of which our vocabulary is made up. The same is true of the lesser articulate entities into which we divide most of our words, namely syllables: every syllable also must contain a vowel, or a sound doing duty as such. Upon this point we must dwell for a time: the distinction of vowel and consonant stands so intimately related with the theory of the syllable, that the latter positively requires at our hands some explanation and definition, in order to the comprehension of the former.

The historical study of language has proved that the syllables composing our present words are, for the most part, elements originally independent, by the combination and fusion of which polysyllabic words were produced. Each such syllable was composed of, or else necessarily contained, a vowel, and after their composition their identity as separate syllables is often still preserved. But in what does this syllabic identity consist? When the separate individuality of the elements is lost so far as meaning is concerned, why is it still phonetically preserved? Why do not the two words become one syllable when they become one word? or why not always, as they do sometimes? What, in short, is the phonetic distinction between a monosyllable and a polysyllable?

None of the definitions of a syllable which I have met with have seemed in all respects accurate and satisfactory. The most usual and current one amounts nearly to this: a syllable is that part of a word which is uttered by a single effort of the voice. Such an account of the matter is not of the slightest value. Just as much is a whole word, a whole sentence, uttered by a single effort of the voice, when the speaker knows what he is going to say, and says it at once in conscious connection. It takes a certain amount of reflection to recognize a word as composed of separate syllables. The untaught speaker, who has not learned to examine and theorize about what he says, utters his word without any thought of analyzing it into parts, without feeling a succession of efforts as necessary to the enunciation of the separate syllables, any more than of the separate letters. Indeed, even upon reflection, it is much more proper to speak of the letters than of the syllables as formed by so many efforts of enunciation. Take, for instance, the word *blend*. It is, as every one perceives, a single syllable; but it is a unity of a very complex composition. In its utterance, the organs of the mouth put themselves in no less than five different positions in succession. First, with the lips closed, a little breath is forced up from the lungs into the closed cavity of the mouth, intonated on its way through the larynx by being made to set the vocal cords in vibration. This lasts but for the briefest moment; before the cavity is so filled as to stop the expulsion, the lips are unclosed, and the *b* is heard. At the same instant, the tongue has been made to touch the roof of the mouth at its tip, while the unintermitted current of sonant breath streams out at its sides, giving the *l*-sound. Next, the tongue changes its position: its point is released from contact and depressed in the mouth, resting against the lower teeth, its upper flat surface approaches the palate, and the *e* makes itself audible. Once more the tongue shifts place; its tip is again applied as in forming the *l*; but this time no opening is left at the sides: contact along its whole length prohibits all emission of air through the mouth; but the passage from the mouth through the nose, hitherto closed, is thrown open, and the stream finds exit there; and the sound is *n*. And lastly, with no change of place on the part of any of the other organs, the passage into the nose is shut again; the intonated breath is expelled a moment longer into the closed cavity of the mouth, and the syllable is closed with a *d* (which, however, requires, in order to be made distinctly audible, a supplemental unclosure of the organs, though without the utterance of any vowel). All these changes, which it has taken so long to describe, are performed with such rapidity and precision, one position of the organs succeeds another so closely and accurately, that no intermediate transitional sounds are apprehended by the ear during the process: it hears five successive sounds only, forming a syllable. In what true sense, now, can this complicated process be called a single effort of the voice? One element of unity, it is true, there is in the word: from its beginning to its end, there has been an uninterrupted emission of intonated breath through the larynx. But in the first place, this is not necessary in order to make the unity of a syllable: *strength* is also a single syllable, composed of six different sounds; but the intonation of the breath begins with the third element *r*, and continues only through the fourth and fifth, *e* and *ng*; the sixth, *th*, like the two first, *s* and *t*, is produced with breath unintonated. In the second place, unbroken continuity of intonation does not suffice to make the unity of a syllable; the word *navy*, for example, requires but four successive positions of the organs of articulation, and is intonated or sonant from beginning to end, yet it is a word of two syllables. The reason for this is, as we usually say, that it contains two separate vowels. But the words *token, able* are also dissyllabic, although they contain but one pronounced "vowel" each: for the *e* in their final syllables is altogether silent; there is nothing after the *k* in the one but an *n*; nothing after the *b* in the other but an *l*. The question to be determined, then, is: What is there in common to these three words which makes them all alike to be reckoned as of two syllables? And the answer, I think, is clearly this: among the four sounds of which each is composed, there are two which are of so much more open position, more sonorous and continuable, than the others with which they are connected, that they make upon the ear the impression of two distinct phonetic impulses, separated and at the same time connected by the closer utterance which intervenes. The distinction of syllables is primarily made, not by the mouth of the speaker, but by the ear of the hearer: the articulating organs are engaged, in the enunciation of any word, long or short, in an unintermitted series of changes of position, from the first letter to the last, and are conscious of no relaxation of effort; the ear apprehends the products of the different positions as so many successive entities, but at once classifies them, arranging them in separate groups, in which the closer sounds are subordinated to the opener. If the word *abragadabra*, for instance, be uttered, while the emission of intonated breath is one and continuous, and while the articulating positions of the mouth-organs are eleven, each giving rise to a separate sound which is distinctly heard, we yet hear five unities, just as if *a* were uttered five times successively, with only a pause, a hiatus, intervening between each two enunciations. So in *endogenously*, or any other like word. The flow of articulated utterance is parted into portions, not only by a complete intermission of utterance, but by that partial check or impediment which is interposed between the opener sounds by the closer ones: and, as the actual hiatus is comparatively infrequent in spoken speech, it is mainly true in practice that the constitution of syllables depends upon the antithesis of opener and closer articulations, the former being their central and necessary constituents, to which the latter are accessories and adjuncts.

Into the details of the construction of syllables, as formed and tolerated in different languages, our present purpose does not require us to enter: these, as every one knows, are very various, depending upon the energy of articulation of the different nations, the degree of effort which they are severally willing to make in enunciation. The Polynesian will not combine more than one closer articulation, or consonant, with each opener articulation, or vowel, which latter, moreover, must always succeed the former; the Englishman, in exceptional cases, and under certain conditions of arrangement, suffers as many as three consonant sounds before the vowel, and four after it, as in *strands, splints, twelfths.*

Now, in the system of spoken sounds, there are some which are of so close position, so little clear and resonant, that they are never used otherwise than as consonants: that is, they appear in actual speech only as combined in the same syllable with the opener sounds. Such are, above all, the mutes; and the sibilants and spirants are, for the most part, in a like case. We may utter or reiterate a *v*, a *th*, an *s*, an *sh*, as much as we please, but we shall not succeed in making upon any ear the impression of syllables. Again, there are others which are so open that they are always vowels and not consonants: they never occupy the position of adjuncts in the same syllable to a yet opener sound which is apprehended as *the* vowel of the syllable. Such, for instance, are *a*, *e*, *o*. But there is also a not inconsiderable class of sounds which are capable of use with either value. Among those which we usually style vowels, *i* (*ee*) and *u* (*oo*) are of this character. They are, as is well known, the vowels which are produced by near approximation of the same organs in the mouth which are used in forming consonants also: in uttering *u*, there is a pretty close approach of the lips, whose complete closure gives *p* or *b*; in *i*, there is a like approach of those parts of the tongue and palate whose contact generates a *k* or *g*. Hence, accordingly, as we are wont to express it, the readiness with which they pass over into the semivowels *y* and *w*: a transition so common, in so many languages, that it is needless to give any illustrations of it here. And what are these "semivowels?" They are nothing but *i* and *u* themselves, deprived of the quantity and stress which belong to a full vowel utterance. They are not distinguished from those vowels by a difference in the position of the mouth-organs, or in the material emitted from the throat through them. Put *u* and *i* side by side, and whether their combination shall require to be written *ui*, or *wi*, or *uy*, will depend entirely upon the force and time which are allotted to each respectively; if both are struck alike, the product is *ui*, two vowels; if the former be made the principal member of the combination, the other being abbreviated and slighted, the result is *uy*, a vowel and following semivowel; if the reverse, a semivowel and following vowel, *yu*. It is true that we are able to pronounce the combinations *ye* and *woo*, putting before each vowel, audibly, its corresponding semivowel: but in such cases, for the sake of preserving the distinction, we make the semivowels closer than usual, approximating the *y* nearly to a sonant counterpart of the German *ch*-sound in *ich*, the *w* nearly to the German *w*-sound in *quellen*—yet not converting them into these sounds: for if the *y* of *ye* and the *w* of *woo* be prolonged, the *i*- and *u*-sounds will be found distinctly apprehensible in them, even though a little friction of the current of air against the nearly closed organs may also be heard; whereas, in the other sounds, which are true fricative consonants, the proper vocalic character is entirely obliterated by the rubbing of the emitted air against the sides of the orifice through which it finds exit; there is resonance, but no vowel. And in our ordinary pronunciation of *y* and *w* we do not—or we need not, and do not except in special cases, when striving after a peculiarly distinct utterance—attain this higher degree of closeness, but only that corresponding to *i* (*ee*) and *u* (*oo*). It is practicable to pronounce a distinct *y* and *w* before a vowel with that yet opener position of the mouth-organs in which are formed our short ĭ (in *pin*) and our short ŭ (in *full*); and even our *e* and *o*, if slighted in the same way before *a*, will make recognizably, though less distinctly, the same impression. To prove, now, that *y* and *w* are not vowels, but consonants, is surely unnecessary: the general consent of alphabetic usage and of the opinions of phonetic theorists is enough to establish their consonantal character. That some nations, as the Latin, have had no peculiar sign for them, but have written them with the signs for *i* and *u*, only proves the economy of their alphabetic systems, and attests the close relation subsisting between these corresponding semivowels and vowels, their virtual identity as articulations.

If the vowels are thus found in part capable of assuming a consonantal value, so, also, some of the consonants are capable of use as vowels. This has already been pointed out and briefly illustrated, and will require but little farther treatment at our hands. The consonants most often employed with vocalic quality are *l, n, r.* Let us notice the circumstances in which they exhibit their different values.

In our two words *talc* and *tackle* (*tak-l*) we have precisely the same four articulations and articulated sounds, with this difference: in the former word, the *l*-sound precedes the *k*-sound; in the latter, it follows it. But in the one case, *l* is a consonant, and the word is a monosyllable; in the other case, the word is a dissyllable, and *l* is the vowel of its second syllable. How is this further difference the result of the one already pointed out? Clearly enough, it is owing to the position and surroundings of the *l. L* is so open and resonant a sound, it has so much of that quality which makes a vowel, which gives a vowel its capacity to stand as the central and essential constituent of a syllable, that it is able to perform the office of a vowel, when put in contrast with a preceding closer sound like *k.* But it is not open enough to maintain a vocalic character when put alongside of the full vowel *a.* The same is the case in the two words *plaid* and *paddle,* which are also made up of identical elements, and differ only in respect to their order. An *l* either before or after an *a* is, by contrast with it, a close sound, consonantal; the ear recognizes the *a* alone as the vowel of the syllable which contains them both; but in combination with the preceding close *k* or *d*, and not followed by any opener sound, it is itself open enough to make the impression of a syllable; it is vocalic. In our previous example, *blend,* there is a regular *crescendo-diminuendo* scale of openness: we begin with the contact-letter *b*, open a little to the *l*, and yet more to the *e*, then close partially in the *n*, and end with the contact-letter *d.* The whole is but one syllable, and furnishes us an illustration of the normal way in which a complex syllable is made up. Change the position of either *l* or *n*, so that they are separated from the full vowel *e* by a sound closer than they themselves are, and we obtain either such combinations as *lbend* or *nbled*—which, though not absolutely unpronounceable, are rejected in practical use as too harsh and difficult—or words of two syllables, *bledn* (like *deaden*) or *bendl* (like *bundle*). In the Lepsian orthographical system, an *l* or *n*, or any other consonant, when thus used with a vowel value, is written with a diacritical point, a little circle beneath; and it is altogether proper to do so; the difference in the office is sufficient to make such a difference in the sign desirable. Only we must be careful not to commit the error of supposing that there is any articulate distinction between the two sounds, any element present in the *l*-vowel, for example, which is wanting in the consonant *l*: the distinction is only, like that of *i* and *y*, *u* and *w*, one of quantity and stress of utterance.

To illustrate the use of *r* as vowel in like manner, out of our own language, is not easy; there are too many controverted points concerning the pronunciation of our *r*, in the detailed discussion of which the attempt at illustration would involve us. In my own opinion, the *r* by itself is not employed by us as a vowel; the neutral vowel almost always comes in either to accompany or to replace it. But in other tongues, the *r* is used as a vowel with much more freedom than is either *l* or *n* in any known form of human speech. The Sanskrit furnishes the readiest exemplification of this use. In Sanskrit, the *r* is a vowel which may stand anywhere: it is not restricted, like *l* or *n* with us, to an unaccented syllable, following accented syllables in the same word, that contain full vowels: it receives the accent, as in *karmakr'␣t;* it is the sole vowel of a monosyllable, as in *hṛd;* it forms an initial syllable, as in *ṛtú.* It is, to be sure, truly regarded as everywhere the historical descendant and representative of a full vowel joined with a semivowel *r*, of an *ar* or *ra*, but that is not material to the point of our present discussion. So our vocalic *l* and *n* are only relics of former syllables containing vowels; and there is doubtless no good reason for believing that any of the "semivowels" or "liquids" has ever come to do duty as a vowel in other than a like way. We are inquiring in virtue of what qualities they do actually come to be called on to perform such duty, while the mutes, as *b*, *d*, *g*, and the spirants, as *v*, *th*, *γ*, are never treated in the same manner.

It must, however, be further noticed that the consonants which we have been considering are not necessarily and inevitably pronounced as vowels, even in the favoring situations where we have seen them assume this character. As in the case of *i* and *u*, a certain degree of stress and quantity is required to make vowels of them. They may be, even after a close letter, so abbreviated and slighted, so subordinated to the preceding syllable, as to form to the ear only a harsh and difficult appendage to that syllable. This is their treatment in French, in the prose pronunciation of such words as *sabre,␣table*, where the "mute *e*" is really mute, and the words are monosyllables. It is usual, indeed, to half or quite whisper the *r* or *l* in such situations, especially when the preceding mute is a surd, as in *lettre, miracle.* Their vocalic quality, then, amounts simply to this: that they are capable of receiving, and under certain circumstances do receive, in many languages, without any change of articulate quality, the full office of a vowel in forming syllables.

A higher grade of vocalic capacity belongs to *r* and *l* than to any other of the sounds usually reckoned as consonantal, in virtue of the more open position assumed by the mouth-organs in their utterance, which gives them a share in the sonorousness and continuability characteristic of the vowels. A next lower degree is shared by the nasals, which derive a like quality from the openness of the nasal passage, even though the mouth is shut while they are spoken. How *n* is used as vowel in English has been already illustrated. There would seem to be no reason in the nature of things why the other nasals, *m* and *ng*, should not be treated in the same way; yet I am not aware that, in English or elsewhere, they are allowed to stand as the vowel of a syllable. In our vulgar colloquial *yes'm*, indeed, for *yes ma'am*, we have a single actual, though a disallowed, instance of *m* as a vowel, which is just enough to show the possibility of so employing it. The difficulty in the way is a historical rather than a theoretical one: *elm, rhythm, chasm, schism* are representatives of considerable classes of English words, but in none of them has the *m* inherited a title to syllabic value, by being the phonetic remnant of an English syllable that once contained a vowel before the *m*; accordingly, while illiterate speakers not seldom make of the *m* an additional syllable, we who are instructed accustom ourselves to force it into combination with the preceding consonants, as the French treat their *r* and *l* in the words cited above. This is the easier, inasmuch as, on the one hand, the *m* never so occurs after mutes, but only after partially open letters; and as, on the other hand, we have reached in the nasals the lowest degree of vocalic capacity. There are words—of which *heaven* is the most familiar instance—in which, after a fricative, even *n* is treated by us sometimes as a separate syllable, and sometimes as a part of the preceding syllable.

In the class of sounds of the next degree of closure, the sibilants, the line which separates the possibly vocalic from the invariably consonantal is already passed. The sibilants are letters whose mode of formation allows of their easy and frequent prefixion and affixion to other consonants, of every class, while yet they are too little open and sonorous to make upon the ear the impression of a syllable, even when separated from a vowel by full contact-letters. Thus, in *tacks, adze, eggs, stain, skein, such* (*sut-sh*), *budge* (*bud-zh*), whatever force and quantity we may give the hissing sound, we feel no impulse to recognize in it a vowel quality, and to estimate the words as dissyllables. The *l* of *draggled* is just as distinctly a vowel as the *e* of *draggeth*, but nothing that we can do will confer the same value on the *s* of *thou drag'st*, though its position, between two mutes, is the most favorable that can be devised for the development of vocalic capacity.* As for the closer spirants, *v, th, γ,* they exhibit no trace whatever of any such capacity.

If, then, certain of the vowels need only to be abbreviated in utterance in order to take on a consonantal character, and if certain of the consonants are capable of performing, under favoring circumstances, the most essential and distinctive office of the vowels, I see not how it can be claimed with justice that vowels and consonants are two separate and independent systems of articulate sounds, the combinations of which produce words, or even two absolute divisions of the general alphabetical system, to be treated apart, and arranged and classified

---

* Yet, by a remarkable exception, it is claimed that in two Chinese words, *sz* and *tsz*, the *z* is obliged to perform the part of a vowel. See Lepsius's Standard Alphabet (second edition), p. 48, note.

without reference to each other. It seems necessary to find some definition of vowel and consonant which shall take due account of and explain these facts, and some mode of arrangement of the alphabet which shall exhibit the relations they imply.

To the same conclusion we are led by a consideration of the insufficiency of the definitions ordinarily given by phonologists of these two classes of sounds. To Prof. Max Müller, for instance (Lectures, second series, third lecture; p. 139 of the American edition), while all vowels are tones, all consonants are mere noises. Of the latter he speaks as follows: "All consonants fall under the category of noises. If we watch any musical instruments, we can easily perceive that their sounds are always preceded by certain noises, arising from the first impulses imparted to the air before it can produce really musical sensations. We hear the puffing and panting of the siren, the scratching of the violin, the hammering of the piano-forte, the spitting of the flute. The same in speaking. If we send out our breath, whether vocalized or not, we hear the rushing out, the momentary breathing, the impulse produced by the inner air as it reaches the outer."

This exposition possesses no more than the semblance of a meaning, if even that; it is worth nothing as affording an explanation of the character of a consonant, or even as helping us better to realize that character. To compare consonants, those essential and highly characteristic parts of our articulated speech, with the unmusical noises of musical instruments, made more or less conspicuous according to the skill of the player, and overborne and silenced altogether in good musical execution, is palpably futile. What is there in the *b* and *l*, the *n* and *d*, of *blend*, for instance, to assimilate them to such noises? Are they, or any other of the twenty or thirty consonants which may gather in groups, even to the number of five or six, about each one of the vowels, in the least degree dependent for their being on the latter, or generated by it? Is not each one as distinct a product of the voluntary action of the articulating organs, consciously directed to its production, as is any vowel? Is there any difficulty in uttering a clear vowel, free from such prefatory or sequent appendages? And are those sounds entitled to the appellation of noises only, as distinguished from tones, which can themselves be musically intoned? There is not a sonant consonant in the system to which a tune cannot be sung, without help from vowels; we are in the constant habit of "humming" a melody, as we call it, which is only singing it to a prolonged *m ;* and an *l* or an *r* may be hardly less easily sung, and with hardly more perceptible friction of the escaping air against the mouth organs, than an *i* or an *u.* The asserted analogy fails of application in every particular.

I have already expressed my regret that Prof. Lepsius has not taken occasion, either in his Standard Alphabet or in his letter respecting it, to give his own view of what makes consonants and what vowels, and why they are to be regarded as forming independent systems. He would unquestionably have given us something far better than the unmeaning comparison cited above. Yet I must confess my inability to see how he would have set about furnishing a solid foundation to his opinion. We may conjecture that he would have put forth some such

definition of a consonant as that furnished by Dr. Brücke (in his Grund-
züge der Physiologie und Systematik der Sprachlaute, Wien, 1856, at
p. 29). No phonetic investigator of the present time is entitled to more
respect and confidence than this gentleman, nor should we naturally
look for a satisfactory determination of the matter here in question from
any other sooner than from him. His account of it is as follows: "In
all consonants, there takes place somewhere in the mouth-canal a closure, or a contraction which gives rise to a plainly audible and self-sub-
sistent rustling, which is independent of the tone of the voice; while
in the vowels neither of these two things is the case."

To the correctness of this statement less exception is to be taken than
to its character as a sufficient definition. It appears to me hardly to
possess a right to be regarded as a definition: it is rather a specification—a specification of the two principal sub-classes into which consonants are divided, and a description of their respective characteristics.
Some consonants, it declares, are formed by a complete closure of the
mouth-organs, others by such an approximation of them as produces
an audible rustling. This specification, however, does not appear quite
exhaustive. In the sub-class produced by closure are included sounds
as different as mutes and nasals (or "resonants," as Dr. Brücke, with
much reason, prefers to call them); the latter implying, indeed, a closure of the mouth, but combining with this an unclosure of the nasal
passages, in such wise as to give a very different character as consonants
to the sounds produced. It might have been better, then, to specify
the three sub-classes of mutes, fricatives, and resonants, as joint constituents of the class of consonants. And our account of the alphabetic system would be of this sort: sounds possessing such and such
and such characteristics, of three kinds, are consonants; the rest, not
possessing any of them, are vowels. Is not this a superficial account of
the matter? Does it give us any common characteristic as belonging
to our consonantal subdivisions, combining them into a class together,
and distinguishing them from the vowels? Why do we set up the
vowels as a distinct grand division of the alphabet, and not as well, for
instance, the mutes; saying, The alphabet is divided into mutes and
non-mutes; the non-mutes being continuable sounds, and accompanied
with the expulsion of breath, through either the lips or the nose; the
mutes implying the closure of both, and being explosive only? If it
be replied, that the distinction of vowels and consonants is shown by
universal linguistic usage to be one of primary and fundamental consequence, the construction of an important phonetic unity, the syllable,
depending upon it, we should retort by alleging the difficulties already
shown to beset the distinction of the two classes upon this basis: that
i and *u*, vowels, are convertible into *y* and *w*, consonants; that *r, l, n,*
and so on, are sometimes vowels, and not consonants. We might even
claim it as questionable whether *l*, and *r* when untrilled, are full fricatives; whether they do not come quite as near to being tone-letters,
like the vowels, as letters whose essential element is a rustling, such as
is plainly and incontrovertibly heard in *z* and *s*, in *v* and *f*. Out of
which of all these difficulties are we helped by Dr. Brücke's definition
of a consonant?

It seems to me evident that, in order to avoid such difficulties, we need a definition of a consonant, a determination of its relation to a vowel, of a different character from any heretofore given. We do not need to supersede or alter any of the definitions of single sounds, or even of the principal groups of sounds, already prevailing: we only want to find the tie which unites these into more comprehensive classes, and the principle on which the whole alphabet of articulated products may be arranged as a single system, with the connection of its parts duly set forth. Nor can I think the principle difficult to find, nor, when found, of doubtful application.

This needed principle is the antithesis of material and form, the respective part played in the production of the different alphabetic sounds by the organs of the lungs and throat, which produce the vibrating column of air, the tone or breath, and by the organs of the mouth, which modify this tone, giving it various individuality. The different groups have their limits determined by the different degree of action of the mouth-organs upon the throat-product—in other words, by the different degree of closure of the former. If the throat-product be given forth with all the freedom and purity of which it is capable, the mouth being set wide open, so that none of its parts stand in the way of the sonant expiration otherwise than as our physical structure renders unavoidably necessary, the tone produced is *a* (in *far*). This is the true description of *a* as a constituent of the spoken alphabet: *a* is the simplest and purest tone-sound which, in virtue of its peculiar structure, the human throat brings forth. To determine the fundamental and secondary vibrations which give to *a* its acoustic character, to ascertain the length of pipe, or the degree of orificial closure, needful to generate it when the tones of the human throat are imitated by means of artificial constructions—these and other like investigations have, it is true, a high theoretic interest, while yet, in their bearing upon linguistic phonology, they are only of subordinate consequence: sounds are produced for the purposes of human speech by the voluntary efforts of human organs, and are to be estimated and classified according to those efforts.

If, now, we go on to modify this pure sound by the action of the mouth-organs, we find at once that we can and do produce certain series of related sounds by different degrees of the same kind of modification. When, for instance, after pronouncing *a*, we round and protrude the lips a very little, the sound becomes *a* (in *all*, *awe*). By rounding them a little more closely, we convert the tone into *o*; and if the approximation is made quite a near one, we give utterance to an *u* (in *rule*, *fool*). There is really an infinite number of sounds intermediate between *a* and *u*, made by infinitely varying degrees of approximation of the lips (not, perhaps, without auxiliary motions at the back part of the mouth, the orifice of the throat—at least it is possible to make tolerable imitations of these vowels by tongue-motions alone, the lips remaining unchanged in position—but these are of secondary importance, concomitants and consequences of the lip action, which alone is consciously performed); and some of these infinite possibilities become realized in the varying utterance, in different languages or within the limits of the same language, of the three we have noticed; yet the latter constitute practically the series of "labial vowels"—as they are denominated, from the organs principally instrumental in their production. The *u* is the closest tone-sound which we can make by labial approximation; however closely we may press the lips toward one another, the vowel generated is still *u*, until they actually touch, when, if their contact be made so loosely that we can still force out the intonated breath between them, we utter a *v*—a *v*, it is true, of a somewhat different kind from our common one, in pronouncing which we press the upper teeth upon the lower lips, but one which is only slightly distinguished from this, and which is found in German, for instance, as a regular constituent of the spoken alphabet. In this sound, the tone or throat-product is no longer the main audible element; but, rather, the friction of the escaping column of intonated air against the edges of the obstacles that so nearly confine it: the form has become more important than the material. So decidedly is this the case that, even if the tone be altogether withdrawn, and mere unintonated breath expelled, the friction is still distinctly audible, sufficiently so to be capable of use in spoken language, as one of the products of the articulating organs: we call it the letter *f*. It was not so with the vowels *a, ạ, o, u*: expulsion of unintonated breath through the four apertures of the mouth-organs by which these were uttered did not give four employable articulate sounds; it gave only a single uncharacterized aspiration, or breathing. But the labial interference may be carried one step farther, to complete closure; then, of course, there is no longer any expulsion of breath; there is neither tone nor friction to make a perceptible sound; there is silence: sound is produced only as the contact is broken, and a fricative or tone-sound follows: but the breach itself forms an appreciable element of articulation, and we reckon it as a *p*; or as a *b*, if it be momentarily preceded by an extrusion of intonated breath from the throat into the closed cavity of the mouth.

Here, at last, we have evidently reached the limit of possible modifying action of the labial organs of the mouth upon the pure tone or throat-product. By their gradully increased interference we have obtained the series of sounds *a, ạ, o, u, v-f, b-p*. It may be called the labial series.

Another similar series is produced by the gradual approximation of other organs, at another point in the mouth. If, from the position in which *a* is uttered, the upper flat surface of the middle part of the tongue be slightly raised toward the roof the mouth, in its highest portion and farther back, successive degrees of elevation and approach will give us the vowels *ạ* (in *fat*), *e* (in *they*), *i* (in *pique*). The accompanying closure of the jaws and lips is here absolutely unessential, and does not contribute to the characterization of the sounds; it is made merely for the convenience of the tongue, helping its access to the palate. The closest sound with predominating tone producible by this method is *i*; a next further degree of approximation gives birth to a pair of fricatives, the German *ch* in *ich, pech*, etc., and its corresponding intonate, which is a very rare alphabetic constituent: Prof. Lepsius writes them with *χ* and *γ*. Then follow, by complete closure, the intonated and unintonated mutes g and k. Thus we have a series which we may call palatal, composed of a, $\underset{e}{a}$, e, i, γ-χ, g-k.

Now I maintain that these two are real series throughout, and that no schematic arrangement of the alphabet can be accepted as complete which does not represent them as such. They are wont to be so presented, as far as to the limits u and i respectively, in the now well-known vowel-triangle or pyramid. But why stop at these limits? As regards their articulation, there is no greater difference between i and γ, between u and v, than between i and e, u and o; not so great as between either i or u and a. It is true that the vowel-pyramid faithfully represents a fact, and one of prime consequence in phonology and in linguistic history. But this is not the only fact that we have to regard in laying out the system of spoken sounds. It is true that, in passing from i to γ, or from u to v, we have to cross an important and well-marked division line. But it is not on that account anything more than a division line in a series, like the equally well-marked line which parts the classes of fricative sounds from the mutes. It is a line representing the undeniable truth that, with the same organs, approximation short of a certain degree produces vowels, and beyond a certain degree produces consonants—and this is not less a conjunctive than a disjunctive difference; while it holds the two classes apart, it at the same time binds them together into one system. The vowels are the opener sounds in the system, of varying degrees of openness, yet all showing a preponderance of tone over its modification, of material over form: the consonants are the closer sounds in the system; also of varying degrees of closeness, and thereby divided into classes; but all of them sounds of the mouth-organs rather than of the throat, the modification or form prevailing in them over the material. Vowels and consonants, then, are the opposite poles of a series; not divided and dissimilar kinds of sounds, but passing into one another, and separated by a border-land of doubtful belongings.

Besides the two series, composed of vowels and consonants, which have already been described in detail, the ordinary alphabets contain another, including consonants only. It is produced by the tip of the tongue, seeking approach and contact with the roof of the mouth in its forward part. If the tongue be turned upward at its point, and brought toward the parts at or behind the upper front gums, no series of gradually changing tone-sounds is brought forth: the only vowel heard is the neutral vowel (u in *burn*), until the approximation of the organs is close enough to generate the r—which, as has been explained above (note 8, p. 341), may be either trilled or left smooth. The next degree of approach, at the same place and with the same organs, gives rise to a fricative sound, a z (or, if far enough back in the mouth, a zh), in which the friction or buzzing is very conspicuous, and which has, like v and γ, its unintonated counterpart, s. One more degree of closure gives a complete stoppage of the voice, and produces the pair of sounds d and t, full mutes, like g and k, b and p. By a peculiar condition of things, now, while the tip of the tongue generates no vowels, it generates two different sounds of its own openest class: namely, the r, produced by an opening of a certain aperture between itself and the roof

of the mouth, and an *l*, produced by a closure at the tip and an opening
at the sides of the tongue. The ready convertibility of these two
sounds, *r* and *l*, in the history of language, is a well-known fact, nor
would any one think of putting them into different classes. Though
not vowels, they are also not properly fricatives: they are the openest,
most resonant, and most continuable, of all the consonantal sounds;
they have not, like the sonant fricatives and mutes, their surd counter-
parts, employable with equal frequency and freedom for the uses of articulate speech. Whether, in their production, the part taken by the
throat or by the mouth-organs should be regarded as predominant,
seems to me a debatable question: I should not dare to say with confidence whether there is in them more tone or more form. No name is
so applicable to them as that of *semivowels*, by which they are also
most frequently called: they do, in fact, stand as nearly as possible
upon the line of division between vowels and consonants. Hence their
capacity of employment as vowels, and their frequent use in that character, as has been sufficiently pointed out above.

There is another important class of sounds, the nasals, whose relations
to the other classes, and consequent position in the alphabetic system,
require a few words of explanation. As regards the position assumed
by the mouth-organs in their utterance, they stand upon the footing of
full mutes, the closure of the oral passage being complete. They are
far, however, from being mute sounds, because in pronouncing them the
nasal passages are opened, and this circumstance gives them no small
degree of openness, resonance, and continuability. They constitute,
then, a peculiar class, and their place in the scheme of articulate sounds
is not to be determined by the position of the mouth-organs only—
which would rank them with the mutes—but by their general character.
And this evidently places them next the semivowels, before the fricatives; since, as we have already seen, they are capable of employment
with the value of vowels, and at least one of them, *n*, is frequently so
employed in our language. The same position is assigned them by
their incapacity to admit a surd counterpart, by their common relation
to the aspiration, the letter *h*. The place and value of this letter in
the general alphabet offer an important confirmation of the truth of our
method of arranging and classifying the alphabetic sounds. The mutes
and fricatives, as we have seen, go in pairs; each sonant letter, produced
by an expulsion of intonated breath with the given position of the
mouth-organs, has its double, produced by an expulsion of unintonated
breath with the same position. In these two classes of sounds, the approximation of the parts of the mouth is sufficient to give a completely
individual character even to an emission of air, without tone: they are
so far from being tone-sounds, the element of form in them so predominates over that of material, that the material may be changed by the
total withdrawal of tone, and what is left is just as much an articulate
sound as it was before. An *f* has fully as much right in the alphabet
as a *v*, an *s* as a *z*, a *k* as a *g*. This is not the case as regards the other
three classes of sounds, the vowels, semivowels, and nasals. An expulsion of mere breath through the three positions, for instance, in which
a, i, u are uttered, produces, it is true, three different sounds, which are

readily to be distinguished from one another by one who listens and compares them; and yet, the three are not different enough, do not possess sufficient individuality, to have practical value as three sounds for the usages of speech; they count together for but a single articulation, namely the breathing or aspiration, represented by the letter *h*. The *h* is thus an anomalous member of the alphabet. Every other letter represents a distinct position of the organs of the mouth, through which alone it can be uttered; the *h* has no position of its own, but is uttered in that of the following letter. When we say *ha*, there is no shifting of place of the mouth-organs, as we pass from the former to the latter sound; there is merely first an expiration of breath, then of sound, through the open throat. So also when we pronounce *he* or *who;* the position of the tongue by which *i* is uttered, or that of the lips by which *u* is uttered, in those two words respectively, is taken up before the utterance of the *h*, not after it; there is again only a change from breath to sound as the material employed, no change as regards the oral modification to which the material is subjected. In whispering the same syllables, the aspiration is distinguished from the whispered vowels by a like difference of material, by a free emission of air through the relaxed vocal cords, which in the vowel are strained up nearly to the point of sonant vibration. *H*, then, has its place in the alphabet as the common surd of all those sonant letters which are too open to have each its own individual surd. And such are not the vowels only, but also the semivowels and the nasals. We do not in English, it is true, use an aspiration corresponding to all the semivowels and nasals, but we easily can do so, and such aspirations are not unusual in other tongues. We put *h* freely before every vowel, pronouncing it always through the position of the vowel; we also use it before the semivowels *w* and *y*, as in *when* (*hwen*) and *hue* (*hyu*)—where, indeed, it is not perceptibly different from the *h* of *who* (*hu*) and *he* (*hi*); and farther, before *m*, in the interjection *hm!** but no word in our language, so far as I am aware, exhibits the combination of *h* with *l* or *r*.

But it is a farther corollary from our arrangement of the alphabetic system that, the closer the sound, the farther its place from the vowel beginning of the alphabet and toward the mute ending, so much the more distinctly characterized will its corresponding aspiration be, so much the nearer will it come to possessing an independent value and availability. The *h* of *hue* verges very closely upon the German palatal *ch*-sound, in *sich, sicher*, etc.; the *h* of *when* is but little removed from an *f* (such as is formed by the lips alone). There are phonetists who maintain that in *when*, as in all other words of the same class, the *w*-sound that originally followed the aspiration (for the etymological history of the words, and the Anglo-Saxon spelling *hw*, leave no room for question by any person that they once began with a semivowel and preceding aspiration) has now become lost, and that only the breathing remains—a breathing of which the character is determined by the for-

---

* A friend reminds me that some persons are in the habit of using *hn!* instead of *hm!* as "the inarticulate symbol of a sneer," and that young children, learning to speak, often say *hnow, hnake*, for *snow, snake*, etc.

merly uttered *w*, and which is therefore, in fact, a surd corresponding to the sonant *w*. If this be so, we have in our spoken alphabet a semi-vocalic aspiration which cannot be properly represented by the indifferent letter *h*, but has acquired an independent *status*, and demands an independent sign. That such a thing is phonetically possible no one could presume to deny; for, in the semivowels, we have arrived at a degree of closure of the organs which gives even to the surd utterances a much more distinctly differentiated quality than belongs to the aspirations of the opener vowels; and we might expect to see them appearing sporadically as elements of articulated utterance, even divorced from the sounds which originally called them out. Thus, the de-intonated *r* and *l* of the French words *lettre* and *miracle* and their like, already referred to, are plainly *r* and *l* still, and not breathings merely. And at least one language, the Welsh, has raised a surd *l* to the rank of an independent constituent of the alphabet, by a withdrawal from the *l*, in certain situations, of the intonation which formerly belonged to it. As a matter of fact, however, I am fully convinced that in the class of words now under discussion we do actually pronounce the *w* after its aspiration, and that those who maintain the contrary wrongly apprehend and describe their own utterance. The English spoken alphabet, accordingly, does not possess that rare anomaly, a surd semivowel; its sounds written with *h* in *when* and *hue*, though different in articulation, have no more title to be treated as separate elements, and marked with separate signs, than have the differently articulated breathings represented by *h* in *harp, hoop,* and *heap*. *H* is, in English usage, merely the corresponding surd to the vowels, semivowels, and nasals, and its relation to them helps to fix the place of the nasals as next after that of the semivowels in the systematic arrangement of the whole alphabet.

The sounds of which we have treated will, then, when arranged according to their physical character and relations, form the following scheme:

Sonant.				*a*					Vowels.
				a̯e		*a̯o*			
			e		*o*				
		i				*u*			
	y			*r, l*			*w*		Semivowels.
ṅ				*n*			*m*		Nasals.
Surd.	*h*								Aspiration.
Sonant.	*γ*			*z*			*v*		Fricatives.
Surd.	*χ*			*s*			*f*		
Sonant.	*g*			*d*			*b*		Mutes.
Surd.	*k*			*t*			*p*		
	Palatal Series.			Lingual Series.			Labial Series.		

I firmly believe that such a scheme exhibits more of the relations, both physical and historical, of the alphabetic sounds, and exhibits them more truly, than any other which can be given, and that by it the spoken alphabets of different languages may be most advantageously compared and judged. In my former article (Journ. Am. Or. Soc., vii. 324) I have given, upon the same plan, a fuller system, embracing all the consonantal sounds which compose the English alphabet.

Our conclusions may be thus summed up. The fully open *a*, on the one hand, and, on the other hand, the absolutely close and silent consonants *k*, *t*, *p*, are the natural and necessary limits between which the sounds of the alphabet are to be arranged, and arranged in order, according as, in their grade of closeness of the modifying mouth-organs, they more nearly approach the one or the other limit. The opener sounds, in which the tone or material predominates, are called vowels; the closer sounds, in which the modification or form predominates, are called consonants. But this distinction, although the construction of the syllable gives to it a higher practical importance than belongs to any other in the alphabetic system, is not an absolute one: while there are sounds which are and can be nothing but vowels, and others which are and can be nothing but consonants, there are also, on the line between the two classes, some which may have either value, according to their situation. Consonant is a comprehensive name, including at least four different classes of sounds, each capable of exact definition;* but no admissible definition of a consonant is to be set up save the one just given—that it is a closer sound than a vowel. Vowel and consonant are the two opposite poles of a series, in which are included all the articulate sounds ordinarily employed by human beings for the purposes of speech.

---

* And, in a fuller scheme, like that referred to above, it may be found convenient to divide the class of fricatives into sibilants and spirants.

I have during the winter taken up in more than one way the defense of European Sanskrit science against Hindu; you will see the papers in due time, and I feel confident of having your judgment on my side.

Letter from Whitney to Rudolf von Roth, June 16, 1893. These later studies of Hindu grammar were published in 1893, one in the *Festgruss an Roth* (Stuttgart, 1893), the reason for Whitney's vagueness. Note the deterioration of handwriting, due to severe cardiac trouble and grippe through winter and spring. (By permission of Harvard University Archives and Mrs. Robert A. Cushman.)

ON LEPSIUS'S STANDARD ALPHABET;*

By WILLIAM D. WHITNEY,

PROFESSOR OF SANSKRIT IN YALE COLLEGE.

Presented to the Society October 17th, 1861.

MORE than once, within no long time past, inquiries have been addressed to us by those to whom the subject was one of practical importance, respecting the "Standard Alphabet" of Prof. Lepsius of Berlin : whether its method was so thorough, its results so correctly deduced, and the system of signs for sounds proposed by it so unexceptionable, that it deserved to be implicitly accepted, and should be made the absolute foundation of the reduction of new languages to a written form, and even allowed to supersede systems of orthography already for some time in use. We have therefore thought that it might be well to bring the matter before the Society at one of its meetings, when it was hoped that there would be those present who had had occasion to consider the orthographical question practically, and to make experience of its difficulties, and when, accordingly, a comparison of opinions might lead to more enlightened conclusions respecting it than are within the reach of a single inquirer. It would have been highly proper if this Society, which maintains so intimate scholarly relations with so large a body of missionaries, scattered over every part of the heathen world, had at the outset given an express examination to Prof. Lepsius's proposed system, and formally sanctioned it, if found worthy of formal

---

* Standard Alphabet for reducing Unwritten Languages and Foreign Graphic Systems to a Uniform Orthography in European Letters. By Dr. R. Lepsius, etc. London : 1855. 8vo. pp. ix, 73. This is a translation of Das Allgemeine Linguistische Alphabet. Grundsätze der Uebertragung fremder Schriftsysteme und bisher noch ungeschriebener Sprachen in europäische Buchstaben. Von R. Lepsius, etc. Berlin : 1855. 8vo. pp. 64.

Since the final revision and preparation for the press of the present Article was completed (Dec. 1861), we have received two additional contributions, of very high importance and interest, made by Prof. Lepsius to the same general subject with that of the work here treated of, in the form of communications to the Berlin Academy on the Phonetic Relations and Transcription of the Chinese and Tibetan Languages, and on the Spoken Alphabet of the Arabic and its Transcription. In both of them reference is made to a second edition of the Standard Alphabet, as in course of

sanction, or else offered criticisms and suggested amendments affecting it. So much might have been regarded as due to the importance of the work, the character of its author, and the auspices under which it was put forth: it having received the express approval of the Berlin Academy, one of the most eminent bodies of learned men, both philologists and physiologists, in the world, and been farther endorsed and recommended by several of the principal English and continental Missionary Societies; as well as, at a later date, by our own American Board. How extensive an actual trial and application the new alphabet has had, and what have been the results of such a practical testing of its merits, we are not fully informed: that it has been substituted at one important mission, at least—that to the Zulus in South Africa—for the alphabet formerly employed, is certain: and it is precisely from that quarter that one remonstrance or expression of dissent has been received. But such remonstrances are by no means to be taken as certain evidence of serious imperfection in a proposed orthographical system. It is a matter of common remark how extremely conservative we are in the matter of the spelling of our own language; what worshippers of the letter as well as of the word; how obstinately unwilling to write a vocable otherwise than as we have been taught to believe was the true traditional way of writing it: and the same tendency to hold fast that which is written does not quit us on foreign soil, and in dealing with strange tongues. Hence a general uniformity of orthographical method is hardly to be hoped for; the end which we may aim to attain is the providing of something like a uniform method for languages still to be reduced to writing, and a norm to which such alterations of existing orthographies as may be found practicable shall be made to conform.

If the missionaries and emissaries sent out to unlettered countries, and destined to be the first introducers there of modes of writing, had from the beginning been only Italians and Germans, the orthographical question would have worn a far less intricate

---

preparation. We greatly regret that we could not have made this the basis of our examination of Prof. Lepsius's system, and had almost decided to cancel our Article, or withhold it until we could take due note of any modifications of his views which their republication should exhibit. But, in view of the fact that our criticism has already (in the Proceedings of the Society for Oct. 1861) been announced as to be published in the present number of the Journal, and considering the uncertainty of the time of appearance of the new work, and that the first edition has been very extensively circulated, in its two versions, among missionaries and others, into whose hands the second may never come, we have concluded not to stop the printer. Such changes or fuller expositions of Prof. Lepsius's views as are brought to light in the two papers referred to will be set forth in marginal notes to this article, and should the revised Standard Alphabet, on its appearance, seem to call for yet farther attention, in justice to its author, we shall make it the subject of a separate treatment.

and pressing phase than now belongs to it. Unfortunately—in this respect unfortunately—they have been, in much the greater part, men to whom was native the English language, a language whose phonetical and orthographical system is more frightfully corrupt and confused than that of any other known form of human speech ; men to whom, accordingly, it seemed not unnatural to write all kinds of sounds almost all kinds of ways; who lacked a distinct conception that each single sign was originally meant to have a single sound, and each single sound a separate and invariable sign, and that, in the history of writing, certain sounds and no others originally belonged to the characters of our own alphabet. Hence, in part, the confusion, to remedy which so much effort has been expended, and with only partial success. But there is also another, and a more deeply seated cause. Our written system is a scanty, and a rigid and non-elastic thing, compared with our spoken systems. The European alphabet, as it may well enough be called now, was invented—or, rather, modified into nearly its present form—to suit the Latin language at a certain stage of its development. Now phonetical systems grow, both by alteration and by extension; a still scantier system of characters would have answered the purposes of the Latin at a considerably earlier period in its history ; but there is not one of the daughters of the Latin which is not both pinched and distorted in the tight and ill-fitting orthographical dress of the mother-tongue. More than this, some languages, or whole families of languages, offer sounds which Latin organs never formed; and these, too, must have their representatives in a general scheme. And yet once more, sounds, occurring in languages either nearly akin with one another or of altogether diverse descent, which to a dull ear, or on brief and imperfect acquaintance, appear quite the same, are yet found, after an intimate familiarity formed with them, to be distinguished by slight differences of quality, dependent upon slightly varying positions of the mouth-organs in their utterance. From these various causes arises the necessity of eking out an imperfect scheme of written characters, in order to make it represent sufficiently a greater number of sounds. This is evidently a thing which cannot be done upon principles commanding universal assent, by the application of rules admitting of distinct statement and impregnable demonstration : it is one into which considerations of history, of usage, of practical convenience, must enter, and which therefore cannot but be differently solved by different people, according to the variations of individual preference: given a system of sounds to be represented, and a system of signs by modified forms of which the representation must be made, and ten different laborers will produce ten different alphabets, each, perhaps, having its advantages, and such that between two or three of them any one may find it hard to select the best. In order, then, to produce an alphabet for general use, two things, of quite diverse character, are requisite: first, a thorough acquaintance with all matters pertaining to the system of articulate sounds and their established representatives—including an understanding of the physiology of the voice and the mode of production of spoken sounds, an acquaintance with the origin and history of alphabets and the primitive and now prevailing values of the characters composing them, and a familiarity with many tongues, of varying type—and second, such prominence before the eyes of the world, such acknowledged weight as an authority, such support from those for whose sake the work is done, as shall give that work at once a general currency, and recognition as a conventional standard. This second requisite is apt to receive less acknowledgment than it deserves; but it must be evident on a slight consideration that where, in the nature of the case, actual completeness cannot possibly be attained, nor universal satisfaction given, it will be better to accept *in toto* a system which has been and is likely to be accepted by a great many others, than either to alter it considerably, to suit our own ideas, or to take another system, which may be more to our mind, but which will probably be known to and noticed by only a few. And it appears to us that the Standard Alphabet of Prof. Lepsius may at least be claimed to unite and embody these different requisites in a higher degree than any other which has hitherto been put forth.

In the first place, as regards its vogue and acceptance. The name itself of Lepsius is sufficient to attract a high degree of attention and favor to anything to which it is attached. Wherever throughout the world there are scholars, there he is known as one of the foremost scholars of the age, distinguished alike in philology, in archæology, and in history. This work of his, moreover, was brought out under most favorable auspices. It was formally discussed and accepted, before publication, at a convention in London of men representing the most important interests to be affected by such a work. It has since been endorsed by the authorized representatives of four English societies, one French, three German, and one American, as we are informed in the Advertisement prefixed to the book as it lies in our hands: what other associations may since have followed their example, we do not know. This general acceptance, while it is a telling testimony in favor of the work itself, furnishes also a powerful reason why we should incline to take the most favorable view possible of it, even overlooking defects of not too serious a character which it may be found to contain, for the sake of securing a uniformity long desired, and now more hopefully in prospect than ever before. Of course, however, if the new system prove false in its fundamental principles, imperfect in its execution, or cumbersome in use, no weight of authority should prevail on us to give it our endorsement. Let us therefore inquire more particularly into our author's qualifications for the task he undertook, and examine critically his method and its results.

That Lepsius, before he threw himself especially into the study of Egyptian antiquity, had distinguished himself by philological and palæographical researches exhibiting great learning and great acuteness, is well known to all students of language. That since that time he has devoted much attention to phonology is less known, but not less true. In the year 1853, he exhibited to the writer at Berlin the nearly-completed manuscript of an extended work on phonetics, and explained its general plan and execution. That work has never yet been published, but the one before us may be regarded as founded upon it, perhaps in part excerpted from it. How wide is the basis of observation and comparison upon which its system has been founded is evidenced by the series of more than fifty languages—half of them African, the rest Asiatic, Polynesian, and American—to which, at the close of the little manual, the standard alphabet is applied. We thus have the fullest assurance that we are not solicited to accept the results of a hasty and half-digested, or of a narrow and one-sided, series of investigations; and we cannot help entering upon their examination with no small degree of prepossession in their favor.

A principal distinctive peculiarity claimed to belong to the Standard Alphabet of our author is that it is founded on a physiological basis. The exposition of this basis is, for the sake of brevity, omitted in the treatise; we are left to judge it from the results it yields, in the classification and arrangement of the sounds of the spoken alphabet offered, and in the selection of the signs allotted to them. The claim means, doubtless, that the alphabet is to be looked upon as underlaid by a correct analysis and description of the whole system of articulate sounds, or as involving an accurate determination of the manner in which each is produced, both absolutely, and relatively to others. This is, of course, a prime requisite, without which no alphabet-maker can be anything but a bungler. It does not necessarily imply, however, a knowledge of the anatomy of the vocal organs, a detailed understanding of the construction and action of the parts of the throat which are concerned in the production of sound— although this subject is a highly interesting and curious one, and well repays study. For the organs employed in giving individual and articulate form to the material—unintonated or intonated breath—furnished by the lungs to the mouth for the purposes of speech, are sufficiently within the reach of conscious observation to enable any one who has trained himself to watch their operations to describe and explain, with sufficient minuteness, the mode of production of the sounds which he utters. There is also another requisite, hardly less fundamental, and which, though not put prominently forward by Prof. Lepsius, is a distinguishing characteristic of his work : one must be thoroughly acquainted with the history, original significance, and various applications of the characters out of which the alphabet is to be constructed. With these two—a thorough comprehension of the sounds for which signs are to be provided, and a complete knowledge of the signs to be employed to represent them—one may hope for a valuable result to his labors : the lack of either would be equally fatal to success.

As we cannot in all points approve and accept the physiological basis upon which our author's alphabet is constructed, we propose to offer here some criticisms upon it, although they may affect only here and there, and in a subordinate degree, the practical result of his work, or the system of signs selected to compose the written alphabet.

In the first place, we object to the division of the spoken alphabet, in a physiological discussion, into the two distinct classes of vowels and consonants. This is a convenient practical classification, but it possesses only a superficial correctness. Even common usage is compelled to bridge over the gulf apparently assumed to exist between the two, by the admission of a class of "semivowels"—that is to say, of sounds which are half vowel and half consonant. In fact, vowel and consonant are only the opposite poles of a continuous line of progression, the successive steps of which are marked by the degrees of approximation of the mouth organs toward a complete closure. All sounds pronounced with more than a certain degree of openness have the quality which we call vocal, and are, to our apprehension, decidedly vowels; all, on the other hand, which have more than a certain degree of closeness possess the consonantal quality only, and are as distinctly consonants. But there is between these two degrees a neutral territory, so to speak ; there are degrees of closure producing sounds which, without change of quality, may have the value either of consonants or of vowels. On this neutral ground stand the semivowels, the nasals, and even, in one or two exceptional cases, the sibilants. We cannot sanction, then, a theoretical system which makes the distinction of vowel and consonant absolute and fundamental, which holds the two classes apart from one another, and adopts for them two different methods of classification and arrangement : the unity which belongs to the alphabet as a whole, as a single concordant system, is thus, in our opinion, quite broken up or obscured. In seeking for a principle of arrangement under which to marshal the whole alphabet, we would adopt the same on which is founded the distinction of vowel and consonant, but we would apply it in a different manner. The ground of distinction is virtually the antithesis of material and form, and the preponderance of the one or of the other. The material is the stream of breath, unintonated or intonated, furnished by the lungs, or by the lungs and larynx, to the mouth organs: the form consists in the modifying action of the latter, converting the material into the greatly varied products which constitute the system of articulate sounds. Now the vowel *a* ("Italian *a*," as in *car*, *father*) is pure material: if the mouth be opened wide, all its organs retained inactive, and the intonated breath suffered to stream forth unimpeded and unmodified, this vowel sound is the result. *A*, then, with this its original and proper value, has a right in theory to stand, as in practice it so generally does stand, at the head of the alphabet. On the other hand, the forming element, the approach and modifying influence of the mouth organs, may be suffered to extinguish the material, as it were, by complete closure, and entire stoppage of the emission of breath, as in the production of the letters we call mutes: these, then, constitute the extreme limit of the alphabet on the consonantal side, as *a* on the vowel side; and between the perfectly open *a* and the entirely close *k, t, p*,* must admit of being arranged the whole system of spoken sounds. And not only do all the other sounds lie between these two extremes, but we shall even find that they arrange themselves approximately along lines joining the two, or drawn from the one point *a* to the three *k, t, p*, respectively. That is to say, there are lines of progression from the neutral openness of *a* towards closure at three different points in the mouth—one produced by a contact of the upper surface of the tongue with the palate in the back part of the mouth, another by contact of the tip of the tongue with the roof of the mouth directly behind and at the base of the upper teeth, the third by contact of the lips with one another; and different degrees of approximation along these lines give rise to the other sounds of the alphabet. On the line of palatal closure, the closest position capable of producing a sound which shall possess a vowel quality gives the vowel *i* (as short and long in *pin, pique*). In like manner, on the line of labial closure, the closest producible vowel is *u* (as short and long in *full, rule*). The line of lingual closure produces no vowels. These two vowels, *i* and *u*, the farthest removed from *a* in their respective directions, are, with *a*, the most primitive and the most universally occurring of all the vowels: and manifestly for

---

* Of course, the consonantal limit may consist, in any given language, of as many different members as there are mutes in that language, or points in the mouth at which complete closure is allowed to take place: for the sake of brevity and simplicity, however, we shall here take notice only of those three which are met with in almost every language, and which in a majority of languages, probably, are the only ones found to occur—namely the palatal, lingual, and labial mutes.

the reason that, in the development of the system of articulations, those sounds were first struck out and employed for purposes of speech which were most broadly and markedly distinguished from one another: the more nicely shaded sounds, the intermediate vowels, as also most of the fricative consonants, are the growth of a later time, the product of a longer training of both voice and ear. Between *a* and *i* on the one hand, and *a* and *u* on the other, the two vowels of intermediate position, *e* (short and long in *then, they*) and *o* (long in *note:* the English has no short *o*, except in the pronunciation, frequent in this country, but unacknowledged by the orthoepists, of a few words, as *home, stone, none*), have been first struck out, and, either in their long or short forms, or both, are present in almost all languages; and finally, a few tongues, our own among the number, have developed between *a* and *e* the sound of *a* in *hat*, and between *a* and *o* the sound of *a* in *all*, usually called by us the "short or flat *a*" and the "broad *a*" respectively. These last are written by our author with an underlined *e* and *o:* thus, *e̱*, *o̱*—a method of transcription to which, as we conceive, no valid objection can be made, and for which we are perfectly willing to relinquish the signs which we have ourselves been hitherto accustomed to use for the sounds in question.

Prof. Lepsius constructs the usual triangle or pyramid of vowels, in the same form as that in which we have here stated it, viz:

but, as we cannot but think, without any due explanation of why they should be thus arranged. Indeed, his treatment of the vowel system is more unsatisfactory and open to criticism than any other part of his work. In the first place, he quits here altogether the physiological basis upon which he professes himself to stand, and, instead of giving us any account of the mode of formation of *a, i, u,* their relations to one another, and the reasons of their prominence in the history of language, he suffers himself to be seduced into drawing out a fantastic analogy between the vowel sounds and the colors, which has not the slightest substantial ground, neither teaches nor illustrates anything, and can only stand in the way of a clear and objective view of the actual phonetic relations of the subject. "There are three primary vowels," he tells us, "as there are three primary colors," and "the other vowels are formed between these three, as all colors between red, yellow, and blue"! And so onward, through his whole discussion of the vowels, we have nothing in the way of description and illustration other than what is afforded by the drawing out of this fanciful parallel: in place of a physical definition of any vowel sound, we are referred to the combination of colors which it may be imagined to represent. We submit that this is not merely a leaving out of sight one's physiological basis, but a trampling it under foot and rejecting it for a foundation of cloud; that it is a backsliding into the old reprehensible method in phonetics, of describing and naming things from subjective comparison, instead of from actual analysis and determination of character; and that the whole color analogy is quite unworthy of a place in our author's phonetic manual. Again— and doubtless as a consequence, in the main, of thus leaving out of account the physical mode of production of the vowels—our author appears to misapprehend the relation in which the German *ü* (French *u*) and the German *ö* (French *eu*) stand to the rest of the vowel system. He speaks of *ü* as standing "between" *i* and *u*, and of *ö* as standing "between" *e* and *o*, in the same manner as *e* between *a* and *i;* and the reason why, between *a* and *i*, language has developed two vowels, *e* and *ę* (*a* in *fat*), while between *i* and *u* it shows but one, is, in his apprehension, that "the distance between *a* and *i* is greater than that between *i* and *u*." But, in fact, the two cases are of entirely diverse character. From *a* to *i* is a line of direct progression, a process of gradual approximation of the organs, in which there are theoretically an infinite number of different points, or degrees of closure, each of them giving a different vowel sound—just as there are between the key-note and the fourth an infinite number of possible musical tones, distinguished from one another by minute differences of pitch; although the natural scale makes use of but two of them, the second and the third, as the spoken alphabet of but two of the vowels intermediate between *a* and *i*, viz. *e* and *ę*. But between *i* and *u*, as being produced by approximation of the organs at two distinct points in the mouth, there is no line of continuous progression, except by going from either of them back to the neutral point *a*, and thence taking a new start in the direction of the other. It is plain, then, that *ü* cannot be a vowel intermediate between *i* and *u*, in the same sense as *e* between *i* and *a*; it is rather a vowel combined of *i* and *u*, or in the pronunciation of which the position of the lips is that in which *u* is uttered, and, at the same time, the position of the tongue is that in which *i* is uttered. It is quite possible to describe this sound, usually so difficult to be learned by those in whose mother-tongues it does not occur, and to make its acquirement a matter comparatively easy, by laying down this rule: fix the tongue to say *i* (as in *pique, machine*), and pronounce that letter; and then, without moving the tongue, fix the lips to say *u* (in *rule*): the combination gives the required sound. To define and teach *ö* is by no means so easy, because the positions assumed by the tongue and lips respectively in its utterance are less distinct and marked, and so are harder to maintain by conscious effort : there is also less persistent uniformity in its pronunciation than in that of *ü:* while the French *u* and German *ü* are absolutely identical in character, a slight difference is generally acknowledged between the French *eu* and German *ö;* both are, without doubt, combinations of a medial palatal with a medial labial approach of the organs, but the degrees of approximation are very slightly different in the two: indeed, French orthoepists also recognize differences in the quality of their *eu* in different classes of words. We can hardly trust ourselves to pronounce a decided opinion upon matters of so delicate distinction between sounds not native in our own mouth ; but we do not think that the differences of quality referred to are greater than subsist between the short and the long *i* in German or English (in *kinn, ihn,* or *pin, pique*), or between the short *i* of the German and English (which is a little more open than the long *i*) on the one hand, and that of the French (which has precisely the same quality as the English, German, and French long *i*) on the other, or that they call for different characters to represent them. And that there is any like combination of the positions of *e* and *ǫ* (*a* in *fat* and *a* in *all*), forming a third vowel of the same class— as is assumed by our author, in order to fill up his system—we do not at all believe; his *ǫ* may be omitted as superfluous.

Prof. Lepsius proposes to write these two combined vowels, vowels of double position, or palato-labial vowels, as we may call them, in a manner analogous to that adopted in German, but with the double point, or diæresis, written below instead of above the letter, in order to leave room above for marks of quantity, accent, nasalization, and the like. This consideration is well worthy of being taken into account; yet we would suggest that, as most fonts of type contain *ö* and *ü*, and not the reversed forms, it be allowed to employ either without incurring the blame of violating the system. In practice, both forms are about equally serviceable, as it is not usual in continuous text to mark accent and quantity; nor could any ambiguity arise from the license, as the two dots are not elsewhere employed as diacritical signs in the alphabet proposed.

In like manner as the separation of *ö* into two sounds (*ǫ* and *ǫ*), and yet more into three (*ǫ, ǫ,* and *ǫ*), seems to us superfluous, so does also that of *e* into *e* and *ẹ*, and of *o* into *o* and *ǫ*.* Our author, indeed, is inconsistent with himself as regards them: now he gives both (p. 26 [24]);† now he gives only one, and at one time only the simple forms, at another (p. 29 [26]) only the dotted.

---

* A single dot beneath the vowel is meant to indicate a closer utterance.

† We cite first, in all references to the Standard Alphabet, the page of the English version, adding in brackets the corresponding page of the German original.

In his list of the vowels with illustrative examples (pp. 47, 48 [42, 43]) he includes both, but virtually admits the uselessness of the distinction, by being forced to leave one of the two forms without an example, or else to illustrate it by setting up as discordant the pronunciation of the English *e* in *men* and the German in *wenn*, between which we defy the keenest living ear to detect a difference of quality. We are thus able to dispense with all those signs which have a twofold diacritical mark below—a great advantage, since they could not but be found very cumbersome in practical use.

The vowel usually known in English as "short *u*" (the *u* of *but, current,* and the like; the *o* of *son*) is one of the hardest matters with which the constructor of a phonetic alphabet is called upon to deal. Its distinctive character is the absence of character; it is the neutral, the indefinite, the uncharacterized vowel, a product of the intonation of the breath alone, with the lips just parted to give it exit. It differs from *a*, in that for the utterance of the latter the mouth is opened with the honest design and effort to give forth a sound, while for that of the other it is indolently left as nearly shut as may be: both are alike free from any consciously modifying and individualizing action of the mouth organs. The opinion referred to by our author (p. 26 [24]) as held by "some scholars," that the other vowel sounds issued forth and grew into individuality from this one, seems to us to lack even the semblance of a basis. We know of no historical evidence supporting it, nor can we regard it as called for by, or consistent with, sound theory. When an untaught race begin to learn to paint, they do not use neutral tints, but the brightest and most startling colors. The beginnings of speech were attended with hearty effort and labor; the most strongly characterized and broadly distinguished sounds composed its first alphabet; it no more began its vowel system with the neutral vowel than its consonant system with sibilants and spirants. The vowel in question comes in rather by the corruption of other vowels, by the process of slighting them, and robbing them of their distinctive qualities. It can hardly be said to appear at all in the best style of German pronunciation; in French it occurs only as the lightest and briefest possible succedaneum of an *e* which is to be made as nearly mute as may be, or as nasalized in the combination *un*; the English is the only modern European language, so far as is known to us, which elevates it to an entire equality with the other vowels, allows it in accented as well as unaccented syllables, and gives it both a short and a long value (as in *hut, hurt*). It is also found extensively in the languages of India, as the result of the dimming of an original short *a*, and it abounds in the idioms of the aborigines of this continent, the general pronunciation of whose vowels, except in accented syllables, is peculiarly dull and indistinct. The practical question is, what sign shall we choose to represent it? the *u* which to the English apprehension is its most natural sign, the *e* to which alone it belongs in French and German, or the *a* out of which it has generally grown in countries farther east? Our author decides for the second, and writes it as an *e* with a little circle beneath as diacritical point: thus, *ẹ*. This will answer well enough; we have no such objections to urge to the sign as should lead us to reject it entirely; yet we confess that we should ourselves have rather chosen the *a* as a basis, for the reason that there is a nearer relationship between *a* and the sound in question than between the latter and *e*. *E* is a palatal vowel: *a* is neither palatal nor labial, but is, like the neutral vowel, uncharacterized; only in the one case the mouth organs have been by a conscious effort removed, that they may not affect the uttered stream of intonated breath, while in the other, though they contribute nothing by conscious action to the production of the sound, yet, by being left in the way of the breath's free passage, they dim and dull it, producing this grunting sound, the most ungraceful of the whole vowel system—or only less ungraceful than the nasalized form which it assumes in the French *un*.

There are some other points in the scheme of vowel-signs and examples given by our author (pp. 47, 48 [42, 43]), besides those we have already noticed above, which seem to us open to criticism. The English vowel sounds, the special difficulty of which Prof. Lepsius alludes to in another place (p. 25 [23], note), are not always well placed and properly paralleled. The designation of the diphthongs and nasal sounds is also in various instances defective in point of consistency with the rest of the alphabet. To represent, for example, the English *oi* in *join* by a simple *oi*, while the first constituent of the compound is not the sound to which the system assigns *o* for a sign, but that represented by *ō̤*, is an undesirable inaccuracy. So also the French nasal sound in *bien, vin,* cannot properly be written with *ē̃*, as our author proposes, since the vowel sound which receives the nasal quality is that to which *ẹ̆* has been before assigned as representative.

We come now to the consonants. And, having already expressed ourselves as not entirely satisfied with our author's general treatment of them—as a class altogether separate from the vowels, and requiring a diverse method of arrangement—we will here first proceed to set forth our own ideas as to how both classes may and should be presented in one harmonious and concordant system.

As has been remarked above, *i* and *u* are the two vowels of closest possible position on the side of the palate and of the lips respectively. In them we are on the very borders of the consonantal territory; so that even *i* and *u* themselves, when coming before an opener vowel, as *a*, in the same syllable, take on a character no longer purely vocal, and become the "semivowels" *y* and *w*. That the latter are not at all closer in position than their corresponding vowels, we are not prepared to maintain: indeed, it is certain that they are sometimes made so, else we could not utter the syllables *ye, woo:* but it is questionable whether they have this greater degree of closeness except when it becomes necessary to distinguish them from a following *ī* and *ū*; and, at any rate, the difference between them and *ī* and *ū* respectively is not greater than between long and short *i*, long and short *u*, as pronounced by English and Germans; it is so insignificant that some languages, as the Latin, have no more thought of distinguishing by a different character *y* from *ī*, and *w* from *ū*, than *ī* from *ĭ*, and *ū* from *ŭ*. It is practically more convenient, however, to have separate signs for the consonantal values of these two vowels, and the great majority of orthographers will agree with our author in adopting such. With *y* and *w* are to be classed, as semivowels, *r* and *l*. In these sounds we begin, at last, the lingual series. We have already noticed that the lingual approximation of the organs, or that of the tip of the tongue to the fore part of the roof of the mouth, gives rise to no vowels proper. The modifying action seems too far from the throat to act with effect upon the stream of intonated breath. It is to be observed that in the production of the labial series of vowels the approach of the lips is not solely the immediate, but in part also the mediate producing cause, by the action which it accompanies and facilitates at the base of the tongue. For it is possible, by a violent effort to change the position of the tongue at its root, to pronounce a pretty clear *a*, even with the lips in the position in which *u* is ordinarily uttered; and, on the other hand, one may bring forth, by a like effort, the whole series of labial vowels, with the lips and teeth held immovably in the position in which one naturally pronounces *i*. But if the lingual position produces no sounds which are solely or prevailingly vocal in their character, its semivowels have in many languages the value of vowels, and it is also much more fertile of consonants than either of the others. Thus, in the rank now under consideration, we have, instead of one semivowel only, two different ones; which, however, are very closely allied, most frequently pass into one another, and in etymology, as is well known to all students of historical philology, hardly count together for more than one letter. They are described by Prof. Lepsius (p. 30 [27]) as both "formed by a contact, which is vibrating in *r*, and partial in *l*." This is not altogether satisfactory: for, as any one who speaks English can perceive, vibration is not necessarily characteristic of *r;* that sound may be uttered as smoothly over the tip of the tongue as any other; and what a "partial contact" is, as distinct from a

near approximation of the organs, such as is universally characteristic of fricative sounds, it is not easy to see. The real definition, if we are not mistaken, is this: *r* and *l* are both breaches of
the close position in which a *t* or *d* is produced; in the *r*, the
breach is made at the tip of the tongue; in the *l*, it takes place
at the sides, the tip remaining in contact with the palate.* Both
may be formed at many different positions along the roof of the
mouth: wherever a *d* can be uttered, there it can be broken into
an *r* and an *l*. In English, as in Sanskrit, the *r* is ordinarily
uttered with the tip of the tongue reverted into the dome of the
palate, and is not vibrated or trilled, as it hardly admits of being
in that position: in languages which have developed a "cerebral"
series, *r* is properly placed at the head of that rank; where there
is none such, it may well enough be left with *l*, in the lingual
series. There is also another *l*—not referred to, we believe, by
Prof. Lepsius, but forming an important constituent of more than
one modern alphabet—which possesses a markedly palatal character, and stands in intimate relations with *y*. It has the distinctive and indispensable characteristic of an *l*, that it is produced by an opening at the sides of the tongue; but the intervening closure is made by the middle surface, and not by the tip,
of the tongue: it is the breach of such a *d* as is formed by pressing the flat of the tongue against the roof of the mouth, well
within the dome of the palate.

From *y* and *w* respectively, a very slight additional degree of
closure gives us the full stoppage of the breath represented by
k and *p*. And if there is any reason why our author should have
arranged the vowels in the triangular method adopted by him,
there is precisely the same reason why he should have prolonged
the sides of his triangle to their natural terminations in the mutes.
If we may follow down the line of progression from *a* to *ẹ*, from
ẹ to *e*, from *e* to *i*, why not keep on in the same direction, from
i to *y*, and from *y* to *k?* and why not, in like manner, from *a* to
p, instead of stopping short at *u?* If the triangle be thus completed, *t* will properly enough occupy the middle of its base, as
belonging in the same rank with *k* and *p*, and as being produced
by closure of the organs at a point between the labial and the
palatal. But before we proceed to construct the triangle, it is
necessary to take account of two matters which have not yet
been considered. First, though the aperture of the mouth be
closed by contact at the three points referred to, there is still a
way for the exit of the breath, namely through the nostrils, and
the permission of its escape in this way gives rise to a distinct
class of sounds, called nasals. There may be, or must be, in any
language, as many sounds of this class as there are mutes;

---

* In his paper on the Arabic (p. 140), Prof. Lepsius explicitly speaks of the *l* as
thus formed.

each letter of complete closure has its corresponding nasal: so to *p, t, k* correspond *m, n,* and the English *ng* (in *sing;* or *n* in *anger, ink*). Observation shows us, however, that hardly any language gives to the palatal nasal the same value, as an independent constituent of the alphabet, as to the other two: it is employed only in a subordinate capacity, either solely before a palatal mute, or also at the end of a syllable, where a palatal mute has in pronunciation been lost after it, as in English and German. Hence it has no sign allotted to it in the Latin alphabet, and one must be devised and applied to its designation. Our author chooses *n* with a dot above as diacritical point: thus, *ṅ*—which seems unobjectionable, if not found to be inconsistent with other signs to be adopted later. The second point to be noticed is that the close positions in which *k, t, p* are uttered give rise, not to those letters only, but also to another set, *g, d, b.* Prof. Lepsius distinguishes the two classes by calling the latter "soft," the former "strong" or "sharp"—terms which he prefers, apparently, to the more natural and usual correlative of "soft," viz. "hard." This whole nomenclature seems to us exceedingly objectionable, as founded on fanciful analogy rather than on physical analysis. The terms hard and soft, once so usual, have of late become in good degree banished from phonetical works, and their re-introduction by our author is a regrettable step in a backward direction. Much as we dislike the color analogy, already spoken of, we would almost as lief see *a, i, u, ü,* etc., habitually called in our author's pages the red, the yellow, the blue, and the green vowel, etc., respectively, as to find *p* and *b,* and *s* and *z,* entitled the strong and the soft mute or sibilant. The use of these terms by our author, however, depends in great part upon an actual defect in his physiological analysis of the sounds to which they are applied: he has no clear, penetrating, and ever-present appreciation of the difference between what he calls the strong and the soft letters. This defect is something rather characteristically German: it is really amazing how some of the most able physiologists and philologists of that nation have blundered over the simple and seemingly obvious distinction between an *s* and a *z,* an *f* and a *v,* a *p* and a *b,* etc. Thus, to cite but an instance or two, the really eminent physiologist Johannes Müller can see no difference between a *p* and a *b* except a difference in regard to the force of utterance; and the noted grammarian Becker can find nothing better to say of them than that the one, the soft, is naturally fitted to stand at the beginning of a syllable, and the other, the hard, at its end: that is to say, that *but* is a correct and normal compound of sounds, while *tub* is something topsy-turvy, an infraction of the order of nature, and ought not, we suppose, to be uttered—as, by most Germans, it cannot be. The more usual way of settling the difficulty is to assume what is implied in the names "hard" and "soft": that *s* differs from *z* in being pronounced with a greater effort of the organs; that it is a hard or strong utterance, while *z* is weak or soft: and this is utterly erroneous, for either can, without alteration of its distinctive character, be pronounced with any required degree of force—with the gentlest possible emission of breath, such as hardly yields an audible sound, or with the most violent expulsion of which the organs are capable—and in ordinary use they do not at all differ from one another in this respect. Our author should have allowed himself to be instructed as regards the point in question by the Hindu grammarians, to whom he finds just occasion to refer more than once as distinguished for their skill in phonetic analysis, and capable of becoming our guides to the understanding of the sounds of our own languages (p. 15 [14]): none of them, so far as we know, fails to define correctly the difference between "hard" and "soft" letters. He himself comes very near the true explanation once or twice, as where he notices (p. 27 [24]) that all the soft fricative consonants include in themselves an intonated sound, or vowel: such a sound is, indeed, included in them, as well as in the soft explosives, and it is precisely this that makes them soft, for "soft" differs from "hard" solely in being uttered with intonated breath, instead of unintonated; that is to say, with sound, instead of breath alone. It may seem a contradiction to speak of a mute letter—for instance, a *b*—as uttered with intonated breath; but the difficulty is only an apparent one. Intonated breath, as any one may readily convince himself by experiment, can be forced up into the mouth even when closed, until the cavity of the mouth is filled with the air so expelled. Thus, with the lips compressed, and no exit permitted through the nose, one may make a sound, in which, even without the closure broken, the ear will recognize a *b* quality, and which will last until the cheeks are fully distended, perhaps a second or two: time enough, though short, to utter a dozen *b*'s in. The syllable *pa* differs from *ba*, then, in this: in the former case, the intonation of the breath, the expulsion of sound, begins the instant that the labial contact is broken; in the latter case, it begins the instant before: *apa* differs from *aba* in that, in the one, the breath loses its sonant quality during the instant of closure represented by *p;* in the other, there is no cessation of intonation from beginning to end of the utterance. In the fricative or continuous letters, as *s, z,* or *f, v,* the case is yet more conspicuously clear; and no one, we are confident, can fail to convince himself by a very little trial that the only difference between any such pair of sounds lies in the difference of the material which is furnished from the lungs and throat to that position of the mouth organs which is characteristic of both. The only proper names, then, by which the two classes of sounds should be distinguished are intonated and unintonated, vocal and aspirate, sonant and surd, or the like, and such terms ought to be substituted throughout for our author's "soft" and "strong," to the rigorous exclusion of the latter.*

---

* In his papers on the Chinese and Tibetan and on the Arabic, Prof. Lepsius recognizes the difference in respect to intonation between the two classes of sounds here in question, and more usually calls them by names which are measurably free from the objections we have urged against "soft" and "strong." But in the latter paper (pp. 106-10), after an elaborate discussion of the phonetic relations of the two classes, he comes anew to the conclusion, which we cannot but deem an erroneous one, that, while intonation does indeed constitute a usual distinction between strong and soft sounds, it is not, after all, the primary and fundamental one: this being, rather, the difference in strength of the emitted breath. Without entering into a detailed analysis of his argument, which would necessarily occupy several pages, we would point out that there are two circumstances by the misinterpretation of which he seems to be especially led astray. The first is, that there is actually a less emission of breath in the production of the intonated than in that of the unintonated letters. If there is no intonation, if the vocal cords remain relaxed, the whole aperture of the larynx is left open for the escape of breath, and the lungs may in a very brief moment be entirely emptied of their content: if there is intonation, the aperture is almost closed by the elevation and approximation of the membranous valves the vibration of whose edges produces the tone; a mere slit is left for the passage of the breath, and this cannot be completely expelled from the lungs until after a prolonged utterance of sound. Thus, other things being equal, a surd letter will cause a greater expenditure of breath than a sonant; but it is, we are sure, a direct reversal of the true relation of things to make the diminution of the column of breath the primary, and the intonation the secondary and subordinate circumstance. We understand Prof. Lepsius, by his scale of *maxima* and *minima*, to admit that more breath may be expended in the violent utterance of a sonant than in the gentle utterance of a surd; yet to hold that the strength of utterance is the main thing, because, through the whole scale of degrees of force, the surd sound would employ more breath than the sonant of corresponding strength. Is not this very much as if one were to say that the essential physical difference between male and female lies in the inferior strength of the latter; since, though a man of *minimum* power may be weaker than a woman of *maximum* power, yet a *maximum* man is stronger than a *maximum* woman, and a *minimum* man than a *minimum* woman? If we may increase and diminish the force of utterance of either a surd or a sonant letter, and to a marked degree, without alteration of their distinctive character, then it seems clear that force of utterance cannot be their distinguishing characteristic: while, on the other hand, if it be true, as we confidently maintain, that the element of intonation cannot possibly be introduced into an *f*, for instance, without immediately and necessarily converting it into a *v*, nor the element of intonation taken away from a *v* without at once making an *f* of it, we cannot hesitate to regard the presence or absence of intonation as determining absolutely the distinctive character of the sounds in question.

The other circumstance to which we regard Prof. Lepsius as giving a false value is that in whispering we are able, to a certain extent, to make audible the distinction between surd and sonant. In whispering, the place of tone is taken by a rustling of the breath through the larynx—we presume, between the edges of the vocal cords, which are approximated, but not sufficiently so, nor with tension enough, to produce actual sonant vibration, although approaching this in proportion to the effort which is made to attain loudness and distinctness. It may be compared to the first hoarse rush of steam through an imperfect steam whistle, approaching, and finally passing over into, clear sound. There is enough of resonance in it to make all the vowels and semivowels distinctly audible, and it can in some measure perform the same office for the sonant consonants: yet very imperfectly; it requires a labored effort at distinctness of utterance, and the close attention of an ear not too far removed, to distinguish a whispered *saza* and *fava* from *sasa* and *vafa*. We cannot see that the possibility of this partial substitution of an imperfect for a perfect intonation militates at all against the theory which regards intonation as the essential distinction of the sonant letter from the surd.

We would construct as follows the complete tableau of the principal sounds thus far treated of:

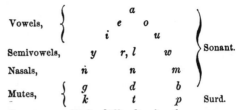

The nasals create a little difficulty in the arrangement of the alphabet, inasmuch as they introduce an element which has no part in the formation of the other letters, and, while in position of the mouth organs they are close, like the mutes, they are nevertheless, in virtue of the freedom of the passage which they unclose, quite open letters, having many important analogies with the semivowels and vowels. Thus, both *n* and *m* are sometimes used as vowels, like *r* and *l*. For this reason we place them next the semivowels, between these and the mutes. Again—and this is perhaps the most marked common characteristic which unites them into one class—the vowels, semi-vowels, and nasals have altogether but one corresponding surd, the letter *h*. This letter our author refers to a new class which he sets up, and calls the "faucal": he describes it as produced "behind the guttural point immediately at the larynx" (p. 39 [34]). We cannot quite agree with this treatment of the *h*, which seems to imply that it has a characteristic position of its own, or is pronounced with the mouth organs fixed in a certain way, which we think is plainly not the case. Our European *h*, although in great part of guttural origin, has become a mere breathing, and is always uttered in the same position with the next following letter, which letter can be no other than a vowel, semivowel, or nasal. The *h* which precedes an *ĭ*, as in the word *he*, is an emission of unintonated breath through the same position of the organs which belongs to the *ĭ*, or through the close palatal position; before *ū*, as in *hoot*, it is uttered through the close labial position; the same is true of the *h* which precedes the semivowels *y* and *w*, as in the words *hue* (*hyū*) and *when* (*hwĕn*); and the Greek rough breathing before ε was doubtless of like character. That is to say, in the production of the vowels, semivowels, and nasals, the approximation of the organs is not so close that the utterance through them of unintonated breath can give sounds individually characterized and capable of being employed as independent members of the alphabetic system: all their positions together add but a single surd to the alphabet, the simple breathing or aspiration *h*. In the rest of the system, on the other hand, each position of the mouth organs adds to the alphabet two sounds, produced by the emission, the one of intonated breath, the other of unintonated

And this distinction seems to us to draw through the system a more marked line of separation, to divide it into two classes more decidedly different from one another, than that between vowels and consonants. If we were to separate the alphabet into two great classes, it would be rather here than there.

In proceeding to fill in the other classes of sounds which help to make up the complete alphabetic system, we may commence with the sibilants. The sibilant most universally found to occur, and the oldest and only primitive one in our family of languages, is the lingual *s*. This is, like *r*, a breach, made at the tip of the tongue, of the position of closure in which *t* is pronounced: the breach is a less open one, and the material expelled through it is the unintonated breath. Hence the so frequent historical transition of *s* into *r ;* and hence even, in the Sanskrit, the prevailing phonetic relation of *s* and *r* as corresponding surd and sonant. The *s*, however, has its precise sonant correlative in *z*, which is pronounced with exactly the same position and degree of closure, and differs only in the material expelled, which is intonated. The other common sibilant is that which in our language is written, though a simple sound, with the compound sign *sh*. Prof. Lepsius does not expressly define it, yet we gather from what he says of it on page 45 [40], and from his classing it as "dental," that he would describe it in a manner with which we could not agree. The most instructive and decisive experiment which one can try in his own mouth upon the sibilants, is to apply the tip of the tongue to the roof of the mouth in front, just behind the upper teeth, uttering an *s* there, and then to pass the tip slowly backward along the palate, continuing the sibilant sound. It will be perceived that, for a brief space, the resulting sound is clearly such as we should call an *s*, but that, as soon as the tongue passes the ridge at which the dome of the palate rather abruptly rises, the sibilant assumes the character of an *sh*, and maintains it, with unimportant change of quality, as far back as the tongue can reach in the mouth. The ridge referred to forms the dividing line between the region where *s* and that where *sh* is uttered, and this difference of region constitutes the essential distinction between the two sounds. The tip of the tongue is not necessary to the formation of either: its upper flat surface, applied in front of the ridge, is used by some persons in their ordinary utterance of *s ;* while the usual *sh* is always produced by that part of the organ, applied within the dome: the *sh* sound, slightly different in quality from this, which is brought forth by turning the tip of the tongue back into the dome of the palate, is the Sanskrit "cerebral" *sh*—a distinct cerebral, like all the other letters of its class, and not identical with our *sh*, although so nearly akin with it. The position of the *sh* and its corresponding sonant *zh* (*z* in *azure:* the French *j*) is thus between the palatal and the lingual letters, but very decidedly more akin with the former. The term "dental" is an incorrect one as applied to it, since not only are the teeth not at all concerned in its production, but it is even originated at a point quite distant from them. We have carefully avoided the use of the term dental throughout, because we think it a misnomer, even as allotted to *s*, *z*, *d*, and *t*. By long and careful trial, we have convinced ourselves that the close approach and contact which give origin to these sounds are not upon the teeth themselves, but immediately at their base and behind them. Even though the tip of the tongue touch the teeth in the utterance of *t* and *d*, the determining contact is upon the gum: the only sound producible between the tongue and the teeth themselves is that of *th;* the teeth are not tight enough to make a mute closure.

In his selection of a sign for this pair of sibilants, our author has not been quite so happy as usual. After rejecting the *s* with a *spiritus asper* above it (thus: *ś*), because the latter has a value of its own, which would not belong to it as thus used, he adopts as diacritical mark the usual sign of a short vowel, which is liable to precisely the same objection, and writes *š*, *ž*. We should have chosen *s'*, for just the analogy on account of which our author rejects it—because we regard the sound as properly palatal, and think it identical with the Sanskrit palatal sibilant. A dotted *s*, or *ṡ*, would also have pleased us better than the sign adopted, as being more easily written, and not suggesting a value which it does not possess. Still, the point is one of inferior consequence, and we should not think of seriously quarreling with the method of representation proposed by Prof. Lepsius.*

The sounds of the English *ch* in *church*, and *j* and *g* in *judge*, are represented in our author's system by *tš* and *dž*, as being evidently compound sounds, containing as their final elements the surd and sonant sibilants just treated. These signs, however, include a slight inaccuracy, which we presume did not escape the notice of Prof. Lepsius, but was neglected by him as of insignificant importance. The *t* and *d*, namely, which form the first constituents of the compounds, are not the ordinary *t* and *d*, as uttered close behind the teeth, and with the tip of the tongue: they are brought forth within the dome of the palate, and by the flat of the tongue—that is to say, by a contact of the same organs, and at the same point, where a near approximation gives the *sh* sound. We properly require, then, some diacritical point to distinguish them from the common linguals, from which they differ quite as much, and in very nearly the same way, as the

---

* In his later papers, we observe that he substitutes an angular mark, like a circumflex inverted, for the circular one: thus, *š*—following, apparently, the Slavonian usage to which he refers on page 35 [31].

Semitic sounds written by our author with a line beneath (*ṭ* and *ḷ*)—perhaps still more nearly as the Sanskrit palatals (according to his understanding of their character), which he represents by *k'*, *g'*. The inaccuracy, it is true, is in great measure excused by the practical inconvenience of adding a second diacritical mark to the compounds, and by the awkwardness of introducing two new characters into alphabets which know the sounds represented by them only in these combinations ; yet we should be inclined to draw from it an argument in favor of a yet simpler mode of representation. Considering the peculiar intimacy with which the elements of the sounds in question are combined—such that some orthoepists still persist in regarding them as simple, and that more than one language, elsewhere very careful to make its vowels long before double consonants, does not allow them to constitute position—we should not be unwilling to turn to account in their representation the otherwise useless *c* and *j* of the Latin alphabet. To write *c* for the sound *ch*, and to retain *j* with its English value would, indeed, involve the inconsistency of writing compound sounds with simple signs ; but this inconsistency may be set off against the inaccuracy of writing *tš*, *dž* ; and if we are dealing with a matter so knotty as to compel us at any rate to a violation of our system, is it not better to err on the side of practical convenience ?*

The labial series has no sibilants; for its pair of fricatives, surd and sonant, expressed in our author's system by *f* and *v*, with their English values, so lack the hissing quality which distinguishes the lingual, palatal, and cerebral sibilants, that it seems preferable to put them into another class ; which, for lack of a better name at hand, we will call the " spirants." Of these two, the *f* is more universally found, and of earlier development—which is apt to be the case, as between surd and sonant letters of the same organic position. In their ordinary pronunciation, the upper teeth are placed directly upon the lower lip, and the breath, unintonated or intonated, forced out between them. They would be most accurately described, then, as dento-labials. The German utterance of these sounds, however (and the same thing is claimed by some for the Latin *f*), brings the teeth much less distinctly into action : the German *f* and *v* (*w*) are almost purely lip sounds, crowded in upon the labial series between *w* and *p, b*.

---

* The later papers of our author, already more than once referred to, show that he appreciates the force of this argument, and that the second edition of his Standard Alphabet will permit the use of *c* and *j* to represent the compound sounds here in question—yet with the addition to them of the same diacritical mark which he finally adopts for the *sh* and *zh* sounds : thus, *č*, *ǰ*. These signs are quite an improvement, in our view, on the *tš* and *dž* which they replace, yet we hardly appreciate the necessity of writing with diacritical points characters not elsewhere employed in the alphabet.

The spirants of the lingual series are the two sounds, surd and sonant, of the English *th*, as instanced in the two words *thin* and *this*. They are properly dento-linguals, being, unlike the other letters commonly called "dental," actually produced between the tongue and the upper teeth. What part of either shall be used is a matter of indifference : the same sound is originated, whether the tip of the tongue be set against the inner surface of the teeth (only not so as to form a contact upon the gums), or whether its tip or any part of its upper surface be applied under the points of the teeth. For foreigners, who are wont to find great difficulty in catching and imitating this sound, it is a method infallibly attended with success to seize the end of the tongue between the teeth, and hold it firmly there, while the breath is forced out over it.

Before examining the characters adopted by Prof. Lepsius for the lingual spirants, it will be well to consider the rules which, at the outset of his treatment of the consonants (pp. 31–2 [28]) he lays down as necessary to be followed in the work of fitting signs and sounds to each other. The first two of these rules— that every simple sound is to be represented by a simple sign and that different sounds are not to be expressed by one and the same sign—are of obvious propriety, and their generally binding character will, we are sure, be universally assented to—yet even to the first of these we have been ready above to admit a single exception (or rather, to replace by it an exception admitted by our author himself to the second), in a peculiar case, and in order to gain what seemed to us an important practical advantage. The third rule is to the effect that those European characters which have a different value in the principal European alphabets are not to be admitted into a general alphabet. This shuts out from all employment such letters as *c, j, x*. To such a rule we are very loth to yield assent. With so scanty an alphabet as the Latin for material to make our system of characters of, it is very hard to have any part of it ruled out of use in advance, unless for more cogent reasons than can be urged in favor of this rule. The multiplication of diacritical points, the introduction among the familiar letters of our alphabet of others of a discordant form and style, like the Greek, are both very inconvenient and very distasteful, and if they can possibly be avoided, wholly or partly, by a judicious use of Roman letters which would otherwise be left idle, practical good sense would seem to teach us so to avoid them. The value of the signs composing the general alphabet must, of course, be learned by every person who is to use it : not a single language possesses all its characters in the signification it attributes to them ; it is but a small matter to add one or two more to the list of those which each person must teach himself to apply in a different way from that to which he has been accustomed, or to adopt one or two convenient signs which in their assigned value must be learned by a majority instead of a minority, or a larger instead of a smaller majority, of those who use the alphabet. In fact, Prof. Lepsius himself furnishes a sufficient argument against his own rule, by palpably violating it in more than one instance : we will not insist upon the circumstance that he presumes to write the vowels and diphthongs by characters used according to their Italian values, while the English language, and in a less degree the French, gives them in many cases a quite different signification : but he also adopts *w* for the labial semivowel, in spite of the more usual value of the sonant spirant (*v*), which it has in other languages than English ; he takes *y* for the palatal semivowel, although it is vowel, vowel and semivowel combined, and diphthong, one or all, in the principal languages of Europe: he represents the deeper palatal of the Semitic languages by *q*, which has not that value in a single European language; nor is his use of *v* and *z* free from similar objections. In every one of these cases, we heartily approve of the choice which he has made; but we do not approve of his cutting himself and us off from other such convenient adaptations, by the peremptory action of a rule which he observes so imperfectly. The fourth rule runs as follows: Explosive letters are not to be used to express fricative sounds, and *vice versa*. That is to say, for instance, *c*, of which the original sound was that of *k*, an explosive, or full mute, must not be used as a base upon which to form a character to represent the fricative, or continuable, sound of the German *ch ;* *t* must not be altered to express the *th* sound, and so on. It is difficult to see why this should be made a peremptory rule, the binding force of which is not to be set aside by any opposing considerations. On the contrary, since the spirants, for example, historically develop themselves in numerous instances from the mutes, there would seem to be a peculiar propriety in developing their representative signs also from those of the mutes—if practical considerations be found to favor rather than oppose such a process. Our author's last two rules, we think, might better have been stated as important leading principles, not to be set aside without good and sufficient reasons.

But to return to the lingual spirants.—For the surd *th* sound, as heard in *thin, throw, path*, Prof. Lepsius adopts the Greek ϑ as representative: not without reluctance, for he feels the great undesirableness of introducing foreign characters into the Latin alphabet, and also allows that the primitive sound of ϑ was not fricative, like our *th*, but an aspirated *t*, or a *t* with an *h* closely following it. He is restrained, however, by his fourth rule from accepting any diacritically distinguished form of our explosives *t* and *d* to indicate the fricative spirants. We, on the other hand, do not see why, if the rule is a good one, it ought not to hold good in dealing with the Greek as well as with the Latin alphabet, and we should have decidedly preferred to see our author devise some modification of *t* and *d*, of a different kind from those assumed to represent the "cerebral" and "palatal" *t* and *d*—for instance, a *t* and *d* with a stroke drawn through them—to stand for the sounds in question. But there are objections yet more powerful to his manner of dealing with the sonant sound, the *th* of *this, though, with*. Recurring to his erroneous explanation of the difference between surd and sonant letters, and regarding the sonant as a weaker or softer utterance of the surd, he proposes to mark the former with the same Greek letter ϑ, only writing a *spiritus lenis* above it to indicate its gentler pronunciation. Here, for the first time, we must positively decline to accept his proposal. It is hard enough to have to borrow a Greek letter for the surd sound; but to take the same sign for the sonant also, while everywhere hitherto surd and sonant have had different characters, and then to mark their difference by a sign which is founded upon and implies a false theory—this is more than we can possibly consent to do. Far better were it to follow the course for which our author himself expresses a preference, but, from an underestimate of the difficulties attending the other course, does not venture to adopt: namely, to take the Greek δ for the sonant character. If we must accept ϑ, let us by all means have δ also, in its Modern Greek value: that is even a less violation of the proprieties of the Ancient Greek than to set the smooth breathing over a consonant, and with a value in no way belonging to it.*

The two sounds of the German *ch*—the one following *a*, and the labial vowels *o, u*, the other following the vowels of palatal position, *e, i, ü, ö*, and those compounds of which the final element is palatal, as *ei, eu*—are allotted by Prof. Lepsius to the guttural and palatal classes respectively. The distinction between the two in respect to mode of formation is sufficiently clear: each is a rough *h*, as we may call it, rasped through the organs with the least possible change from the position of the preceding vowel. If the vowel is a palatal one, uttered between the upper surface of the tongue and the roof of the mouth, the succeeding *ch* is of the same character; it is produced by an expulsion of unintonated breath through the same position made a little more close: or it may even be by a more violent expulsion through the unchanged position, a throwing out of more breath than can pass the organs without audible friction. The *ch* after *a, o, u* is brought forth farther back, at the deepest point in the

* We note that Prof. Lepsius has himself later definitively adopted δ and γ as signs for the dental and palatal sonant spirants.

throat, as it seems to us, where the organs can be so approximated as to yield a fricative sound, or at the point where the familiar and ungraceful operation of clearing the throat, or hawking, is performed. The former of the two, we think, approaches decidedly more nearly than the other to the point at which *k* and *g* are produced, and it is to be reckoned as of the same class with them. Prof. Lepsius calls *k* and *g* "gutturals," according to a very generally received nomenclature, and he ranks with them the deeper *ch* sound. We have all along avoided the use of the term guttural, as applied to the series in which the two mutes referred to belong, because it seems to us to suggest and imply a point farther back in the mouth than that at which they are actually produced. We entirely agree with our author (p. 40 [36]) in locating the place of utterance of *k* upon the soft palate, close upon where it joins the hard palate: their junction seems to be the line of division between lingual and palatal mutes, and behind it, even with the tip of the tongue, one produces a sound which is rather a *k* than a *t*. But the anterior part of the soft palate is hardly entitled to be called "guttural", or regarded as generating "guttural" letters: that term should rather be reserved for the deeper place of origin of the other *ch;* at or very near which is also produced, if our author's description be correct, the Semitic *koph* (Arabic ﻕ, Hebrew ק), very properly written by him with *q*, its graphic, though not its phonetic, equivalent in the European alphabet.

To represent the *ch* sounds, our author proposes to make use of the Greek letter χ, writing the deeper or guttural sound with the simple character, χ, and the higher or palatal with the same character accented, or χ́. Precisely the same objections lie against this expedient as against the adoption of ϑ, already treated of; and for our own part, at least, we should have preferred to take another course. There is a Latin letter still left unemployed in our author's proposed alphabet, which, although its usual signification is quite different from the sound now sought to be represented, has that signification in at least one of the principal languages of Europe, the Spanish; and which, moreover, is the graphic correspondent in Latin of the Greek χ: we mean the letter *x*. Prof. Lepsius has considered the question of applying this letter to signify the *ch* sounds, and he rejects it, pronouncing it (p. 33 [30]) "altogether improper" for such a use. It is true that there are considerations of weight against it, of which we are by no means sure that they will not with many or with most judges have a preponderating influence, and cause the rejection of our proposal: but, in our own apprehension, they are all overborne by the signal advantage of taking a proper Latin sign, and turning to account all the characters of the Latin alphabet. The two points of connection between the sound and the sign which are furnished by the Spanish value of the latter, and by its graphic relation to χ, we are ready to accept as sufficient, scanty though they are. It were, in fact, a great pity to come so near to adopting x, and yet not quite take it. If our author's proposal is followed, we shall, whenever his character is to be written as a capital, use the Latin X: why not accept the other form also—calling it, if we choose, latinizing our χ, in order to adapt it to being written and printed with the other Latin letters?

The sonant corresponding to the surd *ch* sound is comparatively rare, and, if we are not mistaken, chiefly restricted to the deeper or guttural pronunciation: the palatal would pass too readily into y to be easily kept distinct from that semivowel. If the surd is to be written with χ, we should unhesitatingly take γ for the sonant, as is half proposed by our author; the $\dot{\gamma}$ which he finally decides to adopt is to be rejected, like θ, and for the same reason.* If x should be accepted as the sign of the surd, it would be necessary, probably, to devise some modification of g for the sonant.

We have, then, the following, as a more complete scheme of a developed alphabet than was the skeleton formerly given: it contains the consonantal sounds most widely met with, including all those found in the English spoken alphabet:

	Palatal Series.	Lingual Series.	Labial Series.	
Sonant		a $\underline{e}$ $\overset{\circ}{\underline{e}}$ $\underline{o}$ e $\ddot{o}$ o i $\ddot{u}$ u		Vowels.
	y	r, l	w	Semivowels.
	$\dot{n}$	n	m	Nasals.
Surd	h			Aspiration.
Sonant	$\breve{z}$	z		Sibilants.
Surd	$\breve{s}$	s		
Sonant	γ	δ '	v	Spirants.
Surd	χ	ϑ	f	
Sonant	g	d	b	Mutes.
Surd	k	t	p	
Sonant	j			Compound.
Surd	c			

Some things in this scheme require explanation, since it is not in all points so theoretically exact as the simpler one before presented. The vowels of double position, $\ddot{u}$ and $\ddot{o}$, are placed

---

* See the preceding note.

where they stand for the sake of convenience, and not as belonging in any manner to the lingual series: this is indicated by the line drawn below them, from which the lingual series is to be regarded as commencing. For the same reason, the neutral vowel is given a position under the *a*, with which, as explained above, it has the nearest relation. The labial spirants might suitably enough be set somewhat to the left, and the lingual spirants somewhat to the right, of the places allotted to them respectively, since each pair brings in a new organ, the teeth, intermediate in position between the lips and tongue. For a like reason, the palatal sibilants are entitled to a position farther to the right: they might, in a yet more fully expanded scheme, be set in an independent column. That the labial and lingual spirants are letters of closer position than the sibilants, and therefore to be placed between these and the mutes, is very clear. In their production, the teeth are actually in contact with the lip and with the tongue respectively, and it is only because the teeth are too open among themselves to be capable of making a close position that the resulting sounds are fricative, and not explosive. This is not the case with the *ch* sounds, which we have put in the same rank; these have, in many respects, closer analogies with the sibilants than with the spirants, and would be quite as properly ranked with the former; yet, as they lack the full measure of sibilation, are certainly somewhat closer in position than their nearest relatives among the sibilants, the *sh* sounds, and have historical analogies with the spirants—coming, in great part, from *kh*, as *ϑ* from *th*, and *f* from *ph*—we have ventured to give them the place they occupy in the scheme.

The alphabet, as thus drawn out, by no means includes all the sounds which our author treats, and for which he provides representatives. Some languages present whole series of consonantal sounds differing from those we have thus far considered. In most cases, however, they admit of being arranged without difficulty within the same general alphabetic frame-work. Thus, the series representing the Arabic ﻆ, ﺽ, ﺹ, ﻂ would come in just at the left of the common lingual series, being uttered, according to our author's description of them,* by applying the flat of the tongue, instead of its tip, to the same part of the palate where the tip produces the lingual letters, and being also, by general acknowledgment, uttered with greater effort, or stress of enunciation: they are very suitably represented in our author's system by the ordinary lingual letters, *t, d, s, z*, with an underscored line: thus, *t̩, d̩, s̩, z̩*. The Sanskrit so-called "cerebrals" would come next in order to the left; they have been already referred

---

* See his special paper on the Arabic for a more penetrating investigation of these sounds, leading to somewhat different views respecting their character.

to, as uttered by turning back the tip of the tongue within the dome of the palate : Prof. Lepsius represents them in the usual manner, by lingual letters dotted beneath: thus, t, d, s, n.   To the left of these, again, would have to be ranged the letters of the Sanskrit series usually called the " palatal," if our author's view of them, as simple sounds, be accepted as the true one. They are now pronounced like the English *ch* and *j*, and are more usually regarded as having had that signification from the beginning.   It is not the proper place here to enter into a discussion of this difficult point: we will only say that the considerations adduced by our author in opposition to the common view, though very weighty, do not appear to us entirely convincing; and that we cannot regard the mutes of the series in question as differing from the English *ch* and *j* in such a manner and degree as to require other representatives than the signs already provided for those sounds.   As for the sibilant of the class, we have already expressed our belief in its virtual identity with our English *sh*.   Prof. Lepsius adopts the acute accent as sign of the peculiar palatal quality inherent in these letters, and writes the mutes, sibilant, and nasal as follows: $\acute{k}$, $\acute{g}$, $\acute{x}$, $\acute{n}$.   To the two last, as representing the palatal *ch* sound of the German, and the English *n* in *inch*, *hinge* (if the latter is worth expressing by a peculiar character at all), we have no objection—except that, as already explained, we would substitute x' for $\acute{x}$—the other two we do not think well chosen, even allowing the correctness of our author's explanation of their quality : for sounds produced by pressing the broad middle of the tongue against the middle of the hard palate (p. 42 [38]) would not have anything of that quality which we represent by k, g, but would be distinctly a kind of t, d: no letter produced farther forward than the soft palate can be entitled to use k or g as its representative.   The difference between our alleged "palatal" pronunciation of k before *e*, *i*, and our "guttural" before *a*, *o*, *u*, is exceedingly slight, and by no means such as would be made in any alphabet the foundation of a distinction of classes and characters : the only way to establish a valid distinction between a palatal and a guttural k and g in the Sanskrit system would be to regard the latter class as uttered at the deep guttural position of our author's q (Semitic *koph*), and the former as corresponding to our customary k, g.

Finally, Prof. Lepsius gives us a class of "faucal" sounds, which has not, so far as we know, been recognized by any other author as a distinct and connected series.   As constructed by him, it has a very regular and normal look, comprising a pair of fricatives and a pair of explosives, each pair being composed, as elsewhere, of a " soft" and a "strong" sound ; insomuch that the series seems quite analogous to the lingual *s*, *z*, *t*, *d*, or to the

labial *f, v, p, b.* But the analogy turns out, on closer examination, to be only apparent, and there are such weak points in
the construction of the class as forbid us to accept it and place it
parallel with those already received into the general alphabetic
scheme. The first member of the series is the common aspiration *h.* Of this we have already sufficiently spoken, showing
why we cannot regard it as "faucal": it is faucal in no other
sense than as all voice, intonated or unintonated, must of course
come through the fauces; and so, if there is no modifying action
on the part of the mouth organs, the sound produced might, in
a negative way, be styled a throat-sound, or a faucal, or a laryn-
gal. But the *h* is plainly no member of a faucal series in the
sense in which the other sounds we have been considering are
members of a palatal series, a lingual series, and so on—namely,
as having received a distinctive character by the action of the
organ from which it derives its name; it is simple unintonated
material, breath uncharacterized, or insufficiently characterized.
The next member of the series is the Greek smooth breathing.
This is regarded by Prof. Lepsius as a consonant, which necessarily and invariably precedes and ushers in a vowel not immediately preceded by any other consonant; he defines it as consisting in a slight explosion produced by the opening of the throat
for the effort of utterance. Now we are quite unable to convince
ourselves that there is any such thing as this alleged smooth
breathing, having a positive and necessary existence. It is,
indeed, possible to shut the throat and open it again before a
vowel with an audible click (and yet the click will hardly be
audible unless the following vowel is whispered only, instead of
being intonated, or unless between it and the click a little emission of unintonated breath be suffered to intervene); but it is
equally possible to substitute for the click a very slight open
breathing, an infinitesimal *h;* and not less so, again, to commence the vowel without any prefix whatever which the nicest
ear can remark. Why should it be necessary to close the throat
as a preliminary to articulate speech? cannot one pass in the
very midst of a breath from simple breathing to intonation and
articulation? and are the vocal cords so sluggishly obedient to
the will, that their approach to the vibratory position and the
expulsion of the breath in the effort of speaking may not be
made truly simultaneous? We can credit either of these things
only when our own mouth bears witness to our own ears of
their truth; and this we have been thus far unable to make it
do. Our author assumes that this consonant comes in where-
ever we suppose ourselves to be pronouncing two vowels in succession, but uncombined, as in "the English *go 'over.*" This is
the same thing as to say that it is identical with the hiatus: but,
if we can trust our own organs, this is a case where the closing

and reopening of the throat would not take place, but, instead of it, merely an instant of silence, an actual hiatus of sound. We can hardly believe that the use of the *spiritus lenis* by the Greeks was owing to their having noticed, and desiring to represent, the sound which our author defines: in our view, it was employed rather by way of antithesis to the *spiritus asper :* just as we, sometimes, for more marked distinction from a negative quantity, write a positive quantity with a *plus* sign, setting $+1$, instead of simply 1, over against -1. The use of the Semitic *aleph* is sufficiently explained by the syllabic character of the alphabet, and does not necessarily imply any recognition of the smooth breathing as a member of the spoken system of sounds. Our author even sets down the Sanscrit ह as representing this breathing; but we do not understand upon what ground; for the sign stands distinctly for *a*, and for nothing else; and we are not aware that the Hindu grammarians themselves—acute and hair-splitting as they were in catching and noting the finest shades of sound, and much as they would have been delighted with, and have made the most of, just such a nicety as this— ever took any notice of a smooth breathing. It has not, to our apprehension, any claim to be recognized as a distinct element in the spoken system, and as requiring a sign for its representation.

Of that most difficult and puzzling sound, the Semitic *ain* (Ar. ع, Heb. ע), which is the third in our author's faucal class, we shall not venture to speak, as we must confess ourselves unable either to utter or to describe it. So much as this we seem to see, that the definition given by Prof. Lepsius is not entirely satisfactory. He makes it a "hard" sound, corresponding to the *spiritus lenis* as "soft." According to the general meaning of the terms hard and soft, as used by our author, this would signify that the *spiritus lenis* was sonant, and this its corresponding surd—which is, of course, impossible. If, on the other hand, it mean that the *ain* is produced by an actually more violent and audible unclosing of the throat before a vowel, we do not see how this is to be brought into accordance with the descriptions of it given by the grammars.

The Semitic strong *h* (Ar. ح, Heb. ח), our author's fourth faucal, has more claim to the title, probably, than any of the others, as an *h* which, instead of being left in the condition of uncharacterized breath, is, by some degree of approach at the deep guttural point, made slightly fricative, although not to the degree of the *χ*-sound, with which it is most nearly allied in character.*

---

* See the article of Prof. Lepsius on the Arabic, p. 127 etc., for a reexamination and more careful description, of the "faucal" sounds.

We have thus gone over nearly the whole of our author's system, turning our chief attention, as was natural, to those points in which we could not agree with him, and making our criticisms upon them with entire freedom, while at the same time cherishing the highest respect for the work as a whole, and deeming it in many important regards superior to any other of the kind with which we are acquainted. In no other, to our seeming, are learning and practical good sense—the want of either of which is equally fatal to the success of such a work as is here undertaken—united in the same degree. With Prof. Lepsius's view of the general method in which the standard alphabet is to be constructed we are fully agreed; it is to be by the employment of the Latin alphabet to the farthest possible extent, and by the application of diacritical signs to the most suitable bases to fill up its deficiencies; rather than, as some have proposed, by the introduction of italics and capitals among the ordinary "roman" letters; or, according to the method of others, by turning letters topsy-turvy or wrong side before, by cutting away parts of characters, manufacturing arbitrary signs for sounds, and the like, forming compounds even more offensive to the eye than that artificial and incongruous *pot-pourri* of characters, the Russian alphabet. As has been seen above, we only wish that he had gone yet farther in the carrying out of this principle, doing without Greek characters altogether, and pressing into active service the three anomalous letters *c*, *j*, and *x*, as well as *q*. We heartily approve, also, of Prof. Lepsius's moderation in the distinction of sounds and the setting up of signs for them. To compose a complete universal alphabet, offering a sign for every shade of sound which human lips utter, however slightly differentiated, and requiring the use of that sign for that sound in all cases without exception, forms no part of his plan. Even if the execution of such a work be allowed to be possible, the resulting alphabet would be lifted far out of the domain of practical availability, in which our author desires it to rest. The varieties of possible pronunciation are well-nigh infinite, and the signs of a general alphabet must be allowed to cover and designate each a certain territory, as we may call it, of articulation, rather than a single point. It might be laid down as a general rule, that no two modes of pronunciation of a sound require to be distinguished by separate signs, unless they may and do coexist as independent sounds in the same spoken system. Thus, for instance, notwithstanding the difference in mode of pronunciation between the English and the German *f* and *v* (*w*), they are not to be regarded as demanding different signs: it must belong to the description of the methods of utterance of each language to point out their distinction. And yet farther, if a language were found to lack the more usual and normal pronunciation of a letter or a series of letters, and to substitute for it one of those modes of utterance which are indicated in the general alphabet by a diacritical mark, it would yet be superfluous to use, in writing that language, the diacritical point. If, for example—for no actual instance now occurs to us—the Arabic had no *t, d, s, z* but ط, ض, ص, ظ, which are written in our author's system with the underscored line, it would be proper, in transcribing the language, to use for them the simple lingual letters, it being left for description to explain their peculiarity of utterance. Careful and detailed description must necessarily accompany any and every application of an alphabet to a new language, and even when that has done its utmost, there will remain much which only oral instruction can impart, much that cannot be learned but by long practice and familiar usage, and probably even much that can never be perfectly acquired by one to whom the language is not native.

It is evident that adherence to a uniform standard of orthography is not in all cases to the same degree requisite and necessary. The adoption of one alphabetic system throughout is most to be insisted upon where independent laborers are reducing to writing, for practical use, the same or nearly kindred idioms. Here, a diversity of characters employed leads to a confusion of which the consequences may be long and keenly felt. Where languages are quite independent of one another, minor inconsistencies in the mode of writing them are of comparatively small account, since, in the acquisition of a new language, whether for practical or scientific purposes, its phonetic and orthographic systems must receive an amount of attention and study in which such little incongruities will almost entirely disappear. In isolated articles, essays, and treatises, in the making up of empirical alphabets for collectors of vocabularies, and the like, greater freedom may very properly be allowed: convenience of writing and printing, conformity with the previous usages of those for whose information or practical employment the alphabet is devised, leading to its greater intelligibility, or accuracy of application—these and other like considerations rise to an importance which authorizes and justifies deviation from strict theory. It may be well here to review and classify the Standard Alphabet in a summary manner, with reference to the greater or less authority and availability of its signs.

First, as regards the vowels. Here the most important and imperative rule is, that the five vowel sounds of almost universal occurrence, illustrated by the English words *far, prey, pique, note, rule,* should be written by the characters *a, e, i, o, u,* which originally and properly belong to them, and by no other; in other words, that the vowels should receive the "Italian" sound. No alphabet, under any circumstances whatever, is to be tolerated, if it neglect this rule. The same rule implies and requires that the diphthongal sound which we call "long *i*" (as in *pine, aisle, buy*) should be represented by the digraph *ai*, and the diphthong *ou* (as in *house, how*) by *au*. It is much less easy to lay down peremptory rules for the other five vowel sounds which most frequently call for representation. But the vowels of double position, the German *ü* (French *u*) and *ö* (French *eu*), can hardly be better written than with the two dots, either above or below, and we should think that a virtual unanimity as regards them might be pretty easily established. The neutral vowel (in English *but, burn*) will occasion much greater difficulty, and probably no sign can be suggested for it which will not encounter strong opposition in many quarters. Our author's proposal will seem a strange one to most of those who come to it from English usages, and we have ourselves not been able to assent to it without some misgivings: but we have had nothing preferable to suggest, unless to transfer the diacritical point from *e* to *a*, writing *a̤*. The vowels intermediate between *a* and *e* and *a* and *o* respectively, represented in the English words *cat* and *call*, are also hard subjects for unanimity of treatment: and the more so, as they vary more in quality, in different languages, than the others. As said above, we should be very willing to see our author's signs generally adopted as their representatives. As the sign of long quantity, our author, with entire reason, prefers the horizontal line above the vowel (thus, *ā*): the circumflex (*â*) is also available for this purpose: but the use of the acute accent (*á*) to denote the length of a vowel, which has most unfortunately become very prevalent among the English, is contrary to all analogy, and unsupported by any consideration of fitness, convenience, or neatness of appearance, and it ought to be summarily suppressed. The only customary and available sign of short quantity is the concave line above the vowel (*ă*). Whether it be necessary or desirable to distinguish long and short quantity in writing must be determined for each language by itself: it can hardly ever be advisable, we should think, to employ the diacritical marks of both classes in the same system. To indicate the nasalization of a vowel, by the expulsion through the nose of part of the breath by which it is uttered, Prof. Lepsius employs the Greek circumflex above it (as *ã, õ, ũ*), a very suitable sign: where this is for practical reasons not available, a postposed superior *n* (as a^n, o^n, u^n) is a very good substitute.

Secondly, as regards the consonants. We feel confident that almost no one to whom English is native will find any difficulty in assenting to our author's adoption of the signs *k, g, t, d, p, b, f, v, s, z, h, m, n, y, w, r, l* to represent the values which those letters have in the English words *kick, gig, tit, did, pap, bib, fife, valve, sauce, zeal, hat, mum, nun, ye, woo, rare, lull:* and the larger and more important part of the consonantal system is thus disposed of at a blow. Of the remaining members of the system, those which most press for uniformity of representation, being of widest occurrence, are the palatal nasal and sibilants, the English *ng* in *singing*, *sh* in *she*, and *z* in *azure*. With our views of the connected nature of these sounds, we should prefer to see them distinguished from the lingual *n*, *s*, *z* by the same diacritical sign, a dot or an accent; yet this is not a point which needs to be pressed, and, as above remarked, we should have no difficulty in accepting our author's proposals. Next in consequence are the lingual spirants, the English *th* in *thin* and in *this*. To those who are unwilling to adopt our author's ϑ and δ, the linguals with affixed rough breathing—as *t'*, *d'*—might seem natural and convenient substitutes: evidently, if a *t* is made the basis of the surd sound, a *d* should be that of the sonant. So also with the palatal spirants: if χ and γ be rejected, and if *x* be deemed inadmissible, a *k'* and a *g'* would not be unsuited to take their places. The compounds *ch* and *j*, most accurately represented by the prefixion of a diacritically distinguished *t* and *d* to the signs adopted for the palatal sibilants *sh* and *zh*, may have the diacritical distinction omitted, as by our author, or they may, as exceptional cases, be written by *c* and *j*.

Although the use of compounds with *h* to represent simple sounds is a violation of strict theory, and discordant with the rules by which it is desirable to be governed in the construction of an alphabet, yet there may be cases where practical considerations shall justify the employment of the whole series of such compounds, *sh, zh, th, dh, kh, gh, ch*.

Cases beyond these will be of so exceptional and isolated occurrence that they may, with less danger of serious inconvenience, be left to the good judgment and enlightened insight of those who are called upon to construct alphabetic systems for practical use. No slight responsibility, however, rests upon him who first puts into written characters a virgin tongue, since it is impossible to say of how many individuals and generations the convenience depends upon his work. There can be no better preparation for this than a thorough physical comprehension of the sounds of one's own native speech, and a correct understanding of the history of the signs with which it is written; and a searching and intelligible analysis of the English spoken alphabet must be the most valuable phonetical assistant to any one who, having the English for his mother tongue, is required to study the phonetic system of another language, whether for description or for reduction to a written form.

X.—*The Principle of Economy as a Phonetic Force.*

By W. D. WHITNEY,

PROFESSOR IN YALE COLLEGE.

From the very beginning, early in this century, of the scientific study of Indo-European language, the history of the phonetic form of words has taken a leading place as subject of investigation. And from the beginning, also, has been recognized as a principal factor in that history, a tendency to economy, to the saving of effort, in the work of articulate utterance. It might not be easy to tell precisely how and by whom the recognition was first made, and by what steps it arrived at distinct formulation. Perhaps its inception lay, as much as anywhere, in Bopp's demonstration of *i* and *u* as "lighter" vowels than *a*. As a matter of scientific history, the question is not without interest; but I do not propose to enter into it at the present time. Enough for our purpose that the law of economy, as we may call it, has established itself in current linguistic science as the one most unmistakably exhibited, and most widely and variously active, in the transformations of the external form of speech: some, indeed, are prepared already to pronounce it the only existing or possible one. Among these are (as is natural) included not a few of those whose way it is to make easy and confident solutions of difficult questions. Like every other popular dogma, this has its unintelligent partisans and defenders. It would not be hard to cite striking examples of scholars whose application of the law is purely mechanical—who, for example, deduce empirically the prevailing order of succession of sounds in phonetic growth, and then cast about for reasons why the later sound may be declared easier than the earlier; or who endeavor to account for intricate and puzzling phenomena, like the Germanic rotation of mutes, by an arbitrary and baseless classification of the mutes in respect to intrinsic difficulty of utterance. There is hardly a possible abuse of the principle which has not been exemplified in recent discussions of language. And then, by a natural reaction, there have been and are those who deny not only the exclusive domination of the law, its power as a universal solvent of phonetic difficulties, but also its predominant importance, if not its very existence. Perhaps, therefore, a brief discussion of some of the matters involved may be found not untimely or undesirable.

It is evident enough, we may remark at the outset, that those who carry their skepticism so far as to refuse to the principle of economy at least a first-rate place in the external history of speech, display an unreasonableness not excelled by that of the most unenlightened partisan of the principle. Its existence and effects lie upon the very surface of the best understood facts of language. Nothing else is needed, or can be devised, to account for the whole body of phonetic changes falling under the two heads of abbreviation and assimilation. And—especially if we give the latter its full extension, as will be pointed out farther on—this includes the great mass of phonetic changes: those that remain are, whatever their importance and interest, the comparatively rare exceptions.

As much as this, too, may be inferred on appealing to what we know of the processes of the transmission, acquisition, and use of speech. These are matters now sufficiently understood to make them a fair test of the admissibility and adequacy of any general principle claimed to exercise a wide influence in linguistic history.

At present, and as far back in the life of language as our historical researches carry us, every living tongue has been kept in existence by a process of learning, of apprehending and reproducing what was already in currency. The child—and, in his own way and measure, the adult also—hears words and phrases which have come into use he knows not how, and which are brought to his sensorium by a physical agency totally obscure to him; and, when he understands their meaning well enough to use them himself, he reproduces them, as well as he is able, by a physical apparatus which operates, it is true, under the direction of his will, but of whose construction and mode of working he as a child knows nothing, and as an adult very little more. By experience, the possessor and manager of this apparatus acquires great dexterity in the execution of familiar movements; any combination of sounds accordant with those to which he is accustomed he becomes able to imitate with wonderful exactness. But he labors under two disabilities, of which one diminishes and the other increases with his growing age. Until experience has given dexterity, much in utterance is found difficult; the young learner bungles his first speech-imitations terribly, even to the extent of being wholly unintelligible, except to those who know him best. Some sounds are harder to catch and reproduce than others; and it would be practicable, and highly interesting, to determine by a wide observation and deduction what is the general scale of difficulty of acquisition among alphabetic elements. A certain degree of difference would be found between individuals : whether also between communities or races is a much more difficult question : I know of no facts which should lead us to expect to find it of appreciable amount. In general, certainly, it would be found that the sounds, and even the combinations, of all the various languages would be learned with practically equal ease, on an average, by speakers of any and every kindred. It is even more in the combinations than in the individual sounds that the difficulty of reproduction lies—in the quick and nice transition from one articulating position of the organs to another. The child, like the adult learner of a new language, is "thick-tongued" at first, and, even when he can speak correctly, cannot speak rapidly.

And then, the perfection of his conquest of this difficulty ushers in the other. He has begun with being equally awkward, and equally able to overcome his awkwardness, in dealing with the phonetic structure of any language; but when he has schooled his organs to the adjustments and changes required by one system of sounds and combinations, he is less able to adapt them to those required by another; and this new disability, the positive result of habit, grows with every added year of practice, until, after arriving at a certain (not exactly definable) age, one is utterly unable to acquire otherwise than rudely the pronunciation of a strange language.

Thus the attitude of every speaker toward the language which he uses is simply this : he hears, by means which he does not comprehend, signs whose reason is a mystery to him, and, by an apparatus of unknown character in his own throat and mouth, reproduces those signs, at first imperfectly, but later with exactness. Of the *rationale* of the whole process he is both ignorant and careless; to him the practical result is alone of importance. What he knows and realizes is that by such a process of action he makes himself understood by others, even as he understands them ; of the advantage which his own mental acts derive from the possession of this instrumentality he is, for the most part, wholly unconscious.

The question is, now, how there should ever come about any change in the uttered form of the signs thus learned and reproduced.

And I think it must be sufficiently clear, in the first place, that to ascribe to sounds themselves an action of change, or a tendency to variation, in any other than a figurative sense, or for brevity (as when we say that the sun rises), is wholly destitute of reason ; it is a retrogression from the scientific method to the mythological. Sounds are the audible results of the acts of human beings, and of acts which have no instinctive character (though, like everything else made habitual, they may come to be performed with absence of reflection), but are made by volition, in imitation of the similar acts of others. They can suffer no alteration which has not its ground in the action of the human will. And such action is always determined by motives—motives, often, which are not present to the consciousness of the actor, but which may nevertheless be brought to light and demonstrated. What we have to seek, therefore, is the motive or the variety of motives underlying the acts of men in the phonetic changes of speech. There is no question here of a difference of human capacities, making one individual unable to reproduce with accuracy the sounds made by another. Apart from rare individual peculiarities, of habit oftener than of constitution, of which the effect is completely lost in the accordant action of the community, the form of every word as at present used is capable of being perfectly learned and reproduced, and that from generation to generation; there is in the nature of things no necessity that it should ever change; and it never will change if there be not some inducement to its alteration, of a kind that is calculated to affect human action, being either identical or akin with motives that are found operative also in other departments of human action.

It does not need to be pointed out how entirely different all this would be, provided our sounds and their combinations were inherently significant; provided we made them as they are because our mental and physical constitutions are so correlated that certain particular movements of the mind lead naturally to certain particular movements of the organs of speech. Then, of course, changes of significance would be the motives that led to changes of form, and the latter would be the record in which we should study the former. It may be added that, as each person's conceptions are somewhat unlike those of every other, and are all the time changing with his changing knowledge and character, there could neither be unity of speech in a community nor persistency in an individual; the diversities and fluctuations of every language would be illimitable.

As things actually are, it is hard to see what motives can be brought to bear upon the outward framework of language save such as are connected, in one way or another, with increased convenience of use—all of which may be conveniently and fairly summed up in the one word "economy." All changes, indeed, both internal and external, are for the purpose of increased convenience of use; it is not, however, the part of phonetic change to provide new material for the expression of thought; but only to take what is provided in other ways and work it over into more manageable shape. Changes of form are not entirely unproductive of new material—as when phonetic variants of the same word are turned to account by being made to fill different offices: but such things are not only exceptional, they are also inorganic, unintended; they are happy accidents. The almost exclusive direction of movement in phonetic history is toward demolition and decay. Words which had been made up of separate elements first lose their etymologic distinctness, then are fused together, and even shrink into fragments of their former selves. Signs of modification and relation, made in the first place by phonetic change out of independent words, are worn out and drop off again. And what is true of words is also true of the elements which compose them. Mutual adaptation of sound to sound, with rejection of what will not adapt, is the prevailing law. By processes which are completely explainable as results of the tendency to economy, whole classes of sounds are lost from a language or are converted into others.

Just how widely this tendency works, what are the limits to its action, where the line is to be drawn between its effects and those of any other tendency or tendencies, or whether there are such other tendencies, no one has the right to claim to decide at present. That there are phenomena in phonetic history which have not yet been traced to the economic force, and which seem to offer little prospect of ever being so traced, is true enough. But this is by no means equivalent to saying that they never can or will be brought under it. While they resist, they forbid us to maintain with confidence —still more, with dogmatism—that convenience of use, in the form of economy of effort, is the demonstrated sole force at work, and suggest that other minor tendencies may be brought to light; but it will be quite time enough to accept those others when they shall be clearly made out.

The objections hitherto raised, in appearance, against the principle of economy itself have really only lain against the misunderstandings and abuses of that principle—which are common and conspicuous enough. Let us look to see some of the things involved in it.

In the first place—as a matter so much of course that it hardly needs to be pointed out—we have to avoid carefully any views which should imply a conscious and intended economic action on the part of the users of a language. No speaker or set of speakers says: "This word is too long, let us shorten it; this combination is too hard, let us ease it." Such action is totally opposed to all that we know of the past history and the present use of speech. What we need in order to explain the transformations we see is only a motive of permeating, steady, insidious force, which is all the time making in a certain direction, though always liable to be rendered nugatory by a resisting force. Of precisely this character is the tendency to ease. It has been fitly compared to the attraction of gravitation, which constantly tends to level everything high, and draw all substances to the common centre: while, nevertheless, whatever occupies a favoring position, has stamina in itself, or is supported from beneath, keeps up; and while some things even rise, or are projected upward. The economic tendency threatens everything, and reduces whatever is not guarded—or rather, reduces most rapidly what is least guarded: for nothing in language is absolutely insured against its attacks. Every word which is established in use will answer its purpose practically just as well, even if it be not kept up to the full measure of expenditure of force with which it was launched into life, or which it has thus far maintained; and relaxation of the tension of effort at any point allows a weakening to slip in. There is no item of the elaborate structure of speech which cannot be dispensed with; for language is not so poor as to possess only one way of expressing a thing. In a given word it is, other things being equal, the accented syllable that resists best; among words, it is the fully significant ones, as compared with the more enclitic connectives; in an inflective system, it is those formative elements of which the value is most clearly apprehended by the speakers—and so on.

Of far higher importance is it, in the second place, to see clearly that the action of the economic tendency is not toward substituting for sounds in use other sounds which in themselves are easier of production: to no small extent, its effect is just the contrary of this. The problems of phonetics are not going to be helped to a solution by establishing a scale of harder and easier utterances. To draw up such a scale, indeed, would be found a delicate and difficult task. In general, to a given speaker, all the sounds which he is accustomed to make are alike easy; all to which he is unused are hard, in varying degrees, depending mainly on their distance from what he already familiarly knows. If we are to make a scale, it can hardly be otherwise than by the method hinted at above—by observing what comes easiest to the unpracticed organs of young children. And we should find, on applying this test, that the sounds which were dominant in earliest Indo-European, and which phonetic development, through its whole course, has been turning into "lighter" and "weaker" forms, are those with which the untrained speaker at the present time naturally begins. We cannot find a syllable which the infant (etymologically *in-fans*) will sooner and more readily reproduce than *pa:* yet its *a* is the "strongest" of the vowels; and the class (surd mutes) to which its *p* belongs holds a like rank among the consonants. The sounds which the child leaves out or mutilates are apt to be the fricatives, the semi-vowels *y* and *w*, the intermediate shades of vowel utterance. To reverse King Herod's famous deed, and cut off all speakers *except* those of "three years old and upward," would go a good way also towards reversing the alphabetic growth of ages, and restoring an ancient system. So far as children's imperfections of speech exert any influence on phonetic progress, they work against the prevailing current. But their influence is, in reality, only small. They are learners; imperfection is expected from them, and while it is excused, it is also not imitated: age brings practice; and, as adults, they have learned to speak as adults speak. What determines the history of growth of language is the convenience of its adult and practiced speakers.

And what governs the convenience of adults is—so prevailingly that we may almost say exclusively—compatibility, ready combinability in the processes of rapid speaking: not facility of production in the condition of isolated utterance. The succession of different articulating positions, the constant transitions of the organs from one combination to another—these make a modifying influence of far higher importance than the differences of intrinsic ease. Hence, apart from abbreviation, almost all phonetic history consists in adaptation ; and this is mostly assimilation, although in special cases it may be dissimilation likewise ; it may involve omission for the relief of a difficult combination, or, on the other hand, insertion of a transitional sound—and so on.

The phenomena ordinarily reckoned as assimilative are too familiar to be worth illustrating ; but there are others, less generally recognized as belonging to the same class, to whose consideration a brief space may well be devoted.

We are wont to call our human speech "articulate," and to regard the fact that it is so as its most fundamental and distinctive characteristic. And this with good reason ; only there are few who can tell what they really mean by *articulate ;* and even many most reputable authorities are unclear or mistaken in their apprehension of the term. Articulation does not at all signify production by certain definite successive positions and actions of the organs: all utterance, human or brute, is of that nature ; musical utterance would admit the same definition. Articulation is in reality what its etymology makes it: the breaking up of the stream of utterance into distinct parts, into *articuli* or 'joints'—which joints are the syllables : articulate and syllabic are essentially synonymous with each other. And the syllabic effect is produced by the constant alternation of closer and opener utterances ; the closer, or consonants, serve as separators, and at the same time connectors, of the opener and fuller vocal tones, or vowels. The vowels are the main audible substance ; but the aid of the consonants is required to give it articulate character : these divide it into individual parts, separate, but indefinitely combinable. Hence the transition from the close or consonantal positions to the vowel positions, and the contrary, is constant ; and it is a fact of the very first consequence in the phonetic history of speech. For, in its performance, an obvious advantage is gained by making the transitional movement shorter, by reducing the vibrating distance of the organs : that is to say, by shutting less closely the organs which have immediately to open again, and by opening less widely the organs which have immediately to close again. It is only when we give it this interpretation that we can accept as of any force or value the principle often laid down—that the utterances least remote from the medial or neutral position of ordinary breathing are easiest to make. That utterances of this class are easier in themselves, or in isolated use, is disproved by the testimony of young speakers, of early alphabets, and of the ruder existing alphabets. But when the power of swift and ready utterance is acquired, implying a degree of rapidity and accuracy of movement in the organs of speech which appears wonderful and almost incredible to one who looks at it closely enough to see what it is, then the amount of departure each way from the medial position becomes an element of importance. Then the medial sounds, though harder for the untrained speaker to catch and imitate, are found by the advanced and dexterous speaker a lightening of his task. No other reason than this, I believe, can be given why the *a*-sound (of *far*), which is the openest of the vowels, tends always to pass into the closer *i* and *u*, either directly or through the intermediate *e* and *o;* while, by an apparently contrary but really coincident tendency, the mutes are converted into fricatives : and so the medial classes of the alphabet are filled up. Sharpness of distinction and full resonance of tone thus give way to greater pliancy, smoothness, and ease. And the movement is evidently capable of being carried to the extreme of indistinctness and dimness ; there is no necessary limit to the destructive action of the economic tendency ; as it may strip a language once highly synthetic of nearly all its inflectional apparatus, so it may also reduce a clear and full phonetic structure to something approaching the mumbling murmur of one who is trying to speak faster than his organs will let him.

There is not in the phonetic history of our family of languages a movement of more constant action and wider reach than this. And its essentially assimilative character is obvious. It is a mutual assimilation of vowel and consonant: each great class exerts an influence to draw the other toward itself; the vowels are made somewhat closer or more consonantal, while the consonants are made somewhat opener or more vowel-like. I have pointed out in another place (above, p. 57) that a similar assimilative character belongs also to the ordinary interchanges of surd and sonant; thus, and thus only, are they to be brought under the action of the economic tendency; they stand in no natural and inherent relation of comparative ease or difficulty.

In the third place, while we may expect considerable accordance among different languages in the wider and more general results of phonetic change, there is nothing in the law of economy which should necessitate a correspondence in details. The minor movements depend on peculiarities of habit which can neither be prescribed nor foreseen, because they involve as an element the freedom of human action. Such peculiarities may be initiated no one knows why or how —by accident, as we say : and, from wholly insignificant beginnings, they may grow, with the aid of circumstances and under the shaping influence of other habits, into something very definite and marked ; and, in their turn, they may exert a shaping influence on other habits, and lead to consequences which shall seem quite out of proportion to their own import-ance. In learning how movements of this character go on, the minute study of living modes of utterance, especially in what we call their dialectic varieties, will doubtless be of essential assist-ance; it is perhaps the most important result for the study of language which is to be expected from the modern science of phonology. But neither this nor anything else will do more than enable us to follow with fuller appreciation the recorded facts of linguistic history. The varieties of linguistic growth will always be of the same character as other varieties of histor-ical development: incorporations of the varieties of human character and capacity, working themselves out under direction of the varieties of circumstance ; to be traced out with more or less thorough comprehension, but not to be determined *à priori.*

If the law of economy be properly understood, it will be found fairly liable to none of the objections brought against it, and possessed of nearly all the importance ever claimed in its behalf. At present there appears to be no prospect that any other having the tithe of its importance will ever be put alongside it. We have, however, only to wait patiently to see what, in this respect, the future will bring forth, content with noting the absence thus far of any hostile or rival principle.

As to the main question, I do not think that you can (as my brother could not) set before me the many attractions of the place you offer me more strongly than I myself see them. I cannot think of any other offer that would seem to me a temptation to leave here, or would throw me into a state of indecision, like the present. As things are, I cannot make up my mind until my friends here have been able to see what they could do for me if I were to remain. Fifteen years of earnest and interested labor, among colleagues so friendly and helpful, and so worthy in all respects of my regard, have rooted me here very strongly: nor have I for many years had a serious thought of ever quitting this field for another.

Letter from Whitney to C. W. Eliot, October 6, 1869. The discussions that were to lead to a secure appointment at Harvard became public knowledge in New Haven, and Whitney, mortified, wrote apologetically to Eliot asking for time to see whether or not Yale would induce him to remain (see pp. x, xii, xiii). (By permission of Harvard University Archives and Mrs. Robert A. Cushman.)

II. — *On the Nature and Designation of the Accent in Sanskrit.*

By WILLIAM D. WHITNEY,

PROFESSOR OF SANSKRIT AND COMPARATIVE PHILOLOGY IN YALE COLLEGE.

This paper was originally intended only to give such an exposition of the nature of the Sanskrit accent as should illustrate and support the views presented by Professor Hadley in the preceding paper respecting the Greek accent. It has seemed best, however, to treat the subject somewhat more comprehensively than that intent would demand, because full and correct knowledge of Sanskrit accentuation is less accessible to scholars in America than it ought to be. The Sanskrit grammars in English which are most used among us (Monier Williams's and Max Müller's) hardly touch accent at all;[*] and the older works ignore it altogether; while to the treatment of the matter by Oppert and Bopp (and even, in a less degree, by Benfey) much exception is to be taken. To the student of classical Sanskrit merely, accent is a matter of subordinate consequence; no one pretends to give the Sanskrit words their proper tone, and it is the general custom among Western scholars to pronounce them according to the rules of Latin accentuation. This is because the accented syllable is, in the majority of words, unknown; the written texts are not marked for accent, and the notices of the native grammarians are not sufficient to supply the lacking knowledge. With the Vedic student, the case is otherwise; the Vedic texts of the first class (namely, the original Sanhitâs of the Rig, Sâma, Yajur, and Atharva Vedas) are completely accented, and also several works of the second or *brâhmana* class (namely, the two principal *brâhmanas* of the Yajur-Veda, the Çatapatha and Tâittirîya Brâhmanas, and the Tâittirîya-Âranyaka);[†] and the accent is a highly important element in aiding

---

[*] Müller's second edition, which has appeared since the above was written, accents its paradigms, and gives an Appendix on the general subject.

[†] All the works here mentioned are either published or publishing, and will be soon accessible in printed form, complete.

both the grammatical and the lexical comprehension of the texts. And, of course, every student of the history of the Sanskrit language, or of the history of Indo-European language by the aid of the Sanskrit, requires to understand thoroughly a part of the phonetic structure of the latter which is so fundamental in its character, and has exercised so powerful an influence in the shaping of words and forms.

In investigating the nature of the Sanskrit accent, we are not limited to the drawing of inferences from the facts of accentuation laid before us in the texts; our chief sources of knowledge are the Hindu grammarians, who have treated the subject, as they have most other departments of grammatical theory, with great fullness and acuteness. The great grammarian Pâṇini, whose work has become the acknowledged authority for all after time, is clear and intelligible in his statements as to accent; and upon the foundation of his work and its commentators alone, without access to any accented texts, Böhtlingk gave in 1843* an acute, intelligent, and very correct account both of the theory and of the main facts of Sanskrit accent, one that in many respects has not been surpassed or superseded by anything that has since appeared. But the brevity of Pâṇini is most acceptably supplemented by the more detailed statements of the Prâtiçâkhyas. These are treatises which attach themselves each to a single Vedic text, as phonetic manual of the school to which that text belongs. They deal with all the elements of articulate utterance — with the mode of production and the classification of articulate sounds, with accent and quantity, rules of euphonic combination, and the like; and they prescribe how the various forms of text in which their Veda is preserved are to be constructed, cataloguing its slightest irregularities of form, and endeavoring to fix its readings beyond the reach of question or change. Four such treatises have come to light: one belonging to the Rig-Veda, one to the White Yajus or Vâjasaneyi-Sanhitâ, one to the Black Yajus or Tâittirîya-Sanhitâ, and one to the Atharva-Veda; for the Sâma-Veda alone none has yet been found.

---

* *Ein erster Versuch über den Accent im Sanskrit,* von Otto Böhtlingk, in the Memoirs of the St. Petersburg Academy, vol. vii., series 6th, 4to.

Prior to the publication of any of them, the teachings of the
first three with regard to accent were summarily presented by
Roth (who was the first to call the attention of scholars to this
class of works) in the Introduction to his edition of Yâska's
Nirukta (Göttingen, 1852, pp. lvii.–lxxii.). All have been since
edited in full; the Rik-Prâtiçâkhya by Regnier (in the Journal
Asiatique, Paris, 1857–9) and Müller (Leipzig, 1856–69), the
Vâjasaneyi-Prâtiçâkhya by Weber (in his Indische Studien,
vol. iv., Berlin, 1858), the Atharva-Prâtiçâkhya and the Tâittirîya-Prâtiçâkhya by myself (in the Journal of the American
Oriental Society, vols. vii., 1862, and ix., 1871). I have also
discussed—with more fullness, I believe, than any one else
has found occasion to do—some of the general questions relating to the subject, in a critique on Bopp's *Accentuationssystem*,
in the Journ. Am. Or. Soc. (vol. v., 1856, pp. 195–218), and
in the note to Ath. Prât. iii. 65 (Journ. etc. vii. 494 ff.) ; and
have set forth the rules respecting the accent of the verb in
the sentence, with illustrations from the Atharva-Veda, in the
same Journal (v. 387 ff.).

The information which we derive from all these enumerated
sources is full enough, not only to let us see clearly the views
held by the ancient Hindu grammarians (their age, unfortunately, is not ascertained, but is generally believed to precede
by some centuries the Christian era) respecting the accent of
their learned and sacred language, but also to enable us in
some measure to trace the development of their accentual theory, and to criticize it in its details. For, though we cannot
help admiring and respecting, and in a very high degree, the
acuteness and sagacity of those oldest known students of phonetics, we cannot accept for truth what they give us without
first carefully questioning it, and testing it by fact and by theory ; and we shall be likely to find in their treatment of more
than one point their characteristic and national weaknesses,
and to be led to modify and amend their doctrines.

The general name given to accent is *svara*, which means
literally 'tone;' and, in virtue of this meaning, is applied also
to designate other things beside accent. Thus, it is the name
of a 'vowel,' as being a *tone*-sound, an utterance in which the

element of tone predominates over that of articulation ; and it
is in the Prâtiçâkhyas used a dozen times in this sense to once
in any or all others. It designates, moreover, the 'tones' or
musical notes which compose the scale. There is, then, nothing about the word that necessarily implies a particular theory
respecting the nature of accent; although the absence of any
reference in it to stress or force of utterance, and its connection with musical pitch, are distinctly suggestive of a musical
theory.

This suggestion is made a certainty by the names and definitions of the separate accents or "tones." Of these, three
are recognized, and they are called respectively *udâtta, anudâtta,* and *svarita.*

Udâtta (passive participle of the root *dâ,* with the prepositions *ut* and *â*) means literally 'taken up, raised, elevated.'
And the description of the accent by all the authorities corresponds with this title ; it is defined everywhere, in nearly iden
tical terms, as being utterance *uccâis,* 'in a high tone.' (Se
Ath. Prât. i. 14; Vâj. Prât. i. 108; Tâitt. Prât. i. 38; Pân.
i. 2. 29; the Rik Prât. alone, iii. 1, is less explicit, but it
whole doctrine accords with that of the rest.)

Anudâtta is the same word with the negative prefix, and so
means 'not elevated.' The authorities define it as signifying
utterance *nîcâis,* 'in a low tone.' (See Ath. Prât. i. 15; Vâj
Prât. i. 109; Tâitt. Prât. i. 39; Pân. i. 2. 30; the Rik Prât.
defines *udâtta* and *anudâtta* as characterized respectively by
"tension" and "relaxation" — i. e. of the organs of articula
tion.) This lowness of tone does not imply, of course, a fall
from the ordinary pitch of voice ; the tone is low as compared
with *udâtta;* it is the simple negation of that uplifting of
pitch which marks the positively accented syllable.

The name of the third tone is *svarita,* and it is uniformly
explained as consisting in a combination of the other two
Thus, Pânini and the Tâittirîya-Prâtiçâkhya say, in identica
phrase, *samâhârah svaritah,* 'the combination [of the two oth
ers, just defined] is *svarita;*' the Vâjasaneyi-Prâtiçâkhya ha
ubhayavân svaritah, 'one [i. e. a vowel] possessing both [the
two tones as already defined] is *svarita;*' the Rik-Prâtiçâkhy

is more elaborate in its statement: "in case of the occurrence together of the two preceding [tones] in one syllable, the accent is *svarita;*" the Atharva-Prâtiçâkhya alone is here ambiguous, using a term (*âkshiptam*) which is not explanatory, but itself requires to be explained in accordance with what we know by other means of the theory involved. The further specifications added in nearly all the treatises make this definition still more unequivocal. Thus, Pâṇini (i. 2. 32) says, " half [the quantity of] a short vowel at its beginning is *udâtta;*" the Ath. Prât. (i. 17), "half the quantity of a *svarita*, at its beginning, is *udâtta;*" the Vâj. Prât. (i. 126), "at its beginning, half the quantity of the vowel is *udâtta.*" The other two Prâtiçâkhyas complicate the definition with a further development of the accentual theory, to be explained hereafter ; but in regard to the essential characteristic of the accent, that it is a union of higher and lower tone in the same syllable, they accord entirely with those already quoted. The Rik Prât. (iii. 2, 3) says "half a mora, or half the quantity, of this [*svarita*] is higher than *udâtta;* the following remainder is *anudâtta*, but is heard as *udâtta*"—that is to say, the descent of tone, instead of being from *udâtta* to *anudâtta*, is from a higher pitch than *udâtta* down to something sensibly equivalent to the latter. And the Tâitt. Prât. (one of whose peculiarities it is everywhere to quote conflicting opinions on controverted points) says, yet more at large (i. 41–7): " of this *svarita*, when it immediately follows an *udâtta*, the beginning, to the extent of half a short vowel, is uttered in a higher tone than *udâtta ;* the remainder is equivalent to *udâtta ;* or, this following part is in a lower tone; or it is equivalent to *anudâtta ;* the teachers say that the first part is equivalent to *udâtta* and the rest to *anudâtta ;* some hold that the whole is a downward slide."

We thus see that there is no discordance whatever among the ancient Hindu grammarians with regard to the nature of the *svarita* accent, as being the union of a higher and lower tone upon the same vowel, or within the same syllable. No hint of a different explanation is given us, nor do we discover any traces of the former prevalence of another view, crowded

out and replaced by this. Of the name *svarita*, however, by
which it is called, it is exceedingly difficult to find a satisfactory explanation. The word is most likely a quasi-participial
formation from *svara* itself, and means ' toned ;' possibly it was
applied to the syllable because this exhibited all the tones
which have to be taken account of in accentuation ; or because
the element of tone was most conspicuous in it; its change of
pitch gave it a sing-song or cadenced effect. That it signifies
' accented,' in our sense of that term, there is no reason whatever for supposing. Other conjectural explanations, of which
not a few have been ventured, may be left here unnoticed.
What is unmistakably clear with regard to it is the view which
the Hindus unanimously held as to the nature of the accent
which it designated ; and any interpretation which we may
try to put upon it must be subordinated to this ; we have no
right to make an etymology of the name, and then force it into
a definition of the thing.

Such being the defined character of the three tones, their
accordance with the Greek acute, grave, and circumflex, as
defined above, in Prof. Hadley's paper, is clear and undeniable ; and the accentual system either of the Greek or the Sanskrit, if it needed any support from without, would find it
abundantly in this close parallelism with the other. There
being no possibility of a copying of the accentual theory on
either side, both must be regarded as independently founded
upon the facts of the two languages, and as faithfully and fairly
representing them. And we are justified in setting aside
when speaking of the Sanskrit accents, the outlandish Sanskrit
terms, and employing instead of them the familiar designations " acute," " grave," " circumflex."*

Unless, indeed, we shall find sufficient evidence somewhere
in the phenomena of accentuation of either Greek or Sanskrit
to convict the native grammarians of having blundered in
their observations and deductions. And that this is not the

---

* These were used by Böhtlingk, in the essay which first opened to Europe the
knowledge of the Sanskrit accent; and the more the latter is understood, the more
generally will they be adopted.

case as regards the Sanskrit, I shall endeavor to show by a concise exhibition of the rules for the occurrence of the *svarita* or circumflex in that language.

The circumflex in Sanskrit is a rare and inconspicuous phenomenon as compared with the Greek. Only a very small class of words have it as their proper accent, and it arises chiefly in the course of the combination of words into phrases, by the peculiar euphonic system of the Sanskrit, which, as is well known, does not leave its words to stand independently side by side, but adapts their final and initial elements to one another, avoiding the hiatus, or any collision of incompatible consonants.

The first class of circumflexes arises when an acute *i* or *î*, or *u*, is converted into *y* or *v* before an unaccented dissimilar vowel. Thus, *ví* and *evá* are combined into *vyèvá**; *nadí'* and *asya* into *nadyàsya; apsú* and *agne* into *apsvàgne.* That is to say, the single syllable into which the higher and lower tone are combined still retains the double pitch belonging to its constituent parts. This kind of circumflex is in all the Prâtiçâkhyas† styled *kshâipra*, literally 'hasty, quick,' as being accompanied with an abbreviation of quantity, in the contraction of two syllables into one.

One of the most peculiar and problematical processes in the whole Sanskrit euphonic system is that by which a final *ê* or *ô* absorbs or elides an initial *ă* of the word that follows. This, which has become the regular and necessary mode of combination in the later or classical Sanskrit, was only an occasional license in the older Vedic language ; in the Atharva-Veda, for instance, the *a* was elided in only a little more than onesixth of the cases in which it followed *e* or *o*. Wherever, now, the *e* or *o* was acute and the *a* grave, the accent of the former after the absorption of the latter was made circumflex. Thus, *té abravan* became *tèbravan; só abravît* became *sòbravît.*

---

* For want of means to do better, I signify the circumflex accent by what we ordinarily call the sign of grave ; the sound represented (in accordance with usual custom) by *v* is that of our *w*.

† The distinction, namely, of the kinds of circumflex, with the corresponding nomenclature, is unknown to Pânini.

Here, again, the acute and grave tones of the constituent elements are both represented in the circumflex given to the syllable that results from their combination. This second circumflex is styled *abhinihita* (or, by the Tâitt. Prât., *abhinihata*): the literal meaning and ground of application of the term are not very clear.

In case, however, the accent of the two elements is other than has been defined, no circumflex arises; if the second element is acute, the combination is acute; if the first as well as the second is grave, the combination, of course, is grave also.

If, moreover, two vowels are fused together into a single vowel or diphthong, then, if either was acute, the resulting combination, as a general rule, is also acute: that is to say, the acute element is powerful enough to assimilate the other, raising the whole syllable to the higher tone. Thus, *sá'* and *asti* become *sá'sti*, *sá'* and *eshá'* become *sá'ishá'*, *sá'* and *út* become *sót; nayati* and *índrah* become *nayatî'ndrah; stha û'rjam* becomes *sthórjam;* and so on. This is the rule laid down in all the Prâtiçâkhyas; and all the Vedic texts of the first rank, the Sanhitâs, conform to it. Pâṇini, however (at viii. 2. 6), also permits the result of combination of a final acute with an initial grave to be circumflex; that is, he allows *sá' asti* to become either *sá'sti* or *sá'sti*, and so on. And there is a single Vedic text of the second order (the Çatapatha-Brâhmaṇa, belonging to the White Yajur-Veda) which makes its combinations in this manner circumflex. Of course, this is just the exception which we might expect to see made, considering the nature of the circumflex; and that it is not universally recognized in Sanskrit usage indicates the very different position which the circumflex takes in the Sanskrit system, as compared with the Greek: the latter language has a predilection for it, and lets it appear in innumerable cases where it has no etymological justification; the former has a prejudice against it, and exhibits it only where compelled, as it were, to do so.

But there is one exceptional and infrequent case where the Prâtiçâkhyas require, and Vedic usage shows, a circumflex as result of the fusion of an acute vowel with a grave into one.

It is where two short *i*'s are combined, forming long *î*. Thus, *diví iva* becomes *divî'va*, *abhí ihi* becomes *abhî'hi*, and so on. This appears very arbitrary, as we can see no reason why *î* under such circumstances should receive a circumflex accent any more than *â*, or *û*, or the diphthongs *e, ái, o, áu*. And the impression of arbitrariness is increased when we come to notice that one Prâtiçâkhya (the Tàitt. Pràt., at x. 17) denies the circumflex to *î*, but gives it to *û*, combining *mâsú ut* into *mâsû't*, and so on. This is equivalent to restricting still further the occurrence of the circumflex in question: there are no more than sixteen cases of *î'* in the whole ample text of the Atharva-Veda; but there are only five of *û'* in the yet ampler Táittiríya-Sanhitâ (which contains about thirty passages in which *î'* would appear, if the usage of the text permitted). This rare and anomalous circumflex is styled *praçlishta* (or *prâçlishta*), 'resulting from fusion.'

Such, then, are the cases in which a circumflex arises by the combination into one syllable of a preceding acute and a following grave element. Besides these, there is a limited class of words which show a circumflex as their proper and sole accent: for example, the nouns *svàr*, 'heaven,' and *kanyâ'*, 'girl,' the particle *kvà*, 'where ?', the adjective *budhnyà*, 'fundamental,' and so on. But every word of this class contains a *y* or *v* before the vowel of its accented syllable; that is to say, the syllable is of the same kind with those which in combination receive the *ksháipra* circumflex; and it is obvious that the circumflex is indeed essentially a *ksháipra*, its origin lying merely a step further back. By this I mean, that *kanyâ'* and *kvà*, for example, stand for more original *kaní-â* and *kú-a*, so that the circumflex of *kanyâ'* is precisely analogous with that of *nadyàsya* from *nadî' asya*. And the Vedic verse clearly shows that the fusion of the two syllables into one, with consequent circumflex, is a fact not yet accomplished in Vedic times: such syllables are more often to be read as two than as one, *kvà* becoming dissyllabic, *kanyâ'* trisyllabic, and so on. Indeed, the Tàittiríya-Sanhitâ (which has a peculiar orthographic usage with regard to a part of these words) regularly writes *sávar* instead of *svàr*, *budhníya* instead of *budhnyà*, and so on — while, on the other hand, it resolves *indrágnyós* into *indrágniyós*, *báhvós* into *báhuvós*, and so in other like cases.

To the circumflex accent which thus appears as the original accent of a word, and does not arise in the course of the euphonic combination of words into phrases, most of the Hindu grammarians give the name of *játya*, 'native, natural;' the Tâitt. Prât. alone calls it *nitya*, 'constant, unchanging.' We may class the cases of its occurrence under four heads:

a. Words like *svàr* and *kvà*, of which the derivation is obscure or without extended analogies.

b. Words having the circumflexed suffix *yà* (representing *í-a* or *î-a*), like *kanyâ`*, *vîryà*, *dhanvanyà*, *saṁsrávyà* : this class is a pretty large one.

c. Forms of declension made by adding an unaccented case-ending to an accented final *î'* or *û* : thus, *svâdhyàs* from *svâdhî'* ; *lalâmyàm* from *lalâmî'* ; *tanvàs*, *tanvàm*, *tanvè* from *tanû'* (these last are especially frequent ; the Tâittirîya-Sanhitâ writes them *tanúvas*, *tanúve*, etc.), *prdâkvàs* from *prdakû'*. These are mostly nominatives singular dual or plural, or accusatives singular or dual, since the endings of all the cases except these five tend to draw the accent forward upon themselves ; and so we have, for example, from *nadî'*, the nom. dual *nadyâù* and nom. pl. *nadyàs*, but in other oblique cases *nadyâ'i*, *nadyâ's*, etc., just as we have from *nâ'us* the nominatives *nâ'vâu* and *nâ'vas*, but the oblique cases *nâvé*, *nâvás*, *nâví*, etc.

d. Accented vocatives, like *dyâ`us*, *jyâ`ke*. It is the rule, namely, in Sanskrit, that the vocative, if accented at all, is accented on its first syllable. If, now, this syllable, as written, is one of which a semivowel preceding the vowel has in the metre the value of a syllable by itself, that element alone takes the acute tone, and the written syllable is circumflexed. The words given above, therefore, are equivalent to *dí-âus*, *jí-âke*, and have to be so read in scanning the verses in which they occur. The case is quite a rare one ; it occurs, I believe, only twice in the Atharva-Veda (at i. 2.2 and vi. 4.3: but in the latter passage the edited text reads incorrectly *dyâ'us*), and I presume there are hardly more than that number of cases in the Rig-Veda.

To illustrate the degree of frequency of the circumflex accent in actual use, in its different kinds, it may be stated that in the first twenty hymns of the Rig-Veda (about two hundred lines, mostly of twenty-four syllables each; a part, of thirty-two), there are but ten cases of it, namely six *kshâipra*, one *abhinihita*, and three *jâtya;* of which last, there is one case each falling under *a*, *b*, and *c*. In the first *praçna* or chapter of the Tâittirîya-Sanhitâ, again (a somewhat less body of text, chiefly prose), there are six *kshâipra's*, eleven *abhinihita's*, and three *jâtya's* (all falling under *b*). In the first book of the Atharva-Veda (having about the same extent as the passage from the Rig-Veda already reported), once more, there are forty-six cases; eleven *kshâipra's*, three *abhinihita's*, and thirty-two *jâtya's;* of which last, ten fall under *b*, twenty-one under *c*, and one under *d*.

The diversity thus appearing between the different passages compared is in part accidental, in part characteristic of the texts from which they are respectively taken: in general, it will probably be found that the *kshâipra* circumflex appears oftenest, and the *jâtya*, its nearest kindred, next; the *praçlishṭa*, as already explained, is by far the rarest of the four.

So far, there is nothing difficult or questionable either in the theory or in the practice of Sanskrit accentuation, and all the phenomena are of a nature to favor and establish the truth of that description of the nature of the *svarita* or circumflex accent which is given by the grammarians. But we have next to consider an addition to the theory which is of a very problematical character. The native authorities, namely, teach unanimously that a syllable naturally grave, if it follows an acute, in any part of a word, or in a succeeding word in the same phrase, takes the circumflex tone. Thus, the Rik-Prâtiçâkhya, which makes the fullest statement, says (iii. 9) "a grave syllable preceded by an acute is circumflexed, whether separated from it by a hiatus or by a consonant;" and the others teach virtually the same thing.* That is to say (as

---

* See Vâj. Prât. iv. 134, Tâitt. Prât. xiv. 29, 30, Ath. Prât. iii. 67, Pâṇ. viii. 4. 66.

we may state to ourselves the virtual meaning of the doctrine), the voice, when once raised to the higher pitch of acute, is not able to descend to the general level of utterance in the interval between the acute syllable and its successor, but slides down in the course of the latter; it occupies a syllable in its descent. Thus, *íti* is not grave, but circumflex, on its final; *sâ'* and *asya* become *sâ'sya* with circumflex on the last *a ;* the *bru* of the toneless *bruvanti* is circumflexed in the combination *té bruvanti*, and so on. This circumflex, by European grammarians, is conveniently distinguished from those which have been described above by being called the "dependent" or the "enclitic" circumflex: the term, however, has no correspondent in Sanskrit, nor do the Hindu grammarians, by description, classification, or designation, intimate a recognition of any difference in character between the enclitic and the independent varieties of this accent. The Prâtiçâkhyas divide the former, as they do the latter, into sub-varieties, calling *tâirovyañjana*, 'having consonants interposed,' a circumflex vowel between which and the occasioning acute consonants intervene (as in the examples above cited), and *pâdavṛtta*, 'with word-hiatus' (or, in the Rik Prât., simply *vâivṛtta*, 'with hiatus'), one that is separated from the acute by the hiatus that sometimes intervenes between two words (as in the *u* of *yâ' u ca*, from *yâ'ḥ u ca*, and of *tá ucyante*, from *té ucyante**). No attempt is made to describe these two varieties as exhibiting

---

* There are unimportant differences among the different Prâtiçâkhyas in regard to the classification of the enclitic circumflexes. The Vâj. Prât. (i. 118) makes a special class, *tâirovirâma*, 'with intervening pause,' of those which are separated from the occasioning acute by the pause which in *pada*-text divides the two parts of a compound word : thus, *gó patâ-ı* or *yajñá-patim* has tḷi̇ kind of circumflex on *pa ;* and it is probable that the Tâitt. Prât. (xx. 3) intends to designate the same as *prâtihata*, though the native commentary understands the case otherwise, and makes *prâtihata* signify a circumflex standing in another word than the acute and separated from it by consonants, like the *â* of *yás trâ*, or the *u* of *té bruvanti*, as given above. The Tâitt. Prât. further confines the name *pâdavṛtta* to cases involving a hiatus between two independent words, and in the exceedingly rare cases where there is a hiatus within the word itself (as in *prầṅgam*), classes the circumflex as *tâ'rovyañjana*, though there is no 'intervention of consonants' at all here. And the Vâj. Prât. (i. 120) has a peculiar name, *tâthâbhârya*, for the very uncommon and somewhat anomalous case of an enclitic circumflex between two acutes.

any difference of character, and their distinction is evidently only an example of that tendency to over-refinement in classification which is characteristic of Hindu systematists.

It is not possible to accept the teachings of the Sanskrit grammarians as to the enclitic circumflex with the same trust as those respecting the independent circumflex. Even the Greek, which shows a marked predilection for the circumflexed tone, never admits it save in an actually long vowel, not finding room elsewhere for the exhibition of the double tone or downward slide. And the Sanskrit, as we have seen, has so much less inclination to this tone, or capacity for it, as to admit it only in very rare cases even upon a long vowel or a proper diphthong: to bring it out, there is needed an improper diphthong, as we may fairly call it—a vowel-group in which the first element is an *i* or *u* sound, written as a *y* or *v*, but still evidently retaining in good measure its vowel value and its capacity of tone. In a language of this habit, then, it is next to incredible that we should find a circumflex tone developed with the utmost freedom even in short vowels (as the finals of *íti* and *mádhu*) by the simple neighborhood of an acute. We cannot, so it seems to me, avoid suspecting the accuracy of the observations which underlie the whole theory of the enclitic circumflex. The Tâittirîya-Prâtiçâkhya is ingenuous enough to inform us (xiv. 33) that some authorities denied this circumflex *in toto*. If we do not carry our own skepticism so far as that, we shall be likely to take refuge in the theory of a "middle tone," like that assumed by Misteli and Hadley (see the preceding article, p. 11.) in explaining the peculiarities of Greek and Latin accent. This would imply that the enclitic tone which was perceived to lead down from acute pitch to grave was in reality a step intermediate between the two, and was hastily and inaccurately apprehended by the Hindu grammarians as a combination of the two, or a slide, and so identified with the independent circumflex, of which the origin and character were too clear to admit of any doubt or question. Through this modification of the Hindu theory, we may win from the Sanskrit enclitic circumflex a degree of support for the "middle tone;" but it is necessary that we understand and confess the fact of the modification. Quietly to assume, as Misteli does, that the whole Sanskrit circumflex, in both its independent and its enclitic varieties, is only a middle tone, is wholly unallowable, being opposed to the plain and unanimous statements of the Hindu grammarians, and, not less, to the teachings of a sound accentual theory.*

A single exception is made by all the Hindu text-books to the rule that a grave syllable following an acute takes the enclitic circumflex: if, namely, an acute or a circumflex (of course, independent) immediately follows, the grave retains its proper quality. Thus, in *yé ca*, *ca* is circumflexed; but in *yé ca té* or *yé ca svàr* it is grave (Rik Prât. iii. 9, Vâj. Prât. iv. 135, Tâitt. Prât. xiv. 31, Ath. Prât. iii. 70, Pân. viii. 4. 67). The Tâittirîya-Prâtiçâkhya (xiv. 32) reports a single gramma-arian (Âgniveçyâyana) as disallowing this exception, and maintaining the circumflex even before a syllable having or beginning with high tone; and Pânini (viii. 4. 67) mentions three authorities (Gârgya, Kâçyapa, and Gâlava) as holding the same doctrine. I do not see that theoretical considerations teach us anything with definiteness upon this point; we should quite as naturally, however, in my opinion, expect the enclitic tone, whether slide or middle tone, to maintain itself before an acute or circumflex as well as before a grave.

These are the principal features of the system of Sanskrit accentuation. We need, however, to follow it out into one or two further details, important as regards the native theory; and, before we can do this, we must take note of the Hindu

---

* It would almost seem that Misteli's view was to be looked upon as the Italian one, since Ascoli also, in his lately published lectures on comparative philology (*Corsi di Glottologia* etc., first part, Comparative Phonology of the Sanskrit, Greek, and Latin, p. 15), expresses himself upon the subject as follows: " The syllable, finally, that follows the acute, becomes *svarita*, ' tonic,' or, in other terms, assumes the *svarita* accent—which some European grammarians (infelicitously, as it appears to me) have called ' circumflex'—; that is to say, it has a tonality higher than the ordinary, but not so high as is that of the syllable with acute." A scholar of Ascoli's rank and claims to respect should not allow himself thus summarily to set aside the carefully deduced results of his predecessors, without bringing up a single consideration to support the view he takes.

mode of designating accent. This is in the main the same
in all the accentuated texts: some minor differences will
appear as we go on; others may be passed over as of no importance to our purpose.*

By a striking — and as I think, an ill-judged and unfortunate — peculiarity of usage, the Hindu does not designate
directly the really accented or acute syllable, but, instead, its
surroundings, or the preceding grave and the following circumflex. Or, as we may express it, the acute syllable is left
unmarked; but the grave syllable is marked, by a horizontal
stroke beneath the syllable; and the circumflex (whether enclitic or independent), by a perpendicular stroke above. In
the manuscripts (so far as I know, without exception), these
strokes are added in red ink; in printed text, of course, they
have to be represented by black lines.

Thus, examples of single words (with transliteration, accented according to our method, written below each word) are

1. अग्निना । करिष्यसि । चोदयित्रीभिः ।

 a-gní-ná *ka-ri-shyá-si* *co-da-yi-tri'-bhih*

An independent circumflex is generally to be distinguished
from an enclitic (of which latter kind are those in the above
examples) by having no unmarked acute before it: thus

2. स्वः । कन्या । यातुधान्यः ।

 svàh *ka-nyà* *yâ-tu-dhâ-nyàh*

A word that is unaccented has the mark of grave under
every syllable; an acute monosyllable has no mark at all; and
an initial acute has, of course, no grave mark before it, nor a
final acute any circumflex mark after it: thus

3. च । वक्षति । सः । पोषम् । अग्निम् । सुरूपकृत्नुम् ।

 ca *va-ksha-ti* *sáh* *pó-sham* *a-gním* *su-rú-pa-kr-tnúm*

We may conjecture plausibly enough that these marks are
symbolical: the horizontal line below intimates the lower tone

---

* The designation of the independent circumflex in the White Yajur Veda is
in sundry points peculiar; see Weber's edition, Preface, p. x.

at which the voice moves on; the other directs the voice downward from a higher key.

This mode of accentuation would seem to involve an excessive repetition of the sign of grave tone; but the difficulty is avoided (as we may provisionally say) by omitting all signs of grave after a circumflex except under a syllable that precedes another acute or an independent circumflex. In this way, there is no repetition of the grave sign under successive syllables except at the beginning of a word or phrase, before the first accented syllable is reached. Thus,

4. होतारम् । रत्नधातंमम् । चित्रश्रवस्तमः ।

hó-tá-ram　　　ra-tna-dhá'-ta-mam　　　ci-trá-çra-va-sta-maḥ

The same rule is followed, of course, where words are combined into phrases; and

5. अग्ने । यम् । यज्ञम् । अध्वरम् । विश्वतः । परिभूः । असि ।

á-gne　　yám　　ya-jñám　　a-dhva-rám　　vi-çvá-taḥ　　pa-ri-bhú'ḥ　　á-si

becomes, as a sentence,

6. अग्ने यं यज्ञमध्वरं विश्वतः परिभूरसि ।

In this phrase, it is to be noted, the *e* of *ágne*, which was enclitically circumflex when the word stood alone, becomes grave again (by the rule stated above, p. 33) when the acute syllable *yám* comes to stand after it: and, on the other hand, the grave initial *a* of *adhvarám* takes the enclitic circumflex when conjoined with the acute final of *yajñám*. The penultimate and antepenultimate syllables of the line, as both alike standing between grave and circumflex signs, are both acute, the voice when once sent up by the former sign remaining raised until sent down again by the latter. In the same manner, when conducted down by the circumflex sign, it continues at the lower pitch till the other directs it to go up: an example illustrating more fully this effect is

7. ओमासश्चर्षणीधृतो विश्वे देवास आ गंत ।

ómásaç　　carshaṇidhṛto　　víçve　　devása　　á'　　gata

where the first four words are vocatives, and the last a

finite verb in an independent clause—both of which classes of words are toneless in Sanskrit, except when, like the first and third words, they stand at the head of a sentence or of a primary division of a verse.

I will note here but one other peculiarity of the mode of designation: namely, that if an independent circumflex follows an acute, it is in no way distinguished from an enclitic circumflex; so that, for example, in

8. ताः स्व॑र्व॑तीः

it is impossible to tell whether the latter word is a toneless vocative, *svarvatîh*, or a nominative or accusative with its regular accent, *svàrvatîh*.

It thus appears that two classes of syllables in accentuated text are left unmarked: first, those which are properly acute or *udâtta* (as *ó*-, *víç*-, and *á'*, in the last example but one); and second, those which are properly grave or *anudâtta*, but which neither receive the enclitic circumflex as following an acute, nor are marked by the grave sign, as preceding an acute or circumflex. But there is a strange and perplexing addition to the Hindu theory which virtually identifies these two classes with one another in respect to tone: and this we have next to examine.

The point is thus stated in the Tâittirîya-Prâtiçâkhya (xxi. 10, 11): "in continuous text, after a circumflex, a series (*pracaya*) of grave syllables has the tone of acute (literally, 'sounds, or is heard, as acute'), except the syllable that is followed by an acute or circumflex." The other Prâtiçâkhyas have equivalent rules (Rik Prât. iii. 5, 11, 12; Vâj. Prât. iv. 138–40; Ath. Prât. iii. 71, 74).*

---

* The Vâj. Prât., in describing the character of the accent, uses the term *udâttamaya*, 'made of, or of the same material as, acute,' instead of (like the rest) *udâttaçruti*, 'having the audible quality of acute.' The Rik Prât. states the rule twice over, calling the tone once (in verse 11) *udâttaçruti*, and once (in verse 5) *udâtta*, 'acute,' outright; it also adds one or two peculiar items, the first to the effect that "some, however, depress (to grave tone) one syllable, or more than one, at the end of the series; or even all but one or two;" the other (verse 13) is too obscure to be made intelligible without more exposition and discussion than we have room for here.

To this accent is given the name *pracaya*, 'accumulation, indefinite series,' or *pracita*, 'accumulated, indefinitely continued,' from the way in which it is liable to run on, to the extent, sometimes, of ten or a dozen syllables, or more.*

According to the Prâtiçâkhyas, then, the treatment in continuous text of syllables naturally grave is as follows: a single such syllable following an acute before a pause becomes an enclitic circumflex, but before another acute or circumflex retains its grave character (compare *ágne*, above, illustrations 5 and 6); of two such syllables, the first always has the circumflex, the second is either grave before another accented syllable (as *-dhva-* in illustration 6), or *pracaya*, with acute tone, before a pause (as the finals in the last two words in 4 and the last in 7); of more than two, either all but the first and last, or all but the first, are *pracaya* (as *-saç carshaṇîdhṛ-* and *devâ-* in 7, or *-vastamaḥ* in 4) ; — after a circumflex, the treatment is the same, with the exception that the first syllable is not circumflexed, but remains grave or becomes *pracaya*, according to the character of what follows it; — finally, any number of grave syllables coming before the first acute or circumflex in a phrase retain their grave character.

The striking result of this is, that there comes to be a complete accordance between the theoretical tone of each syllable and the way it is marked. Every syllable that has the perpendicular stroke above it is circumflex, and of the same tone, whether the circumflex is independent or enclitic; every syllable that has a horizontal mark beneath is grave, or of low tone ; every syllable that has no mark at all is of high tone, whether it be properly acute, or originally grave and converted to *pracaya*.

An interesting and important question now arises: What is the ground of this complete accordance? Is the mode of designation posterior to the theory? Did the Hindus leave the *pracaya* grave syllables unmarked, like acute, *because*

---

*For example, in the series of toneless vocatives *ágne dudhra gahya kiṁçila vanya*.

they gave them the tone of acute, so that their identity of treatment is due to a perceived identity of character? or, on the other hand, was the omission of a part of the marks indicating grave tone made for the sake of convenience, of brevity (as I have, provisionally, assumed above to be the case), and is the theory an afterthought, suggested by the identity of designation, and aiming to establish a corresponding identity of character?

To many scholars, perhaps even to nearly all, the question I have raised will seem strange, and the latter of the two suggested explanations one altogether to be rejected, as implausible and incredible. Nevertheless, I am convinced that the matter merits a serious discussion. And, in the first place, we shall not, I think, be doing the ancient Hindu grammarians an utter injustice, in supposing them capable of fabricating a theory like that of the *pracaya*-accent, under the inducement stated above. The "schools" of Vedic study in which the Prâtiçâkhyas originated were far removed from the period in which their sacred texts had grown up, or even had been brought into their present shape; and these texts had begun to be treated in more than one respect in a somewhat formal, arbitrary, and unintelligent manner. The acuteness of observation, and the skill in combination and systematization, displayed by the grammarians, as by the Hindu workers in other departments of science, are worthy of high admiration: but we cannot equally commend their moderation, nor is their soundness to be trusted to the end. They never knew where to stop; and their systems, as has been said elsewhere, always tended to take on a prescriptive character where they were intended to be descriptive only — putting violence upon the facts which they set out simply to examine and classify. I should not be restrained from regarding the *pracaya*-accent with acute tone as a later and artificial addition to the original accentual theory by any exaggerated faith in the infallibility of the authorities who report it to us.

A single scholar, of high rank, and especially conversant with the Prâtiçâkhyas,* has, it is, true, maintained that the

---

* M. Müller, in his History of Ancient Sanskrit Literature, p. 497ff.

Prâtiçâkhyas antedate the use of writing in India, and do not presuppose any recorded text at all. But, if I am not mistaken, this view of his is generally rejected as paradoxical. The Prâtiçâkhyas do, indeed, like most of the sacred litera· ture of India, and some of its literature in other departments, studiously and successfully ignore everything written, and acknowledge only the oral tradition of the schools as the lawful channel for the conveyance of knowledge from generation to generation; but, in the view of most men, such phonetic analysis as they make, and such fixation of the nicest details of reading as they imply, would be more than wonderful, it would be absolutely miraculous, without the aid of writing. A race that had made advanced and recondite studies in every department of grammar without even possessing an alphabet would be a greater prodigy than "the Anthropophagi, and men whose heads do grow beneath their shoulders."

The obstacle in the way of our accepting the doctrine of the *pracaya*-accent is the seeming impossibility of working it in as a part of the general accentual system, such as this has been described above. The acute is a syllable which is accented or rendered conspicuous by being lifted above the lower or grave tone of utterance: but what does this distinction amount to, if the grave syllables also are to be raised, even in masses, to the same level? What a strange grave tone is that which can only maintain itself by the help of an immediately following acute! What are we to think of the independent circumflex, made by the combination of an acute and a grave element, when the grave syllable, even without the encouragement of an acute joined with it, can hardly be held down at grave pitch, but is constantly rising to the higher plane of utterance? Yet worse, what sort of an enclitic accent is that which leads down the voice from acute pitch nowhither, since, the moment the transition is past, the voice leaps back again to acute?

The last of these difficulties, and the most insurmountable of them, seems to have been felt by the Hindu theorizers themselves, who have made a very curious attempt to avoid it: namely, by shifting the circumflex itself to a higher plane.

Thus, the Rik Prâtiçâkhya says (iii. 2, 3) " of this [circum-
flex], a half-mora, or the moiety, is more acute than acute;
the following remainder is grave, but sounds like acute"
(literally, ' is *udâttaçruti*,' which is the same term that is used
in describing the *pracaya*). That is to say, the circumflex
begins higher than acute, and descends only to acute pitch,
thus conducting the voice to the level at which it then runs
on in *pracaya*. And the Tâittirîya-Prâtiçâkhya (i. 41, 42, 44,
45) declares " of this [circumflex], when it follows an acute,
the beginning, to the extent of half a short vowel, is higher
than acute; the remainder is the same with acute; or the remaining part is still lower; or it is the same with grave." Of
these rules, the first two state the theory squarely; the others
appear to express the scruples of those who are struck by its
inconsistency with the fundamental principle, that circumflex
is the combination of acute and grave within the same syllable.
The remaining two Prâtiçâkhyas take no notice of any such
modification of the nature of the circumflex. And, we may
say, with very good reason; for nothing is really gained by it.
On the contrary, it would be no less strange that the enclitic
accent, the transition step from an acute to a following grave,
should rise a grade above acute, and come down to acute itself, than that the grave to which it led should spring to the
height of its first element. And, according to the Rik form
of the theory, we should have the independent circumflex,
arising out of the union of an acute and a grave element, and
having no existence except as the result of such union, lifted
up in all or nearly all its substance above acute pitch; while,
in the Tâittirîya form, whether it were so lifted or not would
depend upon the accidental circumstance whether it were preceded by an acute or a grave syllable. There would be no
sense in our assuming that even an independent circumflex
after an acute might be raised in pitch for the sake of clearer
distinction from that acute; for it is sufficiently distinguished
by its sliding tone; and, if it had any right to be further distinguished, an acute following an acute would have much
more right; while, nevertheless, any number of acutes are

allowed to succeed one another, without modification of their natural character.

To my own mind, I must acknowledge, the difficulties that encompass the Hindu theory of a *pracaya* accent, giving to grave syllables the tone of acute, are more numerous and formidable than those involved in its rejection. If there be found any one, skillful enough to smooth these difficulties away, or to devise an explanation of the setting up of the theory other than that which I have suggested, no one will rejoice in his success more than I shall. But for the present, I shall discredit the existence of a fourth or *pracaya* accent, and shall hold it to be at least probable that this was fabricated merely in order to establish an identity of character in those syllables which, according to the current method of accentuation, agreed in their mode of designation — or rather, in being alike undesignated.

In what has been said of the *pracaya*, regard has been had only to the teachings of the Prâtiçâkhyas, since they alone distinctly recognize and name this accent. But in Pâṇini also appears a somewhat kindred doctrine. The great grammarian, namely, has the rules (i. 2. 39, 40) that "grave syllables, following in continuous text a circumflex, are uttered in monotone (*ekaçruti*); but one that is followed by an acute or circumflex is more depressed (*sannatara*, which the commentators explain by *anudâttatara*, 'more grave,' i. e. 'lower than grave')." Precisely what is intended, now, by *ekaçruti*, 'monotone,' is less clear than were to be desired. It is by the commentators defined to mean, 'without distinction of acute, grave, and circumflex'; but, if it signified only this, there would seem to be no good reason for declaring it to belong to a series of grave syllables anywhere; these would of course all be uttered in the same tone, unless there should be given express direction to the contrary. The first mention of *ekaçruti* is a little above (in rule 33) where it is declared to be the tone used "in calling to a person from a distance;" and it is further prescribed in the rules that follow, for certain conjunctures of sacrificial ceremony from which we can infer nothing definite respecting it. But certainly, in shouting to a distance a raising of the voice would seem to us a natural and almost necessary accompaniment of the obliteration of ordinary distinctions of tone. We have, then, both a negative and a positive reason for suspecting in Pânini's *ekaçruti* a peculiar and a higher tone, instead of a mere negation of varied tone; and so for recognizing a nearer relationship between his teaching and the *pracaya*-doctrine of the Prâtiçâkhyas than appears at first sight. An unequivocal sign of the same relationship is the prescription of a lower tone for the syllable, naturally grave, that precedes an acute or circumflex. Whether this actually means, as is generally assumed, a yet lower tone than grave, or only a lower tone than the heightened monotone of *ekaçruti*, it seems to me an equally unacceptable part of a sound accentual theory. I cannot recognize a positive sinking of the voice as a necessary or natural preparation for its rise to the pitch of acute.

I am not aware that any one has ever undertaken an investigation of the modes of accent usual among the modern languages of India for the purpose of casting light upon the ancient systems, as laid down in the grammatical text-books and exemplified in the Vedic texts. The mode of recitation of the Vedic texts themselves, however, as practiced by the native scholars of the present day, has been carefully observed by an eminent European Sanskritist, Dr. Haug (now of Munich), and reported in the Journal of the German Oriental Society (vol. xvii., 1863, pp. 799–802). I quote the most important paragraph:

" The fundamental law of the Vedic accent is a triplicity of tone. In by far the greatest number of cases the voice begins with a strong tone, the low tone, called *anudâtta*, rises in *udâtta* — which, however, has absolutely no perceptible tone [i. e. stress]—and only reaches its full height and force in the *svarita*, or high tone. The real chief accents are the *anudâtta* and *svarita* alone, which are also constantly interchangeable, as is sufficiently shown by a comparison of the *pada* or word-recitation with the continuous or *sanhitâ*-recitation. The *udâtta* is only a kind of auxiliary accent, and I could never, with the closest observation of the mode of recitation, perceive

that the syllable having *udâtta* is really an accented syllable.....
The *udâtta* is only imperceptibly distinguished from the *pracaya* or entirely accentless syllable."

A very cursory comparison of this description with the
teachings of the Prâtiçâkhyas, reported above, will show
how far the rules of utterance laid down and followed in
the ancient schools of Vedic study are maintained in their
modern successors. The identification of the unmarked acute
with the unmarked grave, in point of tone and character, is
the same now as of old. The distortion of the circumflex, by
pushing it up to a higher position in the scale of tones, which
had begun to appear in the Prâtiçâkhya period, has now become complete. And, partly under the influence of these two
causes, there has come about an absolute inversion of the
original accentual relations. The effort has been to mark and
distinguish by the voice the two tones that were marked and
distinguished by writing. And so the old accented syllable,
the acute — the central and determining point of the whole
system, out of which and in strict subordination to which the
others have their being — since it has no written sign, has sunk
into insignificance, and become a mere "auxiliary" to the
other two, which were fortunate enough to be plainly designated. The influence of the written sign on the theory and
practice of the spoken accent here exhibited is an important
support to the explanation suggested above of the origin of
the so-called *pracaya* accent.

There is one further point in the theory and designation of
the Sanskrit accent which it is desirable to consider, in order
to make our view of the subject more complete. It is the
kampa (literally 'trembling, shake, trill'), or the peculiar
modification undergone by an independent circumflex when
followed by another circumflex or by an acute. This modification consists, according to the Prâtiçâkhyas, simply in a
depression of the last portion of the circumflexed syllable to a
lower than the ordinary pitch. Its explanation makes a very
small figure in the rules of the different treatises. In the
Vâj. Prât. (iv. 137) it is so obscurely stated, and in such ambiguous connection, that it would hardly be intelligible, but

for the comparison of the other kindred works, and the light
that the written form of the texts throws upon it. In the Rik
Prât., also, it appears only as an exception to the definition of
the ordinary character of the circumflex: the latter part of
the circumflex is grave, but has the tone of acute—"except
when an acute or circumflex syllable is spoken immediately
after it" (iii. 3). The Ath. Prât., however, says distinctly
that, of the varieties of independent circumflex, "when followed by an acute or a circumflex, a quarter-mora is depressed" (iii. 65). And the Tâitt. Prât. (xix. 3) mentions
it as "the opinion of some authorities that, in a circumflex
that is followed by a circumflex [not by an acute, as well], a
quarter-mora is depressed." The mode, however, of designating this peculiarity is in nearly all the texts a very conspicuous one, and involves an element of prolongation of the vowel
suffering *kampa*, of which the Prâtiçâkhyas give no hint, and
which is intimated by writing a figure, 3 or 1, after the vowel.
Thus, the Rig-Veda writes *tishyò yáthâ* and *yò hyò vartaníh* as
follows:

9. तिष्यो३ यथा । यो३ ह्यो वर्तनिः ।

If the affected vowel is short, the Rig-Veda writes a 1 instead of a 3 after it: thus,

10. न्य१न्यं सह्सा ।

ny à-nyáṅ   sá-ha-sà

The Sâma-Veda (to which there is no known Prâtiçâkhya),
however, always lengthens the vowel in such a case—thus,
ny â-nyâm—and so writes a 3 after it, without exception.
What is the proper usage in the Atharva-Veda is somewhat
doubtful, since the known MSS. are very irregular and inconsistent in this whole class of cases; but the editors of the published text have adopted and carried out the method of the
Rig-Veda. In the Tâittirîya-Sanhitâ, the modification is, in
accordance with the doctrine referred to in its Prâtiçâkhya,
restricted to the case of a circumflex followed by a circumflex;
the figure used is always 1, and the affected vowel, if short, is
lengthened: thus,

11. देवत्य॥१५ ह्येतत् । सो१ ऽपो१ ऽभ्यमियत ।

de-va-tyâ'n̄   *hy è-tát*   *sò*   *'pò*   *'bhy à-mri-ya-ta*

devatyâ'n̄ in the first example being from *devatyàm.* The
Vâjasaneyi-Sanhitâ alone leaves the quantity of the vowel
unchanged, and uses no figure, but only a modification of
the usual circumflex stroke beneath the vowel.

Whatever may be the origin of this peculiar doctrine and
designation, it answers in the majority of texts (Rik, Sâman,
Atharvan) a useful purpose by distinguishing in many cases
an acute syllable from a *pracaya* grave after a circumflex.
Thus, in the last examples quoted, the accentuation does not
show us that the final *-tat* in the one case is acute, and that
the final *-mriyata* in the other is *pracaya*, while, as written by
the Rig-Veda — namely,

12. देवत्यं१ ह्ये३तत् । सो१ ऽपो१ ऽभ्यमियत ।

the difference is brought clearly to light. But that this practical advantage had any thing to do with the development of
the theory, is not lightly to be assumed. The designation
seems to signify that the circumflex vowel, in order to the reduction of its latter portion to *anudâtta* tone, or to a yet lower
pitch, requires to be somewhat prolonged in quantity, either
by a single added mora or by extension to three moras. But
the whole subject is quite obscure, and I do not venture to
enter here into the discussion of it, for fear of occupying much
space without sufficient result.

It does not belong to what I have undertaken that I should
consider at all the correspondences and differences of the
Sanskrit and Greek with reference to the actual phenomena of
accentuation — the clear evidences which they exhibit of an
originally identical system, and of the abandonment of this
system in part by the Greek, under the influence of the new
law of cadence set forth in the preceding paper. These correspondences are most fully and clearly stated in Bopp's
"Accentuations-system," a work which, though often wrong
in matters of theory, is to be highly commended as a clear
and comprehensive exhibition of the facts of which it treats.

AMERICAN

JOURNAL OF PHILOLOGY

Vol. V, 3.　　　　　　　　　Whole No. 19.

I.—THE STUDY OF HINDU GRAMMAR AND THE STUDY OF SANSKRIT.

To the beginning study of Sanskrit it was an immense advantage that there existed a Hindu science of grammar, and one of so high a character. To realize how great the advantage, one has only to compare the case of languages destitute of it—as for instance the Zend. It is a science of ancient date, and has even exercised a shaping influence on the language in which all or nearly all the classical literature has been produced. It was an outcome of the same general spirit which is seen in the so careful textual preservation and tradition of the ancient sacred literature of India ; and there is doubtless a historical connection between the one and the other ; though of just what nature is as yet unclear.

The character of the Hindu grammatical science was, as is usual in such cases, determined by the character of the language which was its subject. The Sanskrit is above all things an analyzable language, one admitting of the easy and distinct separation of ending from stem, and of derivative suffix from primitive word, back to the ultimate attainable elements, the so-called roots. Accordingly, in its perfected form (for all the preparatory stages are unknown to us), the Hindu grammar offers us an established body of roots, with rules for their conversion into stems and for the inflection of the latter, and also for the accompanying phonetic changes—this last involving and resting upon a phonetic science of extraordinary merit, which has called forth the highest admiration of modern scholars ; nothing at all approaching it has been produced by any ancient people ; it has served as the foundation in no small degree of our own phonetics : even as our science of grammar and of language has borrowed much from India. The treatment of syntax is markedly inferior—though, after all, hardly more than in a measure to correspond with the inferiority of the Sanskrit sentence in point of structure, as compared with the Latin and the Greek. Into any more detailed description it is not necessary to our present purpose to enter; and the matter is one pretty well understood by the students of Indo-European language. It is generally well known also that the Hindu science, after a however long history of elaboration, became fixed for all future time in the system of a single grammarian, named Pāṇini (believed, though on grounds far from convincing, to have lived two or three centuries before the Christian era). Pāṇini's work has been commented without end, corrected in minor points, condensed, re-cast in arrangement, but never rebelled against or superseded; and it is still the authoritative standard of good Sanskrit. Its form of presentation is of the strangest: a miracle of ingenuity, but of perverse and wasted ingenuity. The only object aimed at in it is brevity, at the sacrifice of everything else—of order, of clearness, of even intelligibility except by the aid of keys and commentaries and lists of words, which then are furnished in profusion. To determine a grammatical point out of it is something like constructing a passage of text out of an *index verborum:* if you are sure that you have gathered up every word that belongs in the passage, and have put them all in the right order, you have got the right reading; but only then. If you have mastered Pāṇini sufficiently to bring to bear upon the given point every rule that relates to it, and in due succession, you have settled the case; but that is no easy task. For example, it takes nine mutually limitative rules, from all parts of the text-book, to determine whether a certain aorist shall be *ajāgariṣam* or *ajāgāriṣam* (the case is reported in the preface to Müller's grammar): there is lacking only a tenth rule, to tell us that the whole word is a false and never-used formation. Since there is nothing to show how far the application of a rule reaches, there are provided treatises of laws of interpretation to be applied to them; but there is a residual rule underlying and determining the whole: that both the grammar and the laws of interpretation must be so construed as to yield good and acceptable forms, and not otherwise—and this implies (if that were needed) a condemnation of the whole mode of presentation of the system as a failure.

Theoretically, all that is prescribed and allowed by Pāṇini and his accepted commentators is Sanskrit, and nothing else is entitled to the name. The young pandit, then, is expected to master the system and to govern his Sanskrit speech and writing by it. This he does, with immense pains and labor, then naturally valuing the acquisition in part according to what it has cost him. The same course was followed by those European scholars who had to make themselves the pupils of Hindu teachers, in acquiring Sanskrit for the benefit of Europe; and (as was said above) they did so to their very great advantage. Equally as a matter of course, the same must still be done by any one who studies in India, who has to deal with the native scholars, win their confidence and respect, and gain their aid: they must be met upon their own ground. But it is a question, and one of no slight practical importance, how far Western scholars in general are to be· held to this method: whether Pāṇini is for us also the law of Sanskrit usage; whether we are to study the native Hindu grammar in order to learn Sanskrit.

There would be less reason for asking this question, if the native grammar were really the instrumentality by which the conserving tradition of the old language had been carried on. But that is a thing both in itself impossible and proved by the facts of the case to be untrue. No one ever mastered a list of roots with rules for their extension and inflection, and then went to work to construct texts upon that basis. Rather, the transmission of Sanskrit has been like the transmission of any highly cultivated language, only with differences of degree. The learner has his models which he imitates; he makes his speech after the example of that of his teacher, only under the constant government of grammatical rule, enforced by the requirement to justify out of the grammar any word or form as to which a question is raised. Thus the language has moved on by its own inertia, only falling, with further removal from its natural vernacular basis, more and more passively and mechanically into the hands of the grammarians. All this is like the propagation of literary English or German; only that here there is much more of a vernacular usage that shows itself able to override and modify the rules of grammar. It is yet more closely like the propagation of Latin; only that here the imitation of previous usage is frankly acknowledged as the guide, there being no iron system of grammar to assume to take its place. That such has really been the history of the later or classical Sanskrit is sufficiently shown by the facts. There is no absolute coincidence between it and the language which Pāṇini teaches. The former, indeed, includes little that the grammarians forbid ; but, on the other hand, it lacks a great deal that they allow or prescribe. The difference between the two is so great that Benfey, a scholar deeply versed in the Hindu science, calls it a grammar without a corresponding language, as he calls the pre-classical dialects a language without a grammar.[1]   If such a statement can be made with any reason, it would appear that there is to be assumed, as the subject of Hindu grammatical science, a peculiar dialect of Sanskrit, which we may call the grammarians' Sanskrit, different both from the pre-classical dialects and from the classical, and standing either between them or beside them in the general history of Indian language.   And it becomes a matter of importance to us to ascertain what this grammarians' Sanskrit is, how it stands related to the other varieties of Sanskrit, and whether it is entitled to be the leading object of our Sanskrit study.   Such questions must be settled by a comparison of the dialect referred to with the other dialects, and of them with one another.   And it will be found, upon such comparison, that the earlier and later forms of the Vedic dialect, the dialects of the Brāhmaṇas and Sūtras, and the classical Sanskrit, stand in a filial relation, each to its predecessor, are nearly or quite successive forms of the same language ; while the grammarians' Sanskrit, as distinguished from them, is a thing of grammatical rule merely, having never had any real existence as a language, and being on the whole unknown in practice to even the most modern pandits.

The main thing which makes of the grammarians' Sanskrit a special and peculiar language is its list of roots.   Of these there are reported to us about two thousand, with no intimation of any difference in character among them, or warning that a part of them may and that another part may not be drawn upon for forms to be actually used ; all stand upon the same plane.   But more than half—actually more than half—of them never have been met with, and never will be met with, in the Sanskrit literature of any age. When this fact began to come to light, it was long fondly hoped, or believed, that the missing elements would yet turn up in some corner of the literature not hitherto ransacked ; but all expectation of that has now been abandoned.   One or another does appear from time to time ; but what are they among so many?   The last not-

---

[1] Einleitung in die Grammatik der vedischen Sprache, 1874, pp. 3, 4.

able case was that of the root *stigh*, discovered in the Māitrāyaṇi-Saṅhitā, a text of the Brāhmaṇa period; but the new roots found in such texts are apt to turn out wanting in the lists of the grammarians. Beyond all question, a certain number of cases are to be allowed for, of real roots, proved such by the occurrence of their evident cognates in other related languages, and chancing not to appear in the known literature; but they can go only a very small way indeed toward accounting for the eleven hundred unauthenticated roots. Others may have been assumed as underlying certain derivatives or bodies of derivatives—within due limits, a perfectly legitimate proceeding; but the cases thus explainable do not prove to be numerous. There remain then the great mass, whose presence in the lists no ingenuity has yet proved sufficient to account for. And in no small part, they bear their falsity and artificiality on the surface, in their phonetic form and in the meanings ascribed to them; we can confidently say that the Sanskrit language, known to us through a long period of development, neither had nor could have any such roots. How the grammarians came to concoct their list, rejected in practice by themselves and their own pupils, is hitherto an unexplained mystery. No special student of the native grammar, to my knowledge, has attempted to cast any light upon it; and it was left for Dr. Edgren, no partisan of the grammarians, to group and set forth the facts for the first time, in the Journal of the American Oriental Society (Vol. XI, 1882 [but the article printed in 1879], pp. 1–55), adding a list of the real roots, with brief particulars as to their occurrence.[1] It is quite clear, with reference to this fundamental and most important item, of what character the grammarians' Sanskrit is. The real Sanskrit of the latest period is, as concerns its roots, a true successor to that of the earliest period, and through the known intermediates; it has lost some of the roots of its predecessors, as each of these some belonging to its own predecessors or predecessor; it has, also like these, won a certain number not earlier found: both in such measure as was to be expected. As for the rest of the asserted roots of the grammar, to account for them is not a matter that concerns at all the Sanskrit language and its history; it only concerns the history of the Hindu science of grammar. That, too,

[1] I have myself now in press a much fuller account of the quotable roots of the language, with all their quotable tense-stems and primary derivatives —everything accompanied by a definition of the period of its known occurrence in the history of the language.

has come to be pretty generally acknowledged.[1]   Every one who knows anything of the history of Indo-European etymology knows how much mischief the grammarians' list of roots wrought in the hands of the earlier more incautious and credulous students of Sanskrit : how many false and worthless derivations were founded upon them. That sort of work, indeed, is not yet entirely a thing of the past ; still, it has come to be well understood by most scholars that no alleged Sanskrit root can be accepted as real unless it is supported by such a use in the literary records of the language as authenticates it—for there are such things in the later language as artificial occurrences, forms made for once or twice from roots taken out of the grammarians' list, by a natural license, which one is only surprised not to see oftener availed of (there are hardly more than a dozen or two of such cases quotable) : that they appear so seldom is the best evidence of the fact already pointed out above, that the grammar had, after all, only a superficial and negative influence upon the real tradition of the language.

It thus appears that a Hindu grammarian's statement as to the fundamental elements of his language is without authority until tested by the actual facts of the language, as represented by the Sanskrit literature. But the principle won here is likely to prove of universal application ; for we have no reason to expect to find the grammarians absolutely trustworthy in other departments of their work, when they have failed so signally in one ; there can be nothing in their system that will not require to be tested by the recorded facts of the language, in order to determine its true value. How this is, we will proceed to ascertain by examining a few examples.

In the older language, but not in the oldest (for it is wanting in the Veda), there is formed a periphrastic future tense active by compounding a *nomen agentis* with an auxiliary, the present tense of the verb *as* ' be ' : thus, *dātā 'smi* (literally *dator sum*) ' I will give,' etc. It is quite infrequent as compared with the other future, yet common enough to require to be regarded as a part of the general Sanskrit verb-system. To this active tense the grammarians give a corresponding middle, although the auxiliary in its independent

---

[1] Not, indeed, universally ; one may find among the selected verbs that are conjugated in full at the end of F. M. Müller's Sanskrit Grammar, no very small number of those that are utterly unknown to Sanskrit usage, ancient or modern.

use has no middle inflection ; it is made with endings modified so as to stand in the usual relation of middle endings to active, and further with conversion in 1st sing. of the radical *s* to *h*—a very anomalous substitution, of which there is not, I believe, another example in the language. Now what support has this middle tense in actual use? Only this : that in the Brāhmaṇas occur four sporadic instances of attempts to make by analogy middle forms for this tense (they are all reported in my Sanskrit Grammar, § 947 ; further search has brought to light no additional examples) : two of them are 1st sing., one having the form *se* for the auxiliary, the other *he*, as taught in the grammar ; and in the whole later literature, epic and classical, I find record of the occurrence of only one further case, *darçayitāhe* (in Nāiṣ. V 71.)![1] Here also, the classical dialect is the true continuator of the pre-classical ; it is only in the grammarians' Sanskrit that every verb conjugated in the middle voice has also a middle periphrastic future.

There is another and much more important part of verbal inflection—namely, the whole aorist-system, in all its variety—as to which the statements of the grammarians are to be received with especial distrust, for the reason that in the classical language the aorist is a decadent formation. In the older dialects, down to the last Sūtra, and through the entire list of early and genuine Upanishads, the aorist has its own special office, that of designating the immediate past, and is always to be found where such designation is called for ; later, even in the epos, it is only another preterit, equivalent in use to imperfect and perfect, and hence of no value, and subsisting only in occasional use, mainly as a survival from an earlier condition of the language. Thus, for example, of the first kind of aorist, the root-aorist, forms are made in pre-classical Sanskrit from about 120 roots ; of these, 15 make forms in the later language also, mostly sporadically (only *gā, dā, dhā, pā, sthā, bhū* less infrequently) ; and 8 more in the later language only, all in an occurrence or two (all but one, in active precative forms, as to which see below). Again, of the fifth aorist-form, the *iṣ*-aorist (rather the

---

[1] Here, as elsewhere below, my authority for the later literature is chiefly the Petersburg Lexicon (the whole older literature I have examined for myself), and my statements are, of course, always open to modification by the results of further researches. But all the best and most genuine part of the literature has been carefully and thoroughly excerpted for the Lexicon ; and for the Mahābhārata we have now the explicit statements of Holtzmann, in his Grammatisches aus dem Mahabharata, Leipzig, 1884.

most frequent of all), forms are made in the older language from
140 roots, and later from only 18 of these (and sporadically, except
in the case of *grah, vad, vadh, vid*), with a dozen more in the
later language exclusively, all sporadic except *çaṅk* (which is not
a Vedic root). Once more, as regards the third or reduplicated
aorist, the proportion is slightly different, because of the association of that aorist with the causative conjugation, and the frequency
of the latter in use ; here, against about 110 roots quotable from
the earlier language, 16 of them also in the later, there are about
30 found in the later alone (nearly all of them only sporadically,
and none with any frequency). And the case is not otherwise with
the remaining forms. The facts being such, it is easily seen that
general statements made by the grammarians as to the range of
occurrence of each form, and as to the occurrence of one form in
the active and a certain other one in the middle from a given root,
must be of very doubtful authority ; in fact, as regards the latter
point, they are the more suspicious as lacking any tolerable
measure of support from the facts of the older language. But
there are much greater weaknesses than these in the grammarians'
treatment of the aorist.

Let us first turn our attention to the aorist optative, the so-called
precative (or benedictive). This formation is by the native grammarians not recognized as belonging to the aorist at all—not even
so far as to be put next the aorist in their general scheme of
conjugation ; they suffer the future-systems to intervene between
the two. This is in them fairly excusable as concerns the precative
active, since it is the optative of the root-aorist, and so has an
aspect as if it might come independently from the root directly ;
nor, indeed, can we much blame them for overlooking the relation
of their precative middle to the sibilant or sigmatic aorist, considering that they ignore tense-systems and modes ; but that their
European imitators, down to the very latest, should commit the
same oversight is a different matter. The contrast, now, between
the grammarians' dialect and the real Sanskrit is most marked as
regards the middle forms. According to the grammar, the precative middle is to be made from every root, and even for its
secondary conjugations, the causative etc. It has two alternative
modes of formation, which we see to correspond to two of the
forms of the sibilant aorist : the *s*-aorist, namely, and the *iṣ*-aorist.
Of course, a complete inflection is allowed it. To justify all this,
now, I am able to point to only a single occurrence of a middle

precative in the whole later literature, including the epics : that is
ririṣiṣṭa, in the Bhāgavata-Purāṇa (III 9, 24), a text notable for
its artificial imitation of ancient forms (the same word occurs also
in the Rig-Veda); it is made, as will be noticed, from a reduplicated aorist stem, and so is unauthorized by grammatical rule. A
single example in a whole literature, and that a false one! In the
pre-classical literature also, middle precative forms are made
hardly more than sporadically, or from less than 40 roots in all (so
far as I have found); those belonging to the *s* and *iṣ*-aorists are,
indeed, among the most numerous (14 each), but those of the
root-aorist do not fall short of them (also 14 roots), and there are
examples from three of the other four aorists. Except a single 3d
pl. (in *irata*, instead of *iran*), only the three singular persons and
the 1st pl. are quotable, and forms occur without as well as with
the adscititious *s* between mode-sign and personal ending which is
the special characteristic of a precative as distinguished from a
simply optative form. Here, again, we have a formation sporadic
in the early language and really extinct in the later, but erected
by the grammarians into a regular part of every verb-system.

With the precative active the case is somewhat different. This
also, indeed, is rare even to sporadicalness, being, so far as I know,
made from only about 60 roots in the whole language—and of
these, only half can show forms containing the true precative *s*.
But it is not quite limited to the pre-classical dialects; it is made
also later from 15 roots, 9 of which are additional to those which
make a precative in the older language. Being in origin an
optative of the root-aorist, it comes, as we may suppose, to seem
to be a formation from the root directly, and so to be extended
beyond the limits of the aorist; from a clear majority (about three
fifths) of all the roots that make it, it has no other aorist forms by
its side. And this begins even in the earliest period (with half-a-
dozen roots in the Veda, and toward a score besides in the Brāhmaṇa and Sūtra); although there the precative more usually
makes a part of a general aorist-formation: for instance, and
especially, from the root *bhū*, whose precative forms are oftener
met with than those of all other roots together, and which is the
only root from which more than two real precative persons are
quotable. How rare it is even in the epos is shown by the fact
that Holtzmann [1] is able to quote only six forms (and one of these

---

[1] In his work already cited, at p. 32.

doubtful, and another a false formation) from the whole Mahābhārata, one of them occurring twice; while the first book of the Rāmāyaṇa (about 4500 lines) has the single *bhūyāt.* Since it is not quite extinct in the classical period, the Hindu grammarians could not, perhaps, well help teaching its formation; and, considering the general absence of perspective from their work, we should hardly expect them to explain that it was the rare survival of an anciently little-used formation; but we have here another striking example of the great discordance between the real Sanskrit and the grammarians' dialect, and of the insufficiency of the information respecting the former obtainable from the rules for the latter.

Again, the reduplicated or third form of aorist, though it has become attached to the causative secondary conjugation (by a process in the Veda not yet complete), as the regular aorist of that conjugation, is not made from the derivative causative stem, but comes from the root itself, not less directly than do the other aorist-formations—except in the few cases where the causative stem contains a *p* added to *ā*: thus, *atiṣṭhipat* from stem *sthāpaya*, root *sthā.* Perhaps misled by this exception, however, the grammarians teach the formation of the reduplicated aorist from the causative stem, through the intermediate process of converting the stem back to the root, by striking off its conjugation-sign and reducing its strengthened vowel to the simpler root-form. That is to say, we are to make, for example, *abūbhuvat* from the stem *bhāvaya*, by cutting off *aya* and reducing the remainder *bhāv* or *bhāu* to *bhū*, instead of making it from *bhū* directly! That is a curious etymological process; quite a side-piece to deriving *varīyas* and *variṣṭha* from *uru*, and the like, as the Hindu grammarians and their European copyists would likewise have us do. There is one point where the matter is brought to a crucial test: namely, in roots that end in *u* or *ū*; where, if the vowel on which the reduplication is formed is an *u*-vowel, the reduplication-vowel should be of the same character; but, in any other case, an *i*-vowel. Thus, in the example already taken, *bhāvaya* ought to make *abībhavat*, just as it makes *bibhāvayiṣati* in the case of a real derivation from the causative stem; and such forms as *abībhavat* are, in fact, in a great number of cases either prescribed or allowed by the grammarians; but I am not aware of their having been ever met with in use, earlier or later, with the single exception of *apiplavam*, occurring once in the Çatapatha-Brāhmaṇa (VI ii, 1, 8).

Again, the grammarians give a peculiar and problematic rule for an alternative formation of certain passive tenses (aorist and futures) from the special 3d sing. aor. pass.; they allow it in the case of all roots ending in vowels, and of *grah, dṛç, han.* Thus, for example, from the root *dā* are allowed *adāyiṣi, dāyiṣyate, dāyitā,* beside *adiṣi, dāsyate, dātā.* What all this means is quite obscure, since there is no usage, either early or late, to cast light upon it. The Rig-Veda has once (I 147, 5) *dhāyīs,* from root *dhā ;* but this, being active, is rather a hindrance than a help. The Jāim. Brāhmaṇa has once (I 321) *ākhyāyiṣyante ;* but this appears to be a form analogous with *hvayiṣyate* etc., and so proves nothing. The Bhāg. Purāṇa has once (VIII 13, 36) *tāyitā,* which the Petersburg Lexicon refers to root *tan ;* but if there is such a thing as the secondary root *tāy,* as claimed by the grammarians, it perhaps belongs rather there. And there remain, so far as I can discover, only *asthāyiṣi* (Daçak. [Wilson], p. 117, l. 6) and *anāyiṣata* (Ind. Sprüche², 6187, from the Kuvalayānanda); and these are with great probability to be regarded as artificial forms, made because the grammar declares them correct. It seems not unlikely that some misapprehension or blunder lies at the foundation of these rules of the grammar; at any rate, the formation is only grammarians' Sanskrit, and not even pandits'; and it should never be obtruded upon the attention of beginners in the language.

Again, the secondary ending *dhvam* of 2d pl. mid. sometimes has to take the form *ḍhvam.* In accordance with the general euphonic usages of the language, this should be whenever in the present condition of Sanskrit there has been lost before the ending a lingual sibilant; thus: we have *aneḍhvam* from *aneṣ + dhvam,* and *apaviḍhvam* from *apaviṣ + dhvam ;* we should further have in the precative *bhaviṣīḍhvam* from *bhaviṣī-ṣ-dhvam,* if the form ever occurred, as, unfortunately, it does not. And, so far as I know, there is not to be found, either in the earlier language or the later (and as to the former I can speak with authority), a single instance of *ḍhvam* in any other situation—the test-cases, however, being far from numerous. But the Hindu grammarians, if they are reported rightly by their European pupils (which in this instance is hard to believe), give rules as to the change of the ending upon this basis only for the *s*-aorist; for the *iṣ*-aorist and its optative (the precative), they make the choice between *ḍhvam* and *dhvam* to depend upon whether the *i* is or is not " preceded by a semi-vowel or *h :* " that is, *apaviṣ + dhvam* gives *apaviḍhvam,* but *ajaniṣ*

$+$ *dhvam* gives *ajanidhvam*, and so likewise we should have *janiṣīdhvam*. It would be curious to know what ground the grammarians imagined themselves to have for laying down such a rule as this, wherein there is a total absence of discoverable connection between cause and effect; and it happens that all the quotable examples—*ajaniḍhvam, artiḍhvam, aindhiḍhvam, vepiḍhvam*—are opposed to their rule, but accordant with reason. What is yet worse, however, is that the grammar extends the same conversion of *dh* to *ḍh*, under the same restrictions, to the primary ending *dhve* of the perfect likewise, with which it has nothing whatever to do—teaching us that, for instance, *cakṛ* and *tuṣṭu* $+$ *dhve* make necessarily *cakṛḍhve* and *tuṣṭuḍhve*, and that *dadhr-i* $+$ *dhve* makes either *dadhriḍhve* or *dadhridhve*, while *tutud-i* $+$ *dhve* makes only *tutudidhve !* This appears to me the most striking case of downright unintelligent blundering on the part of the native grammarians that has come to notice; if there is any way of relieving them of the reproach of it, their partisans ought to cast about at once to find it.

A single further matter of prime importance may be here referred to, in illustration of the character of the Hindu grammarians as classifiers and presenters of the facts of their language. By reason of the extreme freedom and wonderful regularity of word-composition in Sanskrit, the grammarians were led to make a classification of compounds in a manner that brought true enlightenment to European scholars; and the classification has been largely adopted as a part of modern philological science, along even with its bizarre terminology. Nothing could be more accurate and happier than the distinction of dependent, descriptive, possessive, and copulative compounds; only their titles—'his man' (*tatpuruṣa*), 'act-sustaining' (? *karmadhāraya*), 'much-rice' (*bahuvrīhi*), and 'couple' (*dvandva*), respectively—can hardly claim to be worth preserving. But it is the characteristic of Hindu science generally not to be able to stop when it has done enough; and so the grammarians have given us, on the same plane of division with these four capital classes, two more, which they call *dvigu* ('two-cow') and *avyayībhāva* ('indeclinable-becoming'); and these have no *raison d'être*, but are collections of special cases belonging to some of the other classes, and so heterogeneous that their limits are hardly capable of definition: the *dvigu*-class are secondary adjective compounds, but sometimes, like other adjectives, used as nouns; and an *avyayībhāva* is always the adverbiallyused accusative neuter of an adjective compound. It would be a real service on the part of some scholar, versed in the Hindu science, to draw out a full account of the so-called *dvigu*-class and its boundaries, and to show if possible how the grammarians were misled into establishing it. But it will probably be long before these two false classes cease to haunt the concluding chapters of Sanskrit grammars, or writers on language to talk of the six kinds of compounds in Sanskrit.[1]

Points in abundance, of major or minor consequence, it would be easy to bring up in addition, for criticism or for question. Thus, to take a trifle or two : according to the general analogies of the language, we ought to speak of the root *gṛh*, instead of *grah ;* probably the Hindu science adopts the latter form because of some mechanical advantage on the side of brevity resulting from it, in the rules prescribing forms and derivatives : the instances are not few in which that can be shown to have been the preponderating consideration, leading to the sacrifice of things more important. One may conjecture that similar causes led to the setting up of a root *div* instead of *dīv*, ' play, gamble ' : that it may have been found easier to prescribe the prolongation of the *i* than its irregular gunation, in *devana* etc. This has unfortunately misled the authors of the Petersburg Lexicons into their strange and indefensible identification of the asserted root *div* ' play' with the so-called root *div* ' shine ' : the combination of meanings is forced and unnatural ; and then especially the phonetic form of the two roots is absolutely distinct, the one showing only short *i* and *u* (as in *divam, dyubhis*), the other always and only long *ī* and *ū* (as in *dīvyati, -dīvan*, and *-dyū, dyūta*) ; the one root is really *diu*, and the other *dīū* (it may be added that the Petersburg Lexicon, on similar evidence, inconsistently but correctly writes the roots *sīv* and *srīv*, instead of *siv* and *sriv*).

It would be easy to continue the work of illustration much further ; but this must be enough to show how and how far we have to use and to trust the teachings of the Hindu grammarians. Or,

[1] Spiegel, for example (Altiranische Grammatik, p. 229), thinks it necessary to specify that *dvigu*-compounds do, to be sure, occur also in the Old Persian dialects, but that they in no respect form a special class ; and a very recent Sanskrit grammar in Italian (Pulle, Turin, 1883) gives as the four primary classes of compounds the *dvandva, tatpuruṣa, bahuvrīhi*, and *avyayībhāva*—as if one were to say that the kingdoms in Nature are four : animal, vegetable, mineral, and cactuses.

if one prefer to employ the Benfeyan phrase, we see something of what this language is which has a grammar but not an existence, and in what relation it stands to the real Sanskrit language, begun in the Veda, and continued without a break down to our own times, all the rules of the grammar having been able only slightly to stiffen and unnaturalize it. Surely, what we desire to have to do with is the Sanskrit, and not the imaginary dialect that fits the definitions of Pāṇini. There is no escaping the conclusion that, if we would understand Sanskrit, we may not take the grammarians as authorities, but only as witnesses ; not a single rule given or fact stated by them is to be accepted on their word, without being tested by the facts of the language as laid down in the less subjective and more trustworthy record of the literature. Of course, most of what the native grammar teaches is true and right ; but, until after critical examination, no one can tell which part. Of course, also, there is more or less of genuine supplementary material in the grammarians' treatises—material especially lexical, but doubtless in some measure also grammatical—which needs to be worked in so as to complete our view of the language ; but what this genuine material is, as distinguished from the artificial and false, is only to be determined by a thorough and cautious comparison of the entire system of the grammar with the whole recorded language. Such a comparison has not yet been made, and is hardly even making : in part, to be sure, because the time for it has been long in coming ; but mainly because those who should be making it are busy at something else. The skilled students of the native grammar, as it seems to me, have been looking at their task from the wrong point of view, and laboring in the wrong direction. They have been trying to put the non-existent grammarians' dialect in the place of the genuine Sanskrit. They have thought it their duty to learn out of Pāṇini and his successors, and to set forth for the benefit of the world, what the Sanskrit really is, instead of studying and setting forth and explaining (and, where necessary, accounting for and excusing) Pāṇini's system itself. They have failed to realize that, instead of a divine revelation, they have in their hands a human work—a very able one, indeed, but also imperfect, like other human works, full of the prescription in place of description that characterizes all Hindu productions, and most perversely constructed ; and that in studying it they are only studying a certain branch of Hindu science : one that is, indeed, of the highest interest, and has an important bearing on the history of the language, especially since the *dicta* of the grammarians have had a marked influence in shaping the latest form of Sanskrit—not always to its advantage. Hence the insignificant amount of real progress that the study of Hindu grammar has made in the hands of European scholars. Its career was well inaugurated, now nearly forty-five years ago (1839–40), by Böhtlingk's edition of Pāṇini's text, with extracts from the native commentaries, followed by an extremely stingy commentary by the editor; but it has not been succeeded by anything of importance,[1] until now that a critical edition of the Mahābhāṣya, by Kielhorn, is passing through the press, and is likely soon to be completed: a highly meritorious work, worthy of European learning, and likely, if followed up in the right spirit, to begin a new era in its special branch of study. Considering the extreme difficulty of the system, and the amount of labor that is required before the student can win any available mastery of it, it is incumbent upon the representatives of the study to produce an edition of Pāṇini accompanied with a version, a digest of the leading comments on each rule, and an index that shall make it possible to find what the native authorities teach upon each given point: that is to say, to open the grammatical science to knowledge virtually at first hand without the lamentable waste of time thus far unavoidable—a waste, because both needless and not sufficiently rewarded by its results.

A curious kind of superstition appears to prevail among certain Sanskrit scholars: they cannot feel that they have the right to accept a fact of the language unless they find it set down in Pāṇini's rules. It may well be asked, on the contrary, of what consequence it is, except for its bearing on the grammatical science itself, whether a given fact is or is not so set down. A fact in the pre-classical language is confessedly quite independent of Pāṇini; he may take account of it and he may not; and no one knows as yet what the ground is of the selection he makes for inclusion in his system. As for a fact in the classical language, it is altogether likely to fall within the reach of one of the great

---

[1] For the photographic reproduction, in 1874, of a single manuscript of Patanjali's *Mahābhāṣya* or 'Great Comment' (on Pāṇini), with the glosses upon it, was but a costly piece of child's play; and the English government, as if to make the enterprise a complete *fiasco*, sent all the copies thus prepared to India, to be buried there in native keeping, instead of placing them in European libraries, within reach of Western scholars.

grammarian's rules—at least, as these have been extended and restricted and amended by his numerous successors: and this is a thing much to the credit of the grammar; but what bearing it has upon the language would be hard to say. If, however, we should seem to meet with a fact ignored by the grammar, or contravening its rules, we should have to look to see whether supporting facts in the language did not show its genuineness in spite of the grammar. On the other hand, there are facts in the language, especially in its latest records, which have a false show of existence, being the artificial product of the grammar's prescription or permission; and there was nothing but the healthy conservatism of the true tradition of the language to keep them from becoming vastly more numerous. And then, finally, there are the infinite number of facts which, so far as the grammar is concerned, should be or might be in the language, only that they do not happen ever to occur there; for here lies the principal discordance between the grammar and the language. The statement of the grammar that such a thing is so and so is of quite uncertain value, until tested by the facts of the language; and in this testing, it is the grammar that is on trial, that is to be condemned for artificiality or commended for faithfulness; not the language, which is quite beyond our jurisdiction. It cannot be too strongly urged that the Sanskrit, even that of the most modern authors, even that of the pandits of the present day, is the successor, by natural processes of tradition, of the older dialects; and that the grammar is a more or less successful attempt at its description, the measure of the success being left for us to determine, by comparison of the one with the other.

To maintain this is not to disparage the Hindu grammatical science; it is only to put it in its true place. The grammar remains nearly if not altogether the most admirable product of the scientific spirit in India, ranking with the best products of that spirit that the world has seen; we will scant no praise to it, if we only are not called on to bow down to it as authoritative. So we regard the Greek science of astronomy as one of the greatest and most creditable achievements of the human intellect since men first began to observe and deduce; but we do not plant ourselves upon its point of view in setting forth the movements of the heavenly bodies—though the men of the Middle Ages did so, to their advantage, and the system of epicycles maintained itself in existence, by dint of pure conservatism, long after its artificiality had been demonstrated. That the early European Sanskrit grammars assumed the basis and worked in the methods of the Hindu science was natural and praiseworthy. Bopp was the first who had knowledge and independence enough to begin effectively the work of subordinating Hindu to Western science, using the materials and deductions of the former so far as they accorded with the superior methods of the latter, and turning his attention to the records of the language itself, as fast as they became accessible to him. Since his time, there has been in some respects a retrogression rather than an advance; European scholars have seemed to take satisfaction in submitting themselves slavishly to Hindu teachers, and the grammarians' dialect has again been thrust forward into the place which the Sanskrit language ought to occupy. To refer to but a striking example or two : in Müller's grammar the native science is made the supreme rule after a fashion that is sometimes amusing in its naïveté, and the genuine and the fictitious are mingled inextricably, in his rules, his illustrations, and his paradigms, from one end of the volume to the other. And a scholar of the highest rank, long resident in India but now of Vienna, Professor Bühler, has only last year put forth a useful practical introduction to the language, with abundant exercises for writing and speaking,[1] in which the same spirit of subservience to Hindu methods is shown in an extreme degree, and both forms and material are not infrequently met with which are not Sanskrit, but belong only to the non-existent grammarians' dialect. Its standpoint is clearly characterized by its very first clause, which teaches that " Sanskrit verbs have ten tenses and modes "— that is to say, because the native grammar failed to make the distinction between tense and mode, or to group these formations together into systems, coming from a common tense-stem, Western pupils are to be taught to do the same. This seems about as much an anachronism as if the author had begun, likewise after Hindu example, with the statement that " Sanskrit parts of speech are four: name, predicate, preposition, and particle." Further on, in the same paragraph, he allows (since the Hindus also do so) that " the first four [tenses and modes] are derived from a special present stem."; but he leaves it to be implied, both here and later, that the remaining six come directly from the root. From this we

[1] This work, somewhat recast grammatically, is about to be reproduced in English by Professor Perry, of Columbia College, New York.

should have to infer, for example, that *dadāti* comes from a stem, but *dadātha* from the root; that we are to divide *naçya-ti* but *dā--syati, a-viça-t* but *a-sic-at*, and so on; and (though this is a mere oversight) that *ayāt* contains a stem, but *adāt* a pure root. No real grammarian can talk of present stems without talking of aorist stems also; nor is the variety of the latter so much inferior to that of the former; it is only the vastly greater frequency of occurrence of present forms that makes the differences of their stems the more important ground of classification. These are but specimens of the method of the book, which, in spite of its merits, is not in its present form a good one to put in the hands of beginners, because it teaches them so much that they will have to unlearn later, if they are to understand the Sanskrit language.

One more point, of minor consequence, may be noted, in which the habit of Western philology shows itself too subservient to the whims of the Sanskrit native grammarians: the order of the varieties of present stems, and the designation of the conjugation classes as founded on it. We accept the Hindu order of the cases in noun-inflection, not seeking to change it, though unfamiliar, because we see that it has a reason, and a good one; but no one has ever been ingenious enough even to conjecture a reason for the Hindu order of the classes. Chance itself, if they had been thrown together into a hat, and set down in their order as drawn out, could not more successfully have sundered what belongs together, and juxtaposed the discordant. That being the case, there is no reason for our paying any heed to the arrangement. In fact, the heed that we do pay is a perversion; the Hindus do not speak of first class, second class, etc., but call each class by the name of its leading verb, as *bhū*-verbs, *ad*-verbs, and so on; and it was a decided merit of Müller, in his grammar, to try to substitute for the mock Hindu method this true one, which does not make such a dead pull upon the mechanical memory of the learner. As a matter of course, the most defensible and acceptable method is that of calling each class by its characteristic feature— as, the reduplicating class, the *ya*-class, and so on. But one still meets, in treatises and papers on general philology, references to verbs " of the fourth class," " of the seventh class," and so on. So far as this is not mere mechanical habit, it is pedantry—as if one meant to say: " I am so familiar with the Sanskrit language and its native grammar that I can tell the order in which the bodies of similarly-conjugated roots follow one another in the *dhātupāṭhas*, though no one knows any reason for it, and the Hindu grammarians themselves lay no stress upon it." It is much to be hoped that this affectation will die out, and soon.

These and such as these are sufficient reasons why an exposition like that here given is timely and pertinent. It needs to be impressed on the minds of scholars that the study of the Sanskrit language is one thing, and the study of the Hindu science of grammar another and a very different thing; that while there has been a time when the latter was the way to the former, that time is now long past, and the relation of the two reversed; that the present task of the students of the grammar is to make their science accessible, account if possible for its anomalies, and determine how much and what can be extracted from it to fill out that knowledge of the language which we derive from the literature; and that the peculiar Hindu ways of grouping and viewing and naming facts familiar to us from the other related languages are an obstacle in the way of a real and fruitful comprehension of those facts as they show themselves in Sanskrit, and should be avoided. An interesting sentimental glamour, doubtless, is thrown over the language and its study by the retention of an odd classification and terminology; but that attraction is dearly purchased at the cost of a tittle of clearness and objective truth.

W. D. WHITNEY.

Letter from Whitney to Rudolf von Roth, April 10, 1894. Whitney's last concern was the Atharva-Veda translation and commentary which he had begun as a student under Roth (see pp. xii, 2, 6). Before he died, he had Lanman's assurance of editorial responsibility. (By permission of Harvard University Archives and Mrs. Robert A. Cushman.)

TRANSACTIONS

OF THE

AMERICAN PHILOLOGICAL ASSOCIATION.

1892.

I. — *On the Narrative Use of Imperfect and Perfect in the Brāhmaṇas.*

By Prof. W. D. WHITNEY,

YALE UNIVERSITY.

In the classical Sanskrit, as is well known, imperfect and perfect and aorist are virtually equivalent tenses, freely coördinated in narration. In the Veda, on the other hand, while the imperfect has the same value as later, that of a simple past tense without further special implication of any kind, the aorist is restricted throughout to the proximate past, or answers very closely to our perfect with *have ;* and the perfect is differently treated in the two grand divisions of Vedic text, the *mantra* or sacred song and formula (chiefly hymn-text), and the *brāhmaṇa* or later expository literature (represented especially by the treatises called Brāhmaṇas). In the former of these divisions, the perfect has a bewildering variety of values — that of a simple past or preterit, that of a proximate past (like the aorist of the same period), and that of a present ; in the latter division, it has lost the second of these three values, and has nearly lost (save in certain residual and increasingly infrequent cases) the third ; its general use is, as later, that of a narrative tense, equivalent to the imperfect. In all the Brāhmaṇas, imperfect and perfect are both used in narration, in part separately and in part together ; and the usage of different

Brāhmaṇas, and even of different parts of the same Brāhmaṇa, is considerably different. The matter is one of some interest in the history of development of Sanskrit syntax. In the first edition of my Sanskrit grammar I was able to make (§ 822) only a very brief and general statement respecting it ; in preparing to give this statement more precision in the second edition, I was led (particularly as being able during a part of the time to do no more serious work than this) to note in considerable detail the usage of the different Brāh-maṇa texts ; and it seems worth while to report here the results with some fulness. Delbrück, to be sure, in his Vedic Syntax (1888), has treated the subject, at greater length than it comported with the plan of my grammar to do ; yet he is very far from having exhausted it, nor can I in all points approve the way in which it has been handled by him.

I limit myself throughout, of course, to *brāhmaṇa*-material proper, or expository prose, to the exclusion of all *mantra*-material, whether metrical or non-metrical, and whether con-stituting part of a Brāhmaṇa or merely quoted in its text.

We may best begin our examination with the Sāma-Veda Brāhmaṇa known as the Pañcaviṅça or Tāṇḍya (or Tāṇḍya-Mahā) Brāhmaṇa, because that shows less mixture of the two tenses than any other work of its class. In it the imper-fect is used almost exclusively in narration ; out of near 1450 narrative tenses only 11 are perfects (about 1 to 130). Their distribution through the text is (omitting book i., which is made up entirely of *mantra*-material) as follows :

Narrative Imperfects and Perfects in the Pañcaviṅça Brāhmaṇa.

ii.	4 i.	0 p.	x.	53 i.	1 p.	xviii.	37 i.	0 p.
iii.	2	0	xi.	46	0	xix.	32	0
iv.	47	0	xii.	103	1	xx.	77	0
v.	18	0	xiii.	105	3	xxi.	67	0
vi.	83	0	xiv.	118	1	xxii.	24	0
vii.	138	0	xv.	61	0	xxiii.	26	0
viii.	158	0	xvi.	47	0	xxiv.	38	2
ix.	70	0	xvii.	32	0	xxv.	47	3
							1433 i.	11 p.

Of the eleven perfects, four (at x. 5. 7 : xii. 13. 11 : xiii. 4.
11 : xiv. 1. 12) are cases of *uvāca*, 'he said,' used in reporting
the words of an ancient sage (we shall see hereafter that this
is not uncommon) : e.g. 'O Dṛta, son of Indrota (thus said
[*uvāca*] Abhipratārin, son of Kakṣasena), those who go to
the top of a great tree, what becomes of them then?' The
remaining seven are mingled with imperfects in the same
passage : thus, at xxv. 6. 4–5, we have an imperfect followed
by two perfects, and at xxv. 10. 17–18, two imperfects followed by a perfect, in each case without any traceable difference of meaning; at xxiv. 18. 2 (1 i. followed by 2 p.), we
might conjecture a distinction of continuous (i.) and momentary (p.) action, if this were not unsupported by the usage
elsewhere of the treatise, and by that of the other Brāhmaṇas,
and accordingly lacking all plausibility. At xiii. 6. 9, again,
are two perfects among imperfects : 'that demon Dīrghajihvī
(long-tongue), sacrifice-slayer, used (i.) to lick down the sacrifices ; her Indra had (i.) no hope of slaying by any magic
(*māyā*) whatever. Now there was (p.) a handsome man,
Sumitra, a Kutsa ; to him (Indra) said (i.) : "call her to
thee"; he called (i.) her to him. She said (i.) to him :
"surely that have I not heard (p.), but it is somehow pleasing
to my heart (?). "' And then between them they mastered
and slew her (i.). The first perfect here might be imagined
to have a motive, the direct narrative being broken in upon
by a statement of something that at the time was true ; yet
this has too little support anywhere to be accepted. The
other, a perfect in personal statement, is against the prevailing analogy; and the sense is obscure and the reading doubtful ; the printed text has *nā 'hāi 'va tan nu çuçruba* (which
might be meant for either *çuçruve* or *çuçrava*) ; but the commentary quotes and explains of it only the one word *aha*.
The same story is told, at much greater length and in less
decent fashion, in the other great Sāma-Veda Brāhmaṇa, the
Jāiminīya or Talavakāra (i. 161–3) ; but there is nothing there
to cast any light whatever upon the point here in question.

I add the list of perfect forms with present sense for this
Brāhmaṇa, in order to complete the tale of perfects, and lest

I may have erred in classifying one or another of them, as the distinction is not always altogether clear. They are: *dādhāra*, vii. 4. 7 : x. 3. 13 ; 5. 3 : xi. 5. 12 ; 10. 11 : xii. 9. 16 : xiii. 4. 2 : xxiii. 28. 6. — *ānaçe, -çāte*, iv. 6. 7 : vii. 6. 9, 10 : x. 12. 10 : xi. 1. 4 : xvi. 6. 14. — *dīdāya*, x. 5. 2 : xiii. 11. 23 : xv. 2. 3. — *dadrçe, -çire*, xii. 2. 7 : xxv. 12. 5. — *jāgāra*, x. 4. 4. — *pupuve*, vii. 3. 1. — *bheje*, xx. 16. 1 : in all, twenty-two occurrences, from seven roots, or twice as many occurrences as of the narrative perfects. Such a relation between them is not found in any other text.

In the Tāittirīya-Saṁhitā, again, in the *brāhmaṇa*-parts of it (constituting about three-fifths of the text), we find a similar predominance of imperfects (about 70 to 1), and a similar lack of clear distinction in their use. The two tenses are distributed in the different books (omitting the fourth, which is *mantra* only) as follows :

Narrative Imperfects and Perfects in the Tāittirīya-Saṁhitā.

i.	99 i.	11 p.	iii.	120 i.	0 p.	vi.	472 i.	7 p.
ii.	560	1	v.	338	6	vii.	311	4
							1900 i.	29 p.

Here also, as above, the majority of perfects are cases of *uvāca*, used of the words of a quoted authority : thus, at ii. 6. 2³, 'Keçin Sātyakāmi said (*uvāca*) to Keçin Dârbhya, "to-morrow at the sacrifice I [thou ?] shall use,"' etc. ; other examples occur at v. 4. 2² ; 6. 6³ (*tad ṛṣir abhyanūvāca*) : vi. 4. 5² ; and at vii. 4. 5⁴ (repeated at 5. 4²) such an *uvāca* follows an imperfect in the same narration. At i. 7. 2, *uvāca*, 'said he,' is used eleven times, in a colloquy between two sages ; and a single imperfect is associated with them : 'then they two proceeded to talk about (i. *páry avadatām*) the cow.' Once more, at vi. 6. 2²⁻³, in a brief similar colloquy, we have *uvāca* twice, and *papracha*, 'he asked,' once. But also in the words of one of the collocutors in this story we find a perfect and an imperfect coördinated : '"in truth (? *satyád*) the Sṛñjayas perished (p. *párā babhūvus*)," said (p.) he ; "verily the sacrifice was (i. *āsīt*) to be established in the sacrifice, that the sacrificer might not perish."' Here a distinction between momentary and continuous action might again be conjectured; but (as already pointed out) that distinction is in innumerable cases disregarded, and never attains to expression; whence its recognition here is not to be admitted. Again, at v. 3. 8[1], we have a perfect and an imperfect together in the same sentence: 'this construction Yajñasena Cāitriyāyaṇa knew (i.e. 'devised'; *vidāṁ cakāra*, p.); by it he acquired (i.) cattle': here might be possible a distinction between an act and its after consequences, such as we have glimpses of, but no more than that, elsewhere. The only remaining passage where the two tenses are in any way mixed is vi. 1. 6, where, in the midst of the legend of Kadrū and Suparṇī, narrated in (some 30) imperfects, comes in a single perfect, as follows: 'the divines (*brahmavādín*) say: "in virtue of what truth did gāyatrī, being the least of the meters, compass (*pári 'yāya*, p.) the face of the sacrifice? Even because she formerly (*adás*) brought (i.) the soma, therefore did she compass (i.) the face of the sacrifice,"' etc. (with imperfects only). Here is, to be sure, a break and parenthesis in the story, and we are tempted to render the perfect as if it were an aorist, 'hath compassed'; but that also is a proceeding which finds too little support elsewhere, and the case is a problematical one. The same perfect, *pári 'yāya*, it may be added, is found alone with the same sense in three other passages, namely v. 1. 8[2]; 2. 3[1]; 3. 2[4], where we should expect rather the imperfect (as we actually have it in vii. 5. 8[3]). In vii. 3. 1[3] we find the perfect *ānṛcús* contrasted once with the present *árcanti* and once with the future *arcitáras*, and are again tempted to render 'have sung,' as a perfect used in aoristic sense (perhaps because no aorist from this verb occurs elsewhere); but I do not know why 'sang' would not be equally accordant with Sanskrit usage. Finally, at vi. 1. 11[3], we have the perfect *tatāna*, but it is used in the exposition of a Rig-Veda verse in which the same form appears, and is doubtless only a transfer of this.

Of perfects used in present sense this text has twenty-six occurrences, from five roots: namely, *dādhāra*, i. 7. 2[1,2]: ii. 5. 7[5]; 6. 2[2] (2): v. 1. 10[5]; 2. 7[3], 10[4] (5); 6. 5[1-2] (5); 7. 9[2]:

vi. 6. $7^{2,3}$: vii. 2. 4^3. — *dodrāva*, i. 5. 1^4. — *bibhāya*, ii. 3. 3^4. — *ānaçe*, ii. 5. 4^3. — *dadṛçre*, vi. 4. 2^4 (2).

On the whole, the Tāittirīya-Saṁhitā shows no real example of the substitution of perfect for imperfect as narrative tense, nor any clearly marked distinction between the two tenses in the scattering instances where the perfect is used.

In the Tāittirīya-Brāhmaṇa (of which decidedly the larger part, about as 8 to 5, is *brāhmaṇa*-material), the case is somewhat different. In two of the last chapters the perfect is used instead of the imperfect in narrative, and its proportional frequency is accordingly raised much higher, up to about 1 to 20. The scheme of distribution is as follows :

Narrative Imperfects and Perfects in the Tāittirīya-Brāhmaṇa.

i. 1	159 i.	0 p.	i. 8	17 i.	0 p.	iii. 3	17 i.	2 p.
2	19	0	ii. 1	94	0	8	36	1
3	51	0	2	264	2	9	55	1
4	77	0	3	155	8	10	7	26
5	139	7	7	54	1	11	27	21
6	86	0	iii. 1	104	0	12	61	2
7	36	0	2	63	3		1521 i.	74 p.

In this statement are omitted ii. 4–6, 8 and iii. 4–6, which are *mantra* only ; also iii. 7, which contains no example of either tense.

More than three-fifths of all the perfects, it is seen, occur in iii. 10 and 11. And the largest body of them is found together in iii. 11. 8, in the legend of Nachiketas, on which the Kaṭha-Up. is later grafted (see these Transactions for 1890, vol. xxi. p. 89–90) ; this is told in 16 perfects, among which, however, are intercalated 4 imperfects. The change of tense is not unmotived ; a change of time underlies it. Twice it is Death's inquiry of the boy as to his personal experience : 'Arriving, [Death] asked (p.) him : boy, how many nights hast thou abode (aorist) here ? Three, answered (p.) he. What didst thou eat (i.) the first night ?' etc. The distinction here for the first time illustrated is an important and constant one ; the tenses of personal narration are aorist and imperfect, the former corresponding to our perfect, or proximate past, the latter to our simple preterit, or indefinite past ; the perfect is not favored for either use. The other two imperfects express the after result, outside the story, of something told in the story : thus, 'Death told (p.) him the *nāciketa* fire, and thereafter his good works were not exhausted (i.) . . . and he overcame (i.) the second death.'

Of this latter ground of change from perfect to imperfect we suspected above an instance in TS. (v. 3. 8[1]) ; but it cannot be illustrated by examples from other texts sufficient to give it the character of an established rule. There are, indeed, in the treatise now under discussion, and in the next section (iii. 11. 9[8 7]) to the one quoted above, five similar cases ; some one performed (p.) a certain meritorious act, and after it followed (i.) such and such a recompense. Then, again, in the following chapter (iii. 12 ; its narrative tense is otherwise exclusively the imperfect) is one more similar instance (5[3-4]) : 'these Aruṇa Āupaveçi knew (p.) ; by them he overcame (i.) reproach, also all evil' ; but then unfortunately it is added that 'he went (p.) to heaven,' which goes far toward destroying our confidence in the relation surmised to be intended between the two preceding tenses.

There is at iii. 10. 9[5] another plain case of a quoted imperfect in personal narration among perfects ; a student says, 'thus my teacher [formerly] told (i.) me' ; and the same alternation is made at iii. 2. 9[15], though the statement quoted is not a personal one. In ii. 2. 7[3] (repeated at 11[5]), on the contrary, where a perfect appears in personal quotation among imperfects, we are doubtless to understand it as one of the common cases of perfect used as present : 'those [gods] in yonder world thirsted (i.) ; they said (i.) : verily (*vāí;* printed the first time as if *ké*) we subsist upon (*upa jijīvima*) a giving from yonder.'

In the two or three remaining instances of perfects and imperfects used together no difference of meaning seems recognizable : they are i. 5. 9 (6 p. interspersed among 26 i.) : ii. 3. 10[1-3] (3 i. followed by 8 p.) ; 7. 18[3] (1 p. followed by 1 i.).

Elsewhere the perfect is used alone. In iii. 10. 9[9-15] we find three groups of them (twelve in all), and in 11[3-5] another

group (of eight) : all plain cases of the substitution of perfect for imperfect as narrative tense.   Again, in iii. 2. 5⁴ (repeated at 3. 6¹) are two such perfects (two imperfects follow
in 3. 6², but they belong to a different story).   The remaining
examples are single perfects; they are found at i. 5. 2¹ : iii.
8. 6⁵ ; 9. 15³.

In this text I have noted of perfects having value as
presents only two, with six occurrences : namely, *dādhāra*,
i. 4. 5⁴ (2) : iii. 2. 8³ ; 7. 2⁵. — *dadṛçe*, ii. 1. 2⁹, ¹⁰ ; besides
jijīvima, as quoted above.

Of the Tāittirīya-Āraṇyaka only a small part is *brāhmaṇa*-
material: namely, i. 22–26, 31 (in part), 32 : ii. 1, 2, 7–18 :
v. (all) : vi.–ix. (the Tāittirīya-Upanishad, all) : x. (the Yājñikī-
Upanishad) 13–14, 63–64.   In this the narrative tenses are
not numerous, and the perfects are to the imperfects about
as 1 to 9.   They are thus distributed :

Narrative Imperfects and Perfects in the Tāittirīya-Āraṇyaka.

i. 23.	30 i.	0 p.	v. 72 i.	1 p.	ix.	10 i.	11 p.
ii. 1–2	12	0	viii. 9	0	x.	0	2
7–18	23	3				156 i.	17 p.

At x. 63, two perfects are used together in narration ; in
all the other cases of the occurrence of perfects, they are
mixed with imperfects.   And everywhere there is no distinct
difference of value between the two tenses, unless it be (as
there is reason to conjecture elsewhere) a preference for
beginning a bit of narrative with a perfect or two, and then
continuing it with the other tense.   Thus, we find one perfect followed by an imperfect at ii. 15 and v. 4¹²⁻¹³ ; and in
ix. 1–6 we have five groups of two (once three) perfects followed by two imperfects.   In ii. 7 is found a single introductory perfect followed by nine imperfects ; but after the
first two of these occurs a second perfect, if the *viçus* of the
printed text is for *viviçus* (the commentary unfortunately
gives no help in determining the point) ; its reason would be
wholly obscure.

Of perfects used as presents I find no example.

In the Māitrāyaṇī-Saṁhitā a little more than half (about as 7 to 6) of the material is *brāhmaṇa.* In it the proportion of perfects to imperfects is not far from the same as in the Tāittirīya-Saṁhitā, or as 1 to 64. Their comparative distribution is shown in the following table (in which the purely *mantra*-chapters are omitted) :

Narrative Imperfects and Perfects in the Māitrāyaṇī-Saṁhitā.

i. 4	19 i.	1 p.	ii. 4	100 i.	o p.	iii. 10	69 i.	o p.	
5	32	1	5	144	3	iv. 1	63	o	
6	180	1	iii. 1	45	1	2	138	5	
7	24	2	2	53	5	3	50	o	
8	94	o	3	53	5	4	39	o	
9	99	o	4	60	o	5	87	1	
10	131	2	5	0	o	6	67	7	
11	61	o	6	83	1	7	75	o	
ii. 1	71	o	7	70	o	8	52	o	
2	75	o	8	150	o		2237 i.	35 p.	
3	12	o	9	41	o				

From all this material very little that is of value for the relation of the two tenses is to be won, especially because there is very little mixture of them in the same narration. In a few cases there appears to be a simple substitution (always a brief one) of the perfect for the imperfect as tense of narration : such are i. 7. 3 (p. 112, l. 3 : 2 p. ; perhaps rather used as presents); 10. 12 (152. 1 : 2 p.) : ii. 5. 1 (47. 13 : 3 p.) : iii. 2. 7 (27. 7 : 3 p.) ; 3. 2 (33. 7 : 2 p.), 9 (42. 16 : 2 p.) : iv. 2. 10 (33. 14 : 2 p.) ; 6. 6 (88. 8 ff. : 5 p.) ; and single perfects at i. 4. 12 (62. 4) ; 5. 8 (76. 16) : iii. 1. 3 (3. 20) ; 2. 3 (18. 2) ; 3. 9 (42. 11) ; 6. 5 (65. 12) : iv. 2. 2 (24. 5) ; 6. 2 (79. 18). In a number of these passages it is the actions of sages that are reported (oftenest with *vidāṁ cakāra*) ; but the cases do not seem to form a class, such as was surmised in the Tāittirīya Saṁhitā. Once (i. 5. 8) the perfect is in quoted words ; not, however, relating personal experience.

In the remaining cases, a single perfect is associated with one or more imperfects. Thus, in i. 6. 13 (107. 16), among ten imperfects, a perfect (*vidāṁ cakāra*, 1 sing.) of personal assertion, which is so opposed to all analogies elsewhere that it might seem to call for emendation; in ii. 5. 11 (63. 13), *ānaçe* after one imperfect (used as pres. ? cf. iii. 2. 3 [18. 2]); in iii. 2. 8 (28. 3), a perfect (*uvāca*) after four imperfects; in iv. 2. 2 (23. 6), a perfect (*vidāṁ cakāra*) followed by two imperfects; and 6 (27. 13), the same, by four; at 5. 4 (69. 1), the same, by one; and in 6. 3 (80. 16), a perfect among four imperfects, without any possible reason for the alternation.

Here again, as in the Pañcaviṅça-Brāhmaṇa, the perfects with present value are (if I have not misestimated any of them) more numerous than those with imperfect value, being thirty-six occurrences, from ten roots: *dādhāra*, i. 8. 1 (115. 7), 9 (128. 17) : ii. 5. 1 (48. 2) : iii. 2. 2 (16. 15), 6 (23. 13), 6 (25. 3), 9 (30. 10, twice) ; 7. 4 (80. 11), 5 (81. 10) ; 8. 9 (108. 2) : iv. 3. 7 (45. 19, 20) ; 5. 4 (69. 5, 6) ; 8. 8 (116. 4, 5, 7, 9, 12, 13). — *yoyāva*, ii. 1. 10 (12. 3) : iv. 4. 3 (53. 13), 4 (54. 12). — *lelāya*, i. 8. 6 (123. 12) : ii. 2. 3 (16. 21). — *dadṛçe*, -*çrc*, i. 10. 6 (146. 7) : iv. 4. 1 (50. 13). — *vivyāca*, i. 8. 8 (128. 7) ; 10. 12 (152. 5). — *ānaçe*, ii. 5. 5 (54. 6) : iii. 2. 9 (30. 6). — *duduhre*, iii. 3. 4 (36. 9) : iv. 7. 4 (98. 14). — *āçāte*, iii. 8. 2 (93. 15). — *āpa*, iii. 9. 1 (112. 7). — *jagrāha*, iii. 9. 2 (115. 16).

In the Aitareya-Brāhmaṇa the perfects are decidedly more numerous, being to the imperfects about as 1 to 4, as is shown by the table that follows :

Narrative Imperfects and Perfects in the Aitareya-Brāhmaṇa.

i.	116 i.	6 p.	iv.	186 i.	3 p.	vii.	30 i.	139 p.
ii.	183	5	v.	97	6	viii.	29	51
iii.	347	7	vi.	92	49		1080 i.	266 p.

In the first five books the proportion of perfects (about 1 to 35) is not markedly different from what we have found hitherto ; then the perfects increase rapidly, and in the last two books are even the great majority. The difference is owing to the substitution, on a large scale, of the perfect for the imperfect as preferred narrative tense. Thus, in the seventh book, where are found the majority of the whole number of perfects, it is especially the long story of

Çunaḥçepa (13–18) that gives them their predominance, being
told throughout in (114) perfects. This narrative also includes
(after emending in 14. 8 *prāpnot* to *prāpat*, as palpably required by the sense, and as ÇÇS. in its version of the legend
correctly reads; ÇÇS. has also, just before, *prāpa* for the
blundering *prāpat*) two imperfects, one of which is fully
motived, being of personal narrative in quotation : ' he, assenting, addressed (p.) his son : my dear, he (Varuṇa) verily [long
ago] gave (i.) thee to me ' (14. 8). The other imperfect also
(16. 1) marks a change of time : ' [now at this time] Viçvāmitra
was (i.) his invoker ' ; but it is not one which causes otherwise than in rare and exceptional cases a change of tense (so
at 15. 7 just above : ' he had [p.] three sons) ; and in iii. 49. 5
a perfect appears to be used in a similar way among imperfects (' [now] Bharadvāja was [p.] a lean long gray man ; he
said [i.] ' etc.).

The imperfect of personal narration is further exemplified
in vii. 27–34, where a story at second hand, in the words of
one of the characters, is in (13) imperfects, distributed among
the (21) perfects of the general narrative. Again, in iii. 48. 9
is a quoted imperfect (1st sing.) in a story told in perfects ;
and, at v. 29. 1, 2, two imperfects alternate with two perfects
with a similar distinction. Also at vi. 14. 4 we have an imperfect in quotation, ' ye called to me,' between perfects ; the
imperfect, however (' when at that time *gāyatrī* brought [i.]
the soma '), with which the little legend begins, is unusual
and, for aught we can see, unmotived. In ii. 19. 2, the solitary perfect in the midst of ten imperfects seems intended
only to help the etymology (Parisāraka from *pari sasāra*).
Then in a few passages a change to perfect (*abhyanūvāca*)
occurs when after a narration in imperfects it is stated that a
seer made a verse about the matter : so in ii. 25. 5 ; 33. 6 :
iii. 20. 1 ; but the second of these passages has also another
perfect introducing the story ; and the last has an unmotived
perfect at the end.

In one or two places the Brāhmaṇa text (which is often
faulty, as compared with the other treatises of its class)
plainly calls for emendation. Thus, at vi. 1. 1, 2, where

-*asarpat* apparently occurs twice in a crowd of perfects, it is to be changed once to a participle, -*āsarpan*, and once to a present, -*āsarpati ;* and, in vi. 14. 10, -*avayus* must be -*aveyus* (*ava + īyus*) : the imperfect *abravīt* a little earlier in the same story seems wholly unmotived.

In the remaining passages where the two tenses are mixed, either no reason or only a very doubtful one for the alternation can be alleged. Thus, in i. 18. 1–2 (2 i. followed by 5 p.); 21. 16 (2 i. and 1 p. ; but the former probably a virtual quotation of RV. expressions) : ii. 36. 2 (1 p. in the midst of 14 i.) : iii. 22. 8 (*uvāca* and *abruvan* side by side; in the analogous passage a little above, in 21. 4, only the i. is used) : iv. 8. 3 (1 p. *na dadhṛṣatus,* 'they had not the courage,' among many i.) ; 17. 5 (1 p. following 1 i.) : vi. 15. 11 (1 i., *abravīt,* among several p.) ; 18. 1–2 (1 p. among 6 i.) ; 33. 1–4 (3 i. between 2 p.) ; 34–35 (a jumble of 12 i. and 8 p. in the same story)· viii. 10. 1 (an alternation of 4 *ajayan* i. with 7 *yetire* p., and a *jigyus* p. at the end).

We may note finally the passages where the perfect alone is used, taking the place of the imperfect as narrative tense. Simple perfects are found in iii. 12. 5 (*abhyanūvāca*) : iv. 27. 9 (*uvāca*) : v. 33. 3 (do.) ; 34. 3 (*āsa*) : vi. 20. 17 (do.) : vii. 10. 3 (*ruroha*) ; groups of them in v. 30. 15 (2 p.) : vi. 24. 16 (3 p.) ; 30. 7–15 (10 p.) : vii. 1. 6–7 (3 p., emending *cakrāmat* before *tam* to *cakrāma*) : viii. 21–23 (41 p.) ; 28. 18 (3 p.).

Of perfects with present value are found twenty-one, from four roots (*dādhāra,* which never has anywhere any other than the present sense, making the considerable majority of them) : thus, *dādhāra,* iv. 12. 8 · v. 4. 15 ; 5. 3 ; 6. 12 ; 8. 3 ; 12. 11 ; 13. 4 ; 16. 16 ; 17. 2 ; 18. 15 ; 19. 2 ; 20. 15 ; 21. 5. — *dīdāya,* i. 28. 9 : ii. 40. 2 ; 41. 4 : iii. 8. 2 : iv. 11. 8. — *bibhāya,* v. 15. 9 ; *bībhāya,* v. 25. 17. — *vivyāca,* iv. 12. 8.

In the Kāuṣītaki-Brāhmaṇa the relation of the two tenses is different from anything thus far noticed, the perfects being to the imperfects nearly as 3 to 5. Their distribution in detail is as follows (omitting xi., which contains no example of either tense) :

Narrative Imperfects and Perfects in the Kāuṣītaki-Brāhmaṇa.

i.	11 i.	6 p.	xii.	18 i.	10 p.	xxii.	9 i.	1 p.
ii.	12	4	xiii.	0	6	xxiii.	8	15
iii.	5	1	xiv.	9	0	xxiv.	13	3
iv.	7	2	xv.	20	3	xxv.	5	0
v.	8	1	xvi.	6	5	xxvi.	4	6
vi.	63	15	xvii.	1	0	xxvii.	0	2
vii.	25	10	xviii.	7	1	xxviii.	2	29
viii.	4	2	xix.	3	0	xxix.	2	9
ix.	7	0	xx.	3	0	xxx.	2	17
x.	1	0	xxi.	8	1		263 i.	149 p.

Among all these tenses, however, there are but two well-marked instances of the expression of a distinction of time : namely, in ii. 9 and vii. 4, where an imperfect is found in quotation among perfects. In a few instances may be conjectured to appear the tendency (recognized above, but especially below, in ÇB.) to introduce a story with perfects and finish it in imperfects : such are found in i. 1 ; vii. 6; xii. 1 ; but they are offset by contrary cases, of introductory imperfects, in vi. 13–14; xii. 3 ; xxiii. 2 ; xxx. 6. Passages in which the two tenses are mixed without any apprehensible reason for the alternation are i. 2 ; v. 3 (the solitary perfect here should perhaps be emended to *ajakṣus*, i.) ; vi. 10 (1 p. among 14 i.), 15 (3 p. and 4 i. alternately) ; viii. 8 ; xv. 2 (*uvāca* and *abravīt* alternating twice) ; xxi. 1 ; xxiv. 1 ; xxviii. 2, 4 ; xxix. 1. For the sake of uniformity, the remaining occurrences of perfects may also be noted : we find single ones in iii. 8 ; iv. 4 ; vi. 14 ; viii. 1 ; xv. 1 ; xviii. 9 ; xxii. 4 ; xxix. 2 ; xxx. 1, 3, 9, 9 ; and groups in xiii. 3 (6) ; xvi. 1 (2), 9 (3) ; xxiii. 5 (3) ; xxvi. 5 (6) ; xxvii. 7 (2) ; xxviii. 1 (12), 2 (3), 3 (2), 4 (4), 8 (2) ; xxx. 5 (6).

Of perfects used as present I have found no examples in this Brāhmaṇa.

Of the Çatapatha-Brāhmaṇa, the immense extent, and the number and discordance of the phenomena, make the exhibition of the latter a matter of no small difficulty ; it would be impossible without great expenditure of time and space to set them all forth, as in the case of the works already treated ;

nor would the result repay the labor. Taking the whole text together, the imperfects outnumber the perfects only in the proportion of 2 to 1 ; but the relation of the two tenses is very different in different books, as the subjoined table shows :

Narrative Imperfects and Perfects in the Çatapatha-Brāhmaṇa.

i. 291 i.	306 p.	vi. 547 i.	21 p.	xi. 198 i.	259 p.
ii. 180	192	vii. 281	13	xii. 123	65
iii. 308	196	viii. 462	30	xiii. 132	26
iv. 209	178	ix. 214	91	xiv. 250	337
v. 121	70	x. 319	106	3635 i.	1890 p.

The work begins (i., ii.) with the perfects even somewhat outnumbering the imperfects ; and it ends (xi., xiv.) in the same way ; while in some of the intermediate books (especially vi.–viii.) the preponderance of imperfects is so great (more than 20 to 1) as to remind us of the Brāhmaṇas first described here. While there are numerous passages in which either tense is used to the exclusion of the other, the two are also on a very large scale mixed together, and chiefly without discoverable reason ; in the great majority of cases, no difference of tense-relation is to be apprehended. But the use of the imperfect in quotation, in personal narrative, shows itself (though the examples are fewer than were to be wished, and there are exceptions) to be a pretty well established rule. There seems also to exist an inclination to begin a narration with one or more perfects, as if to give it a proper setting, the details of it then following in imperfects ; but this is far from being a rule — even the contrary sometimes occurs, and in the majority of instances the same tense holds throughout. The apparent indifference as to the use of the two tenses does not go to the extent of total disregard of consistency ; where there is a recurrence of the same passage, or of one closely similar, there is sometimes a striking accordance in the sequence of tenses used, such as to raise the question whether there could not have been, after all, some sense of a difference in the mind of the authors, even though we have not been skilful enough to discover it.

Most of the examples of the imperfect of personal narration occur in book XIV. (also Bṛhad-Āraṇyaka Upanishad). The best is found in XIV. vi. 7, 1–4 (BAU. iii. 7. 1[1]). It is in the account of the noted contest between Yājñavalkya and the other leading Brahmans at the court of king Janaka as to who is superior in sacred knowledge, which is given consistently throughout in perfects (near a hundred of them, the majority being repetitions of *uvāca*). Uddālaka, in his part of the discussion, introduces a narrative of his own former experience as a student, and this is told in imperfects : ' Now Uddālaka Āruṇi questioned (p.) him : Yājñavalkya, said (p.) he, we [formerly] dwelt (i.) among the Madras in the house of Patañcala Kāpya, studying the sacrifice. He had (i.) a wife possessed by a Gandharva. This [Gandharva] we asked (i.) : who art thou ? He said (i.) : Kabandha Ātharvaṇa. He [the Gandharva] said (i.) to Patañcala ' . . . and so on, to the end of the story.

In an earlier section (3) occurs another legend so nearly akin with this that the two seem like two versions of the same tale : ' Now Bhujyu Lāhyāyani questioned (p.) him. Yājñavalkya, said (p.) he, we went about (i.) as wanderers (*caraka*) among the Madras. As such we came (i.) to the house of Patañcala Kāpya. He had (i.) a daughter possessed by a Gandharva. This [Gandharva] we asked (i.) : who art thou ? He said (i.) : Sudhanvan Āngirasa. When we asked (i.) him about the ends of the worlds, then we said (i.) to him : what became (i.) of the Pārikshitas ? what became (i.) of the Pārikshitas ? This I ask of you, O Yājñavalkya : what became (i.) of the Pārikshitas ? He (Yājñavalkya) said (p., as part of the general legend) : he (the Gandharva) doubtless said this (p. again ; we should have expected rather i.) : they went (i.), of course, where the horse-sacrificers go.' What follows is rather problematical. Yājñavalkya seems himself to take up and continue the story of the Gandharva : ' Where, I pray, do the horse-sacrificers go ? [you proceeded to ask him ; and he answered as follows :] this world is . . . (the description may be omitted) ; them Indra, having become an eagle (*suparṇa*),

---

[1] The Kāṇva text of the Upanishad is the one meant in the parallel references.

handed over (i.) to Vāyu (the wind-god); Vāyu, putting them within himself, made them go (i.) to the place where the Pārikshitas were (i.). Somewhat ·in this way, verily, did he (the Gandharva) extol (p.; this accords with the p. used of the Gandharva above) Vāyu; therefore Vāyu is,' etc. Whether the fault be Yājñavalkya's or the Gandharva's, Bhujyu gets no real answer to his question as to where the horse-sacrificers go; but he is at any rate silenced, for the section ends with 'then Bhujyu Lāhyāyani held his peace' (p., as part of the general narration).

Further on in the same book, at XIV. vi. 10 (BAU. iv. 1), is a long passage showing distinctions of the same kind between alternating perfects and imperfects. It is a colloquy between Yājñavalkya and Janaka, told in perfects, as usual, but with change to imperfect whenever one of the collocutors himself has something past to narrate. 'Janaka the Videhan held a session (p.); then Yājñavalkya came up (p.). Said (p.) Janaka the Videhan: O Yājñavalkya, for what purpose hast thou set out (aor.)? seeking cattle, [or] things with subtile conclusions? Both, O great king, said (p.) he; what any one told (i.) you, that let us hear.' We might have expected here an aorist, 'what any one has told you,' but the tense is adapted to that of the king's reply, and, as imperfect, denies the uniqueness and recency of the communication. The king answers: 'Said (i.) to me Udanka Çāulvāyana: breath verily is the *bráhman.* — [Y. goes on.] As one having a mother, a father, a teacher might say, so Çāulvāyana said (i.) this: namely, breath is the *bráhman;* for what would there be of any one without breath? but did he tell (i.) you its support [and] firm standing? — He did not tell (i.) me. — One-footed verily is that, O great king.' Then, after some further exposition, we have, as conclusion of this part of the story: 'a thousand [cows] with an elephant for bull I give [thee], said (p.) Janaka the Videhan. Said (p.) Yājñavalkya: my father was of opinion (i.) [that] one should not take without having instructed (i.e. should not accept reward for a trifling service); who again told (i.) you what?' And then the same series of tenses is repeated five times more, in reporting and answering what so many different Brahmans had said to Janaka.

Further on, at XIV. ix. 1. 8 (BAU. vi. 2. 5), we find again a motived change from perfect to imperfect in a quotation: 'he said (p.) : Acknowledged of me is this boon ; but what thou didst say (i.) in the presence of the boy, that tell to me.' The only admissible alternative here would have been the aorist of proximate action.

An example of mixed character is found in an extremely curious bit of legend at XIV. viii. 15. 11 (BAU. v. 14. 8). Janaka appears to have recognized in a working elephant a former sage, and is astonished to find him in such a condition — transmigrated instead of absorbed or happy in heaven : 'As concerns this, Janaka the Videhan said (p.) to Buḍila Āçvatarāçvi : Since now thou didst then call thyself (i.) a knower of the *gāyatrī*, how, having become an elephant, dost thou carry ? — Because, O great king, I did not know (p. !) its mouth, said (p.) he.' Here the change from the perfect of the general narrative to the imperfect in the first quoted words is perfectly normal ; but the perfect (*vidāṁ cakāra*) in the transformed sage's reply is anomalous, and very difficult to explain.

In another passage further on (XIV. ix. 1. 11 ; BAU. vi. 2. 8), a perfect appears in quoted words : 'how that this wisdom hitherto abode (p.) not with any Brahman soever ; it, however, I will communicate to you.' Here, too, according to the analogy of other similar passages, we should expect instead either an aorist or an imperfect, even though it is not a personal experience that is narrated.

This is all the material of the kind contained in the fourteenth book. But the same shift of tense for a similar reason is met with also in some of the other books.

Thus, in XI. iii. 1, we find Janaka and Yājñavalkya again in colloquy, with perfects as the tense of narration : 'Janaka the Videhan questioned (p.) Yājñavalkya : dost thou know, etc. . . . He (Yājñavalkya) said (p.) : at that time, truly, nothing whatever existed (i.) here ; so then this alone was offered (i.) — truth in faith. — Thou knowest the fire-offering, O Yājñavalkya ; I give thee a hundred cows, said (p.) he.'

Again, at XI. v. 1, the story of Purūravas and Urvaçī is told throughout in perfects; but a pair of imperfects come in at the only point where one of the characters has something past to express: thus (paragraph 7), 'to him the other made reply (p.) : . . . O Purūravas, go away home again; hard to be won, like the wind, am I; verily thou didst not do (i.) what I said (i.) . . .; thus she spoke (p.) to him.' This is as distinct an example as one would wish. But another equally clear is found in XI. vi. 1, in the legend of Bhṛgu's visit to the other world (translated by Weber, Z.D.M.G. ix. 240–241, and *Ind. Streifen,* i. 24–26). In this, again, the general narrative tense is the perfect; but an imperfect occurs four times, namely whenever the words of any of the characters introduced are quoted : thus, 'they said (p.) : Thus, indeed, did these fasten (i.) upon us in yonder world; upon them we now here fasten in return ' — and so on (the same phrase repeated three times more).

In the first paragraphs of XI. v. 5 occurs another series of four imperfects of personal narrative, when the gods give Prajāpati an account of what they have been doing to get rid of the darkness with which the Asuras had afflicted them : 'they said (p.): verily the Asuras, O reverend one, intercepted (i.) us with darkness as we were going upward to the heavenly world; we resorted (i.) to a session,' etc. The example is a less satisfactory one, inasmuch as the introductory part of the legend is in mixed perfects and imperfects (three of each); what follows, however, is in perfects only (nine). The aorist of proximate time is not used in the quotation because of the itemized and successive character of the narration (compare the similar case in TB. iii. 11. 8, above, p. 10; and in ÇB. xiv. 6. 10, p. 20, l. 23); in his answer, Prajāpati sums it all up in a single aorist : 'he said : ye have been going on (aor.) with sacrifices of incomplete ceremony,' etc.

At XII. ii. 2. 13, we are told of one who lived (p.) as Vedic student with a teacher, and 'his teacher asked (p.) him : Boy, how many did thy father think (i.) the days of the year to be ? — Ten, said (p.) he,' and so on.

At XIII. iv. 2. 3 we have an imperfect in quotation between

two perfects : 'Thus said (p.) Bhāllabeya : verily, of two colors this horse may be, black and red ; he originated (i.) from Prajāpati's eye. . . . Then said (p.) Sātyayajñi,' etc.

In the first books of the Brāhmaṇa are also to be found a few examples. Thus, at I. vi. 2. 3 : 'either the gods intimated (p.) it to them or they of themselves conceived (p.) it : go forth (said they) ; we will go to the place from whence the gods attained (i.) the heavenly world.' Further, at I. vi. 3. 17, we have an imperfect in quotation among mixed narrative tenses ; and at I. ix. 1. 26 and II. ii. 3. 7 the same where there is no including narration. Once more, at III. i. 1. 4 : 'thus said (p.) Yājñavalkya : we went (i.) to approve for Vārṣṇya a place of sacrifice to the gods ; then Sātyayajña said (i.) : verily this whole divine earth is a place of sacrifice to the gods.'

But the early books, as well as the later (see the passages quoted above), offer occasional exceptions to the general rule. At I. vii. 3. 26 an imperfect and a perfect are found together in a passage introduced by 'here now these say,' but which perhaps need not be regarded as a proper quotation ; and as of the same character may plausibly be reckoned two perfects at I. ix. 1. 25, in telling of something that was 'overheard by the ṛshis' ; and one in a proverb (*nivacana*) at II. iv. 4. 4. Also, at II. v. 2. 25, *cakṛma* is repeated, in an aoristic sense, from a *mantra*-passage which is undergoing explanation. But *çuçruma* at I. ii. 5. 26 and vi. 4. 11 seems like a remnant of aoristic value from the Vedic use of the tense ; and so does *babhaktha* (emending to *kím ma å babhaktha?* cf. *kim mahyam abhākta* AB. v. 14. 2) at I. ix. 2. 35.

Finally, at XII. ix. 3. 7 are found a series of imperfects in quotation ; but the case is an involved one. In the first place, there is also an imperfect among the preceding (10) perfects of the narrative in which the quotation occurs ; and then the quotation runs off into a long preachment, in which its real character appears to be lost sight of, and mixed perfects and imperfects occur. Thus : 'He said (p.) : how wilt thou manage ? [The other] said (p.) this : with the Asuras in the beginning was (i.) this sacrifice, the *sāutrāmaṇī ;* it went (i.) forth unto the gods ; it came (i.) to the waters ; the waters welcomed (i.) it ; for that reason people [now-a-days] welcome a superior who has arrived.' This practical observation appears to mark the transition to general narrative style ; and the text proceeds : 'they (the waters) said (p.) to it : Come, reverend one. It said (p.) : I am afraid ; lead me forward. Of what art thou afraid, reverend one ? — Of the Asuras. — So be it. — The waters led (i.) it forward ; for that reason,' etc.

These are all the examples which have been noted in the text ; but they seem, especially when taken in connection with the analogous examples from other texts given above and below, quite sufficient to establish the usage as a rule. That the shift of tense is not merely a shift made for the purpose of marking a change of time is shown by the fact that, where the general narrative is in imperfects, a quotation shows the same tense. Thus, at VIII. vi. 3. 1 we find the quoted imperfect *apaçyāma*, 'we saw,' among narrative imperfects ; and similar cases are quotable from other books and from the other Brāhmaṇas : for example, ÇB. I. vi. 4. 4. MS. i. 10. 16 (156. 6) : iii. 8. 6 (102. 14) ; they are not rare.

But a kindred case is found at V. i. 4. 8 : 'the Gandharvas verily in the beginning yoked (p.) the horse ; so then he [virtually] says : let them who in the beginning yoked (i.) the horse yoke thee to-day.' In such passages as this there is no real quotation, but a quasi-one ; the cause of the shift of tense appears to be a change of the point of view : if, as seen in direct relation to the present, so and so happened formerly, the imperfect is preferred for its expression. Not seldom the change of point of view is effected by a 'because' : for example, at I. i. 1. 16 (the first example in the Brāhmaṇa of mixture of the two tenses) : 'the Asuras and Rakshases prevented (p., *rarakṣus*) them ; and because they [then] prevented (i.) them, they are [now] called Rakshases.' Cases of this kind are not infrequent : see, for example, further I. i. 3. 5 ; iv. 1. 34 ; 5. 12 ; viii. 1. 26–7 (in narration of the same facts at viii. 1. 7 the perfect was used) : II. i. 2. 15 ; iv. 4. 2 ; v. 2. 1 : III. v. 1. 23 ; viii. 2. 17 ; 3. 11. It is, however, rather a tendency than an established usage ; one is tempted to explain by it many imperfects among prevalent perfects; but the perfect is also found instead.   For example, in I. i. 3. 4: 'because he lay (p., *çiçyé*) enveloping this all, therefore he [is] by name Vṛtra' (and similarly at IV. ii. 4. 19); we might here, to be sure, conjecture the sense to be 'therefore he *was* called Vṛtra,' but this would not apply at I. vi. 3. 9, where *āhus*, 'they call him,' is expressed; and at I. vi. 3. 10 an imperfect after 'because' is combined with a perfect in the main clause: 'so then, because he said (i.) "increase thou with Indra as enemy," for that reason Indra slew (p.) him.' Doubtless such counter-cases are not rare; no attempt has been made to collect them.

When perfects and imperfects are used in the same story, it often seems (as noted above) that perfects are preferred as introduction, they passing later into imperfects. This has still less the value of a rule (and there are examples of a con- trary character, with imperfects first: thus, II. iv. 2. 1 ff.: III. vi. 2. 2 ff.; IV. i. 5. 1 ff.: VII. iii. 2. 14: XI. 2. 3. 7 ff.), and would not be worthy of any attention save that the cases are so frequent: thus, we find them in the first book at i. 1. 16–7: ii. 4. 1 ff., 8 ff., 17 ff.; 5. 18: iv. 1. 22–3; 4. 8: v. 2. 18, 20; 3. 2 ff., 21 ff., 23 ff.; 4. 6 ff.: vi. 1. 11; 4. 1 ff., 11: ix. 1. 24 ff.; 2. 34–5; and they are met with in similar numbers in the other books.

By way of illustration of the general mode of distribution of the two tenses in parts of the text where the perfects pre- dominate, we may go on and review their remaining occur- rences in the first book. Passages in which both occur without any recognized ground for their alternation are as follows: ii. 3. 1–5, 6–9; 5. 1–11: iii. 3. 13–6: iv. 1. 10–18 (1 i. among 19 p.), 34–5; 5. 8–13: v. 2. 6: vi. 1. 1–8; 2. 1–4; 3. 1–22, 35–7: vii. 1. 1; 2. 22–4; 3. 1–9, 26; 4. 1–8: viii. 1. 1–18 (in 1–9, 29 p. only). Then we find single perfects in i. 1. 7, 9: 2. 3, 7: ii. 1. 6: iii. 1. 5: v. 1. 7: vi. 3. 26: vii. 3. 28; and groups of them in i. 2. 13 (2); 3. 4–5 (6); 4. 1 (3), 14–17 (14): ii. 5. 24–6 (11): iv. 1. 40 (3): v. 1. 20 (3): vii. 3. 19 (5). Single imperfects occur in iv. 5. 3: v. 3. 5: vi. 4. 21 (in a quotation): and groups (oftenest 2 together) in i. 1. 17; 3. 8–9; 4. 18: ii.

4. 6: iv. 2. 1, 5–8: v. 3. 4, 9–13 (2 in each paragraph): vi. 1. 9–10; 2. 5, 7; 3. 28; 4. 8, 9, 12, 17: vii. 2. 25–6; 3. 20, 22; 4. 14: viii. 1. 24, 26–7; 2. 8, 10–13: ix. 3. 11: not a few of these last are capable of being brought under the principle of preference for an imperféct when the past is directly compared with the present.

Per contra, we may take the sixth book as an example of the predominance of imperfects (25 to 1, as in some of the Brāhmaṇas first examined). Here there occur 286 imperfects, or more than half the number in the whole book, before a single perfect makes its appearance; then are found, in ii. 1. 37, two perfects, no reason for the change being discoverable. The same is the case with a perfect in iii. 1. 15, and with five in v. 4. 4–8; but one in v. 1. 7 is the repetition of a *mantra*-perfect quoted from VS. xi. 54; and, of two in viii. 1. 14, one is a similar case (from VS. xii. 34), and the other doubtless adapted to it. The remaining cases are of the two tenses mixed, without perceptible ground: they occur in ii. 2. 17–20 (3 p. and 1 i.); 3. 2, 4, 6 (*uvāca* 3 times among many i.): iii. 1. 31 (1 p. among 4 i.): vi. 3. 2, 3 (3 p. with 4 i.).

A fair example of the unmotived alternation of the two tenses is found in II. ii. 4, of which a part may be here translated by way of illustration:

1. 'In the beginning verily this [universe] was (p.) Prajāpati alone. He considered (i.): how now may I have progeny? He toiled (i.); he performed (i.) penance; he from his mouth generated (p.) Agni. So because he generated (i.) him from his mouth, therefore is Agni a food-eater. He who thus knoweth this Agni as food-eater, a food-eater verily he becometh. 2. So indeed him of the gods he thus generated (i.) in the beginning (*agre*); therefore is he Agni; Agri, namely, is, they say, the same as Agni. . . . 3. He, Prajāpati, considered (i.): verily I have generated (aor.) from myself this one, namely Agni, as food-eater; surely there is no other food here than myself — whom by all means may he not eat! Made bald indeed at that time was (p.) the earth; the herbs were (p.) not, nor the forest-trees; that was (p.) in his mind. 4. So then Agni turned (p.) about toward him with opened

mouth ; of him, frightened, the own greatness departed (p.) ; speech indeed [was] his own greatness ; the speech of him departed (p.). He sought (p.) in himself an oblation ; he rubbed (i.) himself up ; so, since he rubbed (i.) himself up, therefore both this is hairless and this (his two palms?). There he found (p.) either a ghee-oblation or a milk-oblation ; but either is nothing but milk. 5. That (oblation) did not conciliate (p.) him ; mixed with hair, indeed, was (p.) it ; he sprinkled (i.) it out, saying : suck quickly (*oṣaṁ dhaya*) ; then the herbs (*oṣadhayas*) came (i.) into being ; therefore are they called herbs. He rubbed (i.) himself up a second time ; there he found (p.) another oblation, a ghee-oblation or a milk-oblation ; but either is nothing but milk. 6. This conciliated (p.) him ; he was in doubt (i.) : shall I make oblation? or shall I not make oblation? His own greatness addressed (p.) him : make oblation! He, Prajāpati, knew (p.) : my own (*sva*) greatness speaks (*āha*) to me ; he made (i.) oblation, saying *svāhā* ('hail!') ; therefore oblation is made with saying *svāhā*. Thereupon went (p.) up he who burns there (the sun) ; thereupon came (p.) forth he who cleanses here (the wind) ; thereupon, again, Agni turned (p.) about [and] away. 7. He, Prajāpati, by making oblation, both had (i.) progeny and saved (i.) himself from death, from Agni who was going to eat him ; he who, knowing thus, maketh the *agnihotra* libation, hath progeny by that very progeniture by which Prajāpati had (i.) progeny, and just so saveth himself from death, from Agni who is going to eat him.'

Here are 19 perfects and 15 imperfects, quite miscellaneously shaken up together ; the cases in which we might say that the imperfect is used by preference when the past is directly viewed from a contrasted present are spoiled by their occurrence in company with others of which that explanation does not hold good. In the remainder of the chapter (*brāhmaṇa*), the two tenses (14 i., 17 p.) are found rather more distinctly in alternating batches.

An example of the repetition in more than one place of an apparently arbitrary alternation of tenses may be cited from III. i. 4. 3–4 : 'By the sacrifice [it was that] the gods conquered (p.) this conquest which is this conquest of theirs. They said (p.) : How may this of ours be inaccessible to mortals ? They, having sucked the savor of the sacrifice as bees might suck out honey, having milked dry the sacrifice, having blocked (?) [it] with the sacrificial post, disappeared (i.). So then, as they blocked (*yup*, i.) with it, therefore it is by name post (*yūpa*). This verily was (p.) heard of by the seers. They collected (i.) the sacrifice, just as this sacrifice is collected.' . . . While the last two of the imperfects here might be held to admit of explanation by the principle already stated, the other, 'disappeared,' seems wholly coördinate with the perfects that precede and follow. Yet the passage is repeated with the same tenses at III. ii. 2. 2, 11, 28 ; iv. 3. 15 ; and in part at vii. 1. 27 ; while at I. vi. 2. 1–2 it is given more fully (with repetition of the story, down to 'disappeared,' in precisely the same words, as what the seers 'heard of '), but with a different ending : 'That [sacrifice] they began (p.) to seek after ; they went on (p.) praising [and] toiling,' etc. : we might ascribe these last two perfects to the absence of direct antithesis with the present which was found at the close of the version first quoted.

Again, we have at I. vii. 1. 1 a brief sequence of tenses which is repeated at III. iii. 4. 10 : 'When the *gāyatrī* flew (i.) toward Soma, then of her while taking it a footless archer, having taken aim at her, cut off (p.) a feather, either of the *gāyatrī* or of Soma ; that, falling, became (i.) a *parṇa*-tree.' At VIII. ii. 4. 1–15, the alternation of *āpnot* (i.) and *ucca-kramus* (p.) is repeated fifteen times ; and that of *akṣarat* (i.) and *jajñire* (p.) made in XIV. i. 2. 19 occurs again in 3. 11 and 3. 15. In I. ii. 3. 6–7, there is several times a regular change from what the gods did (i.) to what followed (p.) as consequence. At I. v. 2. 6; vi. 3. 35–7 : IV. iv. 1. 16–7, the two tenses seem to be distributed respectively to the two parties concerned in the action.

To set off against such cases as these, on the other hand, we sometimes meet with manifest inconsistencies. Thus, in II. v. 1. 1–3, in a legend of the staple kind about Prajāpati, told in mixed tenses, we have 'he considered' twice in imperfect (*āikṣata*) and once in perfect (*īkṣāṁ cakre*), and 'he created' twice in each tense (*asṛjata* and *sasṛje*); in II. v. 4. 6–7 are used three perfects in opposition to the analogy of preceding and following sections, and against the principle recognized by us above of employing an imperfect when something past is contrasted with something present as the ground of the latter or the like. But, though such examples are doubtless to be found here and there, they are certainly not frequent.

There is but a beggarly array in this Brāhmaṇa of perfects with present value, namely twenty-five occurrences, of three forms : *dadṛçe*, I. iv. 1. 29: vi. 4. 5, 13, 15 (2), 19, 20. II. iii. 4. 22 : iv. 2. 7 (2); 4. 20. VI. iv. 2. 8. XI. i. 5. 1, 4 : ii. 4. 1, 2, 3, 4, 5, 7 ; 5. 3. XIV. viii. 15. 4. — *dīdāya*, I. iv. 1. 32; 3. 7. — *dādhāra*, XIII. i. 4. 3.

Of the immense Jāiminīya- or Talavakāra-Brāhmaṇa (as yet existing only in manuscript) the text is in great part so corrupt and doubtful that the numbers for the two tenses can be given only approximately. Omitting the most doubtful cases (and reckoning the Upanishad-Brāhmaṇa, of which the familiar Kena-Upanishad is a fragment, as a last book ; it is as well entitled to the place as the concluding book of the Çatapatha-Brāhmaṇa), the numbers are as follows :

Narrative Imperfects and Perfects in the Jāiminīya-Brāhmaṇa.

i. 1280 i. 335 p.	ii. 1294 i. 501 p.	iv. 544 i. 200 p.	
	iii. 2324 309	5442 i. 1345 p.	

The general proportion of imperfects to perfects, it will be seen, is very nearly as 4 to 1, and the differences between different parts of the text, though not altogether inconsiderable, are yet only of minor consequence, not comparing at all with those in some of the other texts (as ÇB., or AB., or even TB.). The mode of distribution of the two tenses is also quite other than that in the Çatapatha-Brāhmaṇa. In the vast majority of cases, each tense is used by itself, only the imperfect in one narration, only the perfect in another ; the cases of their mixture are comparatively few, and, where they do occur, usually no reason whatever can be seen for the

alternation. Of a tendency to the introductory use of perfects (as doubtfully recognized especially in ÇB.) there is no
distinct trace. But instances of the change from perfect to
imperfect when some one's words come to be quoted are by
no means rare.

A few examples may be given (one from each book), thus :
i 19. 'If there were no water, with what wouldst thou
make oblation? He said (p.): At that time verily there
existed (i.) nothing at all ; then this was offered (i.): [namely]
truth, in faith. [The other] said (p.) to him,' etc. (we had
the same passage above, p. 21, from ÇB.).

ii. 390. 'Then they flung (p.) him into the fire. Then
came (p.) Vasiṣṭha. He said (p.): what said (i.) my son when
flung in? They said (p.) to him : "O Indra, bring ability to
us, as a father to his sons (SV.)" ; just so much was (i.)
uttered by him, then they flung (i.) him into the fire. He
(Vasiṣṭha) said (p.),' etc.

iii. 64. 'They said (p.) to him : He ascended (i.) indeed
to the heavenly world, reverend sir. He said (p.): Is there
nothing whatever left of him here? They said (p.) to him :
There was (i.) just this horse's head, with which he told (i.)
this to the Açvins; but we do not know what became (i.) of
it. Search for it [said he]. Then they searched (p.) for
it,' etc.

Of examples like these there are as many as thirty in the
whole text, and the cases are sufficiently well marked to show
that the rule which we have already inferred from the other
texts was at least becoming a prevailing one. We cannot
call it established or absolute, for there are also a few
instances (I have noted nine) of a perfect in quotation,
usually among or with other narrative perfects, but in a
couple of cases with shift from narrative imperfect to quoted
perfect : e.g. in i. 283, where (not without considerable emendation) we read : 'Prajāpati created (i.) the gods ; after them
was created (i.) death, evil. Those gods, approaching Prajāpati, said (i.): Why hast thou created (aor.) us, if thou wast
(p.) going to create (*anvavasrakṣyann āsitha*) after us death,
evil? To them he said (i.),' etc.

I have not noted over half-a-dozen examples in this work of perfect-present, all of them forms found elsewhere in the same use, as *dādhāra, dīdāya, ānaçe.*

The facts in the Gopatha-Brāhmaṇa also require to be noticed, notwithstanding the inferior character and textual inaccuracy of that work. Rejecting doubtful cases, the imperfects are to the perfects as somewhat less than 3 to 1.

Narrative Imperfects and Perfects in the Gopatha-Brāhmaṇa.

i.	1	176 i.	39 p.	i.	5	37 i.	22 p.	ii.	4	12 i.	9 p.
	2	98	51	ii.	1	70	4		5	40	5
	3	27	39		2	59	8		6	37	27
	4	12	25		3	58	1			626 i.	230 p.

I have noticed but two cases in which a reason for the variation of tense can be suggested: in i. 4. 24, an imperfect in quotation among many narrative perfects — a clear case; and in i. 3. 8 doubtless a similar one, but the passage is corrupt, and calls for much emendation.

A single example of perfect-present, *dīdāya*, has been noticed at ii. 3. 5.

The Chāndogya-Upanishad may also not less properly be included in an inquiry like this than some of the other Upanishads which form parts of Brāhmaṇas, and so have had their statistics given above. It is a well-marked and peculiar case, showing for the first time a great predominance of perfects, namely as more than 4 to 1 : thus —

Narrative Imperfects and Perfects in the Chāndogya-Upanishad.

i.	6 i.	76 p.	iv.	10 i.	87 p.	vii.	3 i.	4 p.
ii.	6	0	v.	4	63	viii.	0	47
iii.	30	3	vi.	13	39		72 i.	319 p.

For the most part, the two tenses are held distinct, a narrative using either the one or the other throughout; the narratives in imperfects are found in i. 4; ii. 23; iii. 1–5, 19; iv. 17. Real mixture of the two tenses occurs only in one passage, v. 1. 12, where a single imperfect, *akhidat*, appears among twenty perfects (the perfect of *khid* is nowhere met with, but one sees no reason why it might not have been formed here). Then there are a number of passages where imperfects are used in quotation in a narrative carried on in perfects : so in iv. 4. 2 (1 i.), 4 (3 i.); v. 3. 4 (1 i.), 6 (1 i.), 7 (1 i., where the tense indicates a considerable interval between the time of this and that of the preceding sentence); vi. 2–3 (13 i., with a single perfect of the general narration among them in 2. 2, omitted by Böhtlingk in his translation). The chapters vi. 2–7 contain one long preachment ; and possibly it is on this account, and because their being a real quotation had been lost sight of, that *vidāṁ cakrus* (p.) occurs 4 times in 4. 5–7 ; if not, the perfect here is anomalous. The perfect *anuçaçāsa* is also used twice in quotation, in iv. 9. 2 ; 14. 2, where we should expect an aorist rather. Finally, in viii. 11. 3, a perfect, *uvāsa*, appears in quotation, but of a current popular saying, and therefore no real exception. No example of perfect in present sense is to be met with in this Upanishad.

On summing up now the results of the inquiry, we have to confess that they are of a more negative and doubtful character in many respects than we could wish. Still, certain points are brought to light with a fair degree of clearness. The use of the perfect with the value of a present must be viewed, so far as I can see, as a continuation of one of its earlier values as exhibited in *mantra ;* and it stands well up to the use of the same tense for past narration in some of the earlier texts — being twice as frequent as the latter in the Pañcaviṅça-Brāhmaṇa, almost precisely as frequent in the Māitrāyaṇī-Saṁhitā, and nearly as frequent in the Tāittirīya-Saṁhitā ; but it grows rarer, becomes attached especially to certain individual words, and finally disappears. As for the use of the tense with true perfect value (= the Vedic aorist), that makes no figure at all ; it is nowhere distinctly recognizable ; the cases are purely sporadic, and hence everywhere doubtful ; for we also meet occasionally an imperfect where we should decidedly expect an aorist, and these may perhaps be of the same sort. Delbrück, in his Vedic Syntax (§ 170 ; pp. 298–300), treats of what he calls "the perfect as past tense in non-narrative use " — that is, in (Vedic) aoristic sense — translating his examples with 'have,' as true perfects ; but

I cannot accept his interpretation and version; the cases seem to me those of mere narrative use, such as might exhibit imperfects instead of perfects — with the possible exception of the last, from TS. vii. 3. 1³, which has been quoted above (p. 9) as a doubtful instance, possibly but not necessarily (Vedic) aoristic.

The leading and most conspicuous fact is the increasing use, either by substitution or by association, of the perfect as equivalent to the imperfect in narration.   There is no *brāhmaṇa*-work in which the two tenses are not found together in story, although in some the perfects are sprinkled in very scantily, and although the telling of a whole legend with perfects instead of imperfects occurs either not at all or hardly in the (presumably) earlier texts and parts of texts.   Finally, all barriers are broken down, and, the other values disappearing, the perfect gets the use which it maintains through the classical period of the language as a purely narrative tense, exchangeable in almost all situations with the imperfect. We have thought to catch glimpses here and there of attempts made to differentiate the two tenses instead of confounding them with one another as simply equivalent. But we have been every time disappointed, with a single exception — that the perfect is on the whole excluded from personal use; that a quotation, even in a narrative carried on by perfects, is felt to call for imperfects.   Even this is by no means an established rule; exceptions to it are found in almost every treatise, from the oldest to the youngest; but it is at least a distinctly prevalent usage.   We have the more right to lay stress upon it, inasmuch as the native grammar sets up for the classical language a kindred distinction, forbidding the perfect to be used in narrating such facts as have been witnessed by the speaker: that is to say, in the narration of personal experience (compare Speijer's Sanskrit Syntax, p. 247 ff.).   How much attention is paid to the rule in the classical literature is another question; so far as I have myself noticed, it is mainly disregarded, and perfect and imperfect and aorist and (most frequent of all) passive participle used predicatively are jumbled miscellaneously together.   But the existence of such a rule is a voucher for the recognition by highest authority for the later language of that distinction which is seen growing up in the Brāhmaṇas.

One thing more is to be added, in order to complete the history of the Brāhmaṇa perfect: the perfect participle, active and middle, which in *mantra* has the whole range of senses that belong to its tense, inherits that one of the three which in Brāhmaṇa is not shown by the tense, and becomes a truly perfect participle, to be rendered by 'having done' and the like. This is an extremely curious fact, and it has happened to escape the notice of Delbrück (*Vedic Syntax*, p. 375 ff.), who describes the participle as simply past (although he translates it throughout with the auxiliary 'have'), and who further recognizes certain exceptions, having value as present, all of which I think I have proved (*Am. Journ. Philol.*, Oct., 1892; vol. xiii., p. 293) to be misinterpreted by him.

Examples are far from infrequent in all the Brāhmaṇas; a few may be quoted here, to illustrate the usage. Thus, *bahur bhavaty āçvena tuṣṭuvānaḥ*, 'he is multiplied who hath praised with the *āçva*[-sāman]' (PB. xi. 3. 5, and so in very numerous other passages in this work with *tuṣṭuvāna*); *indro 'surān hatvā 'kāryaṁ cakṛvāṅ amanyata*, 'Indra, having slain the Asuras, thought himself to have done a thing that should not be done' (ib. xxii. 14. 2); *yó vāí bahú dadivā́n bahv ı̐jānò 'gním utsādáyate*, 'whoso, having given much and sacrificed much, lets his fire go out' (MS. i. 8. 6; p. 123. 18); *çṛṇvánti hāi 'nam agníṁ cikyānám*, 'they hear of him as having built his fire-altar' (ib. iii. 1. 3; p. 4. 17); *yáthā vāmáṁ vásu vividānó gū́hati tādṛg evá tát*, 'that is as if one, having found valuable treasure, hides it' (TS. i. 5. 2³); *çváḥ-çvo 'smā ı̐jānáya vásīyo bhavati*, 'from one morrow to another it goes better with him who has sacrificed' (ib. ii. 5. 4¹); *yávān hí jakṣúṣīr váruṇó 'gṛhṇāt*, 'for Varuna seized on them when they had eaten the barley' (ÇB. II. v. 2. 16); *pitáram proṣúṣam ā́gatam*, 'a father who arrives after having been absent on a journey' (ib. XII. v. 2. 8). I know of no real exceptions, although the cases are not all so clear and marked as these. In the later language this participle is almost entirely lost.

V.—*A Botanico-Philological Problem.*

By W. D. WHITNEY,

PROFESSOR IN YALE COLLEGE.

A noted writer on language, F. Max Müller, in the course of his researches among the facts summarized in Grimm's Law, brought to light, some years ago, a curious parallelism between certain botanical and certain philological phenomena.

He first observed that the Germanic words *bōka, buche, beech,* and their like, agree in meaning as well as in form with the Latin *fāgus;* while, on the other hand, the same word in Greek, φηγός, signifies ' oak.' He then further found that our *fir*—and the German *föhre* (O. H. G. *foraha*), which has the same sense—is to be regarded as historically identical with the Latin *quercus,* ' oak.' Here, accordingly, if the Greek value of the former word, and the Latin of the latter, be assumed to be the more original, there are evident signs of a transfer of meaning in certain European vocables, from ' oak' to ' beech' and from ' fir' to ' oak,' respectively. This is the philological side.

With these facts in his mind, the same scholar, turning over Lyell's "Antiquity of Man," chanced upon a passage which showed that in the lowest strata of certain peat-bogs in the Danish islands the remains of tree-growth are prevailingly fir, while in the central strata they are oak, and in the upper strata beech ; the whole region showing now, and having shown ever since the Roman conquest, such a marked proclivity to beeches that oaks are uncommon, and firs can hardly be made to grow there. Thus there has been, clearly and incontestably, a change in the arborescent vegetation of the region, from fir to oak, and again from oak to beech. This is the botanical side.

The analogy between the two sets of facts thus stated is a palpable one. After setting them forth, then (Lectures on Language, American edition, ii. 238 *et seq.*), Mr. Müller proceeds to intimate an actual historical connection between them: the " changes of meaning," he thinks, may have been

" as the shadows cast on language by passing events." This poetical and somewhat ambiguous phrase he later puts into more definite shape: "The Aryan tribes, all speaking dialects of one and the same language, who came to settle in Europe during the fir period, or the stone age, would naturally have known the fir-tree only;" and the old name of the fir could not well have been changed to mean ' oak' " unless the dialect to which it belonged had been living at a time when the fir vegetation was gradually replaced by an oak vegetation" (pp. 250–1). And again: " I venture to suggest that Teutonic and Italic Aryans witnessed the transition of the oak period into the beech period, of the bronze age into the iron age, and that while the Greeks retained *phēgos* in its original sense, the Teutonic and Italian colonists transferred the name, as an appellative, to the new forests that were springing up in their wild homes" (p. 252).

This is Müller's theory, in its simple outlines. As to the cautions and reservations which he hangs about it, and the (supposed) analogous facts which he brings up from other quarters in its support, we have for the moment nothing to do with them; we will rather turn our attention first to the acceptableness of the hypothesis considered in itself, taken on its own merits.

In the first place, there seem to be *à priori* difficulties in the way of establishing a cause-and-effect relation between the botanical changes and the linguistic. It is sufficiently obvious, and distinctly pointed out by Müller's quoted authorities, that a complete change of the prevailing tree-growth, from one species to another, would necessarily require many centuries for its accomplishment. There would be, for example, a number of successive generations in whose sight the oaks would be slowly gaining on the firs; other generations before whom the two would be about equally numerous; and yet other generations which would witness the victory of the oak and almost extinction of the fir. How, in this process, should it ever come about that the name of the tree originally prevalent should come to be applied to the tree finally prevalent? If the oak had no name of its own at the outset, during its period of rarity and inconspicuousness, it would gain one, alongside the fir, as it rose to rivalry with the latter; and if, as the fir was reduced to unimportance, any name died out, it would naturally be the old name of the fir, and not that of the conquering oak. The fact that, in times long out of memory, the fir had been predominant and had borne a certain title, would not furnish the dimmest shadow of a ground for giving the same title to the oak, in the day when it predominated. The probability is so overwhelmingly against any such transfer, that we have a right to refuse except to the most direct and cogent evidence our acceptance of a theory implying a causative connection between the supplanting of one tree by another and the conversion of the name of the former into an appellation for the latter: there are many ways in which words arrive at new meanings, but this certainly is not one of them.

If, indeed, the people who witnessed the double process of supplanting never had any specific names for different kinds of tree, but only one word for ' tree' in general, this word would of course have been applied to the fir alone in the period of exclusive fir-growth; in that of mingled firs and oaks, it would have belonged to both; when the oaks reigned alone, it would have designated only the oak—and so on: becoming finally the title of the beech, when that tree had come to the throne and exterminated all its rivals. But the linguistic facts are far enough from being what this theory would demand. To satisfy its requirements, we ought to find the Latin and Germanic peoples in possession of only a single tree-name. And this name should not only have changed its meaning from ' oak' to ' beech,' but it should show signs of having, at a yet earlier period, signified ' fir.' Unfortunately, that is not the case. In the great mass of the Germanic dialects, for example, it is only the ' oak'-name that has been changed into a ' beech'-name; they still possess the word which Müller assumes to have meant ' fir' from the beginning, and they still use it to mean ' fir.' How is this to be explained? Shall we say that the Germanic tribes in general did not witness the supplanting of the firs by the oaks, but only that of the oaks by the beeches, reaching Europe after the former part of the process had been accomplished? But if it had been accomplished, and so effectually that the people who watched it as it went on had been compelled to turn their superfluous 'fir'-name into an 'oak'-name, these Germans had no business to bring in the old 'fir'-name, and cling to it so obstinately, since they could have nothing to which they should apply it.

Or take, again, the case of the Italians. They (with a small and more questionable body of Germans) constitute the main-stay of Mr. Müller's theory; for they have both changed their 'fir'-name into an 'oak'-name (*quercus*), and their 'oak'-name into a 'beech'-name (*fāgus*); if anybody in the world sat by and saw the whole drama of transmutation, in both its acts, they are certainly the men. But, judging from their linguistic effect, the two acts must have been going on at the same time, independently, and each with a permanent result; for the change of meaning has taken place in two different words, and both are left in the language. If there were not firs and oaks together in primitive Europe, how should these "Aryan tribes, all speaking dialects of the same language," have had both the original 'fir'-name *quercus*, which they should proceed to convert into a name for 'oak,' and the original 'oak'-name *fāgus*, which they should proceed to convert into a name for 'beech'? If the meaning of 'oak' came into *quercus* because the oaks had come in and crowded out the firs, why did not the meaning of 'beech' afterward come into it, when the oaks in their turn gave way to the beeches? If the meaning of 'beech' came into *fāgus* because the beeches had come in and crowded out the oaks, why should not the meaning of 'oak' have come into it in a similar manner, as a result of the displacement of the firs by the oaks? And why should these two corresponding processes have gone on after such a different fashion, the one of them stopping in the middle, and the other, so far as our knowledge goes, beginning at the middle?

There are other equally puzzling questions suggested by the attempt to reconcile and combine, according to Müller's theory, the two bodies of facts with which we are dealing; but it is needless to ask them; for we are already in a snarl of difficulties which there seems to be but one way of unraveling. It is this. There was not, as Müller supposes, a double process of displacement and substitution; there were, rather, two independent processes of actual conversion, or transmutation, or transubstantiation. The two did, indeed, take place successively in the Danish isles, and this has led to Müller's slight misapprehension. But in most of Germany only one of them occurred; the firs remained firs, while the oaks were changed into beeches—with an accompanying conversion of the name φηγός, ' oak,' into *fāgus,* ' beech.' In Italy, again, both processes went on to their complete result, and simultaneously: all the firs turned into oaks, and all the original oaks turned into beeches—each species, notwithstanding its changed identity, retaining its old name. If Müller can bring himself to accept this slight modification of his ingenious theory, then the second principal class of obstacles in the way of its success will have been surmounted.

If, however, quitting this line of examination, we try another, we shall encounter another line of obstacles, not less formidable: probably it has already risen before the minds of many or of all who have attended to this exposition. Is it indeed true that the Danish peat-bogs are to be taken as furnishing in their successive layers decisive indications respecting the history of arborescent vegetation through the whole Germanic and Italic territory—not to speak of the rest of Europe? Have the oaks, as Mr. Müller appears to assume, everywhere driven out the firs? and have they been in their turn replaced by the beeches? Mr. Lyell says: "In the time of the Romans, the Danish isles were covered, as now, with magificent beech-forests," almost to the exclusion of any other tree-growth: is this the case with all the European territory, except Greece, occupied by our family of languages?

Doubtless there are many who will answer this question promptly and confidently in the negative, and who will even proceed to moralize on the theory which has called it forth. Here, they will admiringly say, we have one of those ideal

philologists sometimes read of in story, but rarely met with
in actual life: men of the closet, who are so absorbedly
devoted to books and words that these have become to them
the sole realities; who never lift their eyes to the nature
which surrounds them; who care only for the distinctions of
the vocabulary kingdom, and are blind to those of the animal,
the vegetable, and the mineral. Müller is said to have grown
up to adolescence in Germany, and he has probably at least
travelled in Italy; yet, when he finds that *bōka* and *fāgus*
have in these countries changed their meaning from 'oak' to
'beech,' he is at once convinced that the German and Italian
oaks are, and of right ought to be, beeches. And these
persons will probably be confirmed in their view of his
personality by the way in which he expresses his willingness
to put out the question to be decided by a competent scientific
tribunal. "I must leave it," he says (p. 252), "to the
geologist and botanist to determine . . . . whether the changes
of vegetation, as described above, took place in the same
rotation over the whole of Europe, or in the North only." It
will be seen that, not trusting his own eyes, he is also very
particular as to whose eyes shall be allowed to settle the
question. Indeed, I have myself personally experienced that,
to my cost. Being, as I fondly imagined, a little bit of a
"geologist and botanist" in my own right, I ventured, in
criticising Müller's theory eleven years ago, to offer my
scientific testimony in opposition to it. I said that, instead
of firs and oaks and beeches having supplanted and succeeded
each other through the whole region occupied by the Germanic
and Italic races, "we find all of them, or two of them, still
growing peaceably together in many countries."* But Müller,
in a reply recently made to my criticism,† being apparently
unable to comprehend how one who concerns himself especially
with language should presume to know anything on other
subjects, fails to see that what I said was meant as testimony,
and understands me as simply echoing his suggestion that a
scientific oracle, if formally installed and duly inquired at,

---

* Oriental and Linguistic Studies, i. 257.

† Chips from a German Workshop (American edition), iv. 502.

might settle the disputed matter. So he quells me with the remark : " Here Professor Whitney is, as usual, ploughing with my heifer ; " and then, quoting his former words upon the subject, he goes on to say : " I had consulted several of my own geological friends, and they all told me that there was, as yet, no evidence in Central Europe and Italy of a succession of vegetation different from that in the North, and that, in the present state of geological science, they could say no more. In the absence of evidence to the contrary, I said, Let us wait and see ; Professor Whitney says, Don't wait."

Yes, certainly I say, " Don't wait " ; a single moment's unnecessary delay is to be deprecated. How can we sit down and fold our hands over a question that affects the weal and woe of so large and respectable a part of mankind ? If Central Europe and Italy are really covered, exclusively or prevailingly, with " magnificent beech-forests," then there are a great many millions of people, there and elsewhere, whose mental delusions render it unsafe to trust them any longer outside of an insane asylum. In order to do what I can toward determining their condition and fate, I will follow Müller's own example. He has gathered a set of twenty " principal bones of contention " between himself and me, and challenged me to summon a commission of learned professors to deal with them. I will add to the heap one more bone (bigger and more solid than most of those raked together by him), as follows :

21. Whether Central Europe and Italy are covered with beech forests, to the exclusion, almost or quite, of other trees, especially of oaks and firs.

And I appeal to him, in my turn, " to choose from among his best friends three who are *professores ordinarii* [of natural science] in any university of England, France, Germany, or Italy ; and by their verdict I promise to abide " (Chips, iv. 528). I do not feel willing to accept the outcome of his private and confidential consultations with his " own geological friends," as reported by himself, because it has appeared more than once, in connection with other subjects, that those consultations do not yield unexceptionable results. He declares himself (Chips, iv. 498–9) to have been guided in all his phonetic investigations, and controlled in their conclusions, by the advice and approval of the highest authorities in physiology and acoustics; yet the influence of Helmholtz and Ellis could not prevent his declaring his independent opinion (Lectures, 6th [English] edition, ii. 133) that the "neutral vowel," the *u* of *but* or *up*, is a non-sonant or whispered element; even as the aid of Main and Hinds could not keep him, in his astronomical reasonings, from assuming (preface to Rig-Veda, vol. iv., p. lii.) that, to any given observer, the ecliptic is identical with his own horizon.

It ought to be added, perhaps, that there seems to be another method in which this particular "bone of contention" can be ground up and gotten completely out of the way, without summoning an International High-Joint Commission to chew upon it; and we have reason to wonder that that method did not suggest itself to Müller: for it is a linguistic one. We cannot question that he is familiar with the principle, generally accepted among philologists, that the presence in a language of a certain name implies the presence in the minds of the people speaking that language of some knowledge respecting the thing named; indeed, he himself, in the course of his illustrations, frequently applies or implies it. If we could, for instance, catch an untaught and untravelled savage off one of those Danish islands, with their exclusive growth of magnificent beeches, we should find that he had no names for 'oak' and 'fir,' any more than for 'mahogany' and 'palm.' With this test in our minds, let us examine the various Germanic and Italican dialects; if they contain words for 'fir' and for 'oak,' as well as for 'beech,' then we, as linguists, shall have the right to hold, and to maintain before all the world, that in Central Europe and Italy the beeches have not crowded out the oaks, which had before crowded out the firs. And this, even though the decision of the scientific triumvirate should be adverse to us. For if, in the very passage under discussion, Müller teaches us (Lectures, ii. 252), in case of an apparent discordance between linguistic and craniological evidences, to "protest that the Science of Language has nothing to do with skulls," we should be justified *à fortiori* in maintaining that she is above having anything to do with trees. As for the presence in the same European tongue of words for both 'fir' and 'oak,' besides 'beech,' we have already above seen some of the facts bearing upon the matter; it may be commended to Müller for a more careful and exhaustive examination, with the hope that we shall find the results in a later edition either of the " Lectures" or of the " Chips."

Pending their appearance, we may regard the discussion of Müller's theory as brought to an end; and it does not appear doubtful with what conclusion: no theory can stand for a moment which has so many and so various and so powerful objections arrayable and arrayed against it. We ought not indeed, to leave out of sight the modestly hypothetical tone in which its author originally put it forward, adducing against it more than one consideration which, if he had taken the trouble carefully to weigh them, he would have seen to be fatal to it; and ending his whole exposition thus: " I shall be as much pleased to see my hypothesis refuted as to see it confirmed; all that I request for it is an impartial examination." But then he has, after all, written it down and put it forth, for the examination and criticism of scholars; and he must accordingly be held responsible for its character, and has no right to complain if it is treated just as its own intrinsic merits deserve. If he were also to suggest, as a hypothesis, for the discussion of comparative philologists, that a real analogy existed between Grimm's Law of rotation of the three classes of mutes and the nomenclature of these three trees; that the original names for 'fir,' 'oak,' and 'beech' had each been pushed one step around in the series; that, while *quercus* had changed from 'fir' to 'oak,' and *fāgus* from 'oak' to 'beech,' *abies* had also (though, owing to the loss of needed evidence, we could not so clearly prove it) certainly changed from 'beech' to 'fir'—then, with however many *ifs* and *provideds* he might season his exposition, whatever gratitude he might promise to the man who should convince him that his notion was a foolish one, its folly would remain incontestable, and he would deserve to be well laughed at for ever having confessed to entertaining it seriously. Nor would the case be different if he were to put forward, with ever so many allowances that he was perhaps mistaken, the theory that the gradual contraction of the earth's crust had something to do with the universal abbreviation of the vocabular elements of speech: that the latter was, as it were, "the shadow cast on language" by that great event as it passed. Now Müller's modestly indicated hypothesis is just as unreasonable, just as inherently absurd, as either of those others would be; it differs from them only in that its absurdity does not lie so openly and palpably upon its very face. It is one of those queer imitations of a correspondence which now and then call a smile to a man's countenance when he chances upon them over his table; or with the recital of which he, at the utmost, amuses a friend in the course of an evening's walk. To devote to its exposition and support fifteen pages of a treatise on a new "Science," as Müller has done, is to make out of a joke a far too serious matter.

But Müller has done more than this. In a criticism of his volume, published eleven years ago,* I devoted two pages to a complete statement and refutation of the theory; bringing against it, in effect, nearly the same objections which have been here made, though otherwise cast, and in a much briefer form. I had given it, as I knew, a wholly "impartial examination;" and I conceived myself to be fairly earning an expression of the "pleasure" with which its author had promised to greet its refutation. Doubtless this was too sanguine; it might have been suspected that one who could frame and publish such a hypothesis would not be easily accessible to any brief and summary demolition of it; that he might probably enough even show toward it that instinctive special affection which mothers are said sometimes to feel for their weakest and least creditable offspring. At any rate, last year, in an article† which proves him not to have been in a state of mind to profit by any correction of mine, however honestly meant and faithfully administered, he makes what

---

* North American Review, vol. c., 1865; also Or. and Ling. Studies, i. 239–62.

† Chips, iv. 456 *et seq.*

he intends as a stout defense of his bantling. His answer to one of my three main points of objection I have already quoted in full: I had been ploughing with his heifer, and urging the poor beast forward with unseemly haste. *En revanche*, he endeavors, in replying to another point, to impale me upon the horns of a heifer of my own. I have, he says, " unintentionally " offered him the " best illustration " of just such a change of meaning as he assumes in his tree-names, by showing* how the English settlers in America applied the old familiar names of *robin* and *blackbird* to new kinds of bird, somewhat resembling those which had borne them in England. But what is the analogy between this case and the one we have had in hand ? Perhaps we have all along mistaken his meaning, and he has only intended to maintain that the Italican tribes migrated from a country where firs and oaks prevailed to one where, instead, only oaks and beeches were found, and therefore, having the ' fir ' and ' oak ' names idle on their hands, proceeded to apply the former to the oak and the latter to the beech, each being the species nearest like what the same word had before designated. This, and this only, would be a real parallelism. If we are to find one for the theory as originally put forward by Müller, we shall be obliged, it seems to me, to turn the American act of nomenclature the other way, and see the robin and blackbird " transferring the name of ' Indian,' as an appellative, to the new white people that were springing up in their wild homes."

It is needless to spend more time upon Müller's attempt to rehabilitate his hypothesis. About each item which he touches he raises a thin cloud of word-dust, just sufficient to obscure its outlines ; showing an unclearness so curious and puzzling that one almost gives up in despair the endeavor to trace the mental state which it represents. Anything in the nature of a counter-argument no candid and competent person will pretend to discover. But he sings his little song of triumph at the end, and regards his fir-oak-beech theory as established more firmly than ever before the eyes of the students of language.

---

* Namely, in Or. and Ling. Studies, i. 303.

The matter to which we have thus given a few minutes' attention is, in one respect, an almost purely personal one. The scientific question involved is of quite insignificant importance; and no man of real knowledge and penetration is likely to be so far carried off his feet by Müller's persuasive eloquence as to take his hypothesis for an acceptable explanation. The fact that the whole thing is so curiously characteristic of Müller, and that Müller's personality is an element of high importance in the prevailing currents of thought and opinion on a host of subjects, is what gives the subject a wider and impersonal bearing. He has a real genius for exposition and illustration; this very note, "On words for fir, oak, and beech," is full of interesting facts, interestingly grouped, and may be read with lively pleasure by any one who can leave out of sight for what they are marshalled and to what end directed. What its author lacks is inductive logic, the power of combining his facts aright and seeing what result they yield; his collected material dominates and confuses him; often he hits the truth, with a kind of power of genial insight; often he hits wrong, sometimes perversely and absurdly wrong. No man needs to be studied with a more constant and skeptical criticism; no man is less worthy of the blind admiration and confidence, resembling that of a sect in its prophet, with which he has now long been regarded by an immense public, and even by scholars of a certain grade. While he maintains this false position, his influence is harmful, obstructive to the cause of truth; to do anything toward reducing his authority to its true value is a service to truth and to sound science.

There is yet another personal aspect which the controversy bears, personal to both Müller and myself; and I cannot forbear spending a few words upon it in closing. Since, for the reasons just laid down, I have repeatedly controverted views and arguments of his which appeared to me to be false —and sometimes sharply, as I thought they deserved—it was obviously for his interest, in lack of any other more effective method of reply and defense, to represent me as a mere faultfinder and personal vilifier. This he accordingly did, at considerable length, in the Contemporary Review for January,

1875. In the course of his article, he threw out against me this taunt: " He bitterly complains that those whom he reviles do not revile him again" (p. 314). In my answer, in the same Review (May, 1875; p. 728), I said: " If I stated that any one ' bitterly complained ' that he was not answered by those he criticized, I should feel called upon to give chapter and verse for it; and neither Mr. Müller nor any one else can point out any such complaints on my part." It is in answer to the challenge here implied, to authenticate his charge, that Müller returns to the " words for fir, oak, and beech." The way of it is this.

In the preface to the sixth edition of his lectures (1871), Mr. Müller permitted himself a sneering reference to my criticism of an earlier edition, and a sophistical and untenable reply to one or two of the points which I had made against him. I therefore sent to the Review which had printed the original criticism (the North American) a rejoinder,* in which, after setting right the points referred to, and showing that the sneer was a gratuitous one, I went on thus: " We earnestly desire, and heartily invite, a continuation of his exposures. We should be glad, for example, to see him defend his explanation of the phenomena stated in Grimm's Law. . . . We should like, again, to have him try to prove that any one of the three impossible assumptions which we pointed out as involved in his argument respecting the ' names for fir, oak, and beech ' does not vitiate that argument"—and so on. This challenge, now, this invitation to go on and set up again, if he could, the hypothesis which I claimed to have overthrown, is what he brings up, and the only thing that he brings up, to justify his former allegation that I had " bitterly complained " of not being reviled by those whom I had reviled! He does not, indeed, venture to repeat the allegation here in precisely the same terms (though he has reproduced it unaltered in his reprint of the Contemporary article in the " Chips," iv. 433); he speaks, rather, of " a passage where Professor Whitney expressed his dissatisfaction at not being answered, or, as I

---

* North American Review, vol. cxiii., 1871; reproduced in Or. and Ling. Studies, i. 262 *et seq.*

had ventured to express it, considering the general style of his criticism, when he is angry that those whom he abuses, do not abuse him in turn."* Then, in his summing up at the end, he asks, with all the conscious dignity of re-established blamelessness:† "Was I, then, so far wrong when I said that Professor Whitney cannot understand how anybody could leave what he is pleased to call his arguments, unheeded?" We may ask in return, was there ever seen a more beautiful instance of the *diminuendo* in accusation? The documentary and tangible "bitter complaint at not being reviled" first becomes a purely inferential "anger at not being abused"— incapable of absolute refutation, because the accuser, even when driven into the last corner, can still say: "Oh, I am quite sure that he was angry, though he did not show it;" then this is confessed to be a mere adventurous dysphemism for what, when strictly defined, is only a "dissatisfaction at not being answered;" and the last finally dwindles to an intellectual "failure to understand it that one's arguments are unheeded." Surely, the mutual interchanges of oaks and firs and beeches are nothing to this; it could only be paralleled by the transmutation of oaks into alders and of alders into bramble-bushes. In its last form, moreover, the statement, though less widely remote from truth, is not less strictly erroneous, than in its first; for I have not, in fact, ever been at a loss to understand why Müller left my arguments against his views so long unanswered; any more than why, when he finally attempted to answer them, he found nothing to use against them save evasion, misrepresentation, and detraction.‡

---

* Chips, iv. 500.

† Chips, iv. 504.

‡ The character of his charges in reference to points of Sanskrit grammar I have briefly exposed in the Proceedings of the American Oriental Society for May, 1876.

INDEX OF AUTHORS

INDEX OF SUBJECTS

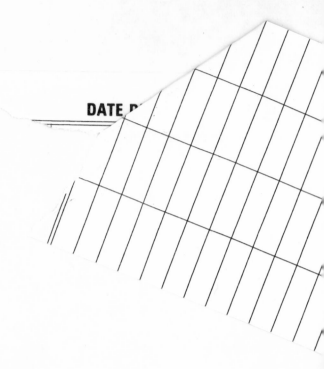

DATE D